ANAXIMANDER
AND THE ORIGINS
OF GREEK
COSMOLOGY

CHARLES H. KAHN

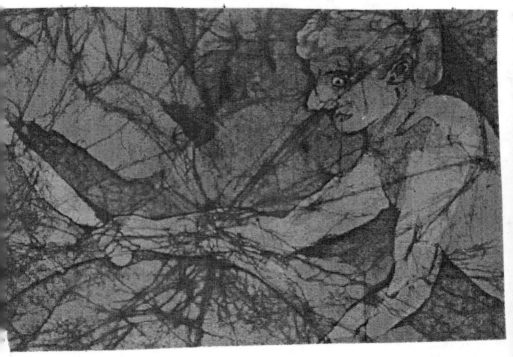

Copyright © 1960 by Columbia University Press

Corrected printing
Copyright © 1985 by Centrum Philadelphia

Reprinted 1994
by Hackett Publishing Company, Inc.

04 03 02 01 00 99 98 97 96   2   3   4   5   6

Printed in the United States of America

Cover photo: Palomar Observatory Photograph
Cover design by Ronald F. Kotrc and Alan E. Singles

For further information, please address

Hackett Publishing Company, Inc.
P.O. Box 44937
Indianapolis, Indiana 46244-0937

Library of Congress Cataloging-in-Publication Data

Kahn, Charles H.
    Anaximander and the origins of Greek cosmology/Charles H. Kahn
        p.   cm.
    Originally published: New York: Columbia University Press, 1960.
    Includes bibliographical references and indexes.
    ISBN 0-87220-256-9 (cloth).   ISBN 0-87220-255-0 (pbk.)
    1. Anaximander—Contributions in cosmology.   2. Cosmology,
Ancient.   I. Title.
B208.Z7K3   1994
182—dc20   94-18778
                                                        CIP

The paper used in this publication meets the minimum requirements of American
National Standard for Information Sciences—Permanence of Paper for Printed
Library Materials, ANSI Z39.48–1984.

♾

To Kurt von Fritz

CONTENTS

Conclusion

Appendices

Indices

ILLUSTRATIONS

PREFACE

THIS essay has grown out of a study of the poem of Parmenides which was begun a number of years ago. I had come to the conclusion that Parmenides' argument was to be understood only against the background of a new rational view of the physical universe, a view which was not his own creation, but which permitted him to take for granted such basic conceptions as the true Nature of things (φύσις) and the ordered structure of the World (κόσμος). What I have tried to do here is to reconstruct this pre-Parmenidean view, proceeding on the assumption that its source must be located in sixth-century Miletus. This assumption is implicit in all the ancient accounts of the origins of Greek philosophy, and seems to be justified by the radical contrast between the physical ideas of Homer and Hesiod on the one hand, and those of Anaximander and Anaximenes on the other.

The view of the historical development presented here differs from the traditional scheme in only two respects. I have discounted the originality of Pythagoras as a figment—or at least an exaggeration—of the Hellenistic imagination. In other words, so far as the study of nature is concerned, I have treated the Italian school as an offshoot of the Ionian philosophy and not as its rival. Furthermore, the scale on which the three Milesians are depicted is not as uniform as it generally appears. In the monumental style of ancient historiography, the Milesians are presented as three statues of the same size and rank, standing at the head of a long gallery of peers. I have tried to adjust the magnitude of the figures to the importance of their role in the history of ideas. Thales and Anaximenes still have their respective places next to Anaximander, as his precursor and disciple. But they are dwarfed by the comparison to the master.

Another deviation from the usual treatment is dictated by the scope of the essay. In dealing with Heraclitus and Parmenides (and, even more, with their successors) I have largely neglected the fundamentally new ideas which are their characteristic achievement. Since this is not a history of early Greek philosophy but a study of the Milesian cosmology, later thinkers must be regarded here primarily as the heirs and debtors of the Milesians.

I would like to mention one recent publication, *The Presocratic*

Philosophers, by G. S. Kirk and J. E. Raven (Cambridge, 1957), which reached me too late for systematic reference in the notes. On several points the authors' close analysis of the evidence has led me to reformulate my own position. Their work provides an important statement on many of the questions discussed here, and should be compared *in extenso*.

A number of other relevant studies have appeared since my manuscript was completed, while a few earlier ones have only recently come to my attention. In one or two cases a new discussion would now be called for. Probably the most important example of this kind is Professor W. K. C. Guthrie's article on "The Presocratic World-Picture," *Harvard Theological Review*, XLV (1952), 87, which I encountered only after the book had gone to press. His suggestion that the κόσμος was from the beginning distinguished from the circumambient divine stuff or περιέχον—and hence that the Stoic distinction between κόσμος and τὸ πᾶν is really pre-Socratic—seems to me very plausible, and I would now want to take up this idea in Appendix I. (I think it is already implicit in Appendix II.) I could scarcely be in more complete agreement with Professor Guthrie's general thesis, that "a common picture of the nature of the Universe, of living creatures, and of divinity was shared by a surprising number of Greek philosophical and religious thinkers of the 6th and early 5th centuries B.C." But I am obliged to part company with him when he goes on: "This world-picture was not the creation of any one of them, but rather seems to have been assumed by all at the outset, as is also suggested by certain indications in Greek literature that it was shared by the unphilosophical multitude." That elements of one or more pre-philosophic views are incorporated in the Ionian cosmology is, I would say, agreed upon by all. But the quality which is lacking in the older world views is precisely what is most essential in the case of the philosophers: the systematic concern for rational clarity and coherence. The recent tendency to assimilate Anaximander to Hesiod—which also underlies Cornford's brilliant treatment of him in *Principium Sapientiae*—can only serve to blur the distinguishing features of each, by confounding the very different attitudes toward Nature that characterize the Greek epic poets and the early philosophers. If these first philosophers had been able to take for granted a coherent, ready-made cosmology, then they would not have been the first after all. On the other hand, once the Milesians and their successors had worked out a consistent cosmic scheme, it naturally exerted a powerful influence on the poets and on the educated public in general. Hence when we find traces of such a scheme in Euripides or in the Potidaea epitaph of 432—or in the undated Orphic poems—we must recognize this as evidence for the diffusion of the Ionian cosmology, not for its pre-existence in the popular imagination.

Acknowledgment is due to the Soprintendenza alla Antichità di Roma I for permission to reproduce the photograph of the frontispiece, to the Trustees of the British Museum for Plate I, to the Archives Photographiques, Paris, for Plate IIA, and to the Austrian National Library for Plate IIB. I wish to thank Professors Otto J. Brendel, Evelyn B. Harrison, and O. Neugebauer, as well as Professor M. Borda of the Museo Nazionale in Rome and Mr. D. J. Wiseman of the British Museum, for information concerning one or more of the monuments reproduced.

As this book is the fruit of some ten years' study, it has been influenced by more teachers and scholars than I can mention here. I think above all of Professors David Grene and Yves R. Simon of the University of Chicago, who first introduced me to Greek literature and philosophy—and first impressions are lasting ones. In a more immediate way, I am indebted to Professor Moses Hadas and the other members of the examining committee who read and criticized the bulk of the manuscript in its original form as a doctoral dissertation for Columbia University. The readability of the whole work has benefited in particular from the comments of Professor Gilbert Highet, who called my attention to many an opaque argument and many a clumsy phrase. My friend Professor Martin Ostwald has often come to my assistance with excellent advice and has in addition read through a full set of proofs.

Special thanks are due to the Stanwood Cockey Lodge Foundation, whose generous grant made this publication possible, and to the staff of Columbia University Press, who have given the author all the co-operation he could have wished for.

Finally, in dedicating the book to Professor Kurt von Fritz, now at the University of Munich, I wish to record my lasting gratitude both for his friendly guidance and for his unflagging interest in this work, despite the various interruptions of time and place.

C. H. K.

Columbia University in the City of New York
April, 1959

INCE this book has been out of print for a number of years but still seems to be in scholarly demand, I am glad that there is now an opportunity to make it available again. A few mechanical corrections have been incorporated into the text, but the conditions of photographic reproduction do not permit any substantial revision. And that is perhaps just as well. Reading the essay again 25 years after its first appearance, I find that I would not want to alter the picture presented here of the origins of Greek philosophy and science: the central theses of the book still seem to me correct. On some points, of course, my thinking has changed. My view of the relationship between philosophy and science in the earliest period is more fully and accurately stated in the 1970 article "On Early Greek Astronomy" (*JHS* 90, pp. 99-116), which should be read as a kind of postscript to this work. And the interpretation of Heraclitean texts given here is entirely superseded by my discussion of the same material in *The Art and Thought of Heraclitus* (Cambridge, 1979). But on the character of Milesian cosmology and its pervasive and permanent influence my views are unrepentant. My emphasis on the personal role of Anaximander may be exaggerated, as I acknowledged at the time. But the nature of our sources does not permit us to correct this emphasis in any way that would be better documented or more insightful. By focussing in this way on the systematic unity of Milesian cosmology as if it were the work of a single mind, but also as the original and persistent background for all Greek natural philosophy, we are able to see connections and continuity that would otherwise escape notice.

My only regret in seeing the book reappear in its original form is that the large number of untranslated passages in Greek and Latin prevent it from being fully accessible to the non-specialist reader. If I were able to alter the text I would make a much more liberal use of translation and transliteration. In this respect the book unfortunately still bears the mark of its origin as a doctoral dissertation in Classics.

I offer the following comments by way of partial updating of scholarship on points of detail.

pp. 16-17. Aëtius may be correct after all in assigning the "Critias" fragments to Euripides. See A. Dihle in *Hermes* 105 (1977), 28-42.

p. 50. Zeller's suggestion that πάντες οἱ οὐρανοί for Anaximander meant the celestial rings no longer seems so plausible, and the interpreters who take this as a reference to a cyclical repetition of world systems are probably right. For a good discussion see J. Mansfeld, *The Pseudo-Hippocratic Tract* περὶ ἑβδομάδων *ch. 1-11 and Greek Philosophy* (Assen, 1971), pp. 44f.

p. 55. In the testimonium from Hippolytus I would now mark ὑγρόν with a crux: neither the transmitted text nor the proposed emendation is satisfactory.

pp. 84f. On the date of the *De Hebdomadibus* see now J. Mansfeld's study cited above (for p. 50). Mansfeld argues for a date in the first century B.C. If he is right, all reference to this treatise should be eliminated from my book. (In addition to pp. 84f., this concerns pp. 94, 207 and 224.)

p. 88. The question of the obliquity of the ecliptic is much more complicated then I realized when I wrote this, and there is reason to doubt whether our sources can be correct in ascribing such knowledge to Anaximander. See "On Early Greek Astronomy", *JHS* 90 (1970), 101-109.

p. 92. My interpretation of the historical import of the quotation from Neugebauer is seriously misleading. For a correction see *JHS* 90 (1970), p. 104, n. 18.

pp. 93-4. For a good astronomical interpretation of Anaximenes' view of the stars turning "like a cap around our head", see the suggestion of Howard Stein quoted in *JHS* 90 (1970), p. 108, n. 34.

p. 108. In Aristophanes' explanation of the thunderbolt (*Clouds* 407) the wind's bursting into flame is probably due not to friction against the cloud, as I suggested, but to rarefaction and conversion into fire as a result of rapid motion. Cf. Anaximenes A 6.

p. 120. For a better account of the early meaning of στοιχεῖον see W. Burkert's article in *Philologus* 103 (1959), 167ff.

p. 125 (and also 157). The interpretation of Empedocles B 38.1 is more controversial than I had supposed. See J. Bollack, *Empédocle* III (Paris, 1969), p. 261 (commentary on his fr. 320).

pp. 153, n. 2 and 157. For divergent interpretations of the cosmogony of Pherecydes see Kirk and Raven, *The Presocratic Philosophers* (Cambridge, 1st. ed. 1957) pp. 55ff. (= 2nd ed. 1983 pp. 56ff.) and M. L. West, *Early Greek Philosophy and the Orient* (Oxford, 1971), pp. 10ff.

p. 156, n. 3. The "greatest god" of Xenophanes cannot be the world itself, since the god is immobile and moves everything else (B 25-26). This cosmic deity presumably lies around the world, like Anaximander's Boundless.

p. 159. My dating Alcmaeon "at the end of the sixth century" was a bit incautious. Barnes' version "probably . . . at the beginning of the fifth century, a younger contemporary of Pythagoras" (*The Presocratic Philosophers* I, 115) is more accurate. But Guthrie's willingness to make him a contemporary of Empedocles (*History of Greek Philosophy* I, 341ff., 357f.) yields too much ground to those who would reject the ancient evidence in favor of their own view of the historical development.

pp. 163-5. The chronological priority of Anaxagoras to Empedocles seems to me just as obvious as it did 25 years ago. Unfortunately this is one of the few points of Presocratic scholarship on which little or no progress has been made, despite much discussion. The interpretation of Aristotle's phrase τοῖς δ' ἔργοις ὕστερος as "later in his philosophical activity" (Ross' translation, following Zeller) is (a) linguistically improbable (ἔργα for Aristotle can scarcely mean "books"; but what else are we supposed to be dating?) and (b) factually indefensible, since (i) Aristotle can have no way of knowing, or supposing that he knew, the exact dates at which books were published (!) or lectures given a century before his own time, and (ii) in fact he everywhere assumes the priority of Anaxagoras (see above all *Met.* 985ᵃ29 where παρὰ τοὺς πρότερον πρῶτος clearly presupposes that Anaxagoras came first), as does Theophrastus (passages cited below, p. 164). For a survey of recent discussion see J. Mansfeld, *Mnemosyne* 33 (1980), 90ff. and D. Sider, *The Fragments of Anaxagoras* (Beiträge zur klass. Philologie 118, Meisenheim am Glan, 1981), p. 5. The phrase in question might conceivably mean that Anaxagoras was "more modern" rather than "inferior" in his philosophical work. What it *cannot* mean is that he was later in writing, publishing, or lecturing about philosophy. The persistence of Ross' translation and Zeller's interpretation in Kirk-Raven-Schofield (2nd ed. p. 353), Guthrie (II, 128 n. 4), and Barnes (II, 4), together with the regular practice of discussing Empedocles before Anaxagoras in histories of Presocratic philosophy, are in my view depressing examples of cultural lag: a bad example set by Zeller has become an inveterate habit.

p. 170. As Guthrie pointed out in his review of this book, in the two texts cited from Herodotus the form τό is not the article (as I imply) but the definite pronoun from which the article developed.

p. 189, n. 2. In support of the dating of the *De Victu* around 400 B.C. see now R. Joly, *Hippocrate, Du Régime* (Paris, 1967), pp. xiv-xvi, with references to his *Recherches sur le traité pseudo-hippocratique Du Régime* (Paris-Liège, 1961).

pp. 219ff. I should have cited the excellent study of the pre-philosophical use of κόσμος by H. Diller in *Festschrift Bruno Snell* (Munich, 1956), pp. 47-60. See also J. Kerschensteiner, *Kosmos* (Zetemata 30, Munich, 1962).

For recent interpretation and bibliography there are now three general histories to consult:

W.K.C. Guthrie, *A History of Greek Philosophy*, Vols. I-II (Cambridge, 1962-63).

J. Barnes, *The Presocratic Philosophers*, 2 vols. (The Arguments of the Philosophers, Routledge and Kegan Paul, 1979).

G. S. Kirk, J. E. Raven, M. Schofield, *The Presocratic Philosophers*, 2nd ed. (Cambridge, 1983).

I would like to express my gratitude to the staff of Hackett Publishing Company for making this reprint possible after the book was again out of print for a number of years.

Charles H. Kahn

Philadelphia
April 1994

ABBREVIATIONS AND SHORT TITLES USED IN CITATION

AJP	*American Journal of Philology.*
Bonitz, *Index*	H. Bonitz, *Index Aristotelicus* (2d ed.; Graz, 1955).
Burnet	J. Burnet, *Early Greek Philosophy* (4th ed.; London, 1945).
CP	*Classical Philology.*
CQ	*Classical Quarterly.*
Diels, *Archiv*	H. Diels, "Ueber Anaximanders Kosmos," *Archiv für die Geschichte der Philosophie*, X (1897), 228.
D.L.	Diogenes Laertius, *Lives of Eminent Philosophers*; text and tr. by R. D. Hicks, Loeb Classical Library (2 vols.; London, 1942).
Dox.	H. Diels, *Doxographi Graeci* (Berlin, 1879).
Harv. Stud.	*Harvard Studies in Classical Philology.*
Heath, *Aristarchus*	T. L. Heath, *Aristarchus of Samos, the Ancient Copernicus* (Oxford, 1913).
Hölscher, "Anaximander"	U. Hölscher, "Anaximander und die Anfänge der Philosophie," *Hermes*, LXXXI (1953), 257 ff. and 385 ff.
Jaeger, *Paideia*	W. Jaeger, *Paideia*, 3 vols. tr. by G. Highet (2d ed.; New York, 1945).
Jaeger, *Theology*	W. Jaeger, *The Theology of the Early Greek Philosophers*, tr. by E. S. Robinson (Oxford, 1947).
JHS	*Journal of Hellenic Studies.*
Kirk, *Heraclitus*	G. S. Kirk, *Heraclitus: The Cosmic Fragments* (Cambridge, 1954).
Kirk and Raven	G. S. Kirk and J. E. Raven, *Presocratic Philosophers* (Cambridge, 1957).
LSJ	Liddell and Scott, *A Greek–English Lexicon* (9th ed., revised by Jones and McKenzie; Oxford, 1940).
Neugebauer, *The Exact Sciences*	O. Neugebauer, *The Exact Sciences in Antiquity* (Copenhagen, 1951).
RE	Pauly–Wissowa, *Real-Encyclopädie der classischen Altertumswissenschaft* (Stuttgart, 1893–).
Reinhardt, *Parmenides*	K. Reinhardt, *Parmenides und die Geschichte der griechischen Philosophie* (Bonn, 1916).
RM	*Rheinisches Museum für Philologie.*

Tannery, *Science hellène*	P. Tannery, *Pour l'histoire de la science hellène* (2d ed.; Paris, 1930).
Vors.	Diels–Kranz, *Die Fragmente der Vorsokratiker* (7th ed.; Berlin, 1954).
Zeller	E. Zeller, *Die Philosophie der Griechen in ihrer geschichtlichen Entwicklung dargestellt*, Part I (in 2 vols.) in 5th ed. (Leipzig, 1892).

BIBLIOGRAPHICAL NOTE

THE fragments of Theophrastus' Φυσικῶν Δόξαι (*Phys. Opin.*) are cited from the edition of Diels in *Doxographi Graeci*; those of Aristotle, according to the numbering of Rose, listed as R³ in the new edition of the *Fragmenta selecta* by W. D. Ross (Oxford, 1955). All references for the pre-Socratics other than Anaximander are to Diels–Kranz (*Vors.*); the system of citation for Anaximander is described below, pp. 25 f. The Greek commentators on Aristotle are cited from the edition of the Berlin Academy.

Titles of Hippocratic works (cited as Hp.) are generally given in Latin, following the abbreviations of LSJ. Works of the Hippocratic Corpus edited by W. H. S. Jones in the Loeb Classical Library are quoted from that edition (abbreviated Jones); otherwise the reference is to Littré. Jones' translation, too, has often been consulted in rendering these texts. For the treatise *De Hebdomadibus*, see the edition of W. H. Roscher, *Die hippokratische Schrift von der Siebenzahl*, Studien zur Geschichte und Kultur des Altertums, VI (Paderborn, 1913), 3–4. The *Anonymus Londinensis* has been cited from the edition of W. H. S. Jones, *The Medical Writings of Anonymus Londinensis* (Cambridge, 1947), abbreviated as *Medical Writings*.

INTRODUCTION

INTRODUCTION

Si nous savions mieux l'histoire, nous trouverions aux origines de
toutes les innovations une grande intelligence.
Émile Mâle, *L'art religieux du XIIe siècle en France*

SINCE the written work of Anaximander is known to us only by a
single brief citation in a late author for whom the original was
already lost, it may well seem an act of folly to undertake a detailed
study of his thought. It is clear that this Greek philosopher of the sixth
century B.C. cannot be the subject of an historical analysis such as we
expect for Plato, Aristotle, or any modern thinker. Anaximander appears to us less as an object for microscopic study than as a kind of
venerable mountain peak looming up in the distance. For what we
catch sight of here is not the countenance of an individual, but the dim
figure of a man who created what the Greeks called περὶ φύσεως ἱστορία,
"the Investigation of Nature."

Firsthand source material for the history of Greek philosophy begins
to be available only at the end of the sixth and beginning of the fifth
century. There, within the compass of a single generation, we find a
number of fragments for Heraclitus and Parmenides, a sentence or two
of Alcmaeon, and a few philosophic verses of Xenophanes. Because of
their brevity or ambiguity, most of these remains offer at best a slippery basis for interpretation. But in the case of Parmenides, the first
few pages of his poem have been preserved as a continuous and almost
integral text. It is here that the serious documentation of Greek philosophy may be said to begin, for it is this text which truly enables us to
judge the quality and complexity of speculative thought at the threshold
of the fifth century. Despite the difference of style and outlook which
separates this period from the classical age, it is impossible to regard it as
one of primitive beginnings. Parmenides' doctrine of the ἐόν, his reasoning to support it, and the physical system which is its complement, all
presuppose a highly cultivated milieu of philosophical discussion. The
other early fragments take on their fullest meaning precisely as representatives of this common intellectual background, this common
climate of ideas, which may be said to constitute the archaic Greek
view of the natural world.

In examining these earliest documents, we find not only that the

Greek philosophy of nature is already in existence, but (rather to our surprise) that it already includes several of the concepts which are most decisive for its classical development. The idea of φύσις itself, for example, of which there is scarcely any trace in the older Greek literature,[1] is taken for granted by both Heraclitus and Parmenides;[2] and it seems also to be implied in the use of the verb φύειν by Xenophanes.[3] The term κόσμος or διάκοσμος for the ordering of the physical world is another momentous novelty, common to Heraclitus and Parmenides.[4] Again, Xenophanes, Heraclitus, and Parmenides all speak of a cosmic deity with functions quite different from those of the traditional Greek pantheon.[5] Alcmaeon joins the other three in distinguishing sharply between complete knowledge—a possession of the gods alone—and the imperfect guesses which men can make about the truth of things.[6] The transformation of the elements is a familiar theme both to Xenophanes and to Heraclitus, who also mentions the change of elemental opposites into one another.[7] And the list might be lengthened.

This common body of ideas, attested for different thinkers of approximately the same date, cannot be explained as the personal innovation of any one of them. Alcmaeon of Croton and Parmenides of Elea on the Tyrrhenian Sea have not borrowed their ideas from Heraclitus of Ephesus; nor can the wandering poet Xenophanes be responsible for this simultaneous flowering of thought at both ends of the Greek world. The resemblance between these widely separated developments may be due in part to an active interchange of persons and ideas; above all, however, it presupposes a common seed from which the regional types have arisen.

The ancient histories of philosophy tell us that the seed was planted in Miletus, in the first half of the sixth century. The new science seems to have been imported into the West by the numerous settlers—such as Pythagoras of Samos—who left Ionia for Magna Graecia in the second half of that century. This Milesian prototype of Greek philosophy has to a large extent disappeared; in its place we have, on the one hand, its

---

[1] The word does not appear in Hesiod and but once in Homer: at κ 303 Hermes shows Odysseus the φύσις of the moly plant, i.e., its bodily form. "The word φύσις is used here like the more common φυή. The Scholiast interprets by τὸ εἶδος" (Merry and Riddell, *Homer's Odyssey* [2d ed.; Oxford, 1886], p. 422). For further discussion of φύσις, see below, pp. 201 ff.

[2] Heracl. B 1, B 106, B 112, B 123; Parm. B 10.5 and B 16.3.

[3] Xenoph. B 32; cf. B 29 and B 38, and ἔφυ in

Parm. B 19.

[4] Heracl. B 30; cf. B 75, B 89, B 124; Parm. B 4.3 and B 8.60, with a play on this meaning at B 8.52.

[5] Xenoph. B 23–26; Heracl. B 32, B 41, B 64, B 67; Parm. B 12–13.

[6] Xenoph. B 34–36; Heracl. B 78–79 (cf. B 1); Alcm. B 1; Parm. B 1.28–32, B 8.50–53.

[7] Xenoph. B 27, B 29–30, B 33; Heracl. B 31, B 36, B 76, B 90, and (for change of opposites) B 126.

various descendants, and, on the other, the doxographical reports and paraphrasing of later authors. In such ancient accounts of early Greek thought, and in the modern histories of philosophy which are based directly upon them, very little attention is paid to the organic relationship between this first age of Ionian philosophy and the much better documented period which stretches from Parmenides to the Hippocratic authors, and to the physical writings of Aristotle. In principle, every student of the subject would be willing to recognize the intrinsic continuity in Greek thought concerning the natural world. In practice, the moderns have generally followed the ancients in treating these early philosophers as so many exalted individualists, whose relationship to one another must be largely a matter of polemic.

Surely more can be done to throw light on the essential unity of early Greek natural speculation. In virtue of such fundamental similarities as those just mentioned, it should be possible to put some semblance of flesh and blood on the dry skeleton of Milesian philosophy preserved for us by the ancient doxography. The historical method should permit us to reconstruct the lost ancestor, as it were, on the basis of a family resemblance in the surviving descendants. The task here may be compared to that of the paleontologist, who, from a fossil, can retrace the form of an extinct predecessor of preserved species; or to that of the linguist, who reconstructs the parent speech revealed by systematic similarities between the early forms of sister languages. The history of ideas naturally poses problems which are even more delicate, for philosophic systems are not handed on as regularly as are the morphological correspondences of words or bones. The task of reconstitution here would no doubt be an impossible one, if we did not possess an outline sketch of the prototype in question. It is for this reason that the ancient doxography of the Milesians must serve as the foundation for any study of the origins of Greek thought. But a foundation it is, and no more. The stones for the superstructure must be quarried elsewhere, from the firsthand documents of Greek thought in the fifth and fourth centuries.

The common traits which these documents present are generally neglected by the ancient accounts of Greek philosophy, which reserve their interest for the points at which one thinker (or group of thinkers) can be contrasted with another. This fact, and the moral to be drawn from it, was clearly pointed out by Paul Tannery seventy-five years ago:

L'histoire de la science restera inintelligible . . . si l'on ne pénètre au delà des contradictions apparentes pour retrouver le fonds commun. Ainsi, tandis que les documents [des doxographes] font surtout ressortir les différences entre les anciens physiologues, le rôle de l'historien doit être aujourd'hui de rechercher surtout les ressemblances; c'est, en effet, leur constatation seule qui peut permettre de rendre raison des différences, d'en préciser le véritable caractère et d'en déterminer l'importance réelle.[1]

The present study is undertaken in the spirit of Tannery's remarks, as an attempt to counterbalance the particularism of our sources by emphasizing those fundamental ideas which bind the early thinkers to one another. It is these common traits which permit us to recognize the Greek philosophy of nature as a unity and as a whole. And this unity can receive an historical explanation only if the common features are shown to result by genetic descent from a common source. In terms of our oldest firsthand documentation, this source may be described as the world scheme which Parmenides presupposes, and against which he is in part reacting. But for a more precise location of the springhead of Greek natural philosophy we must define this scheme as the cosmology of Anaximander.

As one examines the remains of this early period, it is Anaximander who emerges more and more clearly as the central figure in sixth-century thought. It is, in all probability, his work which laid down the lines along which ancient science was to develop and his mind which gave the Greek philosophy of nature its characteristic stamp. In the imperfect state of our documentation, this judgment is obviously beyond the reach of any sort of rigorous proof. What may be affirmed with certainty, however, is that Anaximander is far more accessible to a modern historian than are such fabulous figures as Thales and Pythagoras. It was he who first wrote down his views περὶ φύσεως,[2] and thereby established a new literary form—the first in which prose was employed—which was to serve as the written basis for the new scientific tradition. His work is thus the ancestor for all later specimens of the

---

[1] Science hellène, p. 25.

[2] The expression is current in the fifth and fourth centuries in reference to Ionian physics, and may well have been used by the Milesians themselves. The word φύσις is of particular importance in the first sentence from Heraclitus' book (and compare the other fragments cited in n. 2, p. 4). For περὶ φύσεως as a title see Hp. Anc. Med. 20 (Jones, I, 52): Ἐμπεδοκλῆς ἢ ἄλλοι οἱ περὶ φύσιος γεγράφασιν; De Carn. 15 (Littré, VIII, 604): καὶ εἰσί τινες οἳ ἔλεξαν φύσιν ξυγγράφοντες ὅτι . . . (the reference seems to be primarily to Diogenes); Plato, Lysis 214b.4: οἱ περὶ φύσεώς τε καὶ τοῦ ὅλου διαλεγόμενοι καὶ γράφοντες. Therefore when Aristotle remarks ironically that Empedocles "after all says nothing περὶ φύσεως" (Gen. Corr. 333b18), we may reasonably assume that he was familiar with this phrase as a title for Empedocles' poem.

For the expression περὶ φύσεως ἱστορία, see Phaedo 96a.8, De Caelo 298b2. The two words are associated in Euripides fr. 910 (Vors. 59 A 30), and in Anc. Med. 20; and ἱστορία is used by Heraclitus for the science of Pythagoras (Heracl. B 129, a genuine fragment).

See p. 240 below for Anaximander's priority.

genre, including the *Timaeus*, the physical treatises of Aristotle, and the *De Rerum Natura* of Lucretius. It is this written work which made possible the preservation and transmission of Anaximander's views, their discussion by Aristotle, their summary by Theophrastus, and, finally, their citation by Simplicius in his commentary on the *Physics*. It is, as it were, this act of Anaximander in committing his ideas to writing which brought the history of Greek philosophy into existence. For history implies documents. If Anaximander, Anaximenes, and those who succeeded them had not left behind their thoughts "concerning nature" in written form, early Greek philosophy would no more be a matter for historical study than is, for example, the oral teaching of Pythagoras. On the other hand, Anaximander's significance as an innovator is clearly far greater than that of his younger compatriot Anaximenes, whose doctrines are known to us in the same way, but less completely. It is Anaximander, then, who holds the key to our knowledge of sixth-century thought; and an inquiry into the world view of archaic Greece will best take the form of a study of Anaximander's cosmology.

What the system of Anaximander represents for us is nothing less than the advent, in the West at any rate, of a rational outlook on the natural world. This new point of view asserted itself with the total force of a volcanic eruption, and the ensuing flood of speculation soon spread from Miletus across the length and breadth of the lands in which Greek was spoken. Not all of these derivative streams can be followed here. In particular, the various theories concerning an ἀρχή or first cause have been intentionally neglected, for any adequate treatment of such basic concepts of reality and divinity would have doubled the dimensions of the work. (A partial exception is made, however, in the case of Anaximander's doctrine of the ἄπειρον; see Appendix II.)

Thus the present study is focused on the Milesian cosmology, and on its implications for the Greek view of nature as a whole. The first portion of the work is devoted to a critical analysis of Theophrastus' report on Anaximander. The original text of Theophrastus is lost, but its contents may be recovered from a comparison of the various doxographical accounts which depend upon it in one way or another. The analysis of this material is necessarily involved, but only by such an analysis can we distinguish the questions on which reliable information is available from those which have been hopelessly obscured by the nature of our sources.

The information thus obtained will serve as a basis for the historical discussion of the second part. The first chapter of this discussion outlines the more concrete features of Anaximander's scheme in such matters as the formation of the heavens, the causes of meteorological events, and the origin of life on earth. In the following two sections an effort is made to characterize the more general philosophy of nature within which these theories have their place. Thus the second chapter deals with the classical theory of the elements, its poetic antecedents, and its philosophic origins in the sixth century. The third chapter offers a detailed interpretation of Anaximander's only fragment, considered as the earliest expression for the Greek view of the natural world as a cosmos organized by law. In the Conclusion some permanent aspects of the influence of Milesian ideas will be considered, in particular, the fundamental meaning of φύσις, and the important role assigned to cosmogony in most of the physical schemes of antiquity. Finally, the Appendices deal with two questions whose treatment is too lengthy for a place in the main discussion: the original philosophic sense of the term κόσμος; and Anaximander's conception of the ἄπειρον.

It may be that certain achievements have been claimed for the hero of this story which belong in fact to Thales, to Pythagoras, or to another. If so, there is unfortunately no test by which true paternity can be established. In a sense it might be said that the name of Anaximander stands here as a symbol for the anonymous creative spirit of Ionian thought in the sixth century. The personal features of Anaximander's life and speculation are as completely mutilated for us as is the trunkless remnant of an archaic statue from Miletus which bears his name. But in so far as the earliest coherent view of nature can be deemed the work of any single man, we must truly look upon Anaximander "as the author of the natural philosophy of Greece, and consequently of the Occident."[1]

---

[1] T. Gomperz, *Greek Thinkers*, tr. L. Magnus (London, 1901), I, 49.

The Milesian statue (formerly in Berlin) has generally been interpreted as a portrait, but a recent study suggests that it is a female figure and that "Anaximander" is the donor's name. See W. Darsow, "Die Kore des Anaximandros," *Jahrbuch des deutschen archäologischen Instituts*, LXIX (1954), 101.

Our information concerning Anaximander's life is very meager. Apollodorus gave his age as sixty-four in 547/6 B.C., apparently on the basis of statements in his book (*Vors.* 12 A 1.2). Aelian tells us that he led the Milesian colony to Apollonia

(*Vors.* 12 A 3). A visit to Sparta is mentioned by Diogenes Laertius, who connects it with the establishment there of a γνώμων or sundial (*Vors.* 12 A 1.1, from Favorinus), and also by Cicero, who declares that Anaximander warned the Spartans of an imminent earthquake (*Vors.* 12 A 5a). A second anecdote in Diogenes Laertius—that he tried to improve his singing after having been laughed at by some boys—does not inspire much confidence, nor does the other story in Diogenes, that Empedocles wished to emulate Anaximander by adopting solemn manners and theatrical garb (*Vors.* 12 A 8).

THE DOCUMENTARY EVIDENCE FOR
ANAXIMANDER'S VIEWS

INTRODUCTION TO THE DOXOGRAPHY

A NY treatment of early Greek philosophy is conditioned by the special nature of our sources. In the case of authors such as Parmenides and Empedocles, the original fragments enable us to control many of the statements made by Aristotle and the doxographers. For the sixth-century Milesians, there is no source of information outside the doxographical tradition. Even the fragment of Anaximander is known to us not by direct citation, but as a part of the account of Theophrastus repeated by Simplicius. Since this fragment is the only primary source for Milesian philosophy, its historical value is unparalleled. But the task of exegesis is a delicate one. Embedded as it is in the matrix of a doxographical excerpt, the fragment cannot be extracted and interpreted without a general analysis of its context.[1]

In the first place the doxography itself must be reconstructed as far as possible. Eighty-five years ago Diels showed that all the ancient doxographers who treat of the pre-Socratics depend, in one way or another, on the lost Φυσικῶν Δόξαι of Theophrastus. The principal concern of Diels in his Prolegomena to the *Doxographi Graeci* was to demonstrate the fact and the nature of this dependence. Only incidentally did he compare and criticize the various parallel accounts in order to reconstruct the original version of Theophrastus. Wide use has been made since then of the results of Diels' research, but the attempt to visualize more clearly the lost archetype, and thereby to assay the documentary value of the different epitomes, has not yet been carried to completion.

In dealing with Anaximander, this documentary problem is of particular importance. Although his book was still available to Apollodorus, who made some use of it in his chronology (D.L. 11.2 = *Vors.* 12 A 1), it is not known to have been consulted by any other writer later than Aristotle and Theophrastus. There is then no reason to assign any historical value to a later report of Anaximander's teaching, except in so far as the author relies upon Aristotle and Theophrastus. These are the only two witnesses whose voice deserves a hearing. And before their testimony can be evaluated, one must determine what Aristotle

---

[1] It is therefore most regrettable that in the latest editions of the *Fragmente der Vorsokratiker* this "quotation" from Anaximander has been separated from the surrounding words which alone can specify its meaning. Compare *Vors.* 12 B 1 with 12 A 9.

and Theophrastus have in fact said. The Aristotelian passages which mention Anaximander by name, or where a reference to him may reasonably be inferred, can be cited directly. But in the case of Theophrastus, it is impossible to proceed without a critical reconstruction of his text.

Theophrastus and His Excerptors

There can be no question of restoring a lost work in so far as it is really lost. All we can attempt to do is refine the surviving ore out of the dross which has accumulated through centuries of excerpts and epitomes. Where information given by Theophrastus has not been repeated by an extant author, there is no means of finding out what he said. In fact one may be certain of the original text only in the rare cases where it has been preserved by more than one author, for the necessary and sufficient proof of authenticity is the verbatim agreement of two independent excerptors.

A nice question is posed when information is given by one author alone. Even if the writer is known to make use of Theophrastus elsewhere, that does not prove that he is following the same source at every point, nor that he is reproducing him in accurate fashion. A particular judgment must be formed for each case, in terms of the author's general reliability and on the basis of parallel information given by other sources. A special case is represented by Anaximander's fragment, which cannot very well be explained except as a verbatim repetition by Simplicius of the original quotation in the text of Theophrastus. In other instances we can hardly deal at all with the question of literal faithfulness, but only with the factual reliability of our sources as evidence for what Theophrastus said.

This matter of the relative accuracy of the extant doxographers is decisive for any treatment of Milesian thought, and must be considered here in some detail. In so far as it relates to Anaximander, the Theophrastean account is known to us in four principal versions: (1) the remarks of Simplicius concerning the ἀρχαί of the early philosophers, in the opening pages of his commentary on Aristotle's *Physics* (*Dox.* 476); (2) the brief history of Greek philosophy given by Hippolytus as an introduction to his *Refutation of All Heresies* (*Dox.* 559 f.); (3) the excerpts quoted from the *Stromateis* of "Plutarch" by Eusebius in his *Praeparatio Evangelica* (*Dox.* 579); and (4) the large-scale work on the history of philosophy preserved both as the *Placita* in the manuscripts of Plutarch and as part of the *Eclogae Physicae* of Stobaeus; these two texts were reunited by Diels and ascribed by him to a Hellenistic excerptor called Aëtius (*Dox.* 273 ff.; for Anaximander, see 277 f. and *passim*). Aëtius is little more than a name for us; but this name has the advantage of bringing together two texts which cannot well be separated from one another.[1]

Other doxographies, such as those of Cicero and Diogenes Laertius, give us little real information concerning Anaximander. Two Latin authors, Seneca and Censorinus, do serve to supplement the four primary sources on one or two points. But our knowledge of Theophrastus' account rests essentially upon these four, and it is their reliability which must be examined most closely.

SIMPLICIUS. Pages 22 to 28 of his commentary on the *Physics* constitute our principal source for Theophrastus' chapter on the ἀρχαί. Simplicius repeatedly affirms that he is making use of Theophrastus, and concludes his discussion of the early philosophers with the statement that "this is an abridged outline (σύντομος περίληψις) of what is reported concerning the ἀρχαί" (*in Phys.* p. 28.30 = *Dox.* 484.17). The faithfulness of his excerpts, at least in regard to Anaximander, is clear not only from the citation of the fragment, but also from two verbatim agreements with an independent source, Hippolytus (see below, **2** and **4**; boldface numbers indicate the topical units of the doxography as explained under "Arrangement of the Doxography," pp. 25 f.).

On the other hand, Simplicius does not always limit himself to a slavish copying of one original. We must bear in mind that he is a well-read scholar, whose judgments on early Greek philosophy may also be the fruit of his own reading of Aristotle or other authors. Thus he sometimes quotes the statements of Theophrastus not from a direct consultation of the *Phys. Opin.*, but from the excerpts given by Alexander in his lost commentary on the *Physics*.[2] In describing the doctrine of Xenophanes, Simplicius associates Theophrastus' name with an account so entirely divergent from other Theophrastean sources that Diels concluded that our commentator had no access to the original *Phys. Opin.* but was dependent upon Alexander for all his excerpts (*Dox.* 113).

Now it is difficult to believe that the philosophical library in which Simplicius could find such rare items as the poem of Parmenides and

---

[1] For Diels' unearthing of Aëtius, see *Dox.* 47 f.

[2] As Diels has pointed out (*Dox.* 113), Simplicius cites *Phys. Opin.* fr. 6 (*in Phys.* 38.20), fr. 7 (*ibid.* 115.11), and fr. 15 (*ibid.* 700.18), not from the original text, but from Alexander's commentary, which he must have had continually open before him.

the treatises of Anaxagoras and Diogenes contained no copy of this famous work of Theophrastus; nor is there any reason why Simplicius should not have consulted it for his copious excerpts in pages 22–28.[1] What his section on Xenophanes proves is not that he had never seen the text of Theophrastus, but that this was not his only source, and that he was perfectly capable of ignoring the *Phys. Opin.*, even in these few pages where his general reliance upon it is beyond doubt. It is noteworthy that this strange treatment of Xenophanes occurs at the very beginning of his "abridged outline," before the doctrine of the Milesians, who no doubt figured first in the exposition of Theophrastus. It is only with Thales, Heraclitus, and Anaximander (p. 23.22 ff.) that the systematic dependence on Theophrastus becomes demonstrable. With them, Simplicius had no motive to enlarge upon Theophrastus' account, while in the case of Xenophanes he had already committed himself to a Neoplatonic interpretation (p. 7.1, p. 21.18; cf. p. 29.6), and seems not even to have noticed its incompatibility with the testimony of Theophrastus.[2]

With regard therefore to Anaximander's ἀρχή, the statements of Simplicius on page 24 may rank as an excellent firsthand source for Theophrastus' account. But information given by Simplicius in a different portion of his work—or, a fortiori, in a different commentary— does not necessarily have the same documentary value. These other statements may be based upon the same passages already cited from Theophrastus (as when the comparison of Anaxagoras to Anaximander, first given at p. 27.17, is repeated almost verbatim at p. 154.17), or upon Simplicius' general erudition. The other summaries of Anaximander's doctrines by the same author (*in Phys.* 41.17, 150.22; *in De Caelo* 615.13) do not show literal agreement with parallel sources, and need not presuppose a fresh consultation of the *Phys. Opin.* Nor is there

[1] This paradoxical view of Diels was rightly rejected by Reinhardt, *Parmenides*, pp. 92–94n, followed by O. Regenbogen, *Theophrastos von Eresos*, in *RE*, Suppl. Bd., VII, 1536.52. The hypothesis that such abundant excerpts could have appeared in Alexander's lost commentary is not borne out by the same author's extant work on the *Metaphysics*, which contains only one brief quotation from the *Phys. Opin.* (fr. 6 = Alex. *in Met.* 31.7). There is one other citation, this time not verbatim, in his commentary on the *Meteorologica* (67.11 = *Phys. Opin.* fr. 23). It seems most unlikely that Alexander's practice was radically different in the *Physics* commentary, or that Simplicius would have bothered to repeat such

extensive excerpts if they had already been given by his predecessor.

[2] As basis for his interpretation, Simplicius uses a source which is identical with, or very similar to, the pseudo-Aristotelian treatise *De Xenophane*. But there is no reason to suppose that Simplicius held Theophrastus to be the author of this dialectical exercise. Since he could not hope to find his transcendental interpretation of Xenophanes in the *physical* work of Theophrastus (as he admits, p. 22.29), he had recourse to another, less critical authority. He seems to have been guilty of a simple oversight in failing to recognize the true version of Theophrastus in the view cited by him from Alexander (p. 23.16).

any evidence that Simplicius has drawn upon the other chapters of this work for detailed information concerning Anaximander. It is noteworthy that the latter's speculation concerning the sizes and distances of the heavenly bodies is known to Simplicius not from Theophrastus but from the history of astronomy by Eudemus (see below, under **16**).

For Theophrastus' discussion of the ἀρχαί, Simplicius is thus our best source; for the rest of the *Phys. Opin*, he is scarcely a source at all. In terms of the present numbering of the doxography, Simplicius is the chief authority for **1–7**. Since **8** is not mentioned by him, perhaps it was to be found in a slightly different context. It is doubtful whether **9** comes from the *Phys. Opin*. in the first place; and the information given by Simplicius under **10** cannot represent Theophrastus. His statement under **16** derives from Eudemus. For the rest of the doxography, Simplicius has nothing to tell us.

HIPPOLYTUS. All of the information which this author gives us concerning Anaximander (with the exception of his date, *Dox*. 560.11) comes from Theophrastus and from no other source. He is drawing upon an epitome in which the information spread throughout the sixteen or eighteen books of the *Phys. Opin*. had been grouped under the names of the various thinkers. The account of doctrines has been abbreviated, and some details have been confused and mutilated by careless copying. But no basic blunders mar these excerpts; they are "merae Physicorum Opinionum in epitomen coactae reliquiae" (*Dox*. 144).

The accuracy of Hippolytus, despite his brevity, can be seen in two literal agreements with the text of Simplicius (**2** and **4**). In both cases the minor discrepancies are to be explained by the fact that the version of Hippolytus has passed through more hands. Where the text of Hippolytus is not obviously corrupt, it may in general serve as a direct substitute for Theophrastus. A few instances may suffice to confirm this reliability.

(1) The close verbal parallel between Hippolytus' account of the ἀρχή of Anaximenes (*Dox*. 560 = *Vors*. 13 A 7.1–3), and the same information as given by Simplicius (*Phys. Opin*. fr. 2 = *Vors*. 13 A 5). In this case, the version of Hippolytus is the more complete.

(2) The literal echoes of Anaxagoras B 15 in Hippolytus' paraphrase (*Dox*. 562.2–5 = *Vors*. 59 A 42.2). They can of course be derived only from a faithful excerpt of Theophrastus' own lost paraphrase.

(3) The accurate rendering of Theophrastus' own words (*Phys. Opin*.

fr. 6 = *Vors.* 28 A 7) in Hippolytus' account of Parmenides (*Dox.* 564.19 = *Vors.* 28 A 23).

We need not consider here the inferior source utilized by Hippolytus for the doctrine of Thales, Pythagoras, Empedocles, and Heraclitus. There is no trace of such adulteration in the excerpts used in the present study—those dealing with Anaximander, Anaximenes, Anaxagoras, and Archelaus (chs. 6–9)—where his source is regularly Theophrastus.

PSEUDO-PLUTARCH, *Stromateis*. The documentary value of this text is not on a par with that of Simplicius and Hippolytus. Stylistically, the author is given to very free paraphrase (see below, **2.P.** and **7.P.**). His report is vague, incomplete, and not always free from confusion (e.g., **4.P.**) Nevertheless, he gives some information of great interest which is preserved nowhere else, and whose general accuracy is not open to suspicion (see above all **13.P.**, and the remarks of Diels, *Dox.* 156–58).

AËTIUS. This work on *Placita* (περὶ τῶν ἀρεσκόντων τοῖς φιλοσόφοις φυσικῶν δογμάτων) is the most systematic and the least satisfactory of all ancient histories of philosophy. The material of Theophrastus' sixteen volumes has been compressed into five brief books, which retain the original treatment by subject matter rather than by author. But the rigorous structure of the work has been shattered by a ridiculous subdivision of topics, so that the connected discussion of Theophrastus' chapter *De Sensibus* (*Dox.* 499 ff.) is dispersed into small, almost unrecognizable morsels throughout a dozen sections of Aëtius (*Dox.* 393–409). The loose space between the threads of Aëtius' new fabric has been filled with abundant extracts from later sources (such as those dealing with Stoic and Epicurean views), while even the older doctrines have been remodelled to suit the literary taste of a Hellenistic audience. Thus the typical Peripatetic reserve concerning the undocumented teaching of Thales and Pythagoras gives way before a picturesque presentation of both men as leaders of the two rival choruses in the drama of early Greek thought. Now Pythagoras marches at the head of the Italians as Thales before the Ionians, and each coryphaeus proclaims the doctrines which his followers are to repeat or modify in turn. (See Aëtius 1.3.1, 3.8–9; cf. 1.7.11, 7.18, 8.2, 9.2, etc.) Also characteristic of the writer and his time is the elaborate discussion of the questions, "Whence did men have the notion of gods?" and "What is ὁ θεός?" (*Dox.* 292, 297), neither of which figured in Theophrastus' work on natural philosophy. It is here that the erudition of our author is most ambitious, reaching out to embrace the views of Aratus, Callimachus, and Critias (persistently misquoted as "Euripides"), as well as those of Hesiod, Homer, and the philosophers.

Concerning the exact relationship between Aëtius and the original text of Theophrastus, Diels had an elaborate theory, of which not all the details are convincing, and which presupposes an unknown Hellenistic intermediary called by him the *Vetusta Placita*, presumably composed under the influence of Posidonius (*Dox.* 178 ff.). Whatever the exact textual filiation may have been, a comparison of the *De Sensibus* with Aëtius IV.8–20 makes it plain that the statements of this doxographer can be directly ascribed to Theophrastus only in a small minority of cases. (This comparison is discussed by Diels, *Dox.* 222 f.) Not only does Aëtius make liberal use of later sources; complete distortion is not unknown to him, as one example concerning Anaximander shows very well (see below, on 4.A.).

At the same time it is clear that whatever credible information is given by Aëtius concerning the pre-Socratics must ultimately derive from Theophrastus. Thus the one explicit citation from the *Phys. Opin.* (concerning Xenophanes' explanation of the sun) is set next to another statement on the matter which clearly comes from the same source by way of a freer paraphrase (II.20.3 = *Vors.* 21 A 40); Aëtius himself has apparently not recognized the essential identity of the two versions. Since his work represents the fullest extant epitome of Theophrastus, on many points he constitutes our only authority. In such cases, one must take his testimony for what it is worth. In general, the simpler and more factual matters are likely to be reported by him without serious damage. The more complex or unfamiliar a doctrine may be, the more scope is left to his penchant for confusion.[1] In terms of the following doxography, Aëtius is a very poor source for the philosophic problems of **1–9**; on the other hand, his information is often of great value in the more narrowly physical questions of **10–21**.

Theophrastus as an Historian of Early Greek Philosophy

An equitable judgment of Theophrastus' historical work requires some idea of his method and his purpose in dealing with the predecessors of Aristotle. His dependence upon his master's own work, for

---

[1] For examples of Aëtius' incapacity to give a clear version of any complicated theory, even when plain matters of fact are concerned, see his account of Parmenides' στεφάναι (II.7.1 = Parm. A 37), and of Empedocles' "two suns" (II.20.13 = Emped. A 56). Both of these reports are unintelligible, at least in part, and unfortunately there is no full parallel in either case which would permit us to clear up the confusion.

instance, is often emphasized, but the nature and limits of this relationship have not always been made clear.

The procedure of Theophrastus in dealing with the theories of the early philosophers can best be studied in the one long surviving fragment, De Sensibus (Dox. 499 ff.); and there is no reason to suppose that this text is not typical of the lost portions of the Phys. Opin.[1] His discussion there may be analyzed into three parts: (1) a general statement of the problem, and the principal kinds of solution (De Sens. 1–2, 59–61); (2) the report of individual doctrines (3–11, 25–30, 38–45, etc.); and (3) the critical evaluation of these doctrines, with emphasis on their errors and deficiencies (12–24, 31–37, 46–48, etc.). Sometimes the transition from one section to another—as from the exposition of a doctrine to its criticism—is not plainly marked, but the intrinsic difference between the three procedures is quite clear.

Now, as we can easily see from the De Sensibus, the Aristotelian influence is not equally distributed over the different parts of Theophrastus' discussion. The expository section is in general much fuller than Aristotle's own mention of his predecessors' views, and there is in many cases no Aristotelian reference whatsoever to the doctrine reported by Theophrastus. The case of his critical judgments is similar. Sometimes the objections presuppose an Aristotelian point of view, but more often they are aimed at internal inconsistencies or incompleteness in the doctrines described. It is in the first section, in the statement of the problem, that the Aristotelian influence tends to be most pronounced. And that is precisely what we would expect. Theophrastus may have begun his collection of material as a kind of research project under Aristotle's personal supervision. His master's thought is in any event the starting point for his own philosophical endeavor. It must be remembered that Theophrastus' motive in reporting the views of earlier Greek philosophers is by no means purely historical. The documentary concern with the past is for him above all a tool in the creative search for truth. The sixteen volumes of the Φυσικῶν Δόξαι constituted as it were a prolonged προαπορεῖν—a preliminary analysis of the views of one's predecessors in order to decide the truth for oneself (cf. Arist. Met. 995ᵃ24–ᵇ4).

---

[1] I do not follow the suggestion of O. Regenbogen (RE, Suppl. Bd., VII, 1537.26) that the De Sensibus may not originally have formed part of the Phys. Opin. Our extant text is certainly identical with the basic source on the pre-Socratics followed by Aëtius IV.13 and 16–19. Compare, e.g., the statements concerning Alcmaeon at Aëtius IV.13.12, 16.2, 17.1, 18.1 (= Vors. 24 A 6, A 8–10) with De Sensibus 25–26 (= Vors. 24 A 5).

The sense in which such a work may be regarded as historical is clearly limited. In so far as the problems and concepts of late fourth-century philosophy differ from those of the preceding period, the systematic treatment of Theophrastus (like that of Aristotle before him) tends to distort the original form of the doctrines under consideration. And the gap between Theophrastus and his historical subject matter naturally widens precisely at those points where the Aristotelian school is in possession of an essentially new doctrine and a complex terminology of its own. A conscious effort to free himself of this doctrine and terminology forms no part of Theophrastus' conception of the task before him. The most striking example of such dependence is to be found in his treatment of the ἀρχαί, which follows closely—and even verbally—Aristotle's own discussion in *Metaphysics* A (chs. 3–6). It is clear that here, where Aristotle's analysis of earlier doctrines was particularly elaborate, Theophrastus made no pretense at an independent study. At this point his technique consists essentially in a more thorough documentation of the views expressed by Aristotle.[1]

At the same time, like all good students, Theophrastus is capable of correcting or avoiding an occasional slip on the part of his master. Since the point is an important one, a few examples may be cited.

(1) Aristotle tends to assume that μάνωσις and πύκνωσις are involved in the doctrines of all, or nearly all, the monists (*Phys.* 187ª15, 189ᵇ8). This was probably true, in effect, and Theophrastus expressed himself in a similar way with regard to Heraclitus (*Vors.* 22 A 1.8–9; cf. A 5) and Diogenes (A 1, A 5). At the same time Theophrastus was careful to point out that the theory of Heraclitus was not free from ambiguity (*Vors.* 22 A 1.8: σαφῶς δὲ οὐδὲν ἐκτίθεται), and that it was Anaximenes alone who actually worked out the doctrine in these terms (*Dox.* 477 n.ª2 = *Vors.* 13 A 5).

(2) At *Phys.* 187ª20, Aristotle implies that Anaximander used the term ἐκκρίνεσθαι, while all the doxographers who follow Theophrastus have ἀποκρίνεσθαι for this doctrine. Since the latter word is the only one known from Herodotus and from the fragments of Anaxagoras, it is no doubt the true Ionic form which occurred in Anaximander's text.

---

[1] To this extent, the harsh judgment of J. B. McDiarmid is certainly justified; see "Theophrastus on the Presocratic Causes," *Harv. Stud.*, LXI (1953), 85–156. But I would not subscribe to McDiarmid's general conclusion concerning Theophrastus, that, "with regard to the Presocratic causes at least, he is a thoroughly biased witness and is even less trustworthy than Aristotle" (p. 133).

The dependence of Theophrastus on Aristotle is also emphasized by J. Kerschensteiner, "Der Bericht des Theophrast über Heraklit," *Hermes*, LXXXIII (1955), 385.

(Ἀποκρίνεσθαι is in fact in Homer and Archilochus, whereas ἐκκρίνεσθαι is apparently not to be found before the middle or late fifth century.) Theophrastus' superiority as a documentary source is here apparent.

(3) The same passage of the *Physics* contains a more significant discrepancy between Aristotle and Theophrastus. The former seems to identify the primeval unity of Anaximander (and Empedocles) with the μίγμα of Anaxagoras. Theophrastus accepts the comparison, but qualifies it with the necessary proviso, "if one understands the [Anaxagorean] mixture of all things as one substance indeterminate both in kind and in magnitude" (*Phys. Opin.* fr. 4, cited below under **6**).

There are, furthermore, a surprising number of cases where Aristotle is guilty of strange verbal errors in the interpretation of a text which he cites directly.[1] This kind of carelessness in the use of original documents is not, as far as I can see, attested for Theophrastus.

It would in short be a mistake to suppose that Theophrastus was ever stupidly bound by the obiter dicta of his master. If his own extant metaphysical work does not show the greatness of a creative philosopher, it bears witness at least to the independence of his critical judgment, even when very central points of Aristotelian philosophy are at stake.[2] If in the *Phys. Opin.* he follows the Aristotelian treatment of the causes, it is because he believes such a treatment to be fundamentally correct. The implicit anachronism is as involuntary for both master and disciple as is that of any modern writer who describes ancient philosophy in terms of "Realism," "Idealism," or "subjectivity."

It is nonetheless true that a similarity between Aristotle and Theophrastus on a question like the ἀρχαί does not constitute an agreement of independent sources, and the older interpreters of Greek philosophy (such as Zeller and Burnet) were mistaken in placing so much faith in the schematism of Aristotle's school. Such specifically Peripatetic notions as ὕλη, στοιχεῖον, and ὑποκείμενον are not satisfactory tools for the description of sixth-century ideas. On the contrary, the real historical value of Theophrastus' account appears wherever he diverges from, or goes beyond, the statements of Aristotle. Thus what interests us in his account of Anaximander is not the repetition of the Aristotelian phrase ἀρχὴ καὶ στοιχεῖον τῶν ὄντων (**2**), but the statement that this role was played for Anaximander by the ἄπειρον (which is a fact never expressed by Aristotle, although it is implied by him at *Phys.* 203ᵇ10–15).

---

[1] See the Supplementary Note, pp. 22–24.
[2] See, for example, the discussion of the final

cause in Theophrastus' *Metaphysics*, ch. 9.

Theophrastus also adds the information that Anaximander was the first to introduce the term ἀρχή (2), and that from the ἄπειρον "arise all the heavens and the κόσμοι within them" (4). These statements are important, because they are *not* to be found in Aristotle. Neither of course is the fragment (5), nor the Homeric reference to the ἄπειρον as "unaging" (8.H.). Yet all of this information must have appeared in the discussion of the ἀρχαί. We see that, even here, Theophrastus did not restrict himself to the Aristotelian texts, but referred directly to whatever original sources were available to him.

It seems clear that these writings were carefully studied by Theophrastus, and faithfully represented in the expository sections of his work. The proof of this is not restricted to the direct citations, such as the fragment of Anaximander or an occasional verse from Empedocles or Parmenides. Even where an author is not quoted but paraphrased, the original wording often shows through.[1] This can be demonstrated in detail by a comparison of the views ascribed to Plato in the *De Sensibus* with the corresponding sections of the *Timaeus*.[2] The performance of Theophrastus here, in the sole case where we can fully control his use of source material, is fine enough to justify a modern editor's praise of the "high accuracy" of his "dispassionate and marvellously impartial report."[3] That such verbal accuracy was limited neither to the chapter on sensation nor to the use of Platonic texts is proved by the agreement already mentioned between Hippolytus' account of Anaxagoras (*Vors.* 59 A 42) and that author's fragment 15. There again the method of literal paraphrase reappears. The best extant version of Theophrastus' report on Heraclitus (D.L. ix. 8 ff. = *Vors.* 22 A 1) contains a verbal reminiscence of seven or eight original fragments.[4] If in

---

[1] "Constat in Theophrasteis prisca vocabula velut nobilem aeruginem interdum retineri, velut in fr. de sensu § 50 Democritea ὁμοιοσχημονεῖν, 51 θρύπτεσθαι, 55 vel ionicam formam διαμίμνει" (*Dox.* 219).

[2] Compare *Dox.* 500.9 with *Tim.* 67c.6–7, where φλόγα τῶν σωμάτων . . . ὄψει σύμμετρα μόρια ἔχουσαν is reproduced practically verbatim. The following definitions of "sound" and "hearing" are equally faithful excerpts of *Tim.* 67b.2–5. The many literal reminiscences of the *Timaeus* in *De Sensibus* 83–86 were already noticed by Diels on *Dox.* 524–25. The two texts are printed in parallel columns and discussed in detail by G. M. Stratton, *Theophrastus and the Greek Physiological Psychology before Aristotle* (London, 1917), pp. 160 ff., 203 ff. The exposition of Plato's complex theories contains a few omissions and inaccuracies, due

rather to Theophrastus' habitual brevity than to any misunderstanding of the original. (But see now J. B. McDiarmid, "Plato in Theophrastus' *De Sensibus*", *Phronesis*, IV [1959], 59.)

[3] Stratton, *op. cit.*, p. 16n and p. 53. Theophrastus' exposition may challenge comparison with that of any modern historian of philosophy, but when he turns to criticism, the historical interest of his work naturally fades into the background.

[4] In addition to the four fragments compared in *Vors.* 22 A 1.8 (B 90, B 12, B 91, B 80), compare γίνεσθαι καθ᾽ εἱμαρμένην with B 137 (based, I believe, upon something Heraclitus really said); ὁδὸν ἄνω κάτω with B 60; τὸν κόσμον γίνεσθαι κατ᾽ αὐτήν with B 1 (γινομένων γὰρ πάντων κατὰ τὸν λόγον τόνδε); τὸ ὕδωρ εἰς γῆν τρέπεσθαι with B 31; etc. Whether or not Theophrastus has funda-

this case we possessed the full text of Heraclitus and the original exposition of Theophrastus, we would no doubt find the parallelism as complete as in the excerpts from the *Timaeus*.

These considerations may suffice to justify the inevitable use of Theophrastus' account as the groundwork for any history of sixth-century thought. It is not because the general aim and outlook of his work is truly historical that we may rely upon it; for such is not the case. It is in virtue of his careful and intelligent use of original documents in the exposition of early theories that his account may serve to replace these documents when they themselves have been lost. This use of the original texts becomes apparent precisely at the point where Theophrastus passes beyond the limits of Aristotle's treatment. His own research is therefore least conspicuous in the discussion of the ἀρχαί, although there are distinct traces of it even there. His independent study of the texts is, on the other hand, evident at every point in the detailed exposition of physical theories, such as those treated in the *De Sensibus*.

Aristotle himself may incidentally give us information of great value concerning early Greek philosophy. But the systematic exposition of earlier views plays a much smaller part in his work than in that of Theophrastus, and his negligence concerning documentary details is often in marked contrast to the care and caution of his pupil. In general, we may say that Theophrastus ranks as a documentary source wherever he tells us more than Aristotle does on the same point, and that any apparent disagreement between the two writers may almost invariably be resolved in favor of the version of Theophrastus.

Supplementary Note: On the Relative Accuracy of Aristotle and Theophrastus in the Use of Documentary Material

The frequent errors of Aristotle in the use of documents—even when he cites the text—are well known. One thinks, for instance, of the curious misconstruing of the genitive Διφίλου in the epigram quoted at *Ath. Pol.* 7.4. (See the discussion of Kurt von Fritz and Ernst Kapp in their translation of the *Constitution of Athens* [New York, 1950], p. 155, n. 20. A correct interpretation of the epigram is given by Pollux VIII. 131, cited by Sandys in his edition of the *Ath. Pol., ad loc.*)

---

mentally misunderstood Heraclitus is a question which need not be considered here. What is essential for us is the confirmation of his expository method as one of detailed paraphrase.

Such carelessness is of course not always typical of Aristotle's treatment of documents. The general analysis of early Athenian history on the basis of Solon's poems (*Ath. Pol.* 5–12) is a brilliant example to the contrary. But verbal or mechanical slips in citation are almost too numerous to mention. As one editor remarked, "Our author is very liable to misquotation, as I believe to be the case with all or most of those who, having a wide range of reading and an unusually retentive memory, are accustomed to rely too confidently upon the latter faculty" —E. M. Cope and J. E. Sandys, *The Rhetoric of Aristotle* (Cambridge, 1877), II, 103. Cope was commenting on *Rhet.* 1386ª20, where Aristotle mentions the story of the forbearance of Psammenitus at the death of his son (from Hdt. III.14), but wrongly gives the king's name as Amasis. Comparable examples in quotation from Homer are to be found at *Rhet.* 1417ª14 (where ψ 310–43 are referred to as "sixty verses"; see Munro's note on this passage in the *Odyssey*), and at *Eth. Nic.* 1109ª31, where a speech of Odysseus (μ 219) is assigned to Calypso.

Three cases of similar errors, involving ideas as well as words, occur in connection with quotations from Empedocles: (1) The sense of φύσις in Emped. B 8 is certainly not οὐσία, as Aristotle suggests at *Met.* 1015ª1, but γένεσις (as Plutarch rightly understands it, *Adv. Col.* 1112A). The various modern attempts to justify Aristotle's interpretation all make nonsense of Empedocles' verse. (2) At *Parva Nat.* 473ª17, Aristotle declares that Empedocles speaks only of respiration through the nostrils, and not through the windpipe. This exclusive concern with the nostrils constitutes for him a serious deficiency (474ª18). In illustration of Empedocles' view, he cites a long passage from the former's poem (B 100) in which no mention of nostrils occurs, but which contains the genitive plural ῥινῶν from ῥινός, "skin." The context shows that Aristotle must have misunderstood this as ῥίς, "nose."[1] (3) A third misinterpretation, at *Phys.* 250ᵇ29, has attracted less attention. Here Aristotle quotes Emped. B 26.8–12 as evidence for the alternate cosmic periods of motion and rest. It is clear that he has understood ἀκίνητοι κατὰ κύκλον to refer to the total immobility of things in the divine Sphere, which arises between the destruction and rebirth of the universe (Emped. B 27–28, where μονίη = μονή). But in fact Empedocles is speaking in B 26 of the imperishability of the elements *throughout change* (ἀλλάσσοντα διαμπερές), so that ἀκίνητοι κατὰ κύκλον must be an

---

[1] So Diels on *Vors.* 31 B 100. The error of Aristotle is confirmed by D. J. Furley in a detailed treatment of the passage, "Empedocles and the Clepsydra," *JHS*, LXXVII (1957), 30.

oxymoron, "fixed in a turning circle"; i.e., "undisturbed despite their cycle of transformation."[1]

In so far as we can judge Theophrastus' own use of source material, there is no trace of such carelessness. For example, in his account of Parmenides in *Phys. Opin.* fr. 6 (*Vors.* 28 A 7), we may observe his greater accuracy due to the habit of close paraphrase. Thus the two sections of Parmenides' poem are distinguished κατ' ἀλήθειαν μὲν and κατὰ δόξαν δὲ τῶν πολλῶν, according to the very words of Parm. B 1.29–30: ἠμὲν ἀληθείης . . . ἠδὲ βροτῶν δόξας (and cf. B 8.51). Aristotle's own distinction in terms of λόγος and αἴσθησις or φαινόμενα (*Vors.* 28 A 24–25) is less accurate, for the terms are his own rather than those of the writer in question. On the other hand, the rest of Theophrastus' sentence is based upon Aristotle's treatment of the ἀρχαί, and shares its inaccuracy: δύω ποιῶν τὰς ἀρχάς, πῦρ καὶ γῆν, τὸ μὲν ὡς ὕλην τὸ δὲ ὡς αἴτιον καὶ ποιοῦν. The fragments speak not of fire and earth, but of fire or light and night (B 8.56–59, B 9, B 12), while the contrast between passive matter and the active cause of motion is, in this form, purely Peripatetic. It is characteristic that when Theophrastus came to deal with the cosmology of Parmenides in detail, he seems to have abandoned this Aristotelian schematism for a more accurate paraphrase. Thus Aëtius (who must ultimately depend on Theophrastus for such information) speaks correctly here of φώς and σκότος (Parm. A 37, where the parallel from Cicero also has *lux*), and contrasts them as ἀραιόν and πυκνόν just as Parmenides himself does at B 8.57–59: ἐλαφρόν . . . πυκινὸν δέμας ἐμβριθές τε. In such a case, the agreement of Theophrastus with Aristotle is unhistorical; his additional information comes from a careful study of the texts.

[1] Since this was written, F. Solmsen has called attention to this "howler" in "Aristotle and   Presocratic Cosmogony", *Harv. Stud.*, LXIII (1958), 277.

ARRANGEMENT OF THE DOXOGRAPHY

THE following pages contain what is left of Theophrastus' account of the doctrines of Anaximander, together with a commentary. The text reproduced is essentially that of Diels in the *Doxographi Graeci*, but silently incorporates a few minor changes adopted by him in the *Fragmente der Vorsokratiker*. All conscious deviations from the readings of Diels have been mentioned in a footnote.

To facilitate a point-by-point comparison, the various excerpts have been divided into small units, and these units grouped according to subject matter or topic. The result is a series of cross sections through the different doxographies, permitting at a glance the detailed comparison of their variation and agreement on any given point. Such an arrangement is much more convenient to the task pursued in the commentary, which is to reconstruct (as far as possible) the original version of Theophrastus. Anyone who has tried to compare the doxographers systematically, using only the edition of Diels, knows that the operation is so involved as to be scarcely feasible.

The order of subjects is in general that of Simplicius or Hippolytus, our two best sources, but the aim has been to reproduce the order of Theophrastus' own work, which, I assume, followed Aristotle's plan for the physical treatises outlined at *Meteorologica* I.I. When the statements of any author are given here in a sequence which differs from the author's own, that fact has been noted before each citation. Under each heading the testimonia are listed in order of approximate reliability, but this principle cannot always be applied. The statements of later doxographers are not cited when their information is clearly derived from an earlier extant source. (Thus the testimony of Achilles, *Isag.* 19 = *Vors.* 12 A 21, is omitted here, as a mere distortion of **14.A.2**; see the commentary *ad loc.*)

The doxography proper is restricted to excerpts from Theophrastus, however indirect or confused (but when the confusion is complete enough to render the testimony worthless, this fact has been noted). For convenient reference, the most important parallels in Aristotle or in other authors (when available) are cited directly following the testimonia for each topic.

All passages of Simplicius other than those at *in Phys.* 24.13–25 have been placed in the second category, since they do not appear to be true excerpts (see above, pp. 14 f.). In one case a direct citation from Theophrastus is listed among the subsidiary parallels (*Phys. Opin.* fr. 4, under **7**), as it comes from his discussion of Anaxagoras rather than Anaximander. Under **9** no distinction has been drawn between excerpt and parallel, for reasons given in the commentary on that topic.

In order to read the testimony of a given author as a connected whole, it would be possible to follow his symbol (**S.**, **H.**, **P.**, etc.) through the consecutive items; but, of course, the same thing may be done much more easily by referring to the *Doxographi* or the *Vorsokratiker* of Diels. The corresponding passages in Diels are listed under **1**; the references for all excerpts under later headings are identical with these, unless otherwise indicated. For example, under **7** there are no references given for **S.1**, **H.**, and **P.**, because they are the same as those for Simplicius, Hippolytus, and pseudo-Plutarch under **1**; whereas complete references are offered for **S.2** and **S.3**, which are taken from different passages in Simplicius. For **9** and **20** a single reference is given in the heading since the corresponding texts are listed in one place by Diels.

Translations of the most important texts are presented in connection with the historical discussion, below, pages 76 ff.

The relationship between this arrangement and that of Diels in the *Fragmente der Vorsokratiker* is indicated below in the table of correspondences, following the catalogue of topics and the list of abbreviations.

Topics of the Doxography for Anaximander

1. Anaximander and Thales	**13.** Formation of the Heavens
2. The ἀρχή	**14.** Stars and Sun
3. The ἄπειρον	**15.** The Moon
4. Heavens and κόσμοι	**16.** Size, Position, and Distance of
5. The Fragment	the Rings
6. Reasons for Introducing the ἄπειρον	**17.** Wind
	18. Rain
7. Eternal Motion and ἀπόκρισις	**19.** Lightning and Thunder
8. Cosmic Divinity	**20.** Origin of the Sea
9. Infinite Worlds	**20a.** Earthquakes
10. Position of the Earth	**21.** Origin of Animal Life
11. Form of the Earth	**22.** Descent of Man
12. Antipodes	**23.** The ψυχή

Abbreviations of Authors in the Doxography

A.	Aëtius	**H.**	Hippolytus
Arist.	Aristotle	**P.**	Pseudo-Plutarch
C.	Cicero	**S.**	Simplicius
D.L.	Diogenes Laertius		

Correspondence with the Arrangement in Diels–Kranz, Die Fragmente der Vorsokratiker

Vorsokratiker	This Work	Vorsokratiker	This Work
12 A 1	D.L.: 1–3, 8, 10–11, 14–16, note to 15.A.1	12 A 18	13.A.2; 16.A.1; 14.A.1
A 2	10.Suidas	A 19	16.S.
A 5	Pliny: note to 15.A.1	A 21	14.A.2; 16.A.2; 14.A.3
A 9	S.: 1–7	A 22	15.A.1–3
A 9a	7.Theophrastus	A 23	19.A., Seneca
A 10	P.: 1–2, 4, 7, 11, 13, 22	A 24	17.A.
A 11	H.: 1–5, 7–8, 10–19, 21–22	A 25	11.A.; 12.A.
A 12	7.Hermias	A 26	10.Arist., Theon Smyrnaeus
A 13	C.: 1, 3–4	A 27	20
A 14	A.: 1–6	A 28	20a
A 15	8.Arist.1	A 29	23
A 17	9	A 30	21–22
A 17a	13.A.1		

THE DOXOGRAPHY: TEXTS AND COMMENTARY

1. ANAXIMANDER AND THALES

S. *in Phys.* 24.13 (*Phys. Opin.*, fr. 2 ; *Dox.* 476 = *Vors.* 12 A 9)   τῶν δὲ ἐν καὶ κινούμενον καὶ ἄπειρον λεγόντων Ἀναξίμανδρος μὲν Πραξιάδου Μιλήσιος Θαλοῦ γενόμενος διάδοχος καὶ μαθητής

H. *Refutatio* 1.6 (*Dox.* 559 = *Vors.* A 11)   Θαλοῦ τοίνυν Ἀναξίμανδρος γίνεται ἀκροατής. Ἀναξίμανδρος Πραξιάδου Μιλήσιος.

P. *Stromateis* 2 (*Dox.* 579 = *Vors.* A 10)   μεθ' ὃν (sc. Θάλητα) Ἀναξίμανδρον Θάλητος ἑταῖρον γενόμενον

A. *Placita* 1.3.3 (*Dox.* 277 = *Vors.* A 14)   Ἀναξίμανδρος δὲ Πραξιάδου Μιλήσιος

D.L. *Vitae* 11.1 (= *Vors.* A 1)   Ἀναξίμανδρος Πραξιάδου Μιλήσιος. Cf. the final words of Book 1: Θαλῆς, οὗ διήκουσεν Ἀναξίμανδρος.

C. *Acad.* 11.37.118 (cf. *Vors.* A 13)   Thales . . . ex aqua dixit constare omnia. At hoc Anaximandro populari et sodali suo non persuasit.

Augustine *C.D.* viii.2 (cf. *Vors.* A 17)   Huic (sc. Thaleti) successit Anaximander, eius auditor, mutavitque de rerum natura opinionem.

Theophrastus reported the name of Anaximander's father, his native city, and his position as pupil or successor to Thales. (None of this information is given by Aristotle.) The separate versions show too much variety in the term employed (διάδοχος, μαθητής, ἀκροατής, ἑταῖρος, *sodalis*) for us to recognize Theophrastus' own expression for the relationship with Thales. All of these words imply a personal contact between a younger and an older man ; and all other evidence points to the historical reality of this relationship (see, e.g., below, p. 77). The seniority of Thales is confirmed by his connection with the eclipse of 585 B.C., while the information that Anaximander was sixty-four years old in 547/6 was apparently found by Apollodorus in his book (D.L. 11.2 = *Vors.* 12 A 1).

Burnet (p. 50, n. 4) argued that the agreement between Cicero's *popularis et sodalis* and πολίτης καὶ ἑταῖρος in Simplicius' *in De Caelo*

615.13 (quoted below, **6.S.4**) must represent the original expression of Theophrastus. This is unlikely since in the *De Caelo* passage Simplicius is not following Theophrastus' text as closely as he is here. Although ἑταῖρος would be a natural word, both ἀκροατής and μαθητής are similarly employed by Aristotle. If ἑταῖρος stood here in Theophrastus it is surprising that only pseudo-Plutarch has preserved it, for he is generally the freest in rephrasing his information (see **2**). As for πολίτης, it is a mere stylistic variant for Μιλήσιος, and would be redundant next to the latter expression (which is better attested here).

The point is of no consequence, but it illustrates the hopelessness of any attempt to reconstruct Theophrastus' original words when they are not cited verbatim by our best sources, Simplicius and Hippolytus.

2. THE *APXH*

S. ἀρχήν τε καὶ στοιχεῖον εἴρηκε τῶν ὄντων τὸ ἄπειρον, πρῶτος τοῦτο τοὔνομα κομίσας τῆς ἀρχῆς·

H.a. οὗτος ἀρχὴν ἔφη τῶν ὄντων φύσιν τινὰ τοῦ ἀπείρου,

   b. (after **5.H.**)   οὗτος μὲν οὖν ἀρχὴν καὶ στοιχεῖον εἴρηκε τῶν ὄντων τὸ ἄπειρον πρῶτος τοὔνομα καλέσας τῆς ἀρχῆς.

P. τὸ ἄπειρον φάναι τὴν πᾶσαν αἰτίαν ἔχειν τῆς τοῦ παντὸς γενέσεώς τε καὶ φθορᾶς,

A. φησὶ τῶν ὄντων ἀρχὴν εἶναι τὸ ἄπειρον·

D.L. οὗτος ἔφασκεν ἀρχὴν καὶ στοιχεῖον τὸ ἄπειρον,

The first words of Simplicius recur identically in Hippolytus, with the mere loss of a τε. For the rest of the clause, Hippolytus presents two minor discrepancies: the omission of τοῦτο and the substitution of καλέσας for κομίσας, which is plainly the *lectio difficilior*. (For a similar use of κομίζω, see Plato, *Parm.* 127c.4; Arist. *Met.* 990^b2.) This is one of the rare cases where two doxographers can be compared according to the principles of textual criticism, and from this point of view it is clear that the readings of Simplicius are to be preferred. In fact either Hippolytus himself or some copyist seems to have omitted half of this sentence while transcribing it for the first time (**H.a.**), and therefore to have recopied it afterwards in full (**H.b.**). (This is the simplest explanation of his divergent order, and of the fact that the phrase οὗτος ἀρχὴν ἔφη τῶν ὄντων appears twice in his brief account, but only once in the version of Simplicius.)

The complete agreement of Simplicius and Hippolytus provides us with the original wording of Theophrastus, against which the other doxographers must be judged. None contains the information concerning Anaximander's terminology, but Aëtius and Diogenes Laertius give some of the first part of 2 verbatim. Aëtius omits στοιχεῖον; Diogenes omits τῶν ὄντων; pseudo-Plutarch omits both, and the word ἀρχή as well. Instead the latter gives a general paraphrase which does not correspond exactly to anything in Simplicius or Hippolytus.

It is an old and continuing subject of controversy, whether the phrase πρῶτος τοῦτο τοὔνομα κομίσας τῆς ἀρχῆς refers to the word ἀρχή itself, or to the immediately preceding ἄπειρον. Are we to understand that Anaximander was the first to introduce "this very term of ἀρχή," or "this name ἄπειρον for the ἀρχή"?

Both constructions can be, and have been, defended. It must be admitted that the purely grammatical evidence establishes a prima facie case for the word ἄπειρον. In the first place, οὗτος normally refers to what immediately precedes, in this case τὸ ἄπειρον. Also, τοὔνομα τῆς ἀρχῆς is the regular construction for "the name of something" (with the possessive genitive), while we would expect "this word ἀρχή" to appear in apposition: τοῦτο τοὔνομα τὴν ἀρχήν (cf. τοῦτο τὸ ὄνομα ὁ ἄνθρωπος, Plato Crat. 399c.1, etc.).

However, such evidence cannot be decisive here. For one thing, the use of οὗτος and ἐκεῖνος may reflect not only the relative position of words in a sentence, but also the psychological freshness or remoteness of ideas in the author's mind. (For irregularities in the use of the demonstratives, see LSJ, s.v. ἐκεῖνος 1; s.v. οὗτος C.I.1.) As far as the second point is concerned, the genitive τῆς ἀρχῆς may represent a mere stylistic variant for apposition. This usage is familiar to the poets, above all Euripides (ὄνομα τῆς σωτηρίας = σωτηρία, and the similar phrases listed LSJ, s.v. ὄνομα IV.1). The construction is a rare one in prose, but cf. Thuc. IV.60, καὶ ὀνόματι ἐννόμῳ ξυμμαχίας τὸ φύσει πολέμιον εὐπρεπῶς ἐς τὸ ξυμφέρον καθίστανται; and see in general the "genitivus appositivus" in Schwyzer–Debrunner, Griechische Grammatik (Munich, 1950), II, 121 f. (Unfortunately the example of πηγῆς ὄνομα at Crat. 402c.6, repeated by Schwyzer–Debrunner from Kühner–Gerth, I, 265, is not apt; the meaning there is "the name of a spring," not "the word πηγή.")

Such parallels should show that τοὔνομα τῆς ἀρχῆς is a possible reference to the word ἀρχή, even if it is not the phrase we expect. And the ambiguity which surrounds this expression is, I think, definitively resolved by two other passages in Simplicius, which show that he has himself understood it to refer to the term ἀρχή. The first indication of this is in the words which follow immediately: λέγει δ' αὐτὴν μήτε ὕδωρ μήτε ἄλλο τι . . . εἶναι, where αὐτήν makes clear that it is the word ἀρχή, not ἄπειρον, which is uppermost in Simplicius' mind (and in that of Theophrastus, if his text is faithfully copied here). Furthermore, when Simplicius returns later to the doctrine of Anaximander, his statement is unequivocal: πρῶτος αὐτὸς ἀρχὴν ὀνομάσας τὸ ὑποκείμενον (in Phys. 150.23, cited as 7.S.3). Since this can only mean, "He was the first to give the name ἀρχή to the [infinite body which is the] underlying subject of change," there is no reasonable doubt as to what Simplicius understood by τοῦτο τοὔνομα. No further light is thrown upon this verbal question by the fact that in another work Simplicius describes Anaximander as "the first to posit an infinite substratum" (ἄπειρον δὲ πρῶτος ὑπέθετο [sc. τὸ ὑποκείμενον] in De Caelo 615.15, cited below as 6.S.4). This statement is certainly correct, but it refers to his doctrine, not to his terminology. In all probability, Anaximander was also the first to introduce the term ἄπειρον into a philosophic discussion, but no ancient author bears witness to this fact.

Since Simplicius is our best source for this section of the Phys. Opin., his understanding of Theophrastus' remark must be definitive for us. And the same interpretation seems to underlie the incomplete version of Hippolytus: πρῶτος τοὔνομα καλέσας τῆς ἀρχῆς, "first to call it by the name ἀρχή." Furthermore, as Diels pointed out, such emphasis on the first use of the term ἀρχή is typical of the procedure of Theophrastus, who (like Aristotle) was regularly concerned with questions of originality and priority. (See Diels' brief but important remarks in "Leucippos u. Diogenes von Apollonia," RM, XLII [1887], 7 f.) This entire section of the Phys. Opin. dealt with the ἀρχαί of the various early philosophers and their respective doctrinal innovations. Only in the case of Anaximander, however, is there a clear reference to new terminology. What could be more natural than to mention the earliest use of that term which is at the focus of the entire discussion? The word ἀρχή is continually present in Theophrastus' mind here, and it is this fact which explains the emphasis in τοῦτο τοὔνομα τῆς ἀρχῆς, "this very term of ἀρχή." (The normal apposition would have resulted in a clumsy repetition of the accusative: ἀρχὴν . . . εἴρηκε . . . τὸ ἄπειρον, πρῶτος τοῦτο τοὔνομα κομίσας τὴν ἀρχήν. There would be a new ambiguity, this time with the adverbial expression τὴν ἀρχήν.)[1]

The fact that Anaximander employed the word ἀρχή in reference to the ἄπειρον does not of course prove that he used it in the same sense as Aristotle and Theophrastus. The early history of this term lies outside the scope of the present study, but its meaning for Anaximander will be briefly discussed in Appendix II (below, pp. 235 ff.).[2]

3. THE *ΑΠΕΙΡΟΝ*

S. λέγει δ' αὐτὴν (sc. τὴν ἀρχήν), μήτε ὕδωρ μήτε ἄλλο τι τῶν καλουμένων εἶναι στοιχείων, ἀλλ' ἑτέραν τινὰ φύσιν ἄπειρον,[a]

H. (in 2.H.a.) ἀρχὴν . . . φύσιν τινὰ τοῦ ἀπείρου,

A. (after 6.A.) ἁμαρτάνει δὲ οὗτος μὴ λέγων τί ἐστι τὸ ἄπειρον, [πότερον ἀήρ ἐστιν ἢ ὕδωρ ἢ γῆ ἢ ἄλλα τινὰ σώματα· ἁμαρτάνει οὖν τὴν μὲν ὕλην ἀποφαινόμενος, τὸ δὲ ποιοῦν αἴτιον ἀναιρῶν.][b] τὸ γὰρ ἄπειρον οὐδὲν ἄλλο ἢ ὕλη ἐστίν· οὐ δύναται δὲ ἡ ὕλη εἶναι ἐνέργεια, ἐὰν μὴ τὸ ποιοῦν ὑποκέηται.

D.L. οὐ διορίζων ἀέρα ἢ ὕδωρ ἢ ἄλλο τι.

C. Is enim infinitatem naturae dixit esse

Parallel:
Arist. *Phys.* 203[a]16–18 οἱ δὲ περὶ φύσεως πάντες [ἀεὶ] ὑποτιθέασιν ἑτέραν τινὰ φύσιν τῷ ἀπείρῳ τῶν λεγομένων στοιχείων, οἷον ὕδωρ ἢ ἀέρα ἢ τὸ μεταξὺ τούτων.

[a] *Compare* S. *in Phys.* 41.17 (cited below as **7.S.**2) ἄπειρόν τινα φύσιν ἄλλην οὖσαν τῶν τεττάρων στοιχείων ἀρχὴν ἔθετο . . . .
[b] The bracketed words occur only in the version of pseudo-Plutarch, not in that of Stobaeus.

[1] In support of this interpretation of the phrase, Professor Kurt von Fritz points out that since there is no mention of any other thinker who identified the ἀρχή simply as τὸ ἄπειρον, it would have been pointless of Theophrastus to say that Anaximander was the *first* to do so; whereas this remark applies very naturally to the first use of the term ἀρχή.
[2] The literature on πρῶτος τοῦτο τοὔνομα κομίσας τῆς ἀρχῆς is rather extensive. The principal statements in favor of the view adopted here are those of Zeller (I⁵, 217, n. 2); Diels, "Leucip-

pos u. Diogenes von Apollonia," *RM*, LXII [1887], 7 f.; Heidel, "On Anaximander," *CP*, VII (1912), 215, n. 4; and Jaeger, who deals with the question in detail in *Theology*, pp. 25–29, with nn. 21–28. The contrary view was maintained by G. Teichmüller, *Studien zur Geschichte der Begriffe* (Berlin, 1874), pp. 49 ff., by J. Neuhaeuser, *Anaximander Milesius* (Bonn, 1883), pp. 8 ff., and by Burnet, p. 54, n. 2. It was recently revived by J. B. McDiarmid, *Harv. Stud.*, XLI, 138 ff., and by G. S. Kirk, "Some Problems in Anaximander," *CQ*, XLIX (1955), 21–24.

Here again the words of Simplicius must closely reflect the text of Theophrastus. The parallels prove this, even if they are not quite precise enough to establish the original wording (cf. **A.** and **D.L.**). In general, the text of Simplicius from **1** to **5** can be treated as largely identical with that of Theophrastus.

The version of Aëtius seems to contain a crude pseudo-Theophrastean criticism of Anaximander: "He is mistaken in not declaring what the ἄπειρον is, *whether it is air or water or earth or some other bodies . . . .*" The italicized words occur, however, only in the version of pseudo-Plutarch, and may represent an originally expository remark, which has been confused by him with the more intelligent criticism that follows: "He is therefore mistaken in emphasizing matter, but omitting the active cause. For the ἄπειρον is nothing except matter; and matter cannot be an actuality unless the active cause is present." This Peripatetic argument seems worthy of Theophrastus, and would not be typical of Aëtius' own contributions to the doxography.

The phrase ἑτέραν τινὰ φύσιν in **S.** has sometimes been compared to the passage of **Arist.** that speaks of ἑτέρα τις φύσις, which all the natural philosophers posit as substratum for the ἄπειρον. The contrast expressed by ἑτέρα is, however, entirely different in the two cases: **S.** is distinguishing the ἄπειρον from any one among the elements; whereas **Arist.** is opposing the Ionian doctrine of an infinite material principle (which may be identified with one of these elements) to the view ascribed to Plato and the Pythagoreans, in which the essential form of the Unlimited is considered in itself. This basic discrepancy has recently been cited as a case where Theophrastus distorts or misapplies an Aristotelian remark (G. S. Kirk, *CQ*, XLIX, 21). Perhaps a simpler solution would be to consider the resemblance between the two passages as after all merely verbal. Aristotle too can describe the principle of Anaximander as ἕτερον τούτων (sc. τῶν στοιχείων) in **6.Arist.1.**

For a fuller discussion of the ἄπειρον, see Appendix II, pp. 231–39.

4. HEAVENS AND ΚΟΣΜΟΙ

S. ἐξ ἧς (sc. φύσεως ἀπείρου) ἅπαντας γίνεσθαι τοὺς οὐρανοὺς καὶ τοὺς ἐν αὐτοῖς κόσμους·

H. (after **2.H.a**) ἐξ ἧς γίνεσθαι τοὺς οὐρανοὺς καὶ τὸν ἐν αὐτοῖς κόσμον.

P. ἐξ οὗ (sc. τοῦ ἀπείρου) δή φησι τούς τε οὐρανοὺς ἀποκεκρίσθαι καὶ καθόλου τοὺς ἅπαντας ἀπείρους ὄντας κόσμους.

A. (after **2.A.**) ἐκ γὰρ τούτου πάντα γίγνεσθαι καὶ εἰς τοῦτο πάντα φθείρεσθαι. διὸ καὶ γεννᾶσθαι ἀπείρους κόσμους καὶ πάλιν φθείρεσθαι εἰς τὸ ἐξ οὗ γίγνεσθαι.

C. (infinitatem naturae) e qua omnia gignerentur.

This is the second example of a nearly complete coincidence between the wording of Simplicius and Hippolytus. The discrepancies of the latter consist (1) in the absence of the word ἅπαντας before τοὺς οὐρανούς, and (2) in the singular τὸν κόσμον (where Simplicius has the plural). In both cases we may be reasonably certain that the version of Simplicius mirrors the text of Theophrastus more faithfully. Ἅπαντας reappears in pseudo-Plutarch (applied there to κόσμους, not οὐρανούς); and the phrase πάντας τοὺς οὐρανούς (or πάντας τοὺς κόσμους) occurs elsewhere in reference to Anaximander (see **8.H.** and **8.Arist.4**). A mention of κόσμοι in the plural is also guaranteed by the fact that both pseudo-Plutarch and Aëtius speak here of ἄπειροι κόσμοι. Although we have every right to regard their statements as grossly confused, this is not the kind of confusion which would naturally arise if Theophrastus had spoken of κόσμος in the singular.

Whereas the corruptions of Hippolytus are almost those of a copyist, the deviation of pseudo-Plutarch and Aëtius shows more originality. Obviously neither of these two authors could see what might be meant by plural κόσμοι within the plural οὐρανοί. The κόσμοι most familiar to a Hellenistic excerptor were the infinite worlds of atomic theory, and it seems that both pseudo-Plutarch and Aëtius identified the κόσμοι of Anaximander with this doctrine. Since such infinite worlds could scarcely be said to lie "within the heavens," the original phrase of Theophrastus has in both cases been changed. Pseudo-Plutarch refers vaguely to "the οὐρανοί and in general all the infinite κόσμοι," as if the second term were a more universal synonym for the first. But the procedure of Aëtius is more radical. He simply ignores the original reference to οὐρανοί, so that the doctrine of "infinite worlds" appears in all its splendor. To render their "procreation" more spectacular (γεννᾶσθαι, where the other excerpts have γίνεσθαι), he introduces it with a modified version of the fragment (**5.S**), changing ἐξ ὧν and εἰς ταῦτα to the singular, and referring both terms to the ἄπειρον. Thus the infinite worlds also must "perish into that from which they have arisen." (There is no mention of such a destruction of the κόσμοι in either Simplicius or Hippolytus, but it is implied by Aëtius' comrade in confusion, pseudo-Plutarch, under **2** and **7**.)

In this decisive case, where the original text of Theophrastus may be recognized with confidence, we see that a reference to the infinite worlds and to their destruction is to be found only in those doxographers who diverge most widely from their original source. Their remarks may easily be explained by a contamination with more familiar Hellenistic ideas concerning a plurality of worlds. We are eyewitness here to the progressive distortion of a documentary account as it passes from hand to hand. One is therefore obliged not only to recognize the extreme unreliability of sources such as Aëtius, but also to pose the question, whether any doctrine of "infinite worlds" was in fact ascribed to Anaximander by Theophrastus, or whether this resemblance to the atomists' view is due only to the confusion of our Hellenistic sources (see below, **9**).

5. THE FRAGMENT

S. ἐξ ὧν δὲ ἡ γένεσίς ἐστι τοῖς οὖσι, καὶ τὴν φθορὰν εἰς ταῦτα γίνεσθαι κατὰ τὸ χρεών, διδόναι γὰρ αὐτὰ δίκην καὶ τίσιν ἀλλήλοις τῆς ἀδικίας κατὰ τὴν τοῦ χρόνου τάξιν, ποιητικωτέροις οὕτως ὀνόμασιν αὐτὰ λέγων.

H. (after 8.H.) λέγει δὲ χρόνον ὡς ὡρισμένης τῆς γενέσεως καὶ τῆς οὐσίας καὶ τῆς φθορᾶς.

A. Cf. 4.A.

There is no reason to suppose that Simplicius has here altered the citation as it appeared in the *Phys. Opin.* Even the remark concerning Anaximander's "rather poetic expressions" might very well have been made by Theophrastus.

The parallel sentence in Hippolytus shows traces of the original text, but in a form so badly mutilated that it might represent either a comment by Theophrastus on the fragment, or (more probably) an excerptor's paraphrase of the fragment itself. Even the words are ambiguous as they stand. The most likely sense is: "He speaks of time on the principle that the generation, existence, and destruction [of all things] is determinate [in length]."

6. REASONS FOR INTRODUCING THE *ΑΠΕΙΡΟΝ*

S.1 δῆλον δὲ ὅτι τὴν εἰς ἄλληλα μεταβολὴν τῶν τεττάρων στοιχείων οὗτος θεασάμενος οὐκ ἠξίωσεν ἕν τι τούτων ὑποκείμενον ποιῆσαι, ἀλλά τι ἄλλο παρὰ ταῦτα.

A. (after **4.A.**) λέγει γοῦν διότι ἀπέραντόν ἐστιν, ἵνα μηδὲν ἐλλείπῃ ἡ γένεσις ἡ ὑφισταμένη.

Parallel:

Arist.1 *Phys.* 189ᵇ1–8 ἀναγκαῖον . . . ὑποτιθέναι τι τρίτον (sc. ὑποκείμενον τοῖς ἐναντίοις), ὥσπερ φασὶν οἱ μίαν τινὰ φύσιν εἶναι λέγοντες τὸ πᾶν, οἷον ὕδωρ ἢ πῦρ ἢ τὸ μεταξὺ τούτων. δοκεῖ δὲ τὸ μεταξὺ μᾶλλον· πῦρ γὰρ ἤδη καὶ γῆ καὶ ἀὴρ καὶ ὕδωρ μετ' ἐναντιοτήτων συμπεπλεγμένα ἐστίν. διὸ καὶ οὐκ ἀλόγως ποιοῦσιν οἱ τὸ ὑποκείμενον ἕτερον τούτων ποιοῦντες, τῶν δ' ἄλλων οἱ ἀέρα· καὶ γὰρ ὁ ἀὴρ ἥκιστα ἔχει τῶν ἄλλων διαφορὰς αἰσθητάς· ἐχόμενον δὲ τὸ ὕδωρ. ἀλλὰ πάντες γε τὸ ἓν τοῦτο τοῖς ἐναντίοις σχηματίζουσιν, πυκνότητι καὶ μανότητι καὶ τῷ μᾶλλον καὶ ἧττον.

Arist.2 *Phys.* 203ᵇ18 (τοῦ δ' εἶναί τι ἄπειρον ἡ πίστις μάλιστ' ἂν συμβαίνοι . . .) ἔτι τῷ οὕτως ἂν μόνως μὴ ὑπολείπειν γένεσιν καὶ φθοράν, εἰ ἄπειρον εἴη ὅθεν ἀφαιρεῖται τὸ γιγνόμενον. (Answered, *Phys.* 208ᵃ8 οὔτε γὰρ ἵνα ἡ γένεσις μὴ ἐπιλείπῃ, ἀναγκαῖον ἐνεργείᾳ ἄπειρον εἶναι σῶμα αἰσθητόν . . . .)

Arist.3 *Phys.* 204ᵇ22–29 ἀλλὰ μὴν οὐδὲ ἓν καὶ ἁπλοῦν εἶναι σῶμα ἄπειρον ἐνδέχεται, οὔτε ὡς λέγουσί τινες τὸ παρὰ τὰ στοιχεῖα, ἐξ οὗ ταῦτα γεννῶσιν, οὔθ' ἁπλῶς. εἰσὶν γάρ τινες οἳ τοῦτο ποιοῦσι τὸ ἄπειρον, ἀλλ' οὐκ ἀέρα ἢ ὕδωρ, ὅπως μὴ τἆλλα φθείρηται ὑπὸ τοῦ ἀπείρου αὐτῶν· ἔχουσι γὰρ πρὸς ἄλληλα ἐναντίωσιν, οἷον ὁ μὲν ἀὴρ ψυχρός, τὸ δ' ὕδωρ ὑγρόν, τὸ δὲ πῦρ θερμόν· ὧν εἰ ἦν ἓν ἄπειρον, ἔφθαρτο ἂν ἤδη τἆλλα· νῦν δ' ἕτερον εἶναί φασιν ἐξ οὗ ταῦτα.

Arist.4 *Phys.* 205ᵃ25–29 καὶ διὰ τοῦτ' οὐθεὶς τὸ ἓν καὶ ἄπειρον πῦρ ἐποίησεν οὐδὲ γῆν τῶν φυσιολόγων, ἀλλ' ἢ ὕδωρ ἢ ἀέρα ἢ τὸ μέσον αὐτῶν, ὅτι τόπος ἑκατέρου δῆλος ἦν διωρισμένος, ταῦτα δ' ἐπαμφοτερίζει τῷ ἄνω καὶ κάτω.

Arist.5 *Gen. Corr.* 332ᵃ19–25 οὐκ ἔστιν ἓν τούτων (sc. τῶν στοιχείων) ἐξ οὗ τὰ πάντα. οὐ μὴν οὐδ' ἄλλο τί γε παρὰ ταῦτα, οἷον μέσον τι ἀέρος καὶ ὕδατος ἢ ἀέρος καὶ πυρός, ἀέρος μὲν παχύτερον καὶ πυρός, τῶν δὲ λεπτότερον· ἔσται γὰρ ἀὴρ καὶ πῦρ ἐκεῖνο μετ' ἐναντιότητος·

ἀλλὰ στέρησις τὸ ἕτερον τῶν ἐναντίων· ὥστ' οὐκ ἐνδέχεται μονοῦσθαι ἐκεῖνο οὐδέποτε, ὥσπερ φασί τινες τὸ ἄπειρον καὶ τὸ περιέχον.[a]

S.2 in *Phys.* 36.8 καὶ ὅσοι δὲ ἐν ἔθεντο στοιχεῖον, ὡς Θαλῆς καὶ Ἀ. καὶ Ἡράκλειτος, καὶ τούτων ἕκαστος εἰς τὸ δραστήριον ἀπεῖδεν τὸ καὶ πρὸς γένεσιν ἐπιτήδειον ἐκείνου . . . Ἀναξιμένης δὲ εἰς τὸ τοῦ ἀέρος εὔπλαστον καὶ ἑκατέρωσε ῥᾳδίως μεταχωροῦν ἐπί τε τὸ πῦρ καὶ ἐπὶ τὸ ὕδωρ, ὥσπερ καὶ Ἀ., εἴπερ τὸ μεταξὺ διὰ τὸ εὐαλλοίωτον ὑποτίθεται.

S.3 in *Phys.* 465.5–10 (commenting on *Phys.* 203ᵇ10, cited below as **8.Arist.1**) διὸ οἱ τὸ ἄπειρον μόνον τιθέντες ὡς ἀρχὴν καὶ μὴ προσλογιζόμενοί τινας ἄλλας αἰτίας . . . ἠρκέσθησαν πρὸς τὴν πάντων γένεσιν τῇ τοῦ ἀπείρου φύσει καὶ τῇ ὑλικῇ ταύτῃ ἀρχῇ, ὡς διὰ τὴν ἀνεπίλειπτον τούτου χορηγίαν ἀεὶ γενέσεως ἐσομένης καὶ περιεχομένων πάντων ὑπὸ τούτου καὶ κυβερνωμένων.

S.4 in *De Caelo* 615.13 ἄλλος ἄλλο τι τὸ ἓν ὑπέθετο . . . Ἀ. δὲ Θαλοῦ πολίτης καὶ ἑταῖρος ἀόριστόν τι ὕδατος μὲν λεπτότερον ἀέρος δὲ πυκνότερον, διότι τὸ ὑποκείμενον εὐφυὲς ἐχρῆν εἶναι πρὸς τὴν ἐφ' ἑκάτερα μετάβασιν. (Continued in **9.S.3**.)

[a] For Aristotle's criticism of Anaximander at *Gen. Corr.* 332ᵃ19 (**Arist.5** above), see also, *Gen. Corr.* 329ᵃ10.
In addition to **Arist.1, 4**, and **5** above, the element "in between" is mentioned by him also at: *Phys.* 187ᵃ14 (where it is denser than fire, finer than air); *Phys.* 203ᵇ18 (cited under **3**—where it is between water and air); *De Caelo* 303ᵇ12 (cited below as **8.Arist.4**—where it is finer than water, denser than air); *Gen. Corr.* 328ᵇ35 (where it is between air and fire); *Met.* 988ᵃ30 (denser than fire, finer than air); *Met.* 989ᵃ14 (denser than air, finer than water).
Anaximander's doctrine of the ἄπειρον is also referred to by Arist. at *Met.* 1069ᵇ22 (where his name is linked with that of Empedocles and Anaxagoras, just as at *Phys.* 187ᵃ20, cited under **7**); and it is briefly mentioned without his name at *Met.* 1052ᵇ10, 1053ᵇ16.

After **5**, the version of Simplicius can no longer be shown to follow Theophrastus' text word for word. The parallels under **7** prove only that he is still dependent on Theophrastus in a general way.

Simplicius states that Anaximander refused to identify the material substratum with any one of the four elements, since he had observed the change of these elements into one another. In view of the absence of direct parallels to this remark, and on the basis of rather minute stylistic differences, it has been argued that here "it is not Theophrastus who is speaking, but Simplicius" (Hölscher, "Anaximander," p. 259). But it is not easy to draw such a neat line between a paraphrase of Theophrastus and further commentary added by Simplicius himself. It seems to me likely that Simplicius had found some basis for this statement in the text of Theophrastus, and that for two reasons: (1) the direct connection between this sentence and the fragment, on which it serves as commentary; and (2) the essential agreement between this observation and the reasoning ascribed to Anaximander by 6.Arist.3 (where the Milesian is in fact not named, but obviously intended, as Simplicius confirms *ad loc.*). There is not enough verbal similarity between the two texts to explain 6.S.1 as a mere reminiscence of Arist.3, and the view defined by the two remarks corresponds very well with other early Greek attitudes to elemental change. There is, then, no good reason to doubt that the interpretation of the fragment given in S.1 is based upon the exposition of Theophrastus, and thus ultimately upon the text of Anaximander himself. (For further discussion of the doctrine in question, see below, pp. 186 ff.)

On the other hand, when Simplicius returns later to the discussion of Anaximander's ἀρχή, what he says has no claim to represent new information from Theophrastus, but seems to be based only on his own inference and interpretation (following, perhaps, that of Alexander). Such is the case, for instance, with the statement that Anaximander chose his ἀρχή "in between" the elements in order that it might pass more easily into the other forms (S.2 and S.4). The thought comes from Arist.1. (For the description of Anaximander's principle as "between the elements," see below on 8.)

The considerations mentioned thus far serve to motivate Anaximander's refusal to identify the ἄπειρον with one of the elements. Another question altogether is why he required a boundless ἀρχή in the first place. On this point Aëtius asserts that it was "in order that the existing generation [of things] might not come to an end." The same reasoning is given by Aristotle among the anonymous arguments for an ἄπειρον (Arist.2), and no one else is known to have made use of it. Since it is also recognized by Simplicius as one of the reasons for Anaximander's choice (S.4; cf. S.3), there are no grounds for doubting that in this case Aëtius' version accurately reflects the statement of Theophrastus, and hence, that it is truly Anaximander's argument which is represented in Arist.2. There is nothing to support the suggestion of Diels (*Dox.* 180) that Aëtius drew this information not from Theophrastus, but directly from Arist.2; Anaximander's name is not given by Aristotle in this connection, but only by Aëtius. (These passages have recently been discussed by W. Kraus, "Das Wesen des Unendlichen bei Anaximander," *RM*, XCIII [1950], 364.)

For the anonymous plural τινες with which the view of Anaximander is cited in Arist.3 above (and often), see the remarks of W. J. Verdenius and J. H. Waszink, *Aristotle on Coming-to-be and Passing-away* (Leiden, 1946), p. 56, who note φασί τινες for the citation of Herodotus at *Pol.* 1290ᵇ4–5, and the similar formula at *Rhet.* 1386ᵃ19–20. This is in fact Aristotle's normal way of referring to views for which no name is given, even if only one author is intended. It is therefore unnecessary to invent a school of philosophers to account for every such plural, as some commentators do.

7. ETERNAL MOTION AND ΑΠΟΚΡΙΣΙΣ

S.1 οὗτος δὲ οὐκ ἀλλοιουμένου τοῦ στοιχείου τὴν γένεσιν ποιεῖ, ἀλλ' ἀποκρινομένων τῶν ἐναντίων διὰ τῆς ἀιδίου κινήσεως· διὸ καὶ τοῖς περὶ Ἀναξαγόραν τοῦτον ὁ Ἀριστοτέλης συνέταξεν.

H. (after **2.H.b.**) πρὸς δὲ τούτῳ (sc. τῷ ἀπείρῳ) κίνησιν ἀίδιον εἶναι, ἐν ᾗ συμβαίνει γίνεσθαι τοὺς οὐρανούς.

Hermias *Irrisio* 10 (*Dox.* 653 = *Vors.* A 12) ἀλλ' ὁ πολίτης αὐτοῦ (sc. Θαλοῦ) Ἀ. τοῦ ὑγροῦ πρεσβυτέραν ἀρχὴν εἶναι λέγει τὴν ἀίδιον κίνησιν καὶ ταύτῃ τὰ μὲν γεννᾶσθαι, τὰ δὲ φθείρεσθαι.

P. ἀπεφήνατο δὲ τὴν φθορὰν γίνεσθαι καὶ πολὺ πρότερον τὴν γένεσιν ἐξ ἀπείρου αἰῶνος ἀνακυκλουμένων πάντων αὐτῶν (sc. τῶν ἀπείρων κόσμων). Cf. τοὺς οὐρανοὺς ἀποκεκρίσθαι in **4.P.**, and ἀποκριθῆναι in **13.P.**

Confused:

Augustine *C.D.* VIII.2 (after **1**) Non enim ex una re, sicut Thales ex umore, sed ex suis propriis principiis quasque res nasci putavit. Quae rerum principia singularum esse credidit infinita . . . . (Continued under **9.**)

Parallel:

S.2 *in Phys.* 41.17 Ἀ. ὁ Πραξιάδου Μιλήσιος ἄπειρόν τινα φύσιν ἄλλην οὖσαν τῶν τεττάρων στοιχείων ἀρχὴν ἔθετο, ἧς τὴν ἀίδιον κίνησιν αἰτίαν εἶναι τῆς τῶν οὐρανῶν γενέσεως ἔλεγεν.

Arist. *Phys.* 187ᵃ20–23 οἱ δ' ἐκ τοῦ ἑνὸς ἐνούσας τὰς ἐναντιότητας ἐκκρίνεσθαι, ὥσπερ Ἀ. φησι, καὶ ὅσοι δ' ἓν καὶ πολλά φασιν εἶναι, ὥσπερ Ἐμπεδοκλῆς καὶ Ἀναξαγόρας· ἐκ τοῦ μίγματος γὰρ καὶ οὗτοι ἐκκρίνουσι τἆλλα.

S.3 *in Phys.* 150.22–25 (commenting on the passage just cited, 187ᵃ20) ἐνούσας γὰρ τὰς ἐναντιότητας ἐν τῷ ὑποκειμένῳ, ἀπείρῳ ὄντι σώματι, ἐκκρίνεσθαί φησιν Ἀ., πρῶτος αὐτὸς ἀρχὴν ὀνομάσας τὸ ὑποκείμενον. ἐναντιότητες δέ εἰσι θερμὸν ψυχρὸν ξηρὸν ὑγρὸν καὶ τὰ ἄλλα. καὶ ἡ μὲν ὅλη τῶν εἰρημένων ἔννοια τοιαύτη.

Theophrastus Phys. Opin. fr. 4 (S. *in Phys.* 27.11–23 = *Vors.* 59 A 41) καὶ ταῦτά φησιν ὁ Θεόφραστος παραπλησίως τῷ Ἀναξιμάνδρῳ λέγειν τὸν Ἀναξαγόραν· ἐκεῖνος γάρ φησιν ἐν τῇ διακρίσει τοῦ ἀπείρου τὰ συγγενῆ φέρεσθαι πρὸς ἄλληλα, καὶ ὅτι μὲν ἐν τῷ παντὶ χρυσὸς ἦν, γίνεσθαι χρυσόν, ὅτι δὲ γῆ, γῆν· ὁμοίως δὲ καὶ τῶν ἄλλων ἕκαστον, ὡς οὐ γινομένων ἀλλ' ἐνυπαρχόντων πρότερον. τῆς δὲ κινήσεως καὶ τῆς γενέσεως αἴτιον ἐπέστησε τὸν νοῦν ὁ Ἀναξαγόρας, ὑφ' οὗ διακρινόμενα τούς τε κόσμους καὶ τὴν τῶν ἄλλων φύσιν ἐγέννησαν. "καὶ οὕτω μέν, φησί, λαμβανόντων δόξειεν ἂν ὁ Ἀναξαγόρας τὰς μὲν ὑλικὰς ἀρχὰς ἀπείρους ποιεῖν, τὴν δὲ τῆς κινήσεως καὶ τῆς γενέσεως αἰτίαν μίαν τὸν νοῦν· εἰ δέ τις τὴν μίξιν τῶν ἁπάντων ὑπολάβοι μίαν εἶναι φύσιν ἀόριστον καὶ κατ' εἶδος καὶ κατὰ μέγεθος, συμβαίνει δύο τὰς ἀρχὰς αὐτὸν λέγειν τήν τε τοῦ ἀπείρου φύσιν καὶ τὸν νοῦν· ὥστε φαίνεται τὰ σωματικὰ στοιχεῖα παραπλησίως ποιῶν Ἀναξιμάνδρῳ."

An "eternal motion" was mentioned by Theophrastus as cause of the generation of the heavens (οὐρανοί in **H.** and **S.2**; cf. the rather vague αὐτῶν in **P.**). Eternal motion was also ascribed by him to Anaximenes, as cause of qualitative change (in the passages compared at *Dox.* 135); and much the same thing is asserted of the atomists (*Vors.* 67 A 8, A 10.1, 68 A 40.2).

According to **S.1** the result of this motion is the "separating-out of the opposites." Ἀποκρίνεσθαι is in all versions here, but τὰ ἐναντία are mentioned by Simplicius alone (see also **S.3**). Since ἐναντιότητες occur in the parallel text of **Arist.** (*Phys.* 187ᵃ20), it has recently been urged that Simplicius imported this Aristotelian notion into a more general reference to ἀπόκρισις in Theophrastus, where the opposites would have played no part (Hölscher, "Anaximander," p. 264). It is of course quite possible that Simplicius' wording here—and perhaps that of Theophrastus before him—was influenced by the Aristotelian text. And in the case of **S.3**, it is perfectly clear that he is more concerned to explain Aristotle's text than to describe Anaximander's doctrine in detail. But it is difficult to believe (with Hölscher, *loc. cit.*) that the separation of opposites is a purely Aristotelian interpretation, which was not confirmed in the more circumspect exposition of Theophrastus. In the first place, the fullest excerpt on Anaximander's cosmogony refers precisely to a primordial ἀπόκρισις of "something capable of producing hot and cold" (**13.P.**); and furthermore, this fundamental role of hot and cold in the formation of the heavens is confirmed by a parallel source (**13.A.1**). When, therefore, **S.3** specifies the opposites resulting from ἀπόκρισις as "hot, cold, dry, moist," the second pair may or may not have been supplied from his own erudition; the first pair was certainly given by Theophrastus. And since, on the one hand, the same four primary opposites are recognized by Heraclitus (B 126), while, on the other hand, they also play a central part in cosmic ἀποκρίνεσθαι according to the fragments of Anaxagoras (B 4, B 12, B 15; cf. B 8), there is no reason to doubt the accuracy of Theophrastus' statement on this point. (For the wet and the dry in Anaximander's cosmogony, and their relationship to the hot, see **20–21**; for the role of the opposites in Milesian thought, see below, pp. 100 ff., 109, 160–63.)

The fact that opposing principles or powers arise out of the ἄπειρον by separating-off (*from one another*, as well as from the Boundless itself) does not prove that they were already pre-existent in the ἄπειρον, or that Anaximander thought of the latter as a kind of mixture or blending of opposites. It is true that Aristotle occasionally speaks in this way (*Phys.* 187ᵃ20; cf. *Met.* 1069ᵇ22), but only when he wishes to assimilate Anaximander's doctrine to that of Anaxagoras—and at the same time to that of Empedocles, in whose case the notion of precosmic mixture is clearly inappropriate. (On this assimilation, see Hölscher's pertinent remarks, "Anaximander," pp. 261–64.) When Theophrastus repeats the comparison of Anaximander and Anaxagoras, he is careful to point out that it applies only "if one assumes the mixture of all things to be a single φύσις." He thereby implicitly rejects the interpretation of the opposites as "inhering" (ἐνούσας) in the ἄπειρον before their separating-off. The fact that Simplicius repeats this Aristotelian phrase in his commentary *ad loc.* (**S.3**) does not of course prove that he found it in Theophrastus.

In this connection, it must be pointed out that ἐνῆν and ἐνυπαρχόντων πρότερον in Theophrastus do not refer to the view of Anaximander, since ἐκεῖνος in that sentence is Anaxagoras. (So correctly Zeller, I⁵, 206, n. 2. The contrary view was defended by Heidel, *CP*, VII, 230, n. 3, and recently by Cherniss and McDiarmid.) The use of ἐκεῖνος for an immediately preceding name is well attested (see, e.g., Arist. *De An.* 404ᵃ27), and the words which follow ἐκεῖνος γάρ φησιν were certainly applied by Theophrastus to Anaxagoras, as the parallel versions show beyond a doubt: τὰ συγγενῆ φέρεσθαι πρὸς ἄλληλα reappears as συνελθεῖν τὰ ὅμοια in Hippolytus (*Vors.* 59 A 42. 2), and the example of gold reappears in garbled form in Diogenes Laertius (*Vors.* 59 A 1. 8). As Zeller remarked, the mention of Anaximander probably did not occur until the end of Theophrastus' section on Anaxagoras. That Simplicius has interrupted the excerpt to insert his own comments is clear from the repetitions (viz., the two comparisons to Anaximander, the double mention of gold, and the two appearances of the phrase τῆς κινήσεως καὶ τῆς γενέσεως αἴτιον τὸν νοῦν); and this is well brought out by the spacing of Diels at *Dox.* 478 f.

The fact that an author as far removed from Theophrastus as is St. Augustine should completely confuse the doctrines of Anaximander and Anaxagoras is clearly of no help in restoring the original text. Augustine's testimony here is of exactly the same critical weight as the statement of Diogenes Laertius that for Anaximander the moon was lit up by the sun (**15**).

In summary, it is clear that Theophrastus ascribed to Anaximander an eternal motion as generating cause of the heavens. No text describes the nature of this κίνησις except in terms of the organization of the universe, where its first result is to separate two primary principles from one another: the hot and the cold.

8. COSMIC DIVINITY

H. (after 4.H.) ταύτην (sc. φύσιν τινὰ τοῦ ἀπείρου) δ᾽ ἀίδιον εἶναι καὶ ἀγήρω, ἣν καὶ πάντας περιέχειν τοὺς κόσμους.

D.L. καὶ τὰ μὲν μέρη μεταβάλλειν, τὸ δὲ πᾶν ἀμετάβλητον εἶναι.

Parallel:

Arist.1 *Phys.* 203ᵇ4–15 (= *Vors.* A 15) εὐλόγως δὲ καὶ ἀρχὴν αὐτὸ (sc. τὸ ἄπειρον) τιθέασι πάντες· οὔτε γὰρ μάτην οἷόν τε αὐτὸ εἶναι, οὔτε ἄλλην ὑπάρχειν αὐτῷ δύναμιν πλὴν ὡς ἀρχήν· ἅπαντα γὰρ ἢ ἀρχὴ ἢ ἐξ ἀρχῆς, τοῦ δὲ ἀπείρου οὐκ ἔστιν ἀρχή· εἴη γὰρ ἂν αὐτοῦ πέρας. ἔτι δὲ καὶ ἀγένητον καὶ ἄφθαρτον ὡς ἀρχή τις οὖσα· τό τε γὰρ γενόμενον ἀνάγκη τέλος λαβεῖν, καὶ τελευτὴ πάσης ἔστιν φθορᾶς. διό, καθάπερ λέγομεν, οὐ ταύτης ἀρχή, ἀλλ᾽ αὕτη τῶν ἄλλων εἶναι δοκεῖ καὶ περιέχειν ἅπαντα καὶ πάντα κυβερνᾶν, ὥς φασιν ὅσοι μὴ ποιοῦσι παρὰ τὸ ἄπειρον ἄλλας αἰτίας, οἷον νοῦν ἢ φιλίαν· καὶ τοῦτ᾽ εἶναι τὸ θεῖον· ἀθάνατον γὰρ

καὶ ἀνώλεθρον, ὥσπερ φησὶν Ἀναξίμανδρος καὶ οἱ πλεῖστοι τῶν φυσιολόγων.

Arist.2 *Phys.* 207ᵃ19–20 τὴν σεμνότητα κατὰ τοῦ ἀπείρου, τὸ πάντα
περιέχειν καὶ τὸ πᾶν ἐν ἑαυτῷ ἔχειν . . . .

Arist.3 *Phys.* 208ᵃ3 ἄτοπον τὸ περιέχον ποιεῖν αὐτὸ (sc. τὸ ἄπειρον)
ἀλλὰ μὴ περιεχόμενον.

Arist.4 *De Caelo* 303ᵇ10–13 ἔνιοι γὰρ ἓν μόνον ὑποτίθενται, καὶ τοῦτο
οἱ μὲν ὕδωρ, οἱ δ' ἀέρα, οἱ δὲ πῦρ, οἱ δ' ὕδατος μὲν λεπτότερον ἀέρος
δὲ πυκνότερον, ὃ περιέχειν φασὶ πάντας τοὺς οὐρανοὺς ἄπειρον ὄν.

At this point Simplicius abandons his excerpt concerning Anaximander, and passes on to Anaximenes; Hippolytus thus becomes our
principal source for the rest of Theophrastus' account.

The description of the divine attributes of the ἄπειρον in **H.** is closely
paralleled by one of the rare passages in which Aristotle cites Anaximander by name.[1] The epithets "deathless and imperishable" in **Arist.1**
correspond to Hippolytus' description of the Boundless as "eternal and
unaging" (which has become "unchanging" in **D.L.**). Just which expressions were used by Anaximander can scarcely be determined, but
at least the Homeric ἀγήρως must be his. Ἀίδιος and ἀθάνατος might also
be authentic, while Aristotle's ἀνώλεθρος is paralleled in Parm. B 8.3.

Hippolytus' statement that the Boundless "encompasses (περιέχει)
all the κόσμοι" is echoed by three Aristotelian passages, which describe
it as "encompassing," "encompassing all things," and "encompassing
all the οὐρανοί" (**Arist.2–4**). Did Anaximander speak in this connection
of κόσμοι or of οὐρανοί? The unusual phrase of **4** ("all the οὐρανοί and
the κόσμοι within them") suggests that he used both terms in a closely
related sense, and since the οὐρανοί are said to contain the κόσμοι, anything which "encompasses" the former will clearly do the same for the
latter. Nevertheless there is some reason to think that **Arist.4** is here a
more accurate reflection of Anaximander's phrasing. For the words "all
the οὐρανοί" occur also in **4**, where Theophrastus seems to be following
Anaximander's text rather closely. In other respects the resemblance
between **4.S.** and **Arist.1** is not sufficient to suggest that Theophrastus
has been directly influenced by the latter passage. The agreement

---

[1] Anaximander is mentioned by Aristotle on
three other occasions: *Phys.* 187ᵃ20 (given under
7); *De Caelo* 295ᵇ12 (given under **10**); and *Met.*
1069ᵇ22, where the interpretation of *Phys.* 187ᵃ20
is repeated and generalized.

between the two sentences may indicate the authenticity of "all the οὐρανοί" as a phrase actually used by Anaximander. (In that case, Hippolytus' reading of κόσμους here would represent not the version of Theophrastus, but a verbal corruption of οὐρανούς comparable to καλέσας for κομίσας in **4.H**.)

The assertion of **Arist.1** that the Boundless "governs all things" (πάντα κυβερνᾶν) is not to be found in Hippolytus. That it nevertheless reflects the doctrine of Anaximander is, to my mind, clear from the Aristotelian context, and confirmed by the frequency with which such expressions occur in the early fragments (see Heracl. B 41, B 64; Parm. B 12; Diog. B 5; cf. Anaxag. B 12).

SUPPLEMENTARY NOTE. In what precedes, it has been assumed that the ancient commentators were correct in identifying Anaximander as the author intended by Aristotle in his repeated references to a material principle intermediate between fire and water, between fire and air, or between air and water (as in **Arist.4**, above; for the identification with Anaximander, see Simplicius' commentary *ad loc.*; Alex. *in Met.* 60.8, etc.). Since this view has been contested by Zeller and by other scholars since, the grounds for accepting it may be briefly summarized:

1. Aristotle refers to such an element "in between" on nine different occasions (the list is given in the note to **6.Arist.5**). Its relative position between water, air, and fire varies with the context, but in every case it is named with these three elements alone (or with two of them), i.e., with the principles of Thales, Anaximenes, and Heraclitus. It is Anaximander, and he alone, whom we expect to find mentioned with the other three Ionian monists, and, in eight cases out of nine, such a reference to the μεταξύ corresponds to an omission of Anaximander. (The ninth case will be discussed presently.) For instance, there is absolutely no mention of Anaximander in the entire review of Greek philosophy in *Metaphysics* A, unless it is his doctrine which is meant by the intermediate element at *Met.* 988ᵃ30 and 989ᵃ14. The possibility of this total omission, corresponding to the mention of a comparable but unattested theory, seems too remote to be seriously entertained.

2. Neither Alexander nor Simplicius was able to propose another author for the theory "in between," which proves that no other similar doctrine was described by Theophrastus. (The ascription to Diogenes, mentioned by Simplicius *in Phys.* 149.17–18, is obviously wrong, since Aristotle knew his principle was Air. There is even less to be said for the suggestion of Zeller I⁵, 257 f., that a certain Idaeus is intended.

Such a person is never mentioned by Aristotle, nor, as far as we know, by Theophrastus. See *Vors.* 63.) Now it is scarcely conceivable that Theophrastus should have ignored a doctrine referred to nine times by Aristotle. The τινές in question are therefore identical with Anaximander, or with no one at all. (For the literary plural, see above pp. 38 f.).

3. In two cases Aristotle passes imperceptibly from a substance which is "between" the elements to one which is "different from them" (**6.Arist.1**), or from "something else besides" the elements to "something in the middle" (**6.Arist.5**). This shows well enough that the different expressions are interchangeable from his point of view. Indeed, since he considers matter to be defined by the four elemental forms, a material principle not identical with any one of these forms must somehow fit in between them.

4. In the two cases (**6.Arist.5** and **8.Arist.4**) where the intermediate substance is described in more detail, the terms employed are precisely the same as those used for Anaximander: this principle too is ἄπειρον and περιέχον.

In eight out of nine cases, therefore, the identification is as certain as any can be. The single exception is to be found at *Phys.* 187ᵃ12–21, where Anaximander's view is not only mentioned in addition to the principle "denser than fire but rarer than air," but also apparently contrasted with it. This passage poses a genuine problem, which Simplicius himself does not offer to solve for us. One way out would be to assume that the intermediate principle represents an abstract category, with which the doctrine of Anaximander can be identified (as it certainly is at **6.Arist.1** and **5**; **8.Arist.4**), but from which it may also be separated, as in the present case. Aristotle's actual train of thought, however, seems to be somewhat different.

At *Phys.* 187ᵃ12, he is discussing the proper number of physical ἀρχαί, and he wishes to show that the minimum requirement is a material substratum and a pair of opposite forms. He has thus far demonstrated that reality cannot be *immutably* one as the Eleatics argue (187ᵃ10), and now passes to the two ways in which physical theorists describe the fundamental unity of things: some propose a single underlying body, from which they produce a plurality by condensation and rarefaction (ᵃ15); others separate the opposites out of an original unity in which these already inhere (ᵃ20). It is clear that the model for the first group is Anaximenes, while that for the second is Anaxagoras. We find Anaximander placed in the second group—with the pluralists—

because of his doctrine that the opposites are "separated out," which, from the Aristotelian point of view, implies that they are potentially pre-existent in their source. On the other hand, Aristotle was not ready to separate Anaximander altogether from the other monists. His doctrine is therefore also mentioned, in vaguer form, among those which derive all things from a single underlying body. Just as Anaximander is nearly neglected in *Metaphysics* A, because his doctrine is difficult to fit into Aristotle's neat historical schematism, so here he is, as it were, fixed on both horns of the dilemma posed for Aristotle by this combination of a monistic principle (the ἄπειρον) with a pluralist doctrine of change (as ἀποκρίνεσθαι).

9. INFINITE WORLDS[a]

(= *Vors.* A 17)

S.1 *in Phys.* 1121.5, on 250ᵇ18   οἱ μὲν γὰρ ἀπείρους τῷ πλήθει τοὺς κόσμους ὑποθέμενοι, ὡς οἱ περὶ Ἀναξίμανδρον καὶ Λεύκιππον καὶ Δημόκριτον καὶ ὕστερον οἱ περὶ Ἐπίκουρον γινομένους αὐτοὺς καὶ φθειρομένους ὑπέθεντο ἐπ' ἄπειρον ἄλλων μὲν ἀεὶ γινομένων ἄλλων δὲ φθειρομένων, καὶ τὴν κίνησιν ἀίδιον ἔλεγον· ἄνευ γὰρ κινήσεως οὐκ ἔστι γένεσις ἢ φθορά.

S.2 *in De Caelo* 202.14   οἱ δὲ καὶ τῷ πλήθει ἀπείρους κόσμους, ὡς Ἀ. μὲν ἄπειρον τῷ μεγέθει τὴν ἀρχὴν θέμενος ἀπείρους ἐξ αὐτοῦ τῷ πλήθει κόσμους ποιεῖν δοκεῖ . . . .

S.3 *in De Caelo* 615.16 (after **6.S.4**)   καὶ κόσμους δὲ ἀπείρους οὗτος καὶ ἕκαστον τῶν κόσμων ἐξ ἀπείρου τοῦ τοιούτου στοιχείου ὑπέθετο, ὡς δοκεῖ.

A.1 1.7.12 (*Dox.* 302)   Ἀ. ἀπεφήνατο τοὺς ἀπείρους οὐρανοὺς θεούς.

A.2 II.1.3 (*Dox.* 327)   Ἀναξίμανδρος Ἀναξιμένης Ἀρχέλαος Ξενοφάνης Διογένης Λεύκιππος Δημόκριτος Ἐπίκουρος ἀπείρους κόσμους ἐν τῷ ἀπείρῳ κατὰ πᾶσαν περιαγωγήν.

A.3 II.1.8 (*Dox.* 329)   τῶν ἀπείρους ἀποφηναμένων τοὺς κόσμους Ἀ. τὸ ἴσον αὐτοὺς ἀπέχειν ἀλλήλων, Ἐπίκουρος ἄνισον εἶναι τὸ μεταξὺ τῶν κόσμων διάστημα.

A.4 II.4.6 (*Dox.* 331)   Ἀναξίμανδρος Ἀναξιμένης Ἀναξαγόρας Ἀρχέλαος Διογένης Λεύκιππος φθαρτὸν τὸν κόσμον.

C. De Nat. Deor. i.10.25 Anaximandri autem opinio est nativos esse deos longis intervallis orientis occidentisque, eosque innumerabilis esse mundos.

Augustine C.D. viii.2 (after **7**) et innumerabiles mundos gignere et quaecumque in eis oriuntur; eosque mundos modo dissolvi modo iterum gigni existimavit, quanta quisque aetate sua manere potuerit, nec ipse aliquid divinae menti in his rerum operibus tribuens.

ᵃ For the ἄπειροι κόσμοι, see also 4.P., 4 A., and 7.P. The doctrine is mentioned by Plato *Tim.* 55c.8; and by Arist. *Phys.* 203ᵇ26, 250ᵇ18; *De Caelo* 274ᵃ28, with no name of author.

We saw that in **4**, where the original text of Theophrastus speaks of "all the οὐρανοί and the κόσμοι within them" arising out of the Boundless, the Hellenistic doxographers (pseudo-Plutarch and Aëtius) have assimilated this doctrine to the ἄπειροι κόσμοι of the atomists. Since the version of these late sources differs so patently from that of Theophrastus, it is a moot point whether they can be correct in ascribing a plurality or infinity of worlds to Anaximander. Zeller (I⁵, 230–36) was the first to deny this view for Anaximander. The Hellenistic interpretation was accepted by Burnet (pp. 58–61) and by many authors who followed him, but Zeller's denial was renewed by Cornford in a detailed discussion of "Innumerable Worlds in Presocratic Philosophy," *CQ*, XXVIII (1934), 1. This long and inconclusive debate of the question by modern scholars faithfully reflects the vague and indecisive character of the evidence, and we cannot hope to settle the matter here in any final way. What can be done, however, is to point out (1) the confusion of the doxographic tradition, (2) the vagueness of what Aristotle and Theophrastus (where his version can be recognized) tell us on the subject, and (3) the weight of certain general considerations against ascribing infinite worlds to Anaximander.

1. All late sources, including Simplicius, speak of innumerable κόσμοι for Anaximander, and seem to identify these with the atomistic "worlds." But the error of Aëtius and pseudo-Plutarch has been demonstrated under **4**, and the contamination with later ideas is palpable here in the most detailed statement, **9.A.3**: "Of those who declared the worlds to be infinite, Anaximander said they were equally distant from one another, Epicurus thought the distance between the worlds was unequal." It is possible (though unlikely) that the *longa intervalla* mentioned in Cicero's reference to Anaximander also imply spatial distance. If so, the linking of Anaximander's "worlds" and Epicurean

intermundia was already to be found in the earlier treatise περὶ θεῶν, which must be the common source of Aëtius and Cicero (and also of Philodemus). But this Hellenistic treatise can have drawn only in a general way upon Theophrastus' history of natural philosophy, which did not really deal with θεοί at all. The documentary value of the theological treatise was not very high, judging from what Aëtius and Cicero have to say on the subject of Thales' conception of divinity: νοῦν τοῦ κόσμου τὸν θεόν (Aëtius 1.7.11, *Dox.* 301); *deum autem eam mentem, quae ex aqua cuncta fingeret* (*De Nat. Deor.* 1.10.25).

A different Hellenistic compilation περὶ θεῶν seems to lie behind the report of Augustine, for whom the intervals between Anaximander's worlds are clearly temporal, not spatial: *modo dissolvi modo iterum gigni existimavit, quanta quisque aetate sua manere potuerit* (cf. **7.P.**: τὴν φθορὰν γίνεσθαι καὶ πολὺ πρότερον τὴν γένεσιν). In this view, Anaximander's worlds succeed one another like those of the Stoic doctrine.

Of these two versions, Augustine's is clearly the more credible. It is free of the statement that Anaximander's infinite worlds were so many "gods" (**9.A.1** and **C.**), and of the even more extravagant assertion concerning the divinity of Thales. For Augustine, on the contrary, these two Milesians are both atheistic materialists, while the deity of Anaximenes is represented not as the Air (so Aëtius and Cicero, in *Vors.* 13 A 10), but as its divine offspring, the elements (*Vors. ibid.*)—a statement which is in direct agreement with the version of Theophrastus (cf. *Vors.* 13 A 7.1 and A 5). Here again the report of Aëtius appears as the most unreliable and confused of all extant versions of the doxography.

It would seem that the rather halting testimony of these indirect sources would be confirmed by the authority of Simplicius, who also identifies the doctrine of Anaximander with that of the atomists (**S.1**). But although Simplicius must have had access to the Φυσικῶν Δόξαι, it is revealing that no mention of infinite worlds occurs in his direct excerpt from this source (*in Phys.* 24.13–25 = *Phys. Opin.* fr. 2). The assimilation of Anaximander to the atomists appears much later, when Simplicius is commenting upon Aristotle's reference to "those who declare that there are ἄπειροι κόσμοι" (*Phys.* 250^{b}18). The commentator assumes that not only the atomists are intended by this phrase, but Anaximander as well. Whether or not that is the case, however, depends precisely upon whether or not Aristotle identified the two doctrines; it is of course the atomists whom he has primarily in mind.

Simplicius himself is not as sure of the identification as he seems to be in **S.1**. When he deals with the same question in his commentary on the *De Caelo*, he twice adds a cautious "apparently" to this statement of Anaximander's view (**S.2** δοκεῖ, **S.3** ὡς δοκεῖ). Such hesitation would be meaningless if Simplicius had found a clear-cut statement to this effect in the text of Theophrastus. The natural conclusion is that he was no better informed than we, and has interpreted a reference to "all the οὐρανοί" in the way which seemed to him most plausible.

2. Of much more consequence are the assertions of Aristotle and Theophrastus. In the case of the latter, we are sure that he spoke of "all the οὐρανοί and the κόσμοι within them" as produced out of the Boundless (**4**). In **8**, Hippolytus says that the ἄπειρον "embraces all the κόσμοι"; while **Arist. 4** has the same phrase in reference to "all the οὐρανοί." It makes no great difference whether πάντας περιέχειν τοὺς κόσμους in **8.H.** represents the original wording of Theophrastus, or whether (as I suggested above) κόσμους has been substituted for οὐρανούς by some excerptor. In either case we have a mention by Aristotle and Theophrastus of "all the οὐρανοί" for Anaximander, a phrase which would normally suggest the doctrine of infinite world systems. (Thus when Aristotle refutes the plurality of worlds in *De Caelo* 1.7–9, he speaks indiscriminately of πάντες οἱ κόσμοι, οἱ πλείους οὐρανοί, and κόσμοι πλείους ἑνός—276ᵃ30, ᵇ19, ᵇ21.)

But what are we to make of the plural κόσμοι which lie within these celestial systems? Although κόσμος in the singular can be used by Aristotle for a portion of the universe, and for the sublunary "world" in particular (see below, p. 224), there seems to be no Aristotelian example of κόσμοι in the plural except for the doctrine of other worlds. But that can scarcely be the meaning here of the κόσμοι which lie *within* the οὐρανοί. The phrase is a very unusual one for a Peripatetic, and it has been suggested that ἅπαντας γίνεσθαι τοὺς οὐρανοὺς καὶ τοὺς ἐν αὐτοῖς κόσμους must have been taken by Theophrastus almost verbatim from the book of Anaximander (Reinhardt, *Parmenides*, p. 175, followed in part by Kranz and Gigon). We have seen that close paraphrase was the normal procedure of Theophrastus in the expository sections of his work (above, pp. 18–24). The possibility of such a paraphrase here would explain how κόσμοι could be used for the diverse regions or departments of the world (as in the Hippocratic treatise *De Hebdomadibus*, cited below, p. 224), and this hypothesis is confirmed by the fact that what follows these words in the excerpt of Simplicius is precisely Anaximander's fragment. In all probability, then, **4**, like **5**, contains an exposition of Anaximander's ideas practically in his own words.

Now if it is Anaximander himself who spoke of πάντες οἱ οὐρανοί, the phrase need not mean a plurality of world systems (as it probably would if Theophrastus were its author). The terminology of sixth-century Miletus is largely unknown, and we cannot simply identify it with that of the fourth century. All that we really learn from the statements of Aristotle and Theophrastus is that Anaximander spoke of a plurality of οὐρανοί, which contain a plurality of κόσμοι, and are themselves enclosed within the larger surrounding mass of the ἄπειρον from which they have emerged. It may well be that Anaximander's statement was so brief, and his terminology so unfamiliar, that Aristotle and Theophrastus simply paraphrased his words without venturing to decide whether or not this conception was identical with the κόσμοι of the atomists. The later doxographers, of course, exercised no such restraint.

If Aristotle and Theophrastus were not sure what Anaximander meant by "all the οὐρανοί," it is perhaps rash of us to hazard a guess. But there is a plausible suggestion of Zeller (which Cornford has revived) that the οὐρανοί of Anaximander were the various celestial rings which compose his structure for the visible heavens. Anaximander may have used the plural because no one of these rings was sufficiently unique to deserve the title of οὐρανός alone (see below, **13–16**). On this hypothesis it is clear that the κόσμοι must be some lower "arrangements" of atmosphere or earth, and the Boundless can thus surround both οὐρανοί and κόσμοι within the framework of the one and only world system concerning which the testimonia for Anaximander give us any real information. (In this connection, it may be remarked that in *Vors.* 44 A 16 Aëtius reports a use of κόσμος and οὐρανός by Philolaus for the superlunar and sublunar regions of the heavens, respectively, within the outer stellar sphere which is called ὄλυμπος. There is no other evidence of this particular usage, but one may compare such phrases as ὁ ὀλύμπιος κόσμος for the outer sphere in *De Hebd.* 2.)

3. The interpretation which has just been offered is not the only one which can fit the textual evidence. But it has the advantage of avoiding the very serious difficulties which follow if we attribute a plurality of worlds to Anaximander. In the first place, there is no good evidence of such a doctrine for any other thinker earlier than Leucippus. Furthermore, there is no intelligible reason why the theory of innumerable worlds should have been formulated within the context of Milesian

thought. As Cornford has rightly urged, the only motive for such a theory is the atomist assumption of an infinite, indiscriminate void, in which one point is as good as another for the fortuitous concourse of bodies that may produce a world. The ἄπειρον of Anaximander is of a different order, and his world arises not by chance but, as far as we can tell, by a kind of organic growth (see **13.P.**). Above all, there is the almost insuperable difficulty of conceiving that any Greek could have ascribed the attributes of divinity to such a formless nightmare as the ἄπειρον must be, if it is to encompass innumerable worlds in every direction. The atomists of course recognize such a labyrinthine περι-έχον. But they do not describe it as ageless, deathless, divine, and responsible for the "guidance" of the universe.

SUPPLEMENTARY NOTE. The statement that no other Greek phi-losopher before the atomists believed in a plurality of world systems may come as a surprise to readers of Burnet, who have been told that even Anaxagoras "adopted the ordinary Ionian theory of innumerable worlds" (p. 269). For a point-by-point criticism of Burnet's curious treatment of the evidence, see Cornford's article on the subject (*CQ*, XXVIII, 1). But two points deserve special consideration here.

In Xenophanes A 33.6, Hippolytus tells us that the destruction of mankind (which will result from the sinking of the earth into the sea) and the subsequent new generation of living things constitute a change which takes place "in all the κόσμοι." Burnet accordingly found it "impossible to doubt that Theophrastus attributed a belief in 'in-numerable worlds' to Xenophanes," while admitting that this seemed in contradiction with Xenophanes' view "that the World or God was one" (Burnet, p. 124). In fact there are at least two other meanings for the phrase "all the κόσμοι" in such a context, either one of which would leave the basic monism of Xenophanes intact. In the first place, if the earth eventually disappears into the sea but emerges to support life once more, then there is by that very fact a plurality of κόσμοι or inhabited "worlds" of mankind on earth, one following another. And by saying this happens "in all the κόσμοι," Theophrastus may have meant merely that the process continues indefinitely, each terrestrial κόσμος giving way to another in turn. Or, on the other hand, "all the κόσμοι" may refer to some other organized regions of life on earth, comparable to the "known world" of the Mediterranean basin. (Either of these two senses of κόσμοι, but particularly the second, would be compatible with the use of the same word in **4** for Anaximander.)

Xenophanes is elsewhere represented as believing in "many suns and moons distributed among the regions, sections, and zones of the earth," some of which are "not inhabited by us" (A 41a). The cycle of flood and renewal will then occur in these other κόσμοι, as well as in the world of the Greeks.

The last of these two explanations seems to be confirmed by the parallel evidence for Anaxagoras. In his Theophrastean excerpt on this philosopher, Simplicius declares τῆς δὲ κινήσεως καὶ τῆς γενέσεως αἴτιον ἐπέστησε τὸν νοῦν ὁ Ἀναξαγόρας, ὑφ' οὗ διακρινόμενα τούς τε κόσμους καὶ τὴν τῶν ἄλλων φύσιν ἐγέννησαν (Phys. Opin. fr. 4, under 7). Now it is not likely that the κόσμοι here are "worlds," for in that case there would be little point in adding καὶ τὴν τῶν ἄλλων φύσιν. No other ancient authority ascribes a belief in plural worlds to Anaxagoras; he is even omitted from the very generous list which Aëtius gives of those who professed such a doctrine (9.A.2; cf. Vors. 59 A 63–64). Furthermore, in Phys. 250ᵇ18 ff. Aristotle contrasts Anaxagoras and Empedocles with those thinkers who declare that "there are infinite κόσμοι, some of them being generated and others destroyed"—i.e., with the atomists. Although Aristotle's words do not rigorously exclude the bizarre possibility that Anaxagoras believed in a plurality of worlds, all generated at the same time and never destroyed, their natural implication is that he, like Empedocles, assumed the existence of only one world at any given time. It is true that one fragment of Anaxagoras, hastily read, does suggest a plurality of worlds. Speaking of the mixture of all seeds and forms and of their ἀπόκρισις, Anaxagoras says:

And men were fashioned together, and all the other animals which have life; and these men have organized cities and cultivated fields, as with us (ὥσπερ παρ' ἡμῖν); and they have sun and moon and the rest, as with us; and the earth bears for them many things of every kind, of which they collect together in their dwelling place the ones which are most advantageous, and put them to use.

So much has been said by me concerning separating-off, that things will not separate off only with us, but elsewhere as well. (B 4)

This text has been cited as proof that Anaxagoras subscribed to the theory of innumerable worlds (Burnet, pp. 269 f.). But Simplicius, who quotes the fragment for us, does not even mention this as a possible interpretation. The only suggestion which he makes (other than his own Neoplatonic allegory) is that one might understand Anaxagoras to be speaking of different inhabited regions of the earth. This natural explanation has been defended anew by Cornford, citing the inhabited frog ponds at *Phaedo* 109b (*CQ*, XXVIII, 7–8), and it seems entirely satisfactory. Anaxagoras is stating that the earth has other civilized areas like the Mediterranean basin—the world of the Hyperboreans, perhaps, or the antipodes—and that these areas share our heavenly bodies and our natural order. (The objection of Simplicius that the article would be required for "our Sun" and "our Moon" is of course unfounded. Cornford quotes ἥλιος and σελήνη without the article at Plato *Tim*. 38c.5, and *Laws* 898d.3.)

The κόσμοι formed by separating-off are therefore only the diverse natural "arrangements" of life on earth, and the meaning of the term in Anaxagoras A 41 is entirely parallel to that in Xenophanes A 33.6. (One may compare the usage of κόσμοι for the various political arrangements by which men live together in society; below, pp. 221 f.) But in contrast to Xenophanes, Anaxagoras seems to be insisting that there is only one set of sun, moon, and stars for all these inhabited "worlds."

There is then good evidence of plural κόσμοι in early Ionian philosophy, if these are understood as different constitutions of dry land, sea, and atmosphere in which men may live at other points upon the earth. There is no evidence at all for separate world systems. The latter view is distinctive of Leucippus and his followers (among whom we must count Diogenes of Apollonia, as far as the innumerable worlds are concerned). Leucippus may well have come upon his paradoxical theory by generalizing the idea of plural κόσμοι which we have just described. For if the fertile capacities of land and sea can bring forth at other points a "world" comparable to the one which the Greeks inhabit, a still more magnificent progeny might arise from an infinite number of seminal bodies, scattered at random throughout an endless, indifferent void.[1]

10. POSITION OF THE EARTH

H. (after 7.H.) τὴν δὲ γῆν εἶναι μετέωρον ὑπὸ μηδενὸς κρατουμένην, μένουσαν δὲ διὰ τὴν ὁμοίαν πάντων ἀπόστασιν.

D.L. μέσην τε τὴν γῆν κεῖσθαι, κέντρου τάξιν ἐπέχουσαν

Parallel:

Arist. *De Caelo* 295ᵇ11–16 (= *Vors*. A 26) εἰσὶ δέ τινες οἳ διὰ τὴν ὁμοιότητά φασιν αὐτὴν (sc. τὴν γῆν) μένειν, ὥσπερ τῶν ἀρχαίων Ἀ.· μᾶλλον μὲν γὰρ οὐθὲν ἄνω ἢ κάτω ἢ εἰς τὰ πλάγια φέρεσθαι προσήκει

[1] For further discussion of the use of κόσμος in early Greek philosophy, see Appendix I.

τὸ ἐπὶ τοῦ μέσου ἱδρυμένον καὶ ὁμοίως πρὸς τὰ ἔσχατα ἔχον· ἅμα δ᾽ ἀδύνατον εἰς τἀναντία ποιεῖσθαι τὴν κίνησιν· ὥστ᾽ ἐξ ἀνάγκης μένειν.

Suidas (= *Vors.* A 2) Ἀ. Πραξιάδου Μιλήσιος πρῶτος δὲ ... εὗρε ... τὴν γῆν ἐν μεσαιτάτῳ κεῖσθαι.

Confused:

S. *in De Caelo* 532.14 Ἀναξιμάνδρῳ δὲ ἐδόκει καὶ διὰ τὸν ἀέρα τὸν ἀνέχοντα μένειν ἡ γῆ καὶ διὰ τὴν ἰσορροπίαν καὶ ὁμοιότητα.

Theon Smyrnaeus p. 198, Hiller (*Vors.* A 26 = Eudemus fr. 145, Wehrli) Ἀ. δὲ (sc. εὗρεν) ὅτι ἐστὶν ἡ γῆ μετέωρος καὶ κινεῖται περὶ τὸ τοῦ κόσμου μέσον.

The earth for Anaximander is "aloft," at rest in the center of the heavens. The version of Hippolytus contains two ambiguities. What are the πάντα from which the earth is equidistant? And why is it said to be "not dominated by anything"? The natural answer to the first question is that Theophrastus had a circle (or sphere) in mind, and that πάντα are the points on its circumference, τὰ ἔσχατα in the parallel statement of Aristotle. This is confirmed by κέντρου τάξιν in **D.L.**

For the meaning of κρατουμένην, see below, p. 80.

The assertion of **Theon Smyrnaeus**, that Anaximander's earth moves about the center of the world, is not credible, despite the authority of Eudemus which he invokes at the beginning of the sentence. There is no trace of such a doctrine in the text of Aristotle nor in the excerpts from Theophrastus. The error is probably not due to Eudemus, whose work does not seem to have been utilized by Theon directly. The same context contains other surprising remarks (for example, an ascription to Anaximenes of the doctrine that the moon draws its light from the sun), so that the Eudemian origin of the whole is questionable, as F. Wehrli points out in his discussion of this "fragment": "Eudemus von Rhodos," in *Die Schule des Aristoteles*, VIII (Basel, 1955), 120 f.

Strangely, the statement of Theon is accepted by Burnet (p. 66, n. 3), with no comment except an unmotivated attribution of the same doctrine to Anaxagoras. The source of the confusion is probably to be found in Aristotle's implicit comparison of Anaximander's view to that of Plato in the *Timaeus*, which he has just cited for the theory that the earth, "lying at the center, winds and moves about the axis stretched through the universe" (*De Caelo* 293ᵇ30). The distinction between this doctrine and that of Anaximander was perhaps not carefully drawn by

Eudemus. It is at any rate still a matter for dispute in the commentary of Simplicius (*in De Caelo* 532.2–12). But that is not a sufficient reason for ascribing such a complex celestial model to Anaximander in the sixth century B.C.

The isolated statement of **S.**, that Anaximander explained the earth's stability not only by its symmetrical position but also by the support of the air, occurs in a context which does not suggest a direct consultation of Theophrastus. The assertion has no parallel in the other doxographers, and it is implicitly denied by Aristotle's omission of Anaximander from the list of those who make use of the air in this way (*De Caelo* 294ᵇ13). In addition to these arguments *ex silentio*, we have the express statement of **H.** that the earth is "not dominated by anything." The confusion of **S.** was probably due to the general currency of the air-support doctrine in early Ionian cosmology. (For similar carelessness on the part of Simplicius, see *in Phys.* 1319.21, where he includes Anaximander among the monists who explain generation and corruption by condensation and rarefaction.)

11. FORM OF THE EARTH[a]

H. τὸ δὲ σχῆμα αὐτῆς ὑγρόν,[b] στρογγύλον κίονι[c] λίθῳ παραπλήσιον.

P. ὑπάρχειν δέ φησι τῷ μὲν σχήματι τὴν γῆν κυλινδροειδῆ, ἔχειν δὲ τοσοῦτον βάθος ὅσον ἂν εἴη τρίτον πρὸς τὸ πλάτος.

A. III.10.2 (*Dox.* 376 = *Vors.* A 25) Ἀ. λίθῳ κίονι τὴν γῆν προσφερῆ·

Confused:

D.L. οὖσαν σφαιροειδῆ (sc. τὴν γῆν); cf. **A.** III.10.1 Θαλῆς καὶ οἱ Στωικοὶ καὶ οἱ ἀπ' αὐτῶν σφαιροειδῆ τὴν γῆν.

---

[a] *Compare* D.L. II.2 καὶ γῆς καὶ θαλάσσης περίμετρον πρῶτος ἔγραψεν (cited under **15**), and Suidas ἔγραψε . . . Γῆς περίοδον (*Vors.* 12 A 2). Also Agathemerus I. 1, cited below, p. 82.
[b] ὑγρόν libri: γυρόν coni. Roeper, Diels.　　　　　　[c] χίονι libri: corr. Wolfius, Diels.

A. compares the earth of Anaximander to a stone column. The emendation κίονι for χίονι in **H.** is therefore certain (see *Dox.* 218). The usual change of ὑγρόν to γυρόν is, however, more dubious. As Diels remarked (*Dox.* 218), γυρός means not "circular," but "curving, convex." He understood it to refer to the surface of the earth, while στρογγύλος in **H.** indicates its circumference. But can Anaximander have said that the earth's surface was convex? On the contrary, the only attested Ionian doctrine is that men dwell in a hollow of the earth;

i.e., in the Mediterranean basin. This is the teaching not only of Anaxagoras (A 42.5), but also of Archelaus (A 4.4), of Democritus (A 49), and of Plato in the *Phaedo* (109b. ff., where it is of course combined with the non-Ionic view of the earth as round). Such a hollow may be presupposed by the doctrine of Anaximenes that the sun moves not under but around the earth, and is hidden by the latter's height in the north (A 14). If therefore we accept the correction γυρός, the word must be interpreted as "concave" rather than "convex," and Anaximander introduces the standard Ionic view (so Burnet, p. 65, n. 1). The doctrine in itself is a plausible one for Anaximander. The Chaldaeans too conceived the earth as σκαφοειδὴς καὶ κοίλη (according to Diod. Sic. ii.31.7). But this means building a great deal on what is after all only a conjecture. The term γυρός is not a natural substitute for the usual κοῖλος, and the manuscript ὑγρόν presents no real difficulty. That the earth is moist, and originally much more so, is an authentic doctrine of Anaximander (see 20). The word σχῆμα may mean "form, character" just as well as "shape."

The comparison of the earth to a stone column is correctly interpreted by pseudo-Plutarch as meaning cylindrical in shape. The ratio 3:1 for the diameter and the height, given only by the same author, can scarcely come from any source except Theophrastus.

The spherical earth attributed to Anaximander by **D.L.** represents a Hellenistic confusion, of which the parallel may be found in Aëtius' ascription of the same doctrine to "Thales and the Stoics and their followers." If such blunders require an explanation, one may easily be found in the ambiguous sense of στρογγύλος, "round," which can apply to a sphere as well as to a flat disk.

12. ANTIPODES

H. τῶν δὲ ἐπιπέδων ᾧ μὲν ἐπιβεβήκαμεν, ὃ δὲ ἀντίθετον ὑπάρχει.

A. (with **11.A.**) τῶν ἐπιπέδων****

The essential accuracy of **H.** here is confirmed by the reappearance of the first two words in the mutilated version of **A.** But **H.** too seems to be incomplete. The statement that "the other surface of the earth is set opposite [to the one on which we stand]" suggests that a reference to inhabited antipodes has fallen out of the text (see below, p. 84).

13. FORMATION OF THE HEAVENS

H. τὰ δὲ ἄστρα γίνεσθαι κύκλον πυρός, ἀποκριθέντα ἐκ[a] τοῦ κατὰ τὸν κόσμον πυρός, περιληφθέντα δ' ὑπὸ ἀέρος.

P. φησὶ δέ τι[b] ἐκ τοῦ ἀιδίου γόνιμον θερμοῦ τε καὶ ψυχροῦ κατὰ τὴν γένεσιν τοῦδε τοῦ κόσμου ἀποκριθῆναι καί τινα ἐκ τούτου φλογὸς σφαῖραν περιφυῆναι τῷ περὶ τὴν γῆν ἀέρι ὡς τῷ δένδρῳ φλοιόν. ἧστινος ἀπορραγείσης καὶ εἴς τινας ἀποκλεισθείσης κύκλους ὑποστῆναι τὸν ἥλιον καὶ τὴν σελήνην καὶ τοὺς ἀστέρας.

A.1 ΙΙ.ΙΙ.5 (*Dox.* 340 = *Vors.* Α 17a) *Ἀ.* ἐκ θερμοῦ καὶ ψυχροῦ μίγματος (sc. εἶναι τὸν οὐρανόν).

A.2 ΙΙ.13.7 (*Dox.* 342 = *Vors.* Α 18) *Ἀ.* (τὰ ἄστρα εἶναι) πιλήματα ἀέρος τροχοειδῆ, πυρὸς ἔμπλεα, κατά τι μέρος ἀπὸ στομίων ἐκπνέοντα φλόγας.

Irenaeus *Adv. Haereses* ΙΙ.18.2, or ΙΙ.14 (= *Dox.* 171) A. autem hoc quod immensum est omnium initium subiecit seminaliter habens in semet ipso omnium genesin: ex quo immensos mundos constare ait....

[a] ἐκ Cedr.: om. libri (v. *Vors.* I⁷, Nachtr. p. 487.15).
[b] φησὶ δὲ τὸ libri: corr. Diels ("fortasse"), Hölscher.

The first two or three stages in the formation of the world are described only by **P.** In his text we must understand the phrase τι ἐκ τοῦ ἀιδίου γόνιμον ... ἀποκριθῆναι to mean that "at the origin of this world, something capable of generating hot and cold was separated off from the eternal [Boundless]." (For the ἄπειρον as ἀίδιον, see **8.H.**) That the mention of Hot and Cold in the formation of the heavens goes back to Theophrastus is proved by the vague echo in **13.A.1.** It is possible that the expression γόνιμον should be recognized in *seminaliter habens ... genesin* in the doxography of Irenaeus, as was suggested by Hölscher ("Anaximander," p. 266), who compares Theophrastus' *De Igne* 44, where the sun's heat is γόνιμος καὶ ζώων καὶ φυτῶν. The word may thus have been used by Theophrastus, but probably not by Anaximander (as Diels suggested, on *Vors.* 12 A 10). In such a case fifth-century authors generally speak in concrete terms, of σπέρμα, for example (Anaxag. Β 4), or of ῥίζωμα (Emped. Β 6). The idea is old, the phrasing of **P.** comparatively recent.

The word ἀπορραγείσης in **P.** probably implies that the sphere of flame is torn away from the core to which it was attached, as was pointed out by W. A. Heidel, *Proceedings of the American Academy of Arts and Sciences*, XLVIII (1913), 688, citing Arist. *Hist. An.* 552ᵃ3.

The text of **A.2** shows several verbal peculiarities which cannot be safely ascribed to Theophrastus. **A.2** speaks of στόμια where **H.** (14–15) has ἐκπνοαί and πόροι. While κύκλος is the only term employed by **H.** and **P.** for the astral circles, **A.** prefers τροχός, τροχοειδής. **A.** is also the only author to speak of the "condensations" (πιλήματα) of the air. The word is probably not from Theophrastus, but the notion expressed may be authentic: the originally moist ἀήρ will have hardened and stiffened under the drying action of fire, so as to form a comparatively solid covering around the fiery rings.

14. STARS AND SUN

H. ἐκπνοὰς δ' ὑπάρξαι πόρους τινὰς αὐλώδεις,ᵃ καθ' οὓς φαίνεται τὰ ἄστρα· διὸ καὶ ἐπιφρασσομένων τῶν ἐκπνοῶν τὰς ἐκλείψεις γίνεσθαι.

A.1 11.16.5 (*Dox.* 345 = *Vors.* A 18) Ἀ. ὑπὸ τῶν κύκλων καὶ τῶν σφαιρῶν, ἐφ' ὧν ἕκαστος βέβηκε, φέρεσθαι (sc. τοὺς ἀστέρας).

A.2 11.20.1 (*Dox.* 348 = *Vors.* A 21) Ἀ. κύκλον εἶναι ὀκτωκαιεικοσαπλασίονα τῆς γῆς, ἁρματείῳ τροχῷ παραπλήσιον, τὴν ἁψῖδα ἔχοντα κοίλην, πλήρη πυρός, κατά τι μέρος ἐκφαίνουσα διὰ στομίου τὸ πῦρ ὥσπερ διὰ πρηστῆρος αὐλοῦ· καὶ τοῦτ' εἶναι τὸν ἥλιον.

A.3 11.24.2 (*Dox.* 354 = *Vors.* A 21) Ἀ. τοῦ στομίου τῆς τοῦ πυρὸς διεκπνοῆς ἀποκλειομένου (sc. γίγνεσθαι τὴν τοῦ ἡλίου ἔκλειψιν).

A.4 (Theodoretus IV.16; *Dox.* 329n = *Vors.* 13 A 12) καὶ οἱ μὲν μυλοειδῶς, οἱ δὲ τροχοῦ δίκην περιδινεῖσθαι (sc. τὸν κόσμον) (referred by Diels to Anaximenes and Anaximander respectively).

ᵃ πύρους τινὰς αὐρώδεις Cedr.: τόπους τινὰς ἀερώδεις libri: corr. Diels.

From this point onwards, pseudo-Plutarch abandons us as far as the heavens are concerned, while the account of Hippolytus becomes ambiguous because of its excessive brevity and faulty manuscript tradition.

So far Hippolytus has mentioned only a single circle of fire, yet now he speaks in general of "the heavenly bodies" (τὰ ἄστρα). A reference to eclipses shows that he has the sun and moon primarily in mind. He tells us only that they suffer eclipse "when the exhalation from certain tube-like passages is stopped up." The same account is given for the sun by **A.3**, for the moon by **15.A.3**. No details are given by Hippolytus concerning the "circles of the fixed stars," which he mentions under **16**.

A more elaborate description of the sun's ring is given by **A.2**: the solar κύκλος is like the hollow rim of a chariot wheel, filled with fire; its aperture resembles the mouthpiece of a bellows (πρηστῆρος αὐλός, according to the explanation of Diels, *Dox.* 25 f.). The two images might have been utilized by Anaximander, but the isolated testimony of Aëtius is scarcely enough to prove it. The dimension of the sun's ring (28 times the earth) must ultimately be derived from Theophrastus, but the figure is probably corrupt (see commentary on **16**).

The statement of **A.1** that the movement of the heavenly bodies is due "to the circles and spheres upon which each is placed," implies a distinction between ἀστήρ and sphere which is meaningless within Anaximander's system. The expression has been carelessly repeated from the preceding reference to Aristotle (Aëtius II.16.4, *Dox.* 345; the confusion is then transferred to **16.A.2**).

Equally worthless is the other passage from the same doxography (**A.4**), in which Diels finds a reference to the Milesians. In this case the comparison to the whirling of a wheel would be inappropriate for Anaximander, since **A.4** refers not to the ring of a particular heavenly body, but to the general movement of the κόσμος.

There is no need to discuss the nonsensical report of Achilles Tatius (*Vors.* 12 A 21), according to which it is not the rim but the hub of the sun's wheel which is filled with fire. This is strangely listed by Diels before the corresponding testimonium of Aëtius, without any comment except "aus Poseidonios." This statement is difficult to reconcile with his own proof that Achilles depends directly upon the *Placita* of pseudo-Plutarch, i.e., upon Aëtius, whose words in this case "non excerpuntur, sed ventosa paraphrasi in meras ineptias detorquentur" (*Dox.* 25).

15. THE MOON

H. τὴν δὲ σελήνην ποτὲ μὲν πληρουμένην φαίνεσθαι, ποτὲ δὲ μειουμένην παρὰ τὴν τῶν πόρων ἐπίφραξιν ἢ ἄνοιξιν.

A.1 II.25.1 (*Dox.* 355 = *Vors.* A 22) κύκλον εἶναι (sc. τὴν σελήνην) ἐννεακαιδεκαπλασίονα τῆς γῆς, ὥσπερ ⟨τὸν⟩ τοῦ ἡλίου πλήρη πυρός· ἐκλείπειν δὲ κατὰ τὰς ἐπιστροφὰς τοῦ τροχοῦ· ὅμοιον γὰρ εἶναι ἁρματείῳ τροχῷ κοίλην ἔχοντι τὴν ἁψῖδα καὶ πυρὸς πλήρη καθάπερ τὸν τοῦ ἡλίου, κείμενον λοξόν, ὡς κἀκεῖνον ἔχοντα μίαν ἐκπνοήν οἷον πρηστῆρος αὐλόν.[a]

A.2 II.28.1 (*Dox.* 358 = *Vors.* A 22)   Ἄ. Ξενοφάνης Βήρωσος ἴδιον αὐτὴν ἔχειν φῶς, ἀραιότερον δέ πως.

A.3 II.29.1 (*Dox.* 359 = *Vors.* A 22)   Ἄ. τοῦ στομίου τοῦ περὶ τὸν τροχὸν ἐπιφραττομένου (sc. ἐκλείπειν τὴν σελήνην).

Confused:

D.L.   τήν τε σελήνην ψευδοφαῆ καὶ ἀπὸ ἡλίου φωτίζεσθαι.

[a] I have combined the text of pseudo-Plutarch (up to πυρὸς πλήρη) with that of Stobaeus (for the rest). Instead of κατὰ τὰς ἐπιστροφὰς τοῦ τροχοῦ, Stobaeus has κατὰ τὰς τροπάς, with *v.l.*: κατὰ τὰς στροφάς. The two versions of A. 2 have been similarly combined.
For Anaximander's knowledge of the ecliptic (κείμενον λοξόν), compare Pliny *H.N.* 11.31 (= *Vors.* A 5): "obliquitatem eius [sc. zodiaci] intellexisse, hoc est rerum foris aperuisse, A. Milesius traditur primus Olympiade quinquagesima octava [548–45 B.C.]."
A list of Anaximander's astronomical discoveries is given by D.L. II.1–2 (= *Vors.* A 1): εὗρεν δὲ καὶ γνώμονα πρῶτος καὶ ἔστησεν ἐπὶ τῶν σκιοθήρων ἐν Λακεδαίμονι, καθά φησι Φαβωρῖνος ἐν Παντοδαπῇ ἱστορίᾳ, τροπάς τε καὶ ἰσημερίας σημαίνοντα καὶ ὡροσκοπεῖα κατεσκεύασε. καὶ γῆς καὶ θαλάσσης περίμετρον πρῶτος ἔγραψν, ἀλλὰ καὶ σφαῖραν κατεσκεύασε.
Some of the same information is repeated by Suidas (*Vors.* A 2) and by Eusebius (*Vors.* A 4). The "sphere" is also mentioned by Pliny *H.N.* VII.56.203 (not listed in *Vors.*): "astrologiam Atlans Libyae filius [sc. invenit], ut alii Aegyptii, ut alii Assyrii, sphaeram in ea Milesius Anaximander."

Here Hippolytus gives us only an account of lunar phases by the same opening and shutting of the passages which produce eclipses. (We may reasonably suppose that Anaximander's speculation began here with an explanation of the monthly lunar changes as due to some kind of obstruction, and that he then proceeded to extend the same doctrine to the rarer, but apparently similar, phenomena of eclipse.) That lunar as well as solar eclipses arise in this way is implied by **14.H.**, and stated expressly by **15.A.3**. The divergent explanation of **A.1** is therefore corrupt. Among the several possible emendations, perhaps the simplest is to consider κατὰ τὰς στροφὰς and κατὰ τὰς τροπὰς (Stobaeus) as progressive distortions of κατὰ τὰς ἐπιστροφὰς τοῦ τροχοῦ (in pseudo-Plutarch). The word ἐπιστροφή may itself have arisen as a copyist's error for the original ἐπίφραξις (preserved by **H.**; cf. ἐπιφραττομένου in **A.3**). The scribe or excerptor was misled by his τροχός.

Otherwise, the description of the moon in **A.1** exactly parallels that of the sun. The obliquity of the rings mentioned here applies equally to sun and moon (although this detail was omitted in **14.A.2**). For the dimension of the moon's circle, see commentary on **16**.

The statement (**A.2**) that the moon has her own light, "in some way rarer" than that of the sun, is vague enough, but no doubt represents something Theophrastus said (for it is confirmed by the "purest fire" of the sun, in **16.D.L.**). The contrary assertion of **D.L.** here (that the moon is lit by the sun) is certainly incorrect.

For the moon's light, compare Anaximenes A 18: μὴ πανσέληνον εἶναι (sc. τὴν σελήνην) διὰ παντὸς καὶ ἀσθενέστερον αὐτὴν φῶς ἔχειν τοῦ ἡλίου.

16. SIZE, POSITION, AND DISTANCE OF THE RINGS

H. εἶναι δὲ τὸν κύκλον τοῦ ἡλίου ἑπτακαιεικοσαπλασίονα*** τῆς σελήνης, καὶ ἀνωτάτω μὲν εἶναι τὸν ἥλιον,*** κατωτάτω δὲ τοὺς τῶν ἀπλανῶν[a] ἀστέρων κύκλους.

A.1 II.15.6 (*Dox.* 345 = *Vors.* A 18) Ἀ. καὶ Μητρόδωρος ὁ Χῖος καὶ Κράτης ἀνωτάτω πάντων τὸν ἥλιον τετάχθαι, μετ' αὐτὸν δὲ τὴν σελήνην, ὑπὸ δὲ αὐτοὺς τὰ ἀπλανῆ τῶν ἄστρων καὶ τοὺς πλάνητας.

A.2 II.21.1 (*Dox.* 351 = *Vors.* A 21) τὸν μὲν ἥλιον ἴσον εἶναι τῇ γῇ, τὸν δὲ κύκλον ἀφ' οὗ τὴν ἐκπνοὴν ἔχει καὶ ὑφ' οὗ φέρεται ἑπτακαιεικοσαπλασίω τῆς γῆς.

D.L. ἀλλὰ καὶ τὸν ἥλιον οὐκ ἐλάττονα τῆς γῆς καὶ καθαρώτατον πῦρ.

S. *in De Caelo* 471.1 (*Vors.* A 19 = Eudemus fr. 146, Wehrli) Ἀναξιμάνδρου πρώτου τὸν περὶ μεγεθῶν καὶ ἀποστημάτων λόγον εὑρηκότος, ὡς Εὔδημος ἱστορεῖ τὴν τῆς θέσεως τάξιν εἰς τοὺς Πυθαγορείους πρώτους ἀναφέρων.

[a] "Nach ἀπλανῶν fehlt καὶ τῶν πλανητῶν, wie κύκλους zeigt"; Diels, comparing **A.1**, but see commentary.

The sentence of **H.** appears to be badly mutilated. It gives us (1) the ratio 27:1 between the sun's circle and (if we follow the MSS.) the moon, and (2) the relative order of the rings, with the sun highest and the fixed stars closest to the earth. This order is confirmed by **A.1**, who adds the position of the moon in between sun and stars. The planets, which are not mentioned in **H.**, are placed with the fixed stars in **A.1**. Since, however, the latter refers also to Metrodorus of Chios and to Crates, it is not clear whether this distinction between planets and stars is specifically intended for Anaximander. Diels thought that the plural κύκλοι in **H.** indicated a missing reference to the planets; but in fact a plurality of rings is required simply to account for the visible stellar field. How could all the fixed stars be explained by a single κύκλος? We would then be obliged to interpret the word as meaning "sphere," which would lead to other difficulties for the understanding of Anaximander's view.

The ratio 27:1 reappears in **A.2**, but there it expresses the dimension of the sun's circle with reference to the earth, not the moon. Against this statement, Zeller (I[5], 224, n. 2) prefers the MSS. version of Hippolytus as giving a more plausible celestial model. However, since the text of Hippolytus has clearly reached us in incomplete form, we must accept here the reading of **A.2**, confirmed in this respect by **14.A.2**: the sun's ring is measured by reference to the earth (so Diels, *Archiv*, p. 231). It would in fact be strange if either Anaximander or Theophrastus had used more than one unit in giving the sizes of these circles, but the earth is the only unit which can have served for the dimension of the moon. The measure of the sun is naturally parallel, and there must therefore be a lacuna before τῆς σελήνης in the text of Hippolytus.

It is again the earth's diameter which is implied by the statement (**A.2**) that the sun is equal to the earth. This view is confirmed by Diogenes Laertius, who says that it is "not less than the earth." We naturally understand this dimension to be that of the sun's visible disk, just as when we are told that, for Anaxagoras, "the sun exceeds the Peloponnesus in size" (*Vors.* 59 A 42.8).

In **14.A.2**, the circle of the sun was said to be not 27 but 28 times greater than the earth. This discrepancy has led to some elaborate speculation, based on the assumption that Anaximander (or at least Theophrastus) gave one dimension for the inner edge of the ring and one for the outer diameter: the thickness of the ring taken twice would explain the difference between the two numbers. The chief advantage of this assumption is that it would permit us to replace the awkward figure 19 for the circle of the moon by 18 (performing the same subtraction in order to find the "inner" diameter). This would give us the neat series 27:18:9, whose last term should represent the diameter of the stellar rings (so Tannery, *Science hellène*, pp. 94 f., followed by Diels, Burnet, and Heath). Unfortunately there is little documentary basis for this attractive result; the only one of these three numbers known to the doxographers is 27. Since this figure appears both in **16.H.** and in **16.A.2**, it must be Theophrastus' dimension for the sun's circle; 28 in **14.A.2** is not a different measurement, but a corrupt reading. For the moon's circle, no source offers any figure except 19 (in **15.A.1**). None whatsoever is given for the circles of the stars.

Anaximander's concern for the sizes and distances of the heavenly bodies is cited by **S.** not from Theophrastus, but from the ἀστρολογικὴ ἱστορία of Eudemus. But the reference of **S.** does not prove that any precise figures were given by Eudemus; and there is no reason to doubt that Theophrastus (rather than Eudemus) is the source for the figures quoted by the doxographers.

17. WIND

H. (after **22.H.**) ἀνέμους δὲ γίνεσθαι τῶν λεπτοτάτων ἀτμῶν τοῦ ἀέρος ἀποκρινομένων καὶ ὅταν ἀθροισθῶσι κινουμένων,

A. III.7.1, (*Dox.*374 = *Vors.* A 24) Ἀ. ἄνεμον εἶναι ῥύσιν ἀέρος τῶν λεπτοτάτων ἐν αὐτῷ καὶ ὑγροτάτων ὑπὸ τοῦ ἡλίου κινουμένων ἢ τηκομένων.

According to **H.** winds are formed by a "separating-off" of the finest vapors of the ἀήρ, and by their common motion after being gathered together. What happens to the grosser portion of the air is not specified.

A. speaks of a "flow" of ἀήρ, and mentions the sun as source of this atmospheric movement. (The sun is also given as cause of evaporation in **18.H.** and **21.H.**) **A.** agrees with **H.** concerning the motion of the finest vapors, and adds a reference to the "wettest" portions of air which are "melted" by the sun. This apparently refers to the complementary process of ἀπόκρισις (i.e., of the segregation of like to like): the heavier, moist portion of air is left behind as cloud and mist, after the finest has been exhaled as wind (cf. the account of evaporation given by Hp. *De Aëribus* 8, cited in part below, pp. 161 f., n. 3). This interpretation is confirmed by **19.A.**, where the "thick cloud" is opposed to the fine particles (λεπτομέρεια) of wind. So in the doctrine of Anaximenes "cloud" is distinguished from "wind" by a progressive condensation of the primeval ἀήρ (*Vors.* 13 A 5, A 7.3).

When the dampest portion is "melted" (τηκομένων, **A.**), it is, of course, on its way to precipitation in liquid form.

18. RAIN

H. ὑετοὺς δὲ ἐκ τῆς ἀτμίδος τῆς ἐκ γῆς ὑφ᾽ ἡλίου[a] ἀναδιδομένης·

[a] ἐκ γῆς ὑφ᾽ ἡλίου scripsi: ἐκ γῆς ὑφ᾽ ἥλιον Diels: ἐκ τῶν ὑφ᾽ ἥλιον (v.l. ἡλίου) Cedr.: ἐκ γῆς ἀναδιδομένης ἐκ τῶν ὑφ᾽ ἥλιον libri.

The text of **H.** is corrupt in all versions. The emendation of Diels would imply that the vapor rises "from the earth to the region of the sun." Kirk and Raven (*The Presocratic Philosophers* [Cambridge, 1957], p. 138) accept the reading of Cedrenus and render: "Rain occurs from the exhalation that issues upwards from the things beneath the sun." But since the circle of the sun is the highest of all heavenly bodies for Anaximander, "things beneath the sun" is too general an expression to offer any real sense here. Ὑφ' ἥλιον ἀναδιδομένης seems to correspond to ὑπὸ τοῦ ἡλίου κινουμένων in **17.A.**, and therefore the genitive should also be read here (cf. ἐξατμιζομένου ὑπὸ τοῦ ἡλίου **21.H.**). No matter how the text is interpreted, it is too brief to tell us anything about Anaximander's theory of rain except that it involved both the sun and rising vapors.

19. LIGHTNING AND THUNDER

H. ἀστραπὰς δέ, ὅταν ἄνεμος ἐκπίπτων[a] διιστᾷ τὰς νεφέλας.

A. III.3.1 (*Dox.* 367 = *Vors.* A 23) περὶ βροντῶν ἀστραπῶν κεραυνῶν πρηστήρων τυφώνων. Ἀ. ἐκ τοῦ πνεύματος ταυτὶ πάντα συμβαίνειν· ὅταν γὰρ περιληφθὲν νέφει παχεῖ βιασάμενον ἐκπέσῃ τῇ λεπτομερείᾳ καὶ κουφότητι, τότε ἡ μὲν ῥῆξις τὸν ψόφον, ἡ δὲ διαστολὴ παρὰ τὴν μελανίαν τοῦ νέφους τὸν διαυγασμὸν ἀποτελεῖ.

Seneca *Q.N.* II.18 (= *Vors.* A 23) A. omnia ad spiritum retulit. Tonitrua, inquit, sunt nubis ictae sonus. Quare inaequalia sunt? Quia et ipse ictus[b] inaequalis est. Quare et sereno tonat? Quia tunc quoque per crassum et scissum aëra spiritus prosilit. At quare aliquando non fulgurat et tonat? Quia spiritus infirmior non valuit in flammam, in sonum valuit. Quid est ergo ipsa fulguratio? Aëris diducentis se corruentisque iactatio languidum ignem nec exiturum aperiens. Quid est fulmen? Acrioris densiorisque spiritus cursus.

[a] ἐκπίπτων Cedr., Capelle: ἐμπίπτων f.l., Diels. [b] *ictus* libri: *spiritus* Diels.

H. explains the lightning by a division of the clouds due to the departure of wind (the variant ἐκπίπτων for ἐμπίπτων is confirmed by the sense, and by ἐκπέσῃ in **A**). The same explanation is given in fuller form by **A.**, covering thunder as well. There is little or no significance to the fact that this text speaks of πνεῦμα where **H.** has ἄνεμος; the two terms are used almost synonymously by Aristotle. (See Lee's note in the

Loeb Library edition of the *Meteorologica* [London and Cambridge, Mass., 1952], p. 203.)

The details added by Seneca need not be derived from Theophrastus, even indirectly. Seneca may easily have provided them himself from his own understanding of Anaximander's doctrine. The distinction between *fulguratio* and *fulmen*, for example, is very similar to the definitions of κεραυνός, πρηστήρ, and τυφῶς ascribed to Chrysippus by Aëtius III.3.13 (*Dox.* 370).

20. ORIGIN OF THE SEA
(= *Vors.* A 27)

A. III.16.1 (*Dox.* 381) Ἀ. τὴν θάλασσάν φησιν εἶναι τῆς πρώτης ὑγρασίας λείψανον, ἧς τὸ μὲν πλεῖον μέρος ἀνεξήρανε τὸ πῦρ, τὸ δὲ ὑπολειφθὲν διὰ τὴν ἔκκαυσιν μετέβαλεν.

Alexander in *Meteor.* 67.3 (= *Phys. Opin.* fr. 23), commenting on **Arist.1** below οἱ μὲν γὰρ αὐτῶν (sc. τῶν φυσικῶν) ὑπόλειμμα λέγουσιν εἶναι τὴν θάλασσαν τῆς πρώτης ὑγρότητος. ὑγροῦ γὰρ ὄντος τοῦ περὶ τὴν γῆν τόπου κἄπειτα τὸ μέν τι τῆς ὑγρότητος ὑπὸ τοῦ ἡλίου ἐξατμίζεσθαι καὶ γίνεσθαι πνεύματά τε ἐξ αὐτοῦ καὶ τροπὰς ἡλίου τε καὶ σελήνης, ὡς διὰ τὰς ἀτμίδας ταύτας καὶ τὰς ἀναθυμιάσεις κἀκείνων τὰς τροπὰς ποιουμένων, ἔνθα ἡ ταύτης αὐτοῖς χορηγία γίνεται, περὶ ταῦτα τρεπομένων· τὸ δέ τι αὐτῆς ὑπολειφθὲν ἐν τοῖς κοίλοις τῆς γῆς τόποις θάλασσαν εἶναι· διὸ καὶ ἐλάττω γίνεσθαι ξηραινομένην ἑκάστοτε ὑπὸ τοῦ ἡλίου καὶ τέλος ἔσεσθαί ποτε ξηράν. ταύτης τῆς δόξης ἐγένετο, ὡς ἱστορεῖ Θεόφραστος, Ἀναξίμανδρός τε καὶ Διογένης.

Parallel:

Arist.1 *Meteor.* 353ᵇ5 οἱ δὲ σοφώτεροι τὴν ἀνθρωπίνην σοφίαν ποιοῦσιν αὐτῆς (sc. τῆς θαλάττης) γένεσιν· εἶναι γὰρ τὸ πρῶτον ὑγρὸν ἅπαντα τὸν περὶ τὴν γῆν τόπον, ὑπὸ δὲ τοῦ ἡλίου ξηραινόμενον τὸ μὲν διατμίσαν πνεύματα καὶ τροπὰς ἡλίου καὶ σελήνης φασὶ ποιεῖν, τὸ δὲ λειφθὲν θάλατταν εἶναι· διὸ καὶ ἐλάττω γίγνεσθαι ξηραινομένην οἴονται, καὶ τέλος ἔσεσθαί ποτε πᾶσαν ξηράν.

Arist.2 *Meteor.* 354ᵇ33 διὸ καὶ γελοῖοι πάντες ὅσοι τῶν πρότερον ὑπέλαβον τὸν ἥλιον τρέφεσθαι τῷ ὑγρῷ· καὶ διὰ τοῦτ' ἔνιοί γέ φασιν καὶ ποιεῖσθαι τὰς τροπὰς αὐτόν· οὐ γὰρ αἰεὶ τοὺς αὐτοὺς δύνασθαι τόπους παρασκευάζειν αὐτῷ τὴν τροφήν· ἀναγκαῖον δ' εἶναι τοῦτο συμβαίνειν περὶ αὐτὸν ἢ φθείρεσθαι· καὶ γὰρ τὸ φανερὸν πῦρ, ἕως ἂν ἔχῃ τροφήν, μέχρι τούτου ζῆν, τὸ δ' ὑγρὸν τῷ πυρὶ τροφὴν εἶναι μόνον.

Arist.3 *Meteor.* 355ᵃ21 τὸ δ' αὐτὸ συμβαίνει καὶ τούτοις ἄλογον καὶ τοῖς φάσκουσι τὸ πρῶτον ὑγρᾶς οὔσης καὶ τῆς γῆς, καὶ τοῦ κόσμου τοῦ περὶ τὴν γῆν ὑπὸ τοῦ ἡλίου θερμαινομένου, ἀέρα γενέσθαι καὶ τὸν ὅλον οὐρανὸν αὐξηθῆναι, καὶ τοῦτον (sc. τὸν ἀέρα) πνεύματά τε παρέχεσθαι καὶ τὰς τροπὰς αὐτοῦ (sc. τοῦ ἡλίου) ποιεῖν.

Arist.4 *Meteor.* 357ᵇ19 ὥσπερ φασί τινες, ἀπελθόντος τοῦ πλείστου καὶ μετεωρισθέντος τοῦ ὑγροῦ διὰ τὸν ἥλιον, τὸ λειφθὲν εἶναι θάλατταν.

A. tells us that Anaximander regarded the sea as "a remnant of the original moisture, of which the greater part was dried up by fire, while what was left became changed [i.e., salty] by combustion."

More information is furnished by Aristotle (who does not cite Anaximander by name, but "those who are wiser in the wisdom of men," in contrast to the theological poets), and by **Alexander** in his commentary (who refers the doctrine to Anaximander and Diogenes, on the authority of Theophrastus). In the course of desiccation of the originally moist region of the earth, the portion evaporated produced the winds (cf. **17**), and also the "turnings" of sun and moon (**Arist.1**). There can be no question of interpreting the winds themselves as cause of the τροπαί, much less as cause of the normal astral motions (as Zeller inferred, Iˢ, 223, with n. 3, where Aristotle's text is entirely misconstrued). **Arist.1** and **3** mention winds and turnings not as cause and effect, but as the parallel results of evaporating moisture or "air" (τοῦτον must represent ἀέρα in **Arist.3**, unless we read τοῦτο, "this whole process [of evaporation] produces"). And **Alexander** makes clear that it is not the winds but the vapors and exhalations which are responsible for the τροπαί: "sun and moon turn about the regions where there is an abundant supply of moisture for them."

Arist.1, 3, and **4** clearly represent one and the same doctrine, that of Anaximander and his followers. **Arist.3** mentions the emergence of the οὐρανός, which reminds us that here, as in **13**, it is the process of cosmogony which is being described. The passages under **20** refer to the state of the terrestrial region just after the separation of the sphere of flame. While **A.** speaks of the action of celestial "fire," Aristotle and his commentator specify the sun. This would imply that the individual heavenly bodies have come into existence before the transformation of the earth and sea; but Aristotle's remarks are perhaps too general to be pressed, and **Alexander** simply repeats his expression. In any case we have here a fuller description of what lies within the primordial sphere of flame, corresponding to the brief mention of "the ἀήρ about the earth" in **13.P.**

In **Arist.3** τὰς τροπὰς αὐτοῦ certainly refers to the "turnings" of the sun, i.e., to the solstices: cf. ποιεῖσθαι τὰς τροπὰς αὐτόν in **Arist.2**, twenty-five lines earlier. (The fantastic reference to the "turnings" of the οὐρανός, proposed by Zeller and accepted by Heath, was properly rejected by Burnet, p. 64n., followed by H. D. P. Lee in the Loeb *Meteorologica.*)

Arist.2 gives a parallel explanation of the solstices in terms of evaporated moisture: the sun is nourished by the moist, and must change its path in search of food, just as any earthly fire must be fed or perish. It is difficult, if not impossible, to distinguish this view from the doctrine ascribed to Anaximander and Diogenes by **Alexander**, following Theophrastus. On the other hand, **Arist.3** distinguishes the proponents of this theory from "those who say that at first even the earth was moist" (although he points out that the implications of the two doctrines are the same). Perhaps Alexander has blended two different views into his account of Anaximander and Diogenes (as Kirk and Raven suggest, *The Presocratic Philosophers* [Cambridge, 1957], p. 139). Thus it may be Heraclitus and Xenophanes who spoke of the sun moving about in search of food, while Anaximander and Diogenes had in mind some more mechanical action of vapors upon the paths of sun and moon. Anaximenes (A 15) explains the τροπαί of the heavenly bodies by condensed ἀήρ, which strikes against them and thrusts them off their course. (So also Anaxagoras A 42.9.) It seems possible that these various thinkers are associated by the doxographers with different aspects of what was essentially one and the same theory. The thickening of the atmosphere which Anaximenes mentions is probably to be located in the north (as is explicitly stated for Anaxagoras A 72). It thus accounts for the reversal of direction at the winter solstice, while the depletion of vapor-nourishment applies rather to the arid regions of the south, and thus explains the summer solstice. (Compare Leucippus A 27 and Democr. A 96, where the northern and southern regions of the earth are contrasted from a similar point of view: the former are frozen solid, the latter are rarefied by the heat.) In any case, all of these formulas depend upon the cosmic importance of evaporating or condensing moisture, and they cannot be interpreted independently of one another.

20a. EARTHQUAKES

Ammianus Marcellinus XVII.7.12 (= *Vors.* A 28)   Anaximander ait arescentem nimia aestuum siccitate aut post madores imbrium terram rimas pandere grandiores, quas penetrat supernus aer violentus et nimius, ac per eas vehementi spiritu quassatam cieri propriis sedibus. Qua de causa tremores[a] huius modi vaporatis temporibus aut nimia aquarum caelestium superfusione contingunt. Ideoque Neptunum, umentis substantiae potestatem, Ennosigaeon et Sisichthona poetae veteres et theologi nuncuparunt.

[a] *terrores* libri: corr. Lindenbrog.

The account of earthquakes attributed by Ammianus to Anaximander is listed here only for the sake of completeness. Since the same view is ascribed to Anaximenes by Aristotle (*Meteor.* 365^{b}6 = *Vors.* 13 A 21) and by Theophrastus (in the version of Hippolytus, *Vors.* 13 A 7.8), Ammianus or his immediate source must simply have confused Anaximenes with his better known Milesian predecessor. At *Meteor.* 365^{a}16, Aristotle emphasizes that there were but three explanations of earthquakes offered before his time: those of Anaximenes, Anaxagoras, and Democritus.

On the other hand, Anaximander's interest in earthquakes seems to be attested by the story which Cicero tells, that he warned the Spartans of a violent earthquake which in fact took place (*Vors.* 12 A 5a).

21. ORIGIN OF ANIMAL LIFE

H. (after **16.H.**)   τὰ δὲ ζῷα γίνεσθαι ‹ἐξ ὑγροῦ› ἐξατμιζομένου[a] ὑπὸ τοῦ ἡλίου.

A. v.19.4 (*Dox.* 430 = *Vors.* A 30)   ἐν ὑγρῷ γεννηθῆναι τὰ πρῶτα ζῷα φλοιοῖς περιεχόμενα ἀκανθώδεσι, προβαινούσης δὲ τῆς ἡλικίας ἀποβαίνειν ἐπὶ τὸ ξηρότερον καὶ περιρρηγνυμένου τοῦ φλοιοῦ ἐπ᾽ ὀλίγον χρόνον μεταβιῶναι.

Censorinus 4.7 (= *Vors.* A 30) A. Milesius videri sibi ex aqua terraque calefactis exortos esse sive pisces seu piscibus simillima animalia;

[a] γίνεσθαι ἐξατμιζόμενα libri: corr. Diels.

The text of **H.** is again corrupt, and has been emended by Diels in accordance with *ex aqua terraque calefactis* in **Censorinus**: animals arise from the primeval moisture as it is evaporated by the sun and separated into sea and land. The details are given by **A.**: at first these animals were surrounded by thorny "barks"; upon maturity they migrated to dry land, shed their coverings, and ἐπ' ὀλίγον χρόνον μεταβιῶναι. Since the verb μεταβιῶναι occurs nowhere else, its meaning has been disputed. Burnet renders the phrase "they survived for a short time," and compares the doctrine of Archelaus (A 4.5) that the first animals, produced in the earth and nourished by slime, were ὀλιγοχρόνια (p. 70, following Heidel). But a verbal compound in μετα- normally indicates a change from one condition to another, and μεταβιῶναι should mean "to live a different life" or "to survive in a different form." Either sense is applicable to Anaximander's view. There is, of course, a considerable change in living conditions for these creatures newly transferred from the sea to the land and suddenly exposed to sunlight and air. It is understandable that their constitution was less robust, and their life span shorter, than that of their children who were produced in the normal way.

22. DESCENT OF MAN

H. τὸν δὲ ἄνθρωπον ἑτέρῳ ζῴῳ γεγονέναι, τουτέστι ἰχθύι, παραπλήσιον κατ' ἀρχάς.

P. (after **13.P.**) ἔτι φησίν, ὅτι κατ' ἀρχὰς ἐξ ἀλλοειδῶν ζῴων ὁ ἄνθρωπος ἐγεννήθη ἐκ τοῦ τὰ μὲν ἄλλα δι' ἑαυτῶν ταχὺ νέμεσθαι, μόνον δὲ τὸν ἄνθρωπον πολυχρονίου δεῖσθαι τιθηνήσεως· διὸ καὶ κατ' ἀρχὰς οὐκ ἄν ποτε τοιοῦτον ὄντα διασωθῆναι.

Censorinus (with **21**) in his homines concrevisse fetusque ad pubertatem intus retentos; tunc demum ruptis illis viros mulieresque qui iam se alere possent processisse.

Parallel:

Plutarch *Symp.* VIII.8.4, 730E (= *Vors.* A 30) οἱ δ' ἀφ' Ἕλληνος τοῦ παλαιοῦ καὶ πατρογενείῳ Ποσειδῶνι θύουσιν, ἐκ τῆς ὑγρᾶς τὸν ἄνθρωπον οὐσίας φῦναι δόξαντες, ὡς καὶ Σύροι· διὸ καὶ σέβονται τὸν ἰχθῦν, ὡς ὁμογενῆ καὶ σύντροφον, ἐπιεικέστερον Ἀναξιμάνδρου φιλοσοφοῦντες· οὐ γὰρ ἐν τοῖς αὐτοῖς ἐκεῖνος ἰχθῦς καὶ ἀνθρώπους, ἀλλ' ἐν ἰχθύσιν ἐγγενέσθαι τὸ πρῶτον ἀνθρώπους ἀποφαίνεται καὶ τραφέντας, ὥσπερ οἱ γαλεοί, καὶ γενομένους ἱκανοὺς ἑαυτοῖς βοηθεῖν ἐκβῆναι τηνικαῦτα καὶ γῆς λαβέσθαι. . . . οὕτως ὁ Ἀναξίμανδρος τῶν ἀνθρώπων πατέρα καὶ μητέρα κοινὸν ἀποφήνας τὸν ἰχθῦν διέβαλε πρὸς τὴν βρῶσιν.

P. states that men must have been born "from living things of another kind," for they could not have survived as helpless infants with no parents to care for them. H. tells us one thing more about these proto-men: they were like fish. In the version of **Censorinus** these fish-like creatures are identified with the first aquatic living things (**21**), and adult men and women are represented as emerging in the same way as other animals, when their enclosing membranes are split. (In **Censorinus** the words *ruptis illis* refer grammatically to *pisces seu piscibus simillima animalia*, but in fact it must be the wrappings of the early sea creatures which are meant.)

The statement of **Censorinus** concerning the formation of men agrees so closely with what Aëtius tells us about animals in general (**21.A.**) that we seem justified in identifying the two accounts. In that case Anaximander agreed with the later Greek physicists in considering the origin of man as entirely comparable to that of the other land animals (see below, p. 112). A special reason is given why human beings cannot have originated in their present form, but their original form itself was in no way unique. Like the rest of the animals, they completed their development in the sea within a protective shell.

Plutarch, on the other hand, declares (*Symp.* 730E) that men were born within fish (not fish-like animals), were nourished like dogfish or small sharks, and became self-sufficient before leaving the water. He thus presents an account of man's prehistory which is unlike that of other animals, and which is not confirmed by any other source. (It should be noted that although Censorinus hesitates between "fish or animals very similar to fish," he does not have the dogfish in mind. This is clear from the mere fact of his hesitation, and above all from the expression *ruptis illis*; for the dogfish does not burst when its young are produced.)

In such a case should we follow Plutarch against the testimony of the doxographers? Can men really have been born like sharks, ready to take care of themselves in the sea? I think not. Plutarch has enlarged upon the meager doxographical information in order to make Anaximander's view fit better into a convivial discussion of "why the Pythagoreans rejected fish more than all other animals." We need no more believe that Anaximander thought men were born from dogfish than that he "deprecated the eating of fish, having shown it to be the father and mother of mankind." This playful conclusion draws with it a fallacious premise. Plutarch, like Aristotle, certainly knew that the dogfish (as well as many other sharks) is viviparous, and that "the young are large at birth and prepared to take care of themselves" (D. S. Jordan, *A Guide to the Study of Fishes* [New York, 1905], p. 127). He has made use of this example here to render his version of Anaximander's theory more plausible. But it does not tally with the statements of Aëtius and Censorinus; if Plutarch is right, they are wrong. We are not bound to reject their testimony when it is contradicted only by an after-dinner speaker with an obvious motive for inaccuracy.

There is then no good reason to suppose that the dogfish comparison goes back to Anaximander; or rather, there is every reason to believe that it does not. All appreciations of his theory which emphasize this analogy and its importance for the modern doctrine of evolution (as does Burnet, p. 71) are either irrelevant or misleading.

23. THE ΨΥΧΗ

A. (Theodoretus v.18; *Dox.* 387n = *Vors.* A 29) Ἀναξιμένης δὲ καὶ Ἀναξίμανδρος καὶ Ἀναξαγόρας καὶ Ἀρχέλαος ἀερώδη τῆς ψυχῆς τὴν φύσιν εἰρήκασιν.

In the other versions of Aëtius IV.3.2, Stobaeus has Ἀναξιμένης Ἀναξαγόρας Ἀρχέλαος Διογένης, pseudo-Plutarch simply οἱ ἀπὸ Ἀναξαγόρου. The textual basis for attributing this doctrine of the soul to Anaximander is therefore very weak. Theodoretus (who generally follows Aëtius) has omitted Diogenes from his list by inadvertence, and we are led to wonder whether his reason for including Anaximander was a better one. Of course, it is just possible that Anaximander figured in the original list of Aëtius, and has fallen out of the other excerpts. But the connection with Theophrastus' account would still be a doubtful one.

THE COSMOLOGY OF ANAXIMANDER

I

THE MILESIAN THEORY OF THE
NATURAL WORLD

IN evaluating Theophrastus as an historian of early Greek philosophy, we have seen that his usual method of exposition is to give a careful, detailed paraphrase of the author whose doctrines are under discussion (above, pp. 17–24). The only fundamental distortions which can be discovered in his account are due to the use of Aristotelian terms and concepts as valid tools for the analysis of earlier ideas. This is not so much a question of misunderstanding as of the involuntary projection of more specialized, abstract notions into a period where the modes of thought and expression were simpler and closer to the concrete language of poetry and myth.

Although the procedure of Theophrastus was justified by the original goals of Peripatetic doxography, the results are, from our point of view, anachronistic. And this lack of a fully historical method becomes most serious where fundamental philosophic doctrines are involved, such as those concerning the ἀρχαί. For it is in regard to such basic matters that the variations of language and conception are most significant between one age and another. Thus, the word φύσις was used by Empedocles to refer to the whole process of "growth" (i.e., of natural development) from birth to maturity, but Aristotle misinterprets Empedocles' statement a century later, because in his mind φύσις has come to represent above all the true nature or form of a fully developed thing.

This kind of misunderstanding is much less frequent in regard to specific physical theories, even if they are no longer accepted by Aristotle and his disciple. For example, the fact that Theophrastus regards the earth as spherical does not prevent him from accurately describing the cylindrical shape given to it by his predecessors, just as the Peripatetic conviction that the order of the universe is unchanging does not preclude a fair exposition of doctrines explaining how the sea and dry land have come into existence. In general, the Theophrastean doxography (where it can be reconstructed) is fully reliable for the detailed theories of heaven and earth. But it requires very close scrutiny whenever more general principles of reality and causation are under discussion.

The practical consequence of all this for an understanding of Anaximander is that his authentic "fragment"—which has reached us by way of Theophrastus' account of his ἀρχή—is the last thing which we will be in a position to interpret. For the fragment itself is too brief to provide its own context, and we cannot altogether rely upon the one within which it is preserved. Paradoxically enough, the detailed physical speculations of Anaximander, for which we depend entirely upon later paraphrasing, are more accessible to us than the general philosophic doctrine which has come to us partially in his own words. Indeed it is these specific theories alone which can provide us with an authentic context for the interpretation of the fragment itself. It is therefore with them that we must begin, as offering some firm ground from which the more slippery problems can later be attacked.

Topics **10** to **23** of the foregoing doxography for Anaximander will thus be reviewed here in turn. A translation of the most important testimonies is given in each case.

10. *Position of the Earth*[1]

H. The earth is aloft, not dominated by anything; it remains in place because of the similar distance from all points [of the celestial circumference].

Arist. There are some who say that the earth remains in place because of similarity [or symmetry], as did Anaximander among the ancients; for a thing established in the middle, with a similar relationship to the extremes, has no reason to move up rather than down or laterally; but since it cannot proceed in opposite directions at the same time, it will necessarily remain where it is.

Anaximander's view of the earth as resting in equipoise at the center of the heavens is perhaps the most significant single piece of information which has reached us concerning the development of scientific thought in sixth-century Miletus. Thales' prediction of a solar eclipse, which symbolized to the ancients the scientific attainments of this period, is less impressive for us who know that such a *tour de force* could only have been achieved on the basis of century-long Babylonian observations.[2]

[1] For the texts translated here, see the doxography (above pp. 53 f.).

[2] Although it is generally assumed that the report of Herodotus (1.74) has an historical basis, doubts have been expressed from time to time, most recently by O. Neugebauer (*The Exact Sciences*, p. 136; cf. pp. 113 f.). Even if only a legend, the story would still show how an Ionian of the fifth century pictured the Milesian science of the preceding age. In fact, however, the authority for the story is somewhat greater than its critics suppose. Even Xenophanes seems to have been familiar with it, judging from the vague report in D.L. 1.23 (Thales A 1): "According

For the history of ideas, Anaximander's theory of the earth's position is of an entirely different order of importance. Even if we knew nothing else concerning its author, this alone would guarantee him a place among the creators of a rational science of the natural world. What is most striking in this doctrine is its specifically mathematical character. No matter what terms were used for its formulation, it must, in substance, presuppose the standard definition of the circle as "that which is in every way equidistant from the middle to the extremes."[1] That this clear geometric concept was itself the work of Anaximander is unlikely, and is in fact contradicted by the ancient tradition, which ascribes to Thales a proof that the diameter of a circle divides it into two equal parts.[2] In all probability the rudiments of geometry were an essential part of Anaximander's formation in the "school" of Thales. The definition of a circle in terms of its equal radii might have been suggested by the spokes of a wheel; for the word κύκλος originally had this concrete sense. But the fact that such a notion had been formulated in a precise way is in itself worthy of note.

More important for us is Anaximander's own use of this geometric idea, as a general expression for the principle of symmetry or indifference. It is indeed the same notion which was glorified in modern times by Leibniz as his Principle of Sufficient Reason, according to which everything which is true or real implies a reason why it is so and not otherwise.[3] Such considerations of symmetry have by no means

to some, Thales seems to have been the first to practice astronomy and to predict solar eclipses and solstices, as Eudemus says in the History of Astronomy; for this reason Herodotus and Xenophanes express their admiration for him. And Heraclitus and Democritus also speak in his favor." Since there is nothing marvelous about a prediction of solstices, the natural implication is that Xenophanes, Heraclitus, and Democritus—like Herodotus—had the eclipse in mind.

It is true that the Babylonians had no reliable method of predicting solar eclipses. But they certainly made an effort to foretell such eclipses, apparently with the aid of lunar cycles which informed them when an eclipse was possible. And Thales may very well have offered his prediction on the basis of such information. This is the suggestion of B. L. van der Waerden, who concludes: "Daß sie [the eclipse] wirklich eingetreten ist und in Kleinasien sichtbar war, war natürlich der reinste Zufall." See "Die Voraussage von Finsternissen bei den Babyloniern," *Berichte der sächsischen Akademie Leipzig, Mathematische-Physische Klasse*, XCII (1940), 113, n. 2.

[1] Euclid's classical definition of a circle (I, Def. 15) is naturally limited to the plane figure, but the early references to a figure "whose extremities are equidistant from a central point" do not distinguish between the circle and the sphere (see, e.g., Plato *Epist.* VII. 342b.7). Anaximander had a sphere in mind, but may in fact have referred to it as κύκλος; for this wider use of the term see p. 89, n. 1.

[2] See T. L. Heath, *A History of Greek Mathematics* (Oxford, 1921), I, 130 f. For the basic plausibility of the tradition, see Kurt von Fritz, "Die APXAI in der griechischen Mathematik," *Archiv für Begriffsgeschichte*, I (Bonn, 1955), especially 77 ff. For a parallel tendency to reinstate one of the traditions concerning Thales' scientific accomplishments, see A. Wasserstein, "Thales' Determination of the Diameters of the Sun and Moon," *JHS*, LXXV (1955), 114; *JHS* LXXVI (1956), 105.

[3] The most succinct ancient formula for this is the proposition of Leucippus (B 2): οὐδὲν χρῆμα μάτην γίνεται, ἀλλὰ πάντα ἐκ λόγου τε καὶ ὑπ' ἀνάγκης. The atomists seem to have made use

ceased to play a role in modern mathematical thought. If the geometric
sphere imposed itself with such power on the ancient scientific imagination (and indeed still on that of Galileo), it must be due above all to the
intellectual prestige of this figure as the image par excellence of regularity, order, and rational proportion.[1]

That this cosmological application of a geometric idea was Anaximander's personal achievement, is fortunately beyond doubt. One of
the rare items of information which Aristotle gives us concerning the
thought of Thales is the latter's teaching that the earth does not fall
because it floats on water.[2] The Egyptian and Oriental affinities of this
doctrine have been remarked both by ancient and by modern commentators. It may be considered philosophical only in that it recognizes
a problem to be solved. Anaximander dismisses all such pseudo-solu-
tions at a single stroke and gives the question its decisive form: Why,
after all, should the earth fall? If the universe is symmetrical, there is
no more reason for the earth to move down than up. By this implicit
rejection of the familiar idea of "down" as the direction in which all
bodies tend, Anaximander is well ahead of his time. The use of such
speculative reasons in radical contrast with the evidence of common
sense did not satisfy his successors, who resorted to more solid considerations to keep the earth in its place. Aristotle tells us that Anaximenes, Anaxagoras, and Democritus—the leading Ionian physicists
for a century and a half—all explained the earth's stability by its flatness and its great size, which caused it "not to cut the air below but to
sit upon it like a lid."[3] Their view is in principle the same as Thales',
only air has now replaced water. The alternative theory of the celestial
δίνη which supports the earth is that of Empedocles.[4] Now any such
explanation of the earth's stability, and in particular any notion of a
γῆς ὄχημα, presupposes that "down" would be the natural place for it
to go. It is therefore incorrect to say that the predecessors of Aristotle
"only treated of the relative light and heavy."[5] They may not have

---

of this principle in demonstrating the infinite
diversity of the atomic bodies (*Dox.* 483.17 =
Vors. 67 A 8).

[1] The unique esthetic and hence magical importance of the circle is of immemorial antiquity;
cf. *Il.* Σ 504: ἦατ' ἐπὶ ξεστοῖσι λίθοις ἱερῷ ἐνὶ
κύκλῳ. And children still draw "a magic circle."

[2] *De Caelo* 294ᵃ29 = Thales A 14.

[3] *De Caelo* 294ᵇ13. See also Plato *Phaedo* 99b.8,
and the texts quoted at *Vors.* 64 c 2. The same or a
very similar doctrine seems to have been held by

Archelaus (A 1.17 ᾗ μὲν [sc. γῇ] ὑπὸ τοῦ ἀέρος . . .
κρατεῖται), as well as by Diogenes (A 1 τὴν γῆν . . .
ἠρεισμένην [sc. ἐπὶ τῷ ἀέρι] ἐν τῷ μέσῳ).

[4] *Phaedo* 99b.6; *De Caelo* 295ᵃ17 = Emped.
A 67. A similar view is apparently ascribed to
Leucippus by D.L. ιχ.30 (= Leucippus A 1): τὴν
γῆν ὀχεῖσθαι περὶ τὸ μέσον δινουμένην. But there is
perhaps some confusion here; it is not likely that
Leucippus differed from Anaxagoras and Democritus on this point.

[5] Burnet, p. 343, citing *De Caelo* 300ᵃ9.

defined absolute lightness and weight, but they generally assumed that the earth would fall downwards if left to its own devices.

The fundamentally different point of view proposed by Anaximander reappears in the *Phaedo*, where Socrates presents a description of the earth which is avowedly not his own, but of whose truth he has been convinced by someone else :[1]

I am therefore persuaded that, in the first place, since the earth is round and in the middle of the heaven, it has no need either of Air or of any other Necessity in order not to fall, but the similarity of the heaven to itself in every way and the equilibrium of the earth suffice to hold it still. For an equilibrated thing set in the midst of something of the same kind will have no reason to incline in one direction more than in another. But as its relationship is symmetrical it will remain unswervingly at rest. (108e–109a)

If one disregards the spherical shape of the earth, the essential identity of this explanation with that of Anaximander is clear. It is no doubt this passage of the *Phaedo* (and the corresponding statement in the *Timaeus*[2]) which Aristotle has in mind when he declares, "There are some who say that the earth is at rest because of symmetry,[3] as did Anaximander among the ancients." Who the moderns are, Aristotle does not need to say.

We need not infer that Anaximander is the unnamed "someone" by whom the Socrates of the *Phaedo* claims to have been persuaded. It is on the whole more probable that the point of view of Anaximander, although neglected by the Ionian naturalists, was not entirely forgotten during the fifth century. An explanation of the position of the earth in terms of symmetry may well have been preserved by some Pythagorean astronomers, and was at all events given by Parmenides in his cosmology, if we may rely upon a confused statement of Aëtius.[4] We shall see in a moment that Parmenides certainly made use of the principle

---

[1] ὡς ἐγὼ ὑπό τινος πέπεισμαι, *Phaedo* 108c.8.

[2] *Tim.* 62d.12.

[3] ὁμοιότης here (as in the *Phaedo* passage) implies the geometric sense of "similar," i.e., of the same shape, proportional. Since the earth and the heaven are spheres, they are related to one another as are similar triangles. But this geometric consideration is heaped upon another, the internal symmetry or ὁμοιότης of a sphere in every direction from the center. It is only the second idea (as applied to the heaven) which can go back to Anaximander. For the earliest doctrine of a spherical earth, see the Supplementary Note at the end of this chapter.

[4] *Dox.* 380.13 = Parm. A 44. The confusion of Aëtius is clear from (1) the fact that he blended this information into his discussion of earthquakes, instead of giving it under its correct heading, two chapters earlier (περὶ κινήσεως γῆς, *Dox.* 378), and (2) his attribution of the same doctrine to Democritus, who should have been listed just below with Anaximenes (*Dox.* 380.19). Heath (*Aristarchus*, p. 124) is very ill-advised to follow Aëtius on this point, against the express statement of Aristotle (p. 78, n. 3). The proper explanation of Democritus, according to suspension in air, is presupposed by Aëtius himself at *Dox.* 378.16 (= Democr. A 95).

of symmetry in the first part of his poem, so that the information preserved by Aëtius must be correct. In that case it could be Parmenides
whom Plato had in mind, or he may simply have wished to indicate
that the doctrine was not a new one.[1]

There is one feature of Anaximander's view (as presented by Hippolytus) which does not appear in the statements of Plato and Aristotle,
namely, that the earth remains aloft "not dominated by anything"
(ὑπὸ μηδενὸς κρατουμένην). The authenticity of this idea is confirmed
both by its absence from the fourth-century formulations, and by the
general importance of the idea of κρατεῖν in early Greek cosmology.[2]
Thus it is reported for Archelaus that "the earth is dominated by air,
air by the surrounding rotation of fire" (A 1.17). The author of the
Hippocratic treatise De Flatibus insists that Air is "the greatest poten-
tate of all things" (μέγιστος ἐν τοῖσι πᾶσι τῶν πάντων δυνάστης ἐστίν,
ch. 3; Jones, II, 230); its δύναμις is supreme. So Anaximenes is supposed to have compared the Air surrounding the world to the soul
which dominates (συγκρατεῖ) the body.[3] Anaximander denies that any
elemental body or portion of the world dominates another; for him it is
equality and equilibrium which characterize the order of Nature.

By this radical distinction between the situation of the earth in the
surrounding heaven and the condition of a particular body falling to
the earth, Anaximander's view prepared the way for a purely geometric approach to astronomy, and hence, indirectly, for the helio-
centric hypothesis. This mathematical insight was, as we have seen,
refused by his more empirically minded successors. Their rejection
probably constitutes the earliest recorded conflict between mathematical science and common sense. But if this exalted vision of the harmonious sphere did not impose itself on Ionian physics, it remained
alive in another form. Xenophanes seems to have described the body of
his "greatest god" as "equal in every way," a "symmetrical form,"
which Theophrastus rightly interpreted as meaning spherical in shape.[4]
The same idea appears in the poem of Parmenides, when he describes
Reality (τὸ ἐόν) as marked by "an uttermost limit" and therefore

[1] For E. Frank's conjecture that the "someone"
is Archytas, see the Supplementary Note, pp.
117 f.
[2] See also below, p. 130.
[3] Anaximenes B 2. Although the wording is
almost certainly not that of Anaximenes, some of
the thought is probably authentic; συγκρατεῖν,
περιέχειν, and the conception of the ψυχή as
breath seem to echo Milesian ideas. I suspect,

however, that it was originally not the κόσμος but
the earth which Air was said to dominate by surrounding; cf. Ar. Nubes 264, and Anaxag. A 42.3:
τὸν ἀέρα ἰσχυρότατον ὄντα φέρειν ἐποχουμένην
τὴν γῆν.
[4] See the imitations of Xenophanes by Timon
in Vors. 21 A 35. For the judgment of Theophrastus,
see ibid. A 33.2 (Hippolytus), and the other passages cited by Diels in note on Dox. 481.9.

"completed in every direction like to the bulk of a well-rounded sphere, equally balanced in every way. . . . For, equal to itself on every side, it meets with its end points in symmetrical fashion."[1] Even so the divine sphere of Empedocles, the embodiment of absolute cosmic harmony, is declared to be "equal to itself on every side" (B 28–29). We see here how Anaximander is ancestor not only to the naturalism of Ionia, but also to the geometric philosophy usually associated with the name of Pythagoras, and how his ideas could therefore serve as springboard for the metaphysical flight of Parmenides.

11. *Form of the Earth*[2]

H. The form of the earth is moist,[3] rounded like [the drum of] a stone column.

P. Its form is cylindrical, with a depth one third of its width.

The geometrical turn of mind confronts us with equal distinctness in Anaximander's description of the earth, as a cylinder whose altitude is one third the diameter of its base. Whether or not he made use of the classical term κύλινδρος or "roller" (which was familiar to Democritus, B 155) is not known, but the idea is perfectly expressed by a comparison of the earth to the stocky, rounded stones of which a Greek column is composed. That this image is due to Anaximander himself, and not simply to Theophrastus, is a very likely conjecture of Diels (*Dox.* 219).

The originality of Anaximander's conception of the earth is by no means limited to his precise numerical ratio for the dimensions of the cylinder. The epic, it is true, also conceives the surface of the earth as flat, and even as circular in shape, bounded by the circumjacent Ocean. As one might expect, this view is a good deal older than Homer. But what the early poets lack is any distinct notion of the subterranean regions. The *Iliad* speaks of the Titans seated in the darkness of Tartarus "at the limits of earth and sea" (Θ 478 ff.). This "deepest pit under the earth" is as far below Hades as heaven is from earth (Θ 13–16). The Hesiodic *Theogony* contains several elaborate descriptions of this place, where the "sources and limits" of Earth, Tartarus, Sea, and Heaven converge, while "above grow the roots of Earth and Sea"

---

[1] Parm. B 8.42 ff. The link with Anaximander was pointed out by G. Vlastos, "Equality and Justice in Early Greek Cosmology," *CP*, XLII (1947), 161 f. For a full discussion of the sphere as the symbol or embodiment of divinity, see O. J. Brendel, "Die Symbolik der Kugel," *Mitt. Deutsch. Archäol. Inst. Rom.*, LI (1936), especially 28 ff.

[2] For the texts translated here, see the doxography (above, p. 55). The texts quoted for 12–23 are also to be found in their respective places in the doxography.

[3] Or "concave," if the correction γυρόν is accepted for ὑγρόν in the MSS. See above, pp. 55 f.

(*Theog.* 727 f., 736 ff., 807 ff.). It would be hopeless to draw a diagram to accompany such a description. The poetic Tartarus is vividly and dramatically conceived. A diagram, however, requires not drama but a precise geometric arrangement, and nothing could be more alien to the poet's state of mind when describing such mysterious regions. It is, on the other hand, the characteristic feature of Anaximander's view of the earth that it lends itself directly to geometric representation. We can scarcely doubt that the Milesians were in fact accustomed to discuss such matters with the aid of diagrams or of simple models. And, in Ionia at any rate, the standard model for the earth remained that of Anaximander until the time of Democritus.[1]

The doxographical description of Anaximander's earth as a rather low cylinder can be supplemented by data from a different source. When the Greek geographers looked back to the origins of their science, they recognized the same Milesian as the first to have produced a πίναξ or chart of the inhabited earth. And what little we know about the details of that first Greek map shows the same geometric spirit reigning here as in the rest of the cosmos. We have no description of Anaximander's chart as such, but F. Jacoby has shown that the geographical ideas which Herodotus ascribes to the "Ionians" are essentially those of Hecataeus of Miletus, and he has rightly pointed out that the general lines of Hecataeus' view must already have been those of Anaximander.[2] The fullest statement of the relation between Hecataeus and Anaximander is given by the late geographer Agathemerus, probably on the authority of Eratosthenes:

Anaximander of Miletus, the pupil of Thales, was the first to depict the inhabited earth on a chart (ἐν πίνακι γράψαι). After him Hecataeus of Miletus, a much-traveled man, made it more precise so as to be a thing of wonder. . . . Now the ancients drew the inhabited earth as round, with Hellas in the middle, and Delphi in the middle of Hellas, since it holds the navel (τὸν ὀμφαλὸν ἔχειν) of the earth. Democritus, a man of great experience, was the first to recognize that the earth is oblong, with its length one-and-a-half times its width.[3]

The natural inference is that this circular scheme (with a given point

[1] Democritus changed the model to an oblong solid, the ratio of whose sides was 2:3 (Democr. B 15, A 94). Perhaps this correction applied only to the inhabited region of the earth, ἡ οἰκουμένη γῆ; and even the latter was represented as a circle on maps of the time of Aristotle (*Meteor.* 362ᵇ13).
[2] F. Jacoby in *RE*, VII, *s.v.* Hekataios, cols. 2667 ff., especially sec. 10 on the schematic "Weltbild" (cols. 2702–7). See also W. A. Heidel,

The Frame of Ancient Greek Maps (New York, 1937), pp. 11 ff. Heidel emphasized this aspect of Milesian science in "Anaximander's Book, The Earliest Known Geographical Treatise," in *Proceedings of the American Academy of Arts and Sciences*, LVI (1921), 239.
[3] Agathemerus 1.1–2, in *Geographi Minores*, ed. Mueller, II, 471 (= *Vors.* 12 A 6 and 68 B 15).

at the center) was due to Anaximander, while the contribution of Hecataeus lay chiefly in the more accurate details added from his extensive travels. This view is decisively confirmed by other sources. Thus Herodotus refers as follows to the geographical ideas of his predecessors: "I laugh at the sight of the earth charts which many have drawn up in the past, and which no one has explained in a way that makes any sense. They picture Ocean flowing round about the earth, which is circular as if drawn with the compass; and they make Asia equal to Europe."¹ The oblique reference here to a nonsensical exegesis suggests the travel book of Hecataeus, while the "many" cartographers imply a number of maps in circulation, all constructed according to the same general scheme.

Now these charts were either painted on wood or worked in bronze, like the χάλκεος πίναξ which Aristagoras of Miletus brought to Sparta in 499–98 B.C. in order to win help for the Ionian revolt, on which were engraved the "circumference of the entire earth, the whole sea, and all the rivers."² These Greek maps are of course lost, but by a lucky coincidence we possess one of their Mesopotamian counterparts inscribed in a more durable medium. There is in the British Museum a clay tablet of neo-Babylonian or Persian date (that is, approximately contemporary with the maps of Anaximander and Hecataeus), on which is plainly visible the outline of the earth, surrounded by the "Bitter River," or salty Ocean (Plate I). Precisely as in the maps described by Herodotus, the circumference of the earth and the Ocean are here represented as perfect circles, and there is even a small, deep hole in the center of the chart which was probably left by the scribe's compass.³

¹ Hdt. IV.36: γελῶ δὲ ὁρῶν γῆς περιόδους γράψαντας πολλοὺς ἤδη, καὶ οὐδένα νόον ἐχόντως ἐξηγησάμενον. οἱ 'Ωκεανόν τε ῥέοντα γράφουσι πέριξ τὴν γῆν, ἐοῦσαν κυκλοτερέα ὡς ἀπὸ τόρνου, καὶ τὴν Ἀσίην τῇ Εὐρώπῃ ποιεύντων ἴσην. There is a similar criticism in a fragment of "Epimenides," which denies the existence or knowability of an ὀμφαλός of land and sea (Vors. 3 B 11).

² Hdt. v.49. So, in mentioning Anaximander's chart Diogenes Laertius says, "He was the first to draw the circumference of land and sea" (cited in note to 15.A.1).

³ There is at any rate no other good explanation of this hole, and Mr. D. J. Wiseman of the British Museum was kind enough to verify with me the possibility that it represents the point where the compass pin was fixed. Similar marks are to be found in the mathematical tablets, as Professor O. Neugebauer informs me (in a letter). This map was compared to those of Anaxi-

mander and Hecataeus by B. Meissner, "Babylonische und griechische Landkarten," Klio, XIX (1925), 97 ff. The parallel with Greek cartography may help to explain the most curious feature of the Babylonian map: the triangular extensions beyond the Bitter River. Four such triangles are visible, and there seems to be trace of a fifth. Unger supposes the original number was seven, but it might just as well have been six. In that case, the triangles would correspond to the six cardinal points which Heidel has shown to be fundamental in ancient Greek maps: the three points of sunrise at summer solstice, equinox, and winter solstice, together with the corresponding sunsets. On the tablet, the three western triangles appear at the proper points; two of the sunrise indications have been lost. There is clearly not a triangle in the north, for here (as the inscription indicates) "the sun is not seen," either rising or setting. The legend corresponding to the summer

Just as the Danube for Herodotus cut Europe in the middle (11.33), and the Nile for his predecessors divided Asia (or, with a different terminology, separated Asia from Libya, 11.16), so the Babylonian map shows the Euphrates dividing the world vertically into two nearly equal portions.

This correspondence between early Greek geography and an extant Babylonian map presents several points of interest. It gives a special relevance to the traditional concern of Thales to show that the diameter of a circle divides it into two equal parts.[1] It also reinforces what other sources reveal of the dependence of Milesian science upon a much more ancient Babylonian tradition. At the same time Anaximander no doubt surpassed his Mesopotamian model by the rigor with which he applied the principle of mathematical proportion to the details of his scheme. The symmetrical subdivisions of the earth's upper "inhabited" surface answer to its exact cylindrical dimensions and to its harmonious position in the center of the balanced structure of the heavens.[2]

12. Antipodes

H. We are standing on one surface of the earth; the other is set opposite.

It is difficult to see what considerations other than those of symmetry can have led Anaximander to speak of the underside of the earth as "set opposite" (ἀντίθετον) to that on which we stand. The statement preserved by Hippolytus does not specify that this antipodal region was inhabited, but that is quite possible in view of Anaximander's rejection of absolute up and down. In fact, one may suspect that the notion of a symmetrical existence on the other side of the earth would occur more naturally in the context of a cylindrical model than in that of a sphere, where the idea of antipodes is essentially more artificial. If Anaximander taught that the lower surface of the earth was inhabited, we would have a simple explanation of those strange words of the De Hebdomadibus which seem to constitute the earliest extant mention of the antipodes:

The earth, which lies in the middle of the κόσμος and holds moisture in itself and under itself, is borne in the air so that for those [standing] below things above are

---

setting declares, as we would expect, that "the light of day is greater than the nighttime."

[1] A further link between early Greek geography and geometry can probably be seen in the view of the great rivers (Ister, Nile, Phasis) as drawing their source from the Ocean and emptying into the central sea (Mediterranean plus

Pontus). They thus represent so many equal radii from the circumference to the center. Such considerations no doubt contributed to the Pythagorean view that nature imitates mathematics.

[2] Compare the remarks of Jaeger on Anaximander's geography, Paideia, I, 157 f.

below, while things below are above; there is a similar difference for things at the right and at the left; and this is the case around the entire earth.[1]

This passage has been interpreted as indicating a spherical earth, whereas the statement that it is *borne in the air* seems in fact to presuppose the usual Ionian view of it as flat.[2] The point is that right and left, like up and down, are reversed for someone standing at any point on the upper surface ("around the entire [circumference of the] earth") in relation to someone standing at the corresponding point underneath. This remark is relevant here, because the author has just stated that "the κόσμοι (i.e., celestial spheres or regions) above the earth are equal in number and similar in form to those underneath the earth" (ch. 2.1).

The date of the *De Hebdomadibus* is a subject of considerable dispute, but its cosmology seems to be that of the early or middle fifth century. It is difficult to see from whom the author could have taken the doctrine of antipodes if not from Anaximander.[3] At this point, however, we depend upon a conjecture that goes beyond the reach of the extant testimony.

13. Formation of the Heavens

H. The heavenly bodies arise as a circle of fire which is separated off from the [primeval] fire in the world, and enveloped by air.

P. Something capable of generating Hot and Cold was separated off from the eternal [Boundless] in the formation of this world, and a sphere of fire from this source grew around the air about the earth like bark around a tree. When this

---

[1] *De Hebd.* 2.24: κατὰ μέσον δὲ τὸν κόσμον ἡ γῆ κειμένη καὶ ἔχουσα ἐν ἑωυτῇ καὶ ὑφ' ἑωυτῇ (ὑπὲρ ἑωυτῆς?) τὰ ὑγρὰ ἐν τῷ ἠέρι ὀχέεται, ὥστε τοῖσι κάτω τάδε μὲν τὰ (τὰ δὲ μέντοι vulg.: corr. Boll) ἄνω κάτω εἶναι, τὰ δὲ κάτω ἄνω· οὕτω τε διέχειν τά τε ἐκ δεξιῆς καὶ τὰ ἐξ ἀριστερῆς· καὶ περὶ πᾶσαν τὴν γῆν οὕτως ἔχει. See the discussion of F. Boll in his appendix to "Das Lebensalter," *Neue Jahrbücher für das klassische Altertum*, XVI (1913), especially 141–42.

[2] ἐν τῷ ἀέρι ὀχεῖσθαι is the standard phrase for the Ionian theory of the earth's support; see *Vors.* 64 C 2, and in particular the expression γῆς ὄχημα (Eur. *Troades* 884; *De Flat.* 3). The phrase περὶ πᾶσαν τὴν γῆν no more requires a spherical model than does the γῆς περίοδος of Herodotus and Hecataeus.

[3] Unfortunately, it is not possible in the present state of Hippocratic studies to fix the date of a

treatise like the *De Hebdomadibus*. Suggestions range from the middle of the sixth century (Roscher) to somewhere in the fourth; Diels proposed the general period 450–350 B.C. (*Deutsche Literaturzeitung*, 1911, cols. 1861–66). But in view of its probable reflection of Milesian ideas concerning the ἄπειρον (which Diels recognized), it is difficult to believe that this treatise was composed much later than the middle of the fifth century.

The next mention of the antipodes is in the *Timaeus* (63a.2), where a spherical earth is presupposed. The statement of the *De Hebdomadibus* can scarcely be derived from the *Timaeus*, for it uses "up" for our side of the earth, "down" for the other, in precisely the way which Plato says is "not that of an intelligent man" (63a.6). But this usage is of course natural if the author has a flat earth in mind.

sphere was torn off and closed up into certain circles, the sun and moon and stars came into being.

A.1 The heavens are formed from a mixture of hot and cold.

A.2 The heavenly bodies are wheel-like, compressed masses of air filled with fire, which exhale flames from an orifice at one point.

14. *Stars and Sun*

H. There are some tube-like passages which form vents [in the envelope of air], through which the heavenly bodies are seen; therefore eclipses occur when these vents are obstructed.

A.2 There is a circle 28 times as great as the earth, similar to the wheel of a chariot, which has a hollow rim filled with fire, letting this fire appear through an orifice at one point, as through the mouthpiece of a bellows; and this is the sun.

15. *The Moon*

H. The moon appears now full, now waning, according to the obstruction and opening of the passages.

A.1 The moon is a circle 19 times as great as the earth, filled with fire like that of the sun . . . for it is similar to a chariot wheel which has a hollow rim, and is full of fire like the circle of the sun, lying aslant [the celestial equator] as does the latter, and having a single vent like the mouthpiece of a bellows.

A.2 The moon's light is its own, but somehow fainter [than that of the sun].

A.3 It suffers eclipse when the orifice in the wheel is obstructed.

16. *Size, Position, and Distance of the Rings*

H. The circle of the sun is 27 times as great as [. . .] the moon, and the sun is highest [. . .]; lowest are the circles of the fixed stars.[1]

A.1 The sun is set highest of all, after it the moon, and beneath them the fixed stars and planets.

A.2 The sun is equal to the earth, but the circle from which it has its vent and by which it is carried is 27 times as great as the earth.

D.L. The sun is no smaller than the earth and consists of purest fire.

Our information concerning the early phases of Anaximander's cosmogony is limited to a single source (**13.P.**), and one which is not explicit enough to permit a detailed reconstruction. The first stage seems to have been the secretion of a pregnant seed or germ out of the

---

[1] There seem to be at least two gaps in this text; see above, pp. 61 f.

Boundless, which thus became the parent of the universe. The world seed in turn secretes or "separates off" from itself a sphere of flame "which grew around the air about the earth like bark around a tree." This statement suggests that flame and ἀήρ are the concrete representatives of the hot and cold principles named in the preceding clause: the embryo of the world develops by fission into an inner, cold (and damp) core, and an outer, warm (and dry) spherical skin, which fits tight about it (περιφυῆναι). At this point the earth is mentioned only by anticipation, for the dry land has not yet arisen out of the central vaporous mass. Its emergence, which constitutes a further "separation" of dry from wet, will be discussed below (20). At this stage, what lies within the sphere of flame must be something very much like the primeval Moisture of Thales. Since it is a continuous source of rising water-vapor or ἀήρ, the primary phase of the three Milesian cosmogonies appears as thus much more uniform than would be suggested by the traditional opposition of "water," "air," and "something in between," (i.e., the ἄπειρον).

The next stage in the formation of the heavens occurs when the spherical skin of flame is torn loose from the inner bulk to which it was attached. The details of this operation are most obscure. Presumably the heat of the celestial fire causes the air within to expand and the whole heaven to grow until the outer sphere is burst.[1] Circles (κύκλοι) of fire are separated off from this celestial flame, and enclosed within envelopes of "air," that is to say, of haze or mist, perhaps in a solidified state. It is only the circles of the sun and moon which are described in any detail. Their flame is exhaled by certain tube-like passages or jets that constitute the visible disks of the sky. The light of the moon is thus its own, but of course fainter than that of the sun, which is itself of "purest fire" (16.D.L.). The lunar phases occur according to the opening and closing of such passages (15.H.). A similar obstruction of the passages accounts for the eclipses of both sun and moon (14.H., A.3; 15.A.3). Why or how this takes place is not indicated in our sources.

Aëtius compares these circles to the hollow rims of gigantic wheels, and describes their openings as similar to the mouthpiece of a bellows (14.A.2; 15.A.1). Whether or not these similes are due to Anaximander himself is not at all clear. It seems more likely that they reflect the picturesque style of some Hellenistic popularizer, but there is no reason

---

[1] Cf. 20.Arist.3: "At first even the earth was moist and, as the region about the earth was heated by the sun, air was formed and the whole heaven grew in size."

to doubt the general accuracy of the images. The apparent motion of the sun and moon may have been interpreted as the daily revolution of a wheel, although no reliable information is available on this point. Since the circles of the sun and moon are said "to lie aslant" (λοξὸν κεῖσθαι, **15.A.1**), Anaximander must have been familiar with the inclination of the ecliptic relative to the diurnal path of the stars. Pliny also attributes this knowledge to him, and other sources speak of his interest in solstices, equinoxes, and the measurement of the diurnal "hours."[1]

On Anaximander's theory of the fixed stars and planets, our ignorance is almost total. The only thing which is clear is that the circles of the stars lie below that of the moon, while the sun is farthest of all from the earth (**16.A.1**). If Anaximander specified the magnitude of the stellar circles, the figure is lost. The circle of the sun is given as 27, that of the moon as 19 times the size of the earth (**16**, with commentary). The unit intended must be the diameter of the earth's upper surface, represented on Anaximander's map. The only datum concerning the size of any heavenly body is that "the sun is equal to the earth" (**16.A.2, D.L.**). This must refer to the visible, circular opening from which solar fire breathes forth. The boldness of such an estimate deserves our notice. Several generations later Anaxagoras would only say of the sun that "it exceeds the Peloponnesus in size" (A 42.8).

This is all the information given by reliable ancient sources concerning the celestial model of Anaximander. Many conjectures have been made in order to fill some of the yawning gaps in this account. The one suggestion which is really difficult to resist is Tannery's reconstruction of the simple arithmetic series 9–18–27, for the circles of the stars, moon, and sun respectively. The inherent plausibility of this conjecture is very great, when we take into account the ratio 3:1 for the earth's dimensions as well as Anaximander's general use of mathematical proportion. But the documentary basis for this particular series is weak, and it must remain only a good guess.[2] There are several other problems concerning the details of this cosmology which deserve consideration, even if we cannot hope for certainty in their solution. In the first place, what meaning can be attached to the κύκλοι of the fixed stars? In this case we might expect to find a sphere rather than a

---

[1] See the passages of Pliny and D.L. cited in the note to **15.A.1**.
[2] For Tannery's reconstruction, see above, p.

62. The only number of this series given by an ancient source is 27.

PLATE I

BABYLONIAN MAP OF THE WORLD
Apparently from the Persian period
(sixth to fourth centuries B.C.)
Published in *Cuneiform Texts in the British Museum* (1906),
Part XXII, plate 48 (BM 92687)

PLATE II

B. CREATION WITH COMPASSES

Thirteenth-century French "Bible moralisée," Codex Vindobonensis 2554, folio 1 verso (Austrian National Library)

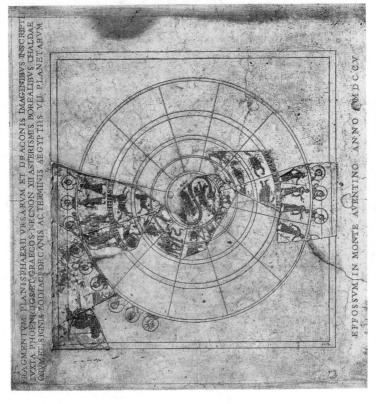

A. PLANISPHERE OF BIANCHINI

Marble table of the second or third century A.D. (Louvre)

circle; and κύκλος in the singular could in fact have this sense.[1] But probably we must think neither of isolated circles nor of a sphere, but of wide bands or "rings" (anneaux, Tannery). The night sky can easily be represented as a series of bands or zones circling the pole. This simple conception was, of course, familiar to the ancients. Some Hellenistic authority followed by Aëtius ascribed the division of the whole celestial sphere into five such bands to "Thales, Pythagoras, and his followers."[2] It is not necessary to believe that the five zones of Hellenistic astronomy were already in use in sixth-century Miletus, but some scheme of this kind is in fact the simplest way of dealing with the visible field of heaven; and a system of three "roads" or belts for the fixed stars was used by the Babylonians in very ancient times.[3]

We are told that Anaximander was not only concerned with astronomical hours and sundials, but that he also contrived a "sphere."[4] This celestial globe was of course not a complicated mechanism of the type constructed by Archimedes and described with such admiration by Cicero (De Republica 1.14), but a simpler, solid model which Cicero says was first constructed by "Thales" and elaborated by Eudoxus. One might even suppose it to be a flat chart of the heavens divided into concentric rings or bands circling the pole, of the sort ordinarily used in ancient representations of the zodiac (Plate II A). Anaximander's map of the heavens, like his map of the earth, must have pictured the universe as organized in a system of concentric circles.[5]

Another question is why he should have placed the stellar circles or rings closer to the earth than are the sun and the moon. The answer

---

[1] Κύκλος is often used for a sphere, and in particular for the sphere of the heavens. Emped. B 38.4: Τιτὰν ἠδ' αἰθὴρ σφίγγων περὶ κύκλον ἄπαντα; Hdt. 1.131.2: (οἱ Πέρσαι) τὸν κύκλον πάντα τοῦ οὐρανοῦ Δία καλέοντες; Plato Tim. 34b.4: κύκλῳ δὴ κύκλον στρεφόμενον οὐρανόν. Compare Hp. De Arte 10 (Jones, II, 208): ὁ τῆς κεφαλῆς κύκλος, ἐν ᾧ ὁ ἐγκέφαλος.

[2] Vors. 11 A 13c (Aëtius): κύκλους πέντε, οὖστινας προσαγορεύουσι ζώνας. Knowledge of the invisible antarctic band seems to me presupposed by Heracl. B 120, although this fragment is notoriously obscure. Posidonius ascribed the invention of the five zones to Parmenides (Vors. 28 A 44a).

[3] Neugebauer, The Exact Sciences, p. 96.

[4] D.L. 11.2 and Pliny VII.20, cited in note to 15.A.1.

[5] The Planisphere of Bianchini (Plate IIA) presents a late, eclectic symbolism and an elaborate system of celestial reference which was probably unknown to the early Greek astronomers. But the general scheme of concentric circles and intersecting radii, focused upon the polar constellations of the Dragon and the Bears, must have been characteristic of all Greek planispheres and globes, including Anaximander's. Such a pattern of rings and radii is basically identical with the cross section of Anaximander's cosmos as sketched by Diels (Archiv, p. 236), and Diels himself remarked the parallel between this plan and Anaximander's map of the earth.

For a detailed discussion of the Planisphere of Bianchini, see F. Boll, Sphaera (Leipzig, 1903), pp. 299–346. Comparable zodiac schemes are known from Egyptian monuments (ibid., plates II and VI), as well as from Greek astronomical manuscripts (ibid., plate I; also A. Schlachter, Der Globus, ΣΤΟΙΧΕΙΑ VIII [Leipzig, 1927], fig. 12; Schlachter discusses Anaximander's sphere pp. 10 ff. with Nachträge, p. 107).

cannot come from an observation of the heavens. For when the moon hides a constellation of fixed stars by passing in front of them, no one would spontaneously imagine that these stars lie between us and the moon. Nor does it seem likely that this curious notion is due to an oriental antecedent.[1] The explanation must, I think, be found in Anaximander's own theory, and there it is not far to seek. Like all Greeks he believed that fire tends upwards. The surge of flame towards heaven is, as it were, a fact of experience, and this view of the matter is confirmed for Anaximander by the mention of a sphere of flame which grows outside of—and hence above—the terrestrial ἀήρ. There would then be a general tendency for fire to collect more abundantly near the periphery of the heavens. If the stars provide such little light, it must be because they contain a smaller proportion of fire and belong rather to the region of air. The bulk of flame is concentrated in the outermost circle of the sun, while the moon's position, like its light, is intermediate. On this view, the surprising position of the stars affords another instance of that all-pervading symmetry which is the stamp of Anaximander's thought.[2]

A question which arises for us more naturally perhaps than for the Greeks is why these lower rings of stellar ἀήρ do not obscure the brighter but more distant bodies. On this point the explanation given by Burnet is probably correct: it is the essential property of ἀήρ from Homer onwards to make things invisible, but not necessarily to be seen itself.[3] It is, on the other hand, very doubtful whether we could therefore see

[1] It is true that a similar arrangement of the heavenly bodies is attested for Sassanid Persia; see ch. 3, sec. 7, of the "Greater Bundahišn," translated by R. C. Zaehner, in *Zurvan, A Zoroastrian Dilemma* (Oxford, 1955), p. 333; and other texts cited by R. Eisler, *Weltenmantel und Himmelszelt* (Munich, 1910), I, 90, n. 3 F. But there is no good reason to assume that the doctrine of these relatively late texts must represent a Persian (or Mesopotamian) view more ancient than Anaximander. Perhaps the most plausible explanation of this curious parallel would lie in the influence of sixth-century Greek ideas upon the religious cosmology of the Achaemenid period. (On the late date and derivative character of the Bundahišn cosmology, see J. Duchesne-Guillemin, "Persische Weisheit in griechischem Gewande?" *Harvard Theological Review*, XLIX [1956], 115.)

On the other hand, what little is known of a more archaic Babylonian theory of celestial layers or spheres seems to indicate that the moon was placed lowest, in accordance with the observed facts (Neugebauer, *The Exact Sciences*, pp.

94–95). This is certainly the case for the Chaldean astronomers described at a later date by Diodorus Siculus (II.31).

[2] So Anaximenes, when he rendered to the stars their proper place, was obliged to point out that (although they are fiery like the sun) "they give no heat because of the magnitude of their distance" (A 7.6, repeated by Anaxag. A 42.7).

No explanation is given for the revival of Anaximander's arrangement in the fourth century by Metrodorus of Chios and Crates (presumably the Theban Cynic), but we may suspect a paradoxical reaction against the more subtle doctrines of the astronomers. It is interesting to see that this whole question of the distance and relative position of the heavenly bodies is one for which Xenophon makes Socrates express strong disapproval (*Mem.* IV.7.5).

[3] Burnet, p. 68. Professor von Fritz suggests (in a letter) that the fixed stars may have had less dense envelopes than sun and moon, so that the stronger fire of the latter could easily break through.

right out into the Boundless, as Burnet suggests.[1] The Boundless no doubt acts as an outer binding limit for the whole structure of the heavens,[2] but there is no reason to believe that we can actually see anything beyond the fire or air of our world.

It is difficult to say whether or not, in the finished state of the heavens, anything remained of that primeval sphere of flame from which the celestial rings had been formed. Both Parmenides and Anaxagoras seem to have identified the αἰθήρ or sky with elemental fire; and for Anaximander too this upper sky might have constituted that "fire in the κόσμος," which is distinguished by one ancient source from the fire enclosed in the rings (**13.H.**). This residual sphere of flame could then form the outer celestial periphery which is presupposed as a reference point in Anaximander's account of why the earth remains in place. But probably this spherical limit was constituted by the Boundless itself, which "surrounds" all things, and there may have been no place for celestial fire outside of the individual rings.

Before discussing the general theoretic importance of Anaximander's scheme, a word may be said concerning the empirical knowledge which it presupposes. Whether or not it is true that Thales was capable of predicting a solar eclipse, it is at any rate clear that the Milesian competence in astronomical matters involved a great deal more than the familiarity with months, solstices, and star risings which we find in the *Works and Days* of Hesiod. From what source did Thales and Anaximander draw their greater technical skill? Later writers often speak in this connection of a voyage of Thales to Egypt. Herodotus, however, is well aware of the Babylonian origin of much Greek astronomical technique.[3] Whatever the direct link may have been, recent studies in the cuneiform texts make it clear that the sixth-century flourishing of science in Ionia was essentially dependent upon the much older Mesopotamian tradition. Among the fundamental tools "available at the

---

[1] Burnet, p. 69. His proposal to identify the fixed stars with the "innumerable worlds" is in flat contradiction with the ancient sources, which place the fixed stars below the moon.

[2] See πάντα περιέχειν and the similar phrases under 8. The ἄπειρον is conceived as a necessary limit in an argument mentioned by Aristotle (*Phys.* 203ᵇ20–22) and used by Epicurus as proof of the infinity of the universe (D.L. x.41). The primary world power is regularly represented as binding all things together; cf. συγκρατεῖ in Anaximenes B 2, and ἅπαντα . . . συνδεῖν καὶ συνέχειν in Plato *Phaedo*, 99c.6 (referring to the

natural philosophers); ἡ δύναμις συναπτική or συνεκτική becomes also one of the Stoic descriptions of the deity.

[3] πόλον μὲν γὰρ καὶ γνώμονα καὶ τὰ δυώδεκα μέρεα τῆς ἡμέρης παρὰ Βαβυλωνίων ἔμαθον οἱ Ἕλληνες, Hdt. ii.109, where the origin of geometry is ascribed to Egypt. For the instruments known as gnomon and polos see Tannery, *Science hellène*, p. 85. The texts concerning Thales' supposed voyage to Egypt are cited by Zeller I⁵, 185, n. 2. The story could easily be a Hellenistic invention, suggested by Herodotus' theory concerning the birthplace of geometry.

end of the 'prehistory' of Babylonian astronomy which extends from about 1800 B.C. to about 500 B.C.," the following have been listed by O. Neugebauer: "The zodiac of 12 times 30 degrees as reference system for solar and planetary motion. A fixed luni-solar calendar and probably some of the basic period relations for the moon and the planets. An empirical insight into the main sequence of planetary and lunar phenomena and the variation of the length of daylight and night."[1] What we know of the ideas of Anaximander shows that most, if not all, of this science had reached Miletus by the middle of the sixth century.

What the cuneiform texts have not yet revealed is a clear geometric model for visualizing and co-ordinating the various empirical data. Here again we may perhaps recognize the original genius of Anaximander, for in his scheme it is easy to find "the first, if still imperfect, indication of the theory of geocentric spheres which dominated the astronomy of antiquity and of the middle ages."[2] It may be that one day the study of Babylonian tablets will introduce us to the precursors of Anaximander in this domain. At present his claims to originality seem to rest intact.[3]

If one looks back over the broad outlines of this scheme for the heavens, what emerges in clearest perspective is its geometric character. In the case of the celestial rings, as in the account of the earth's stable position, the essentially mathematical turn of Anaximander's mind is underscored for us by the apparent unwillingness of his Ionian followers to accept the speculative symmetry of his scheme. The entire spherical view of the heavens seems to have been rejected in the astronomy of Xenophanes and Heraclitus—if this term applies at all to theories of the daily lighting and quenching of the sun, its falling into a hole upon eclipse, or the reversible "bowls" of celestial fire.[4] It is difficult to believe that either Xenophanes or Heraclitus has spent much time in careful observation of the stars. Whatever they know on such matters has been gleaned from the Milesians and their followers.

But even the dominant Ionian cosmology of a scientific character— that of Anaximenes, Anaxagoras, and the atomists—offers a distinct contrast to the geometric scheme of Anaximander. The cylindrical

[1] *The Exact Sciences*, p. 98.
[2] Diels, *Archiv*, p. 230.
[3] For the possibility of one cuneiform text being interpreted in this way, see Neugebauer, *The Exact Sciences*, pp. 94–95, and n. 1, p. 90 above. That

the system of cosmic circles was not known to Thales seems clear from his theory of the earth floating on water.
[4] Xenoph. A 33.3, A 41–42; Heracl. A 1.9–10, A 12; and see Heath, *Aristarchus*, pp. 52–61.

earth at the center of a spherical heaven has been preserved. In between, however, we find no intricate series of circles or rings, but a single, continuous atmosphere (ἀήρ), surrounding the earth and stretching outwards to the limit of the world-sphere or περιέχον. This all-encompassing "air" is not everywhere of uniform consistency, but increasingly hot and bright in the upper astral region, increasingly dull, cold, and damp in the vicinity of the earth.[1] It is this theory of the cosmic atmosphere which survives in Aristotle's description of the sublunary world (in the *Meteorologica*), where no clear line can be drawn between the region of Fire and that of Air. This Ionian scheme is probably a natural development of Anaximander's ideas concerning the distribution of fire and air in the heavens. But whereas in the cosmos of Anaximander the orbits of the sun and moon are represented by definite geometric (and probably mechanical) structures, the atmosphere theory of the later Ionians seems to treat the heavenly bodies as isolated clusters of fiery cloud or incandescent stone, like the solar μύδρος of Anaxagoras (A 72). Anaximenes, too, held that "the sun and moon and other ἄστρα are all fiery, and borne upon the air by their flatness," just as the earth itself is borne (A 7.4). Those thinkers who were familiar with the pressure of air, as demonstrated by the clepsydra, argued that, in a closed space such as our world, the strength of the air would be sufficient to keep bodies aloft.[2] For Anaxagoras and the atomists, the heavenly bodies are aflame primarily because of the speed (and hence the friction) of their motion. They are caught up and borne aloft by the whirling celestial atmosphere.[3] In this view there is no place for a circular orbit of sun or moon, independent of the general celestial rotation. These bodies may fall behind the circling fixed stars, or be pushed from side to side by outside causes. Their own path in the zodiac has no significance as such.[4] For Anaximenes, their path seems

---

[1] See, e.g., Anaxag. B 15–16; Diog. B 5: (ἡ ψυχὴ . . . ἐστὶν) ἀὴρ θερμότερος μὲν τοῦ ἔξω ἐν ᾧ ἐσμεν, τοῦ μέντοι παρὰ τῷ ἡλίῳ πολλὸν ψυχρότερος.

[2] *De Caelo* 294ᵇ18 ff. Aristotle is referring to Anaximenes, Anaxagoras, and Democritus. (Which one first made use of the clepsydra example in this connection, we do not know; it is mentioned in Emped. B 100 in reference to breathing.) This conception of the heavens as an airtight system seems to be alluded to in the αἰθήρ σφίγγων περὶ κύκλον ἅπαντα of Emped. B 38, and in the χιτών or ὑμήν of atomic cosmology (*Vors.* 67 A 1.32, A 23). If W. K. C. Guthrie is correct in interpreting the stellar sphere of Anaximenes as an

external membrane or ὑμήν for the world, this whole idea goes back to Anaximenes; see "Anaximenes and τὸ κρυσταλλοειδές", *CQ*, XLIX (1956), 40. It has its roots of course in the περιέχον of Anaximander.

[3] Anaxag. A 42.6, A 71; Leucippus A 1.33; Democr. A 88.

[4] On the historical importance of this point, and the astronomical "blind alley" into which it leads, see B. L. van der Waerden, *Die Astronomie der Pythagoreer*, Verhandelingen der koninklijke Nederlandse Akademie, XX, 1 (Amsterdam, 1951), especially p. 14.

not even to have been of circular form, if it is true that they pass not under but around the earth, like a cap about our head.[1]

Now the geometric unity of the orbits of sun and moon seems to have been presupposed in Anaximander's scheme, for otherwise it would make no sense to say that their circles "lie aslant" (**15.A.1**). If so, this essential insight was neglected by his successors in favor of a more mechanical explanation, just as they ignored his mathematical account of the earth's stability. In both cases the point of view of Anaximander reappears in the astronomical passages of the Platonic dialogues, bearing witness to a Pythagorean revival or, more probably, to an unbroken preservation of these oldest Milesian ideas. In the course of the intervening century and a half the survival of this geometrical conception is attested by the "rings" (στεφαναί) of Parmenides, which unmistakably recall the κύκλοι of Anaximander. Another, much dimmer echo of this scheme is perhaps intended by the "orders" (κόσμοι) of *De Hebdomadibus*. But from the time of Plato and Eudoxus this mathematical scheme of the heavens reigns supreme. Its victory is, as it were, consecrated by the Aristotelian conception of the αἰθήρ, now no longer a kind of fire but a unique element, scarcely material in form, within which the operation of geometric law proceeds unclogged by any mechanical aid or impediment.[2]

If the geometric quality of Anaximander's general scheme is beyond doubt, a different interpretation has been offered by Diels for the dimensions of the celestial circles. Accepting the plausible series 9–18–27, and pointing out that it can scarcely have been obtained by exact measurement, Diels compared the religious and mythic importance of the number 3 and its simple multiples in the ancient conceptions of many lands, including Greece. He concluded that "this young Ionic science was still very strongly caught in the mystic and poetic enchantment which it attempted by its own rationalism to dispel," and that "the whole numerical speculation is in reality only a poetic representation (*Veranschaulichung*)." At the same time Diels made clear that he considered this imaginative point of view to have its advantages, and even to be more creative scientifically than the exact astronomy of

---

[1] Anaximenes A 7.6, A 14. Heath reasonably suggests that this asymmetrical path can apply only to the sun, moon, and planets (*Aristarchus*, p. 43). But it is by no means clear what is intended by the expression "moving around the earth as a cap turns around our head."

[2] In modern times the Cartesian system of vortices might be regarded as an unconscious revival of the ancient celestial machinery operating by contact, Newton's *Principia mathematica* as a more or less final victory for the strictly geometric view.

Aristarchus or Ptolemy.[1] Sir Thomas Heath (who did not share Diels' preference for Anaximander over Aristarchus) concluded simply that "Anaximander's figures really say little more than what the Indians tell us, namely that three Vishnu-steps reach from earth to heaven."[2]

The general relationship between science and myth in early Greek thought is not a matter which can properly be treated here. But the significance of Anaximander's figures is a question which concerns us directly. Should this first attempt to fix the dimensions of the solar and lunar orbits, and, presumably, of the stellar rings as well, be considered as evidence of a mythic or a scientific point of view? Is it or is it not comparable to the three cosmic steps of Vishnu?

In endeavoring to answer such a question we must be careful to give the devil his due; that is, we must know what we mean by speaking of a mythic point of view. One cannot reduce mythic speculation as it is practiced in the Rigveda either to poetry or to superstition. The finest Vedic hymns clearly represent an effort to give a speculative unity to the world as it is known to the poet and to his audience. There is, I think, nothing comparable in the Greek tradition, which is in this sense already devoid of myth in Homer. The closest parallels would perhaps be Aeschylus or Heraclitus, but they presuppose the development of Ionian rationalism. (Serious speculation seems to me to play very little part in Hesiod's *Theogony*.) Now in the authentic intellectual endeavor of the Veda, number symbolism performs a decisive function. The importance of the number 3, for instance, lies in its role as the representative of plurality in general. This notion finds expression (as Diels saw) in the grammatical classification of all numbers into singular, dual, and plural. The difference between 2 and 3 is essential, that between 3 and 1000 negligible, from the linguistic point of view. The prime numbers 3, 5, and 7 can therefore serve as symbols for the ideas both of "many" and of "all," and their role in expressing a totality can be underlined by playing them against their simple sums and multiples. Since 3 signifies "many" and "all," the force of both ideas

---

[1] *Archiv*, pp. 230 ff. Diels' conclusion is worth quoting at length (pp. 236 f.): "Der Begriff κόσμος selbst entspringt einer ästhetischen Anschauung. . . . In der Tat hat die poetische Abmessung der Anaximandrischen Sphären vielleicht mehr Wert als die bewunderungswürdigen exacteren Berechnungen des Aristarch von Samos. Dem Dichter-Philosophen ist aufgegangen, was den wissenschaftlichen Astronomen des Altertums verborgen blieb, daß der Kosmos durch ein Gesetz zusammengehalten wird, das sich in symmetrischen Zahlen-Verhältnissen anschaulich darstellt. An die somnia Pythagorea hat Copernicus bewußt angeknüpft, und Anaximander steht dem Kosmos Keplers näher als Hipparch und Ptolemaios. Die hellenische Wissenschaft hat eben meines Erachtens darum so ausnahmsweise viel geleistet, weil sie auch der Phantasie in der Wissenschaft ihr Recht gab."

[2] *Aristarchus*, p. 38.

is enhanced in the number 9, which is, as we say, equal to 3 raised in power. The effect of emphasis is given by implicit repetition, just as we emphasize the meaning of "forever" by saying "forever and ever." The use of numbers by the Vedic poets thus constitutes a kind of special language, abstract in meaning but concrete in form, for expressing the grandeur and the perfection of the universe considered as a whole.[1] In particular, the three steps of Vishnu measure the width of the earth, the height of heaven, or the magnitude of all things visible and invisible; and in each case the number 3 counts the beginning, middle, and end, the full extension of the thing measured from Alpha to Omega.[2]

This world measured by the Vedic god is of ritual, mythic, and poetic significance. It contains at the same time some elements of essentially rational character: for instance, the idea that when the Sun sets, it does not cease to exist, but passes the night in a hidden place under the earth. Rational also is the attempt to use numbers as symbols for a complete and unified vision of the world. Now when we compare the scheme of Anaximander, it is only such rational elements which reappear. The secret hiding place of the Sun at night becomes a hemisphere symmetrical at every point to the world in which we live, and here the numbers refer not to the steps of a god but to the diameters of perfect geometric circles laid out upon a common center. It is therefore more fitting to speak of a rational element in Vedic thought than of a mythic element in Milesian cosmology.

It must of course be admitted that (as far as we know) the celestial dimensions given by Anaximander cannot have been based upon any kind of accurate observation or geometric construction, in the style of Aristarchus. But it does not follow that they came from the poets, or even from the poet in Anaximander. I suggest that quite a different inspiration is likely to have led him to these results. In the first place, Anaximander clearly believed that the universe was governed by mathematical ratios, and by ratios of a simple kind. Furthermore, his Babylonian predecessors must have provided him with considerable data concerning the periods in which the various bodies return to the same relative position.[3] It is easy to imagine that he assigned them distances

[1] "Une *totalité*, et une totalité correspondant en principe à l'ensemble des parties de l'univers, voilà en effet ce qu'expriment essentiellement les divers nombres mythologiques," A. Bergaigne, *La religion védique* (Paris, 1883), II, 151. Bergaigne's chapter on "L'arithmétique mytholo-gique" is the fullest treatment of the subject (pp. 114 ff.).

[2] See Bergaigne, *op. cit.*, II, 414 ff., and H. Oldenberg, *Die Religion des Veda* (Berlin, 1894), pp. 227 ff.

[3] Such periods, as known from direct observa-

in some simple relationship to this observational data, just as his dimensions for the earth must have had some connection with known (or supposed) facts. Our fragmentary knowledge of Anaximander's system does not permit us to reconstruct the method by which his numerical results were reached; we are not even sure of the figures he obtained. But that the inspiration was essentially mathematical seems to me beyond reasonable doubt.

In this perspective it is legitimate to consider Anaximander as the earliest known type of a mathematical physicist, at any rate the earliest outside Babylonia. But his century is one in which this type does not appear in its pure form. Geometrical conceptions play only a secondary part in Anaximander's meteorological theories, as will presently be seen, and for him there was no gap between atmospheric events and the study of the stars. We must remember that the age of Anaximander is also that of Pythagoras, and that for both of them the ideas of geometry are embedded in a much larger view of man and of the cosmos. Even the Pythagorean theories known to Aristotle two centuries later still lack (or ignore) the distinction between physical bodies and ideal mathematical constructions, just as they ignore the contrast between rigid geometric form and the vital processes of living things: the Pythagorean heaven, says Aristotle, which is composed of numbers, first takes shape by "breathing in spirit (πνεῦμα) and void out of the Boundless."[1] This concept of a surrounding ἄπειρον is clearly derived from Anaximander, and its identification with Air or πνεῦμα is in fact the doctrine of Anaximenes. In all probability the idea of cosmic respiration is itself of Milesian origin, and is implied by Anaximenes' comparison of the cosmic Breath to our own ψυχή or breath-soul. In the case of Anaximander, no text speaks of breathing in connection with the world as a whole, but the circles of the sun and moon "exhale" their flame from tubular pores (ἐκπνοαί). This archaic idea is echoed much later, in an Epicurean context where we might least expect it. Lucretius, in describing the sudden darkening of the heavens in a storm, alludes to the entry of bodies into our world from the external void: such is their speed that it is no cause for wonder that tempest and darkness should quickly cover land and sea and the whole limits of the sky at every point, while the elemental bodies leave and return again "as if by breathing pores round about the mighty

---

tion, play a great role in Babylonian astronomy from early times; cf. Neugebauer, *The Exact*

Sciences, pp. 95–98.
[1] Arist. *Phys.* 213ᵇ22, fr. 201 (= *Vors.* 58 в 30).

world."[1] It is certain that this conception of the world as breathing in and out must be traced back to the sixth century, for an early attack upon it was launched by Xenophanes.[2]

Here one might be able to speak with better grounds of a mythic element in sixth-century cosmology. For the same tendency to conceive of cosmic life in concrete terms recurs in other Milesian views, as, for instance, in the emergence of the heavens from "something capable of generation" (γόνιμον, 13.P.), that is to say, from a fertile seed. But if such drastic imagery is genuinely characteristic of mythic modes of thought, we must remember that the same idea of the world as a living being reappears, stripped of such imagery, in the *Timaeus*, the *De Caelo*, and in the cosmological doctrines of the Stoics. The Milesian conception of the world as a geometrical organism suffused with life is thus the true archetype of the ancient point of view, and, indirectly, the stimulus to all modern endeavors (such as those of Leibniz and, more recently, A. N. Whitehead) to interpret the total process of nature in terms of organic life.

17–20. *Meteorology*

In questions concerning the great celestial bodies, it is the geometric spirit which seems to dominate Anaximander's thought, and to make of him a precursor of the modern mentality. But when we enter the field of meteorology the prospect changes, as if we had come upon a strange and less attractive landscape. Although we must recognize its rational quality, the meteorology of the ancients fails to awaken our enthusiasm. This lack of sympathy may be due in part to the radical

---

[1] Lucr. VI. 492 ff.:

undique quandoquidem per caulas aetheris omnis
et quasi per magni circum spiracula mundi
exitus introitusque elementis redditus exstat.

It was Diels (*Dox.* 25, n. 2) who first compared this Lucretian mention of cosmic respiration with the ἐκπνοεῖν of Anaximander. The *spiracula* of Lucretius correspond nicely to the πόροι and αὐλός of Anaximander's rings. (For the biological use of αὐλός as "windpipe," etc., see Bonitz, *Index*, 122ᵃ26 ff., whose first example is "spiraculum cetaceorum.") There is an allusion to cosmic "pores" in the description of the outermost sphere in the *De Hebd.*: "the arrangement of the unseparated κόσμος, which contains the passage through which summer and winter pass" (τάξιν τὴν τοῦ ἀκρίτου κόσμου ἔξοδον ἔχοντος [vulgo

ἔχοντα: corr. Diels] θέρεος καὶ χειμῶνος, 1.43). The alternate heat and cold of the seasons are pictured as entering and leaving the world in the course of the year, just as Lucretius describes the entry and exit of the atoms during a storm. (On this passage of the *De Hebd.*, see E. Pfeiffer, *Studien zum antiken Sternglauben*, ΣΤΟΙΧΕΙΑ II [Leipzig, 1916], 31, n. 5.)

[2] Xenoph. A 1.19: οὐσίαν θεοῦ σφαιροειδῆ, μηδὲν ὅμοιον ἔχουσαν ἀνθρώπῳ· ὅλον δὲ ὁρᾶν καὶ ὅλον ἀκούειν, μὴ μέντοι ἀναπνεῖν. The accurate paraphrase of fr. 24 shows the hand of Theophrastus, and thus guarantees the concluding reference to breathing. This attack of Xenophanes on the idea of cosmic respiration is echoed by Plato in the *Timaeus*: πνεῦμά τε οὐκ ἦν περιεστὸς δεόμενον ἀναπνοῆς (33c.3).

transformation which modern ideas concerning the atmosphere have undergone, since Benjamin Franklin showed the identity of the lightning bolt and the electric spark. Perhaps no less important, however, is the fact that here more than elsewhere we miss the scientific requirement of an experimental test.[1] If this field has been so largely neglected by modern students of Greek thought, it is because they were looking above all for the antecedents of modern philosophy and positive science. Now if ancient astronomy is not different in kind from that of Copernicus and Kepler, Greek meteorology bears little resemblance indeed to modern physics. Yet by this very fact the subject can be of unique importance for an historical understanding of the differences between the ancient and the modern view of nature. A full-scale study of meteorological ideas would no doubt bring clarity into much that has appeared obscure in ancient natural thought. The material is abundant, and even the dangers of anachronism are here not very great; the main lines of explanation scarcely vary from Anaximander to Roman times. Perhaps no work of Aristotle is so directly dependent upon his Ionian predecessors as is the *Meteorologica*. Whole pages could have been written by Anaxagoras or Democritus.[2] It might be possible to show that all the meteorological theories of antiquity represent only minor variations on the doctrine of sixth-century Miletus, and that this doctrine represents, as it were, the heart of the ancient view of nature, the vital link between the study of the heavens and that of living things upon the earth.

Such a demonstration lies, of course, beyond the scope of the present inquiry. We must be content here to outline Anaximander's theory, to distinguish its principal features, and to illustrate in one or two cases the permanent importance of the Milesian view.[3]

---

[1] This has been well remarked by H. D. P. Lee, the latest translator of Aristotle's *Meteorologica*, in the Loeb Classical Library (London, 1952), p. xxvii.

[2] This profoundly conservative tendency seems to account for a number of theories put forward by Aristotle which can scarcely have arisen in the context of his own scheme for the universe. See, e.g., his statement that the sun does not pass over the north or south, but always moves from east to west (361[a]7), and that the east is exposed to the sun's heat longer than the west (364[a]25). In both cases the point of view implied is clearly that of Aristotle's predecessors, who presupposed not only a flat earth but one larger than the sun and relatively close to it. Aristotle ridicules such "childish doctrines" (339[b]34), but has not thoroughly expunged them from his own theories.

[3] For a general discussion, see W. Capelle *s.v.* "Meteorologie," in *RE* Suppl. Band VI (1935), cols. 315 ff., who points out that "the history of Greek meteorology is not yet written." The only attempt to treat the whole subject is O. Gilbert, *Die meteorologischen Theorien des griechischen Altertums* (Leipzig, 1907). Gilbert saw the nature of the problem, but his lack of critical judgment prevented him from offering any real solution. By projecting the philosophic theory of the elements back into Homer and the "Volksanschauung," he rendered the historical sequence of ideas unintelligible.

17. Wind

H. Winds are produced when the finest vapors of the air are separated off and move together in one mass.

A. Wind is a flow of air, when the finest parts in it are set in motion by the sun, and the wettest portions are melted [i.e., liquefied].

18. Rain

H. Rainfall arises from the vapor emitted by the earth under the action of the sun.

19. Lightning and Thunder

H. Lightning occurs when a wind (ἄνεμος) leaping forth separates the clouds.

A. Concerning thunder, lightning, thunderbolt, fire-winds (?), whirlwinds: All these arise from wind (πνεῦμα). For, when it is enclosed in a thick cloud and bursts out violently because of its lightness and the fineness of its parts, then the tearing of the cloud produces the noise, the dilatation [or explosion] causes the flash, by contrast with the darkness of the cloud.

Winds for Anaximander are a result of "separating-off" (ἀποκρίνε-σθαι), the same process by which Hot and Cold, the circles of the stars, and the heavens as a whole are produced. The finest vapors are separated from the grosser bulk of ἀήρ, under the influence of the sun's heat. They are thus set in motion and, when a sufficient quantity have been gathered together, constitute a wind. This is described by Aëtius as a "flow of air," although in fact only the finest portions of the air are involved. We are tempted to say, "the finest *particles*," although the connotations of this word are anachronistic.

Our authorities do not make clear what is left over in the ἀήρ when the finest vapors have been removed. However, this residue would naturally be a thick cloud on its way to precipitation in raindrops or some similar form (**17.A.**, with commentary). Wind and water are thus produced by ἀπόκρισις from air under the influence of the sun's heat. To this corresponds the statement from another source (**20.Arist.1**) that "at first the entire region about the earth was moist, but, as it was dried up by the sun, what was evaporated produced the winds (πνεύ-ματα) . . . while the remainder is the sea." In cosmogony, also, the action of celestial fire is thus to separate wind from water. The emergence of atmosphere and sea from primitive moisture is strictly comparable to the production of wind and rain cloud out of the air. The process in both cases is the same: "separating-out."[1]

It may easily be seen that Anaximander's ἀήρ is not quite what we call "air." If, as a matter of convenience, we may translate the word by its direct descendant in our own tongue, it must be remembered that ἀήρ in Homer—and still in some fifth-century texts—means "mist" or "haze." This will be seen in detail in the next chapter. That Anaximander's notion of air is still close to this old sense of the word is clear from the fact that fine vapors (and, presumably, "gross" or thick ones as well) can be separated out from it. Ἀήρ, then, is a gaseous substance of a certain consistency, like smoke or steam. Its resemblance to the primeval moisture which lay about the earth before the sea was formed is probably so great as to fade almost into identity. One text actually speaks of the first appearance of fire above "the air around the earth" (13.P.). The roots of the doctrine of Anaximenes are here apparent: both Milesian cosmogonies begin with "an aery fluid charged with water vapor."[2]

Rain was, of course, derived by Anaximander from the vapor raised by the sun and concentrated in the clouds (18). We have inferred that this atmospheric moisture which tends to condense as rain is identical with the wettest portions of air, whose "melting," i.e., liquefaction, is mentioned by one text (17.A.). Rain and wind then represent the two opposite products of the ἀήρ. The air we breathe is not expressly assigned to either form, but in the nature of the case it must be closely connected with the wind. The very word πνεῦμα applies to both forms of "blowing."[3] Clouds, on the other hand, are naturally associated with the moist ἀπόκρισις leading to rain. Accordingly, we find here in virtual form a theory of the entire atmosphere as ἀήρ, although what is emphasized is not the unity of this medium, but its polar analysis into fine and gross, wet and dry. The primary Hot and Cold (13.P.) do not reappear in our brief meteorological summaries, but their presence here must be taken for granted in connection with solar heat.

It is of thunder and lightning that the most detailed description has reached us (19.H. and A.). The active agent here is wind (ἄνεμος), i.e.,

---

[1] This doctrine is also implied by Xenoph. B 30, where the sea is said to be the source of wind and rain water, and therefore of the rain clouds as well.

[2] The phrase is Tannery's (Science hellène, p. 104). But I cannot follow him in identifying this "fluide aériforme chargé de vapeur d'eau" with the Boundless itself.

[3] It is perhaps an oversimplification on the part of Aëtius to say that ἀήρ and πνεῦμα are synonymous for Anaximenes (B 2), but the connection between human breath and cosmic Air certainly goes back to him (B 1).

a movement of fine air vapors under the influence of the sun. The passive condition or foil is a thick surrounding cloud, the corresponding residue of ἀήρ after wind has been separated out. When some wind is enclosed within this thick envelope, its reaction is to escape outwards in virtue of its fineness and lightness. The consequent ripping and rending of the cloud is cause of the thunder roar; the flash is produced from "the explosion by contrast with the darkness of the cloud." Unfortunately this statement of Aëtius is by no means clear. Seneca speaks in this context of "fire" and "flame." Now the connection between the earthly fire and the bolt of Zeus is age-old. It is presupposed by the theft of Prometheus. Since the burning flame of a thunderbolt reappears as an important element in the classical theory, we can be sure that its absence in the Greek doxographies for Anaximander is due only to the meagerness of the excerpts which have reached us. To contrast with the darkness of a storm cloud, a wind must have acquired the brilliance of a flame. This wind is then an inflammable air current, trapped in the cloud like air in a balloon. When its heat or innate motion causes it to expand, the envelope is torn, the wind shoots outwards and bursts into flame.

It is impossible to mistake the parallel between this meteorological fire and that of the celestial rings. The envelope of obscure cloud or "air," the fire or hot wind within, the flaming emission, all justify the remark of Tannery that the great heavenly bodies resemble a lightning flash which could last indefinitely.[1] In both these cases, as in that of evaporation and the production of winds, the Hot operates as the active cause. In the description of lightning we see that other opposite pairs— fine and thick, bright and dark—also play a decisive role.

20. *Origin of the Sea*

A. The sea is a remainder of the first moisture, of which the greatest part was dried up by fire, while the rest was changed (i.e., made salty?) by the process of heating.

Alexander. Some of the natural philosophers say that the sea is a remnant of the first moisture. For the region about the earth was moist, but then part of the moisture was evaporated by the sun, and winds arose from it and solstices and "turnings" of the moon. This theory supposes that the turnings of those bodies are due to such vapors and exhalations, and that they turn about the places where there is an abundance of moisture for them. But the part of the moisture which was

---

[1] Tannery, *Science hellène*, p. 92.

left behind in the hollow regions of the earth is the sea. Therefore it is continually diminished and dried up by the sun, and will someday finally be dry. Anaximander and Diogenes were of this opinion, as Theophrastus reports.

The sea is produced by a gradual evaporation of the moisture which originally covered the earth. The appearance of water and dry land, as well as that of winds and rain cloud, is thus a result of evaporation under the influence of celestial fire. But this fire is itself dependent upon the evaporating moisture. Having grown out of and around the primeval moist air "like bark around a tree" (**13.P.**), it must receive sustenance from the same source. Aristotle suggests that Thales' emphasis on the priority of water is due to its role as the generating and nourishing source of fire or heat (*Met.* 983ᵇ23), and we know that this principle was commonly accepted in early Greek thought.[1] If Alexander's information here is correct, Anaximander and his followers made use of this notion to explain solstices and lunar "turnings": the sun and moon are fed by vapors and moist "exhalation" (ἀναθυμίασις), and their paths therefore turn about the places "where there is an abundance of moisture for them."

Without entering into the intricacies of this theory of "turnings,"[2] we may point out that here the link between meteorology and astronomy is dramatically established. The apparent irregularity in the paths of sun and moon is interpreted by the Milesians as proof of their mortal nature: like living things on earth, the great heavenly bodies must move about in search of food. As Aristotle points out with some scorn (*Meteor.* 355ᵃ5), this doctrine implies not only that the stars are like earthly flames but that they are in contact with our atmosphere. Still for the late fifth-century thinkers, the paths of sun, moon, and stars pass through the πνεῦμα or air, while the Stoics maintain the pre-Socratic doctrine that the heavenly bodies are nourished by rising vapors.[3]

We may conclude this survey of Anaximander's meteorology with the explanation of earthquakes that one late author attributes to him,

---

[1] See below, p. 132, n. 1.

[2] The details are very obscure, and it is difficult to see how such an interpretation of solstices is compatible with the description of the sun's circle as "lying aslant" the equator (**15.A.1**). See above, pp. 92 ff., and the long and inconclusive discussion of Heath, *Aristarchus*, pp. 33–36. (The idea implied in Alexander's account, that the "turning-points" may be located somewhere on earth, is as old as the epic; *Od.* o 404: Ὀρτυγίης

κατύπερθεν, ὅθι τροπαὶ ἠελίοιο.)

[3] Hp., *De Flat.* 3 (Jones, II, 230): ἀλλὰ μὴν ἡλίου τε καὶ σελήνης καὶ ἄστρων ὁδὸς διὰ τοῦ πνεύματός ἐστιν; so also in Diog. B 5: τοῦ παρὰ τῷ ἡλίῳ (sc. ἀέρος).

For the Stoics, see, e.g., Cicero, *Nat. Deor.* II.46. 118: "sunt autem stellae natura flammeae; quocirca terrae, maris, aquarum vaporibus aluntur iis, qui a sole ex agris tepefactis et ex aquis excitantur."

probably by mistake (**20a**). In this view, earthquakes arise from excessive dryness or moisture in the region underneath the earth. Decisive also is the violent intervention of air or πνεῦμα, sucked down into the subterranean cavities or forced out by evaporation. This doctrine is clearly in agreement with the principles of Anaximander's meteorology, but it seems in fact to have been formulated by his younger compatriot, Anaximenes; the names have probably been confused by our source (Ammianus Marcellinus).

With an explanation of earthquakes we leave the narrower domain of τὰ μετέωρα, "things aloft." But the science is nonetheless felt as one and the same, and hence we find such fuller expressions as τὰ μετέωρα καὶ τὰ ὑπὸ γῆς. In a work devoted to "what all previous thinkers called μετεωρολογία" (*Meteor.* 338ᵃ27), Aristotle does not hesitate to discuss rivers, sea, and earthquake, as well as the phenomena of the atmosphere. This wide framework of discussion is at least as old as Anaximenes and Xenophanes; for the sea, we have the doctrine of Anaximander himself. In its larger as well as in its more restricted sense, "meteorology" is of Milesian origin.

Indeed, meteorology was at first not a distinct subject of research, but an alternative expression for "the investigation of Nature."[1] It included astronomy as well as atmospheric processes, the two domains being regarded as physically continuous. The dominant principles and powers do not vary from the uppermost heavens to the inner regions of the earth. In so far as the early cosmologists directed their attention to living things as well, their treatment was inevitably the same. Division and classification of subject matter developed only in the course of time, when the bulk of accumulated knowledge imposed the need of specialization. Originally there was only one natural world, and but a single science of Nature.

If this science could often be referred to as meteorology, it is because the interest in "things aloft" was particularly keen, and the results of special importance. We shall see further evidence of this fact in the following chapters. Here we may consider two points in the Milesian view: the importance of the sun, as the most concentrated source of the fiery principle in the universe; and the fundamentally new significance of the ἀήρ as source and material of atmospheric events.

The decisive role played by the sun in Anaximander's account of

[1] See W. Capelle, "Μετέωρος–Μετεωρολογία," *Philologus*, LXXI (1912), 414: and O. Gilbert, *op. cit.*, pp. 3 ff.

evaporation and wind formation is clear. Its importance is mirrored by the Milesian interest in solstices, equinoxes, and the measurement of days and hours. Astronomy and meteorology belong together, for the sun's annual progress among the stars marks out the stages of seasonal change in the earth's atmosphere.

This primacy of the sun in the organization of the universe was recognized by all of Anaximander's followers or associates. Of Anaximenes we are told that he attributed all seasonal changes to the action of the sun alone,[1] while Xenophanes declared the sun to be "useful for the generation and administration of the world and of the living things within it, while the moon is superfluous" (A 42). Xenophanes was apparently protesting against popular superstitions concerning the phases of the moon, but the principle of his protest is fully Milesian. Thus he derived all meteorological events "from the heat of the sun, which causes things to rise. For when moisture is drawn up from the sea, the sweet portion is separated because of the fineness of its parts, and it turns to mist and causes clouds to form and rain to fall in drops by its condensation and winds to be evaporated [by its rarefaction]" (A 46). Heraclitus has in mind this same cosmic role of the sun when he insists that Helios will always obey his appointed measures (B 94), and Plutarch cites Heraclitus as an authority for the widespread view that the sun is "overseer and guardian" (ἐπιστάτης καὶ σκοπός) of the cosmic periods and seasons (B 100).

It is this old Ionian view of the sun's physical importance which explains an otherwise surprising remark in Plato's famous comparison of knowledge to vision: "I think you will agree that the sun provides those who see not only with the power of sight, but also with generation and growth and nourishment" (Rep. 509b). Much the same doctrine is developed at length by Aristotle. For him, the cause of continuous generation and corruption in nature is to be found in the eternal movement of the heavens, but since a uniform motion such as that of the outer cosmic sphere would produce a uniform effect, the alternative reign of birth and death must be due to the shifting movement of the sun in its oblique path. When it approaches the earth in spring and summer, it causes generation to occur; when it withdraws in fall and winter, corruption sets in.[2] In the Meteorologica this causal action of the sun is interpreted as atmospheric "separation and combination":

[1] Anaximenes A 14: τὰς ἐπισημασίας τάς τε   ἥλιον μόνον.
θερινὰς καὶ τὰς χειμερινὰς . . . γίνεσθαι . . . διὰ τὸν   [2] Gen. Corr. 336ᵃ23 ff. and the same chapter

The moisture around the earth is borne upwards as vapor by the sun's beams and the heat from above; but when the heat drawing it up fails—in part dispersed into the upper region, in part quenched by the height which it attains in the air above the earth—the vapor condenses again as it is cooled by the region and by the loss of heat, and it turns from air to water; in this form it is borne again towards the earth. The exhalation from water is vapor, that from air to water is cloud; mist is the residue of cloud's condensation to water. . . .

Now this cycle occurs in imitation of the circle described by the sun. For as the sun passes laterally back and forth, this cycle moves up and down. One must think of it as a river flowing in a circle up and down, common to air and to water. . . . So that if the ancients spoke of Ocean with a hidden meaning, perhaps it is this river they meant by saying that it flows in a circle around the earth. (*Meteor.* 346^{b}25 ff.)

Despite the intimate connection of this theory with Aristotle's whole view of the order of nature, its purely Ionian origin is unmistakable. When he speaks of "a river up and down," the parallel with Heraclitus' phrase can scarcely be fortuitous. The question whether Aristotle is consciously echoing Heraclitus here, or whether both make use of an older formula, is of little importance. The doctrine at any rate is that of Anaximander and Anaximenes.[1]

To us for whom the notion of "air" is as banal as the fact of breathing, the emphasis placed upon this idea in some verses of Euripides and in the *Clouds* of Aristophanes appears rather extravagant. Modern commentators tend to interpret these passages by connecting them with a more or less fictitious visit that Diogenes of Apollonia is said to have paid to Athens about this time.[2] Even if such a visit took place, it cannot by itself explain the significance which a tragic and a comic poet ascribe to the divine Air. In fact the originality of Diogenes must not be

(II.10) *passim.* For the vital place of this doctrine in Aristotle's conception of the cosmos, see Joachim's note on 336^{a}14–18.

[1] The Ionian view of the sun's importance for the seasonal order was systematically developed by the Stoics. Cleanthes designated the sun as τὸ ἡγεμονικὸν τοῦ κόσμου (D.L. VII. 139). Similarly Cicero, *Rep.* VI. 17: "Sol . . . dux et princeps et moderator luminum reliquorum, mens mundi et temperatio"; Pliny, *H.N.* II.6.12: "Sol . . . amplissima magnitudine ac potestate, nec temporum modo sed siderum etiam ipsorum caelique rector." This semi-religious view of the sun as ruler or viceroy of the universe is illustrated by the Pompeian painting of Apollo as Helios Kosmokrator (reproduced as frontispiece by A.-J.

Festugière in *La révélation d'Hermès Trismégiste*, II : *Le dieu cosmique* [Paris, 1949]).

[2] The only ancient authority for this visit is the ambiguous statement of D.L. IX. 57 concerning Diogenes: ἦν δὲ τοῖς χρόνοις κατ᾽ Ἀναξαγόραν· τοῦτόν φησι ὁ Φαληρεὺς Δημήτριος ἐν τῇ Σωκράτους ἀπολογίᾳ διὰ μέγαν φθόνον μικροῦ κινδυνεῦσαι Ἀθήνησιν. But the word τοῦτον probably refers to Anaxagoras rather than to Diogenes, as Diels notes on *Vors.* 64 A 1. (Diels had earlier referred the remark to Diogenes, in "Ueber Leukipp und Demokrit," *Verhandlungen der 35. Versammlung deutscher Philologen* [1880], p. 106, n. 32; this article contains the best statement of the case for a link between Diogenes and the *Clouds*.)

overestimated,[1] and it may be fairly doubted whether the Athenians had anything to learn from him after the long residence among them of the master of Clazomenae, after the lessons of Archelaus and the swarm of lesser polymaths, such as those which met in the salon of Callias. We are liable only to dull the point of the Aristophanic parody by directing it too exclusively against the person of Diogenes.

What is most striking in the treatment of Ionian science in the *Clouds* is first, the accuracy with which the physical doctrines are reproduced, and second, the religious sense which is put upon them. It would be a naive anachronism to think of the Ionian naturalists as adopting an attitude like that of modern atheists or agnostics. The ἀσέβεια of the fifth century B.C. is of another sort. If the gods of the poets and of the traditional cult are rejected by these men with contempt, divinity itself—as a fundamental category of speech and thought—is seldom or never called into question. We can see this clearly from the fragments of Xenophanes and Heraclitus in the older period, as well as from the secondary impact on Euripides and on the Aristophanic φροντισταί. The pupil who admits Strepsiades into the school first warns him that "it is not lawful to speak of these things except to those who are disciples. . . . These must be deemed mysteries" (140 ff.). The elaborate parallel to rites of initiation which then follows (252 ff.) is not an empty farce: if the belief in the Olympians is no longer current coin, it is because finer and truer divinities have taken their place (247 ff., 367 ff.).

The authentically Ionian, and even Milesian, provenance of the science taught within the φροντιστήριον is not left in doubt. The first thing which meets Strepsiades' eager glance is an inquiry into "things beneath the earth" singularly combined with an astronomy lesson. He finds perhaps a celestial globe or chart, and certainly a course in geometry, while a world map (γῆς περίοδος πάσης) is posted on the wall (184–206). The disciple has already discoursed to him on the problems of exact measurement, and on the strange power of breath (πνοή, πνεῦμα) forced through fine narrow passages out into hollow

[1] According to Theophrastus *Phys. Opin.* fr. 2 (= *Vors.* 64 A 5), he was for the most part dependent on Anaxagoras and Leucippus. The general doctrines relevant to the *Clouds* are (1) that the ἀήρ is divine, and (2) that it is the cause of our intelligence. Both are also ascribed to Anaximenes (A 10, A 23, B 2) or vaguely to "others" (Arist. *De An.* 405ª21). The ἰκμάς or moist secretion which passes from earth to heaven is part of the Milesian view (Anaximenes A 7.5), and modern scholars have perhaps been too quick to see the influence of Diogenes in the frequent mention of ἰκμάς in the Hippocratic Corpus. Even the theory of moisture as an obstacle to clear thinking (κωλύειν τὴν ἰκμάδα τὸν νοῦν, Diog. A 19.44), which seems to be implied at *Nubes* 233, is also familiar to Heraclitus (B 77, B 117, B 118).

space (144–64). And we recognize the common doctrine of the Ionians, from Anaximenes to Democritus, when the schoolmaster solemnly invokes his "sovereign lord, immeasurable Air, who holds the earth on high" (264).

But if all aspects of Ionian science are pictured or suggested here, it is the theory of the atmosphere which dominates in the poet's mind. So much is evident from the title of his play. Why should air, sky, and clouds be of such overwhelming concern? The answer is clearly given in the work itself. The ideas of traditional Greek religion are centered around Zeus, god of the sky, master of the weather, gatherer of rain clouds on mountain peaks, whose sign to men is the lightning flash and whose voice a peal of thunder. Zeus was, of course, never a *mere* weather god; he was also Ζεὺς βασιλεύς, ξένιος, ἱκέσιος, πατρῷος, σωτήρ, and the rest—the lord of social order as well as of natural processes. But his distinctive personality, his numinous power was that of the god who gives or withholds rain at his pleasure, and hurls the thunderbolt when his temper is aroused. A naturalistic account of these events inevitably took on the proportions of a full-dress attack upon the ancestral conception of the gods. Thus the opening scenes of the *Clouds* reach their climax when Socrates explains rain, thunder, and lightning without the intervention of Zeus. Only then is his new disciple ready to renounce the traditional rites and devote himself wholly to the divinities of the school (425).

Nothing symbolizes better the overthrow of Zeus than does a rational description of the thunderbolt. The account given by Aristophanes may therefore conclude our treatment of Milesian meteorology: "The thunderbolt brilliant with fire" (395) arises "when a dry wind is raised aloft and enclosed in the clouds; it inflates them from within like a bladder and then, breaking through them by necessity, it rushes out with a violence due to their thickness, and bursts into flame from the impact of its surging and rushing"; or, as we would say, from its friction against the cloud.[1]

The essential identity of this explanation with that given by Anaximander scarcely calls for comment. The doxographical report of his theory does not specify the dryness of the enclosed wind, but that must

---

[1] *Nubes* 404–7:

> ὅταν εἰς ταύτας (sc. νεφέλας) ἄνεμος ξηρὸς μετεωρισθεὶς κατακλεισθῇ,
> ἔνδοθεν αὐτὰς ὥσπερ κύστιν φυσᾷ, κἄπειθ' ὑπ' ἀνάγκης
> ῥήξας αὐτὰς ἔξω φέρεται σοβαρὸς διὰ τὴν πυκνότητα,
> ὑπὸ τοῦ ῥοίβδου καὶ τῆς ῥύμης αὐτὸς ἑαυτὸν κατακαίων.

be presupposed. (A damp wind could not ignite. Flame is a product of dry, hot air or πνεῦμα not only for Anaximenes but also for Aristotle, whose "dry exhalation" is scarcely distinguishable from elemental fire.) The explanation of the thunderbolt as an ignited wind or πνεῦμα that tears through a thick surrounding cloud remains the classic view.[1]

Once such a rational theory had been expounded, there was little need for a new one. The goal of a naturalistic explanation had been reached; the most impressive of atmospheric phenomena no longer revealed the hand of an anthropomorphic god. The attention of later thinkers was thus diverted to new problems, or restricted to a re-arrangement of the details. Hence the conservative character of Greek meteorology, and hence the permanent sway of Milesian doctrine throughout antiquity.

In an historical perspective we see that it is not Δῖνος but Ἀήρ, the Milesian concept of the atmosphere, which has taken the place of Zeus. The new view has preserved some of the grandeur of the Olympian pantheon. Although the drama of sunlight and storm no longer represents the work of personalized gods, it appears nonetheless as a great battlefield debated by hostile powers: the cosmic forces of cold and heat, dampness and drought, darkness and light, of which one host is marshalled in the vicinity of the earth, the other arrayed in the outer regions of heaven, alternately descending and retreating according to the command of its princely hero, the Sun. These two realms are bound not only by opposition, but by bands of mutual dependence: the hot element is nourished by the moist, while the lower ἀήρ must draw its power of action from the evaporative heat of the sun.[2]

21. *Origin of Animal Life*

H. Animals arise from moisture evaporated by the sun.

A. The first animals were generated in moisture and enclosed in thorny barks;

---

[1] The explanation of Anaximenes (A 7.8) is identical with that of his predecessor: ἀστραπὴν (sc. γίνεσθαι) ὅταν τὰ νέφη διαστῆται βίᾳ πνευμά- των· τούτων γὰρ διασταμένων λαμπρὰν καὶ πυρώδη γίνεσθαι τὴν αὐγήν. The versions of Metrodorus of Chios (*Vors.* 70 A 15) and Aristotle (*Meteor.* 369ª25 ff.) remain substantially the same. Anaxag- oras (A 84), Empedocles (A 63), Leucippus (A 25), and Democritus (A 93) seem to transfer the role of dry πνεῦμα to celestial fire trapped within a dense cloud, but this distinction may be largely verbal. Thus Lucretius (VI.274–84) combines the roles of *ventus* and *ignis*, while Seneca prefers *ignis*

(*Q.N.* II.21.1) but goes on to speak of *aër mutabilis in ignem . . . cum in ventum conversus est* (II.23.2).

[2] "Fire has the power of moving all things all throughout, water of nourishing all things all throughout." These words of Hp. *De Victu* ch. 3 express no personal view of the author, nor that of any given predecessor, but the common pre-supposition of all Greek natural philosophers. This is in short one of those κοιναὶ γνῶμαι mentioned by the author of *De Carnibus* (ch. 1; Littré, VIII, 584), which must be utilized by anyone who undertakes to treat of such a subject in a scientific way.

as they grew older, they came out onto the drier [land] and, once their bark was split and shed, they lived in a different way for a short time.

Censorinus. Out of water and earth which had been heated arose either fish or living things very similar to fish.

22. *Descent of Man*

H. In the beginning man was similar to a different animal, namely, a fish.

P. In the beginning man was generated from living things of another kind, since the others are quickly able to look for their own food, while only man requires prolonged nursing. Therefore if he had been so in the beginning he would never have survived.

Censorinus. In these [fishes or fish-like animals] men were formed and kept within as fetuses until maturity; then at last the creatures burst open, and out came men and women who were already able to feed themselves.

The early view of the world, in Greece as elsewhere, has no place for compartmentalization. Man and nature, microcosm and macrocosm, are seen together in a single pattern as two facets of the same stone. If the whole universe has undergone a process of birth and development, that is because its existence is comparable to that of a living creature. By the same token, those factors which explain the formation of the universe must also preside over the origin and growth of men and animals. When the author of the *De Victu* speaks of the formation of the human body as "an imitation of the Whole, small things [arranged] according to great ones, and great according to small,"[1] he is expressing no new principle, but only a more conscious and rigorous application of this age-old view.

This parallelism can be easily traced within the theories of Anaximander. Thus the gradual emergence of dry land under the action of the sun was accompanied by the formation of living things within the moist element. Animals arise from the same process of ebullition which separates sea from land, and their transition from a marine existence to life on land forms part of the cosmic trend towards dryness.[2] Living

---

[1] *De Victu* 10 (Jones, IV, 246). See the interesting article of H. C. Baldry, "Embryological Analogies in Pre-Socratic Cosmogony," *CQ*, XXVI (1932), 27.

[2] Thus Anaximander agreed with Thales, and with early speculation in many lands, that moisture is the source of life. At the same time, he may have had in mind some curious observations mentioned by later Ionians. Xenophanes, for example, cited inland deposits of sea shells and marine fossils as evidence of the originally mud-like condition of the earth (A 33). Since Xenophanes' theory of the drying earth is Milesian, some of his facts may have come from the same source. Both facts and theory are known to Herodotus, who mentions shell deposits on the Egyptian hills as proof that the land there was once covered by water (II.12.1).

things are themselves conceived of as a joint product of the wet and dry—that is, of water and earth (21.Censorinus). This is the doctrine repeated by Xenophanes: "We have all arisen from earth and water" (B 33). Much the same view seems to have been held by Anaxagoras and Democritus,[1] and Heraclitus must have had something similar in mind when he said that "life (ψυχή) comes from water" (B 36). The derivation of living things from the primeval moisture is in effect the standard Greek theory on the subject. Later versions are known from several sources, of which the fullest is Diodorus Siculus' introduction to his *Historical Library*. Here, as in the doctrine of Anaximander, the earth was originally "mud-like and thoroughly soft."

It first became hardened under the beaming fire of the sun. Then, as its surface was seething with the heat, some moist portions swelled up in many places, and fermentations arose there enclosed in fine membranes ["like bubbles," says the parallel passage in Hermippus; *Vors.* 68 B 5.2, 6]. . . . While the moisture was thus becoming impregnated with life by the heat, the creatures were directly nourished at night from the mist which descended out of the surrounding atmosphere, and solidified in the daytime by the burning heat. Finally, when the fetuses had reached their full growth, and when the membranes were burnt through and split off, all kinds of animals were produced. (Diod. Sic. 1.7 = *Vors.* 68 B 5.1)

This version goes on to specify that creatures with a high proportion of heat in their constitution became birds, those in which earth predominated were reptiles, while those which contained more moisture flocked to a place which was like them, and were called aquatic.

We do not know who is responsible for the particular form of the theory cited by Diodorus,[2] but the "fermentations" and "membranes" are known from other texts, which show that the doctrine in its main features must belong to the fifth century.[3] There are of course important differences between this account and that of Anaximander. His envelopes are "thorny," while the later membranes are said to be as fine

---

[1] Anaxagoras A 42.12: ζῷα δὲ τὴν μὲν ἀρχὴν ἐν ὑγρῷ γενέσθαι, μετὰ ταῦτα δὲ ἐξ ἀλλήλων. Democritus A 139: ex aqua limoque primum visum esse homines procreatos (Censorinus); πρῶτον τοῦ ὑγροῦ ζῳογονοῦντος (Aëtius).

[2] The doctrine of Diodorus is generally traced back to Democritus. (See K. Reinhardt, *Hermes*, XLVII [1912], 492, and more recently G. Vlastos, *AJP*, LXVII [1946], 51, who cites the literature.) But in fact, as E. Schwartz pointed out long ago, there is no trace in Diodorus' account of anything

characteristic of atomist thought or, for that matter, of any other distinctive cosmological view.

[3] *Phaedo* 96b.2: ἆρ' ἐπειδὰν τὸ θερμὸν καὶ τὸ ψυχρὸν σηπεδόνα τινὰ λάβῃ, ὥς τινες ἔλεγον, τότε δὴ τὰ ζῷα συντρέφεται; *De Carn.* 3 (Littré, VIII, 586): καὶ τῷ χρόνῳ ὑπὸ τοῦ θερμοῦ ξηραινομένης τῆς γῆς ταῦτα τὰ καταλειφθέντα (sc. θερμὰ ἐν τῇ γῇ) περὶ ἑωυτὰ σηπεδόνας ποιεῖ οἷόν περ χιτῶνας. According to Burnet, the theory mentioned in the *Phaedo* passage is that of Archelaus (*Plato's Phaedo* [Oxford, 1911], notes, p. 100).

as bubbles (although this description may apply only to their condition when first formed). Instead of Anaximander's view that living things first arose in the moist element and then shifted to dry land, the later sources suggest a picture of isolated pockets of moisture forming in the half-dry crust of the earth. But the historical continuity between the two views should be clear. In particular the membranes of Diodorus play exactly the same role as the "barks" of Anaximander. If we imagine these pregnant membranes floating in the water while they mature, we will probably have a good picture of those "living things very similar to fish" which constitute the first animals in the Milesian account.[1]

It is significant that Diodorus does not give a special account of the origin of men, but assumes that his formation was the same as that of the other animals. Precisely the same assumption is made in a parallel text of the Hippocratic Corpus (*De Carn.* 1–3). In all probability, Anaximander also thought of the origin of mankind as entirely comparable to that of the land animals in general. At first sight, the contrary seems to be implied by his remark that originally "man was generated from living things of another kind, since the others are quickly able to look for their own food, while only man requires prolonged nursing" (**22.P.**). But these living things "of another kind" (ἀλλοειδῆ ζῷα) are not contrasted with the original form of the other animals, but with human beings as we know them. In the case of man, his helpless infancy is a special proof that he cannot have appeared at first in his present form. But the original human embryos may be safely identified with those floating membranes from which the other animals also developed.[2]

Anaximander's insight that the first men cannot have been born as babies, since there would have been no parents to feed or protect them,

[1] Cornford suggested that Anaximander had the spiny-shelled sea urchin in mind. There is in any case a curious analogy between the shattered "bark" of these creatures (**21.A.**) and the bursting sphere of flame that originally encircled the inner region of the world, which a different author describes precisely by this very term "bark" (φλοιός, **13.P.**). It is difficult to believe that this double use of an unusual image is to be traced to anyone but Anaximander himself, who thus wished to emphasize that "the world develops like a great animal, or the animals like a small world" (G. Teichmüller, *Studien zur Geschichte der Begriffe* [Berlin, 1874], p. 69). When one compares the flame which grew around the primeval air

(περιφυῆναι, **13.P.**), the air which surrounds the fire in the astral circles (περιληφθέντα, **13.H.**), and the wind which is enclosed in a thick cloud before the lightning bursts (περιληφθέν, **19.A.**) with these primitive animals wrapped up in bark (περιεχόμενα), it becomes clear that Anaximander's conception of the Boundless as "surrounding all things" (περιέχειν ἅπαντα, **8**) was carefully paralleled by similar envelopes at every point within the world.

[2] For the reasons for rejecting Plutarch's statement (under **22**) that men were originally born from fishes and nourished "like the dogfish," see above, pp. 70 f.

was a remarkable feat of scientific imagination. But the precedent for a Darwinian concept of organic evolution, which has been so often insisted upon, is at best very vague. There is no hint here of a general evolutionary scale, according to which the higher species would develop out of simpler forms. On the contrary, each species arises independently from the life-giving moisture of slime, according to the same process of spontaneous generation by which mice and other small animals were, until a few centuries ago, thought to be produced from the alluvial mud of the Nile.[1] Nor is there any trace of a struggle for survival by adaptation to environmental conditions. Adaptation of some sort is of course implied for the first animals, who "lived in a different way for a short time." Like a tadpole turning into a frog, these sea-born creatures must adjust themselves to life on land. But their case is unique, and their usefulness is exhausted once a few of them have lived long enough to reproduce and to nurse their offspring to maturity. With this second generation, each species becomes self-propagating in its present form.

When these theories reappear in their classic version, the origin of life is followed by a sketch of man's primitive existence and his earliest experience in social organization. We can follow the development step by step in the poem of Lucretius and in the briefer narrative of Diodorus.[2] There is a hint of similar theories in a fragment of Anaxagoras (B 4), and it seems likely that such speculation concerning prehistoric man dates from the earliest period of Greek natural philosophy. Direct proof of the fact is lacking, but one fragment of Xenophanes does reveal an interest in the origins of civilization: "By no means did the gods reveal all things to mortals from the beginning, but by seeking they find out what is better in the course of time" (B 18). Every hint of a context is lost, but Xenophanes must have had in mind the origin of the arts, and perhaps also of religion, morality, and government— those questions that were later debated by the Sophists in terms of Nature and Convention. From a different point of view, Hecataeus too in his rational study of the human past must have been following in the footsteps of the natural philosophers.[3] In the special as well as the wider acceptation of the term, ἱστορία is a child of Miletus.

[1] Anaximander's view has been described as spontaneous generation and rightly contrasted with modern evolutionary ideas by J. H. Loenen, "Was Anaximander an Evolutionist?" *Mnemosyne*, VII (1954), 215. Loenen accepts Plutarch's shark analogy as part of Anaximander's theory. So also does W. K. C. Guthrie, *In the Beginning* (Ithaca, New York, 1957), p. 33. Pages 31–42 of Guthrie's book should be compared in detail for the theories of the origin of life discussed above.

[2] Lucretius v.780 ff.; Diod. Sic. 1.7–8.

[3] See F. Jacoby, in *RE*, VII, 2749.9, and the remarks of Kurt von Fritz concerning the

23. *The ψυχή*

According to one late ancient source (Theodoretus), Anaximander's investigation of Nature included not only astronomy, meteorology, geography, and biology, but also the beginnings of a theory of the ψυχή or life-principle in men and animals. Despite the slight documentary evidence for Anaximander's view, the statement of Theodoretus that he declared the ψυχή to be "of an airy nature" is intrinsically credible. Thales before him had apparently concerned himself with an explanation of the ψυχή, and had regarded it as a force responsible for motion (*Vors.* 11 A 22). Anaximander's speculation concerning the origin of life would naturally have led him too to pose the question of the ψυχή, and it is this theory which we should expect him to adopt. The conception of the soul as air or breath is independently attested for both Xenophanes (A 1.19) and Anaximenes (A 23; cf. B 2), as well as for the old Orphic poems.[1] It is founded in the age-old sense of the link between respiration and life that is contained in the very etymology of the word ψυχή: the power by which we breathe, and which we "expire" with life itself.[2] Such a view of the ψυχή as a breath-soul is still prevalent in the time of Plato.[3] Considering the importance of πνεῦμα in Anaximander's meteorology and in Ionian physics generally, this notion of the vital spirit in men and animals might almost be taken for granted even if no text could be cited in its support. We may perhaps go a step further and conjecture that this vivifying πνεῦμα was conceived not simply as "air," but also as partaking of the active power of heat. The ψυχή is expressly said by Diogenes to be "air hotter than the external air in which we live" (B 5), and just such a hot vapor or ἀναθυμίασις was identified as the soul by Heraclitus (B 12; A 15). The idea that only possession of a ψυχή permits things to have motive force— presupposed in Thales' remark on the lodestone—would thus be explained by the inherent connection between heat and motion recognized in all Greek natural thought.

relationship of Hecataeus to Anaximander, in "Der gemeinsame Ursprung der Geschichtsschreibung und der exakten Wissenschaften bei den Griechen," *Philosophia Naturalis*, II (1951), 211.

[1] Arist. *De An.* 410ᵇ29 = *Vors.* 1 B 11: τὴν ψυχὴν ἐκ τοῦ ὅλου εἰσιέναι ἀναπνεόντων, φερομένην ὑπὸ τῶν ἀνέμων.

[2] The eccentric attempt of LSJ to separate ψυχή from ψύχω is a rearguard action doomed to failure. For the linguistic proof, see E. Benveniste in *Bulletin de la Société de Linguistique*, XXXIII (1932), 165; P. Chantraine, *La formation des noms*

en grec ancien (Paris, 1933), p. 23. The semantic development is, of course, paralleled by Latin *anima*, and by similar words in many tongues. The fact alleged by LSJ that the Homeric ψυχή can leave through a wound as well as through the mouth proves nothing either against the etymology or against the poet's awareness of its meaning. Even in the fifth century no real distinction is drawn between the respiratory system and the circulation of blood through the limbs; see, e.g., Emped. B 100; Hp. *De Morbo Sacro* ch. 19.

[3] *Phaedo* 70a.5, 77d.8 ff.

Supplementary Note: The Earliest Doctrine of a Spherical Earth

The sphericity of the earth is unknown to Anaximander: his earth is a flat cylinder balanced at the center of a perfect celestial sphere. When this view of the earth's position reappears a century and a half later in Plato's *Phaedo*, its essential symmetry has been rendered more complete by an extension of the spherical shape to the earth itself. Hence not only is the earth as a whole equidistant from the celestial periphery in every direction, but every single point on the earth's surface is equidistant from the corresponding point in the celestial sphere. The sphericity of the earth thus appears as a kind of corollary to that of the heavens, serving to round out Anaximander's vision of the universe as an embodiment of geometric balance. Because of this intimate connection between the spherical earth and the general celestial scheme of Anaximander, the origin of this doctrine is of interest to us here.

Who first declared the earth to be a sphere? Even in antiquity this matter caused some dispute. Diogenes Laertius reports of Pythagoras (on the authority of Favorinus):

ἀλλὰ μὴν καὶ τὸν οὐρανὸν πρῶτον ὀνομάσαι κόσμον καὶ τὴν γῆν στρογγύλην· ὡς δὲ Θεόφραστος, Παρμενίδην· ὡς δὲ Ζήνων, Ἡσίοδον. (VIII.48 = *Vors.* 28 A 44).

That the disagreement refers not to the use of the word κόσμος but to the shape of the earth is clear (as Diels pointed out, *Dox.* 492.7*n*) from the restatement of the same information by Diogenes Laertius in the report of Parmenides' views which he gives from the epitome of Theophrastus:

πρῶτος δ' οὗτος τὴν γῆν ἀπέφαινε σφαιροειδῆ καὶ ἐν μέσῳ κεῖσθαι. . . . καθὰ μέμνηται καὶ Θεόφραστος ἐν τοῖς Φυσικοῖς. . . . (IX.21–22 = *Vors.* 28 A 1)

The text of Theophrastus which served as basis for these two remarks of Diogenes Laertius is clearly one and the same.[1] That by στρογγύλος in the first passage Diogenes Laertius meant "spherical" and not merely "circular" is put beyond doubt by σφαιροειδής in the second; Theophrastus presumably made use of the more precise expression. In any case he could not have said that Parmenides was the first to declare the earth to be circular (but flat), for he ascribed that view to Anaximander (**11**), and these two statements must originally have appeared side by side in the same section of the *Physicorum Opiniones* (where Theophrastus probably pointed out how Plato's doctrine of the

[1] It is therefore regrettable that Diels listed them separately, as frs. 6a and 17 (*Dox.* 482 and 492).

earth's position was anticipated by Anaximander in part, and more fully by Parmenides).

Thus there is no real room for doubt in regard to what Theophrastus said. But two historical problems are posed by the ascription of a spherical earth to Parmenides: What were the grounds which led him to this view? And why was it refused by the Ionian naturalists from Anaxagoras to Democritus, all of whom must have been familiar with the poem in which it was expressed?

The first problem is well discussed by Heath (*Aristarchus*, p. 48), although in reference to the supposed discovery by Pythagoras rather than Parmenides. Heath first mentions the possibility of an inference from the round shadow cast upon the moon in lunar eclipse, but rejects it since "it is certain that Anaxagoras was the first to suggest this, the true explanation of eclipses." The fact does not seem as certain to me as to Heath,[1] but it must be admitted that the evidence from eclipses cannot have seemed decisive, since Anaxagoras combined it with the old view of the earth as a cylinder or disk. Heath continues:

The second possibility is that Pythagoras may have extended his assumption of a spherical sky to the separate luminaries of heaven; the third is that his ground was purely mathematical, or mathematico-aesthetical, and that he attributed spherical shape to the earth for the simple reason that "the sphere is the most beautiful of solid figures."[2] I prefer the third of these hypotheses, though the second and third have the point of contact that the beauty of the spherical shape may have dictated its application *both* to the universe and to the earth. (pp. 48–49)

As Heath remarks, his second and third possibilities collapse into one. Furthermore, they both coincide with the suggestion made above that this doctrine arose as a perfection of Anaximander's view of the position of the earth within the celestial sphere. In fact the statement of Theophrastus, as Diogenes Laertius has preserved it, implies that Parmenides connected the shape of the earth with its position (σφαιροειδῆ καὶ ἐν μέσῳ κεῖσθαι), just as Plato does in the *Phaedo* (108e.5: ἔστιν ἐν μέσῳ τῷ οὐρανῷ περιφερὴς οὖσα).

We do not know whether this corollary to Anaximander's theorem was really formulated by Parmenides for the first time, or whether his

---

[1] Parmenides B 14–15 contain strong prima facie evidence of a correct understanding of the moon's light, cast into the peculiar, allusive style of his hexameters. Theophrastus (in the version of Hippolytus) says only that Anaxagoras was the first to give a clear analysis of the phenomena (οὗτος ἀφώρισε πρῶτος τὰ περὶ τὰς ἐκλείψεις καὶ φωτισμούς Vors. 59 A 42.10). He may himself have felt some doubt about Parmenides' view.

[2] "D.L. VIII.35 attributes this statement to the Pythagoreans" (Heath's note).

poem contains merely the first public statement of a view which might originally have been taught by Pythagoras to the members of his fraternity. An oral tradition more ancient than Parmenides' poem was at all events inaccessible to Theophrastus, and any ancient authority for assigning such a doctrine to the master from Samos is devoid of historical worth. The decision of Burnet, Heath, and others in favor of Pythagoras as author must remain a personal conjecture, beyond the scope of documentary proof or refutation.

If the account given above is correct, it is not difficult to see why the Ionian physicists refused to accept this early doctrine of a spherical earth. It is one more sign of their severely skeptical common sense. Just as they could not be satisfied with a purely geometric interpretation of the earth's position, neither were they impressed by this "mathematico-aesthetic" account of its shape. One sees with one's eyes, as it were, the flatness of the earth. Those for whom the possibility of non-sensual knowledge is a difficult problem (cf. Democr. B 125) must have more compelling reasons to abandon such a clear fact of observation. It is not until the fourth century that the strictly astronomical arguments in favor of a spherical earth (reinforced by the prestige of Plato and Aristotle) become overwhelming.

A widely different account of the question is given by E. Frank, in *Platon und die sogenannten Pythagoreer* (Halle, 1923). Frank begins with a reconstruction of the history of the discovery on the basis of *Phaedo* 108c. Since (in his view) the statement of Plato there implies that the doctrine of a spherical earth is a recent innovation, and since, on the other hand, the earth of Democritus is still flat, the discovery must have been made in the period between these two, most probably by Archytas of Tarentum. This conclusion is stated (Beilage V, pp. 184 ff.) before Frank considers the documentary evidence which we have just discussed. Since he has already reached a decision concerning the discovery itself, Frank must understand the testimony of Theophrastus to mean only that Parmenides was the first to use the term στρογγύλος for the disk-like shape of the earth (Beilage VI, pp. 198 ff.)

This interpretation of what Theophrastus said will not, I think, recommend itself to anyone who reads without preconception the two sentences of Diogenes Laertius quoted above.[1] Furthermore, at *Phaedo*

---

[1] I see, however, that a similar view is taken by J. S. Morrison, "Parmenides and Er," *JHS*, LXXV (1955), 64. But where is the "first" if Parmenides does not differ from Anaximander? It

108c Plato does not state that the doctrine he will present is *new*, but that it is at variance with what is usually taught by the experts on the subject, i.e., by the Ionian natural philosophers (whose views, together with that of Empedocles, have been mentioned at 99b). Nor is Plato referring in particular to the spherical earth, but to the whole half-fantastic cosmology which follows. He has in fact already mentioned a spherical shape for the earth as one of the recognized possibilities (97e.1, where στρογγύλη opposed to πλατεῖα must mean "round," not "disk-like").

The real ground for Frank's view is that the acceptance by a great scientist like Democritus of such a primitive model for the earth seems to him "undenkbar, wenn man zu dieser Zeit auch nur eine Ahnung von der Kugelgestalt der Erde gehabt hätte" (p. 185). He presupposes that the doctrine of a spherical earth must have been introduced as a result of the observed differences in star risings at different latitudes, which constituted then as now "der einzig ernsthafte Beweis für die Kugeltheorie" (p. 187). But the notion of a serious proof was not quite the same in the fifth and fourth centuries as it is today. In Aristotle's demonstration of the earth's sphericity, general cosmological arguments take precedence over τὰ φαινόμενα κατὰ τὴν αἴσθησιν, and among the latter, the evidence from lunar eclipses comes before the star observations (*De Caelo* 297ᵃ8–298ᵃ6). On the other hand, even modern scientists have not always been as quick as Frank supposes to see the truth of a theory which has become obvious to us. Did not Galileo resist to the end the elliptical paths of planetary motion which had been proposed by his friend Kepler?

With regard to Archytas, Frank has made it likely that he did hold to the spherical shape of the earth, although it must be admitted that the documentary evidence is very slight and indirect (Horace, *Carm.* 1.28 = *Vors.* 47 A 3). But Archytas himself lists astronomy and σφαιρική among the subjects on which σαφὴς διάγνωσις has been handed down by his predecessors (B 1). It is in contradiction with his own words to assume that the views of Archytas on such matters could constitute a radical innovation.

There is then no reason to suppose that the doctrine of a spherical earth was a novelty when the *Phaedo* was written, nor any to doubt Theophrastus' assertion that the same view was held by Parmenides a century earlier.

---

is scarcely credible that Theophrastus was referring to a terminological innovation, or that Parmenides should have used the word στρογγύλος in his hexameters.

II

ELEMENTS AND OPPOSITES: THE MEMBERS OF THE WORLD

In the first chapter we discussed the world scheme of Anaximander on the basis of the more strictly factual information given by the doxographers, where the problem of anachronism scarcely arises. If we are now to penetrate more intimately into the philosophical ideas of sixth-century Miletus, we must deal with another kind of evidence, for which this problem is inevitably posed.

The surviving fragment of Anaximander reaches us embedded in the account of his ἀρχή given by Simplicius. The commentator is at this point closely following the text of Theophrastus, and often citing it word for word. The philosophical "starting-point" of Anaximander, we are told, was "neither water nor any other of the so-called elements, but some different, boundless nature, from which all the heavens arise and the κόσμοι within them." There follows the quotation from Anaximander, after which Simplicius concludes: "It is clear that, having observed the change of the four elements into one another, he did not think fit to make any one of these the material substratum (ὑποκεί-μενον), but something else besides these" (3–6.S.). Thus Simplicius distinctly affirms that, for him, the words of Anaximander explain why no one of the four elements can be identified with the "boundless nature from which all the heavens arise."

A very similar interpretation of Anaximander's doctrine is given by Aristotle, when he speaks of the point of view of "those who say that there is an infinite body which is one and simple . . . besides the elements; from which [body] they generate the latter" (*Phys.* 204^{b}22 = 6.Arist.3). We see that for Aristotle, as for his disciple and commentator, the doctrine of Anaximander is defined by reference to the elements.

At the same time, it is clear that the concept of elements has its history, and that the "elements" of the sixth century are not quite the same as those of Aristotle. In order to interpret what Aristotle and Simplicius tell us concerning Anaximander, we must find our way back from the classical conception of the elements to the point of view of Greek natural philosophy in the earliest period.

The term itself of "element"—στοιχεῖον—is of no direct significance for our problem. In Greek, as afterwards in Latin, this expression is based on a comparison of the physical principles to the letters of the alphabet (the primary meaning of τὰ στοιχεῖα).[1] This comparison seems to have been introduced by the atomists. Thus Aristotle repeatedly cites the diverse ways in which letters may be arranged to form words and written texts in order to illustrate the infinite creative power of the atoms, and the same example is regularly employed by Lucretius.[2] Plato was the first to make use of the term in a systematic way, but with him the comparison to the letters was still clearly borne in mind.[3] Only with Aristotle does στοιχεῖα appear as an abstract expression whose metaphorical value has been largely forgotten.

What concerns us here is neither this comparatively late terminology nor the image on which it is based, but the larger conception which both serve to express. This conception is a complex one, and any account of its development must carefully distinguish between those ideas concerning the elements which are so ancient as to be dateless and those which (like the metaphor just mentioned) took shape within the recorded history of Greek thought.

These separate aspects of the concept of elements can best be analyzed in the case of Aristotle. When the latter speaks of "the so-called elements," he has in mind the classic tetrad of earth, water, air, and fire. Since these are for him not true elements, he uses the word with some reserve: τὰ καλούμενα (or λεγόμενα) στοιχεῖα. What Aristotle properly designates as an "element" is the primary, simple ingredient of a composite thing (*Met.* 1014ᵃ26 ff.). In his view, the true elements of the natural world are not these concrete bodies of earth, water, and the rest, but the four chief physical opposites: Hot, Cold, Dry, and Wet. It is from the combination of these opposing principles that the four elemental bodies arise. For Aristotle, then, we must distinguish three things: (1) the tetrad of earth, water, air, and fire, which are described

---

[1] For the history of the term στοιχεῖον, see H. Diels, *Elementum* (Leipzig, 1899); the original sense is discussed there, pp. 58 ff.

[2] Arist. *Gen. Corr.* 315ᵇ14; *Met.* 985ᵇ17; fr. 208 (= *Vors.* 68 A 37): ἐκ τούτων οὖν ἤδη καθάπερ ἐκ στοιχείων, "from the atoms as if from letters" (in reference to Democritus). Lucr. 1.196, 823, etc. Cf. Diels, *Elementum*, pp. 5–14.

[3] "We speak of them [fire, water, air, and earth] as στοιχεῖα of the universe, although they may not be fittingly compared even to syllables" (*Tim.* 48b–c). This terminology is said by Simplicius (on the authority of Eudemus) to have been original with Plato (*in Phys.* 7.13 = Eudemus fr. 31, Wehrli); confirmed by Diels, *Elementum*, pp. 14 ff. For the Aristotelian usage, *ibid.*, pp. 23 ff.

as the "so-called elements"; (2) the idea of an element as such; and (3) the primary opposites, which best deserve this name.

All three of these ideas must be studied here. Of course, we cannot trace in detail the history of each one from Homer to Aristotle. Our attention must be directed to the broad outlines, and to those features which are most important for the earlier cosmology. In dealing with the classical doctrine we shall therefore be less concerned with the individual point of view which distinguishes one author from another, than with those general traits that characterize the theory as a whole.

Empedocles has first claim to our attention, since he is said to have introduced the standard doctrine of the four elements. This assertion is made by Aristotle, and has been generally accepted by modern scholars.[1] In so far as it is correct, the concept of the elements obviously cannot be ascribed to earlier philosophers such as Anaximander. It is the originality of Empedocles which we must put to the test, in order to see where his personal contribution lay and what conceptions had been developed before him.

From the time of Empedocles down to that of Aristotle, Greek views on the subject of the elements are abundantly documented. The conceptions of the earlier period, on the other hand, must be reconstructed from partial and indirect evidence. In order then to pass safely from the known to the less known, we shall begin with an analysis of the classical theory of the elements. Only when these well-attested ideas have been clearly brought to mind can we turn our gaze from Empedocles backwards, in search of the origins of this theory and of the most likely meaning of the "elements" for Anaximander.

The Classic Doctrine

We have distinguished three aspects of the doctrine of elements. (1) the primary importance of earth, water, air, and fire; (2) the idea of an element as such; and (3) the role of the opposites in a general theory of natural change. In the classical view these three conceptions are inextricably combined, but the distinction between them is indispensable for clarity of exposition. Above all, the question of historical origins must be posed separately for each notion in turn, if the complex threads of the development are to be successfully unraveled.

THE FOUR ELEMENTS. The standard conception of the elements presupposes a division of the visible universe into the four great masses of

---

[1] *Met.* 985ª32; cf. 984ª8. See Zeller I⁵, 758 ff.; Burnet, p. 228; Diels, *Elementum*, p. 15.

Earth, Sea, Air, and the upper atmosphere or sky, considered as a form of Fire. The elements thus appear, in the expression of Lucretius, as "the great limbs of the world," *maxima membra mundi* (v.243). This mode of speech is familiar to Plato, who says that the four elements taken together compose the "body" (σῶμα) of the universe, just as our own body is formed of fire, water, breath, and earth (*Phil.* 29a–e). The metaphor derives no doubt from Empedocles himself, who speaks on several occasions of the "limbs" or "members" of the cosmic Sphere.[1] This imagery does not prevent the poet (and those who follow him) from also conceiving the cosmic bodies concretely, as stratified sections of the world. The canonical sequence of the elements, beginning with earth and ending with fire, presents them precisely in this order of ascending layers—more precisely, as concentric rings grouped outwards around the earth. This notion, too, is attested for Empedocles.[2]

The view of the four elements as members or sections of the world's body comes more and more to dominate the natural philosophy of antiquity. There is, however, another aspect of the classic four which, in the earlier period at any rate, is no less important; that is the process of their mutual and continual transformation. Plato, for instance, writes in the *Timaeus*:

In the first place we see what we have just now called water solidifying *as we think*, and becoming stones and earth; and then this same thing melting and decomposed again into breath and air; air then is consumed as fire. But fire in its turn is collected together, quenched, and returns again to the form of air; and air again contracts and condenses as cloud and mist; from these it is yet more compressed and flows as water. But out of water come earth and stones back again, thus handing on, *as it would seem*, their generation to one another in a circle. (49b–c)

By his repeated qualification Plato obviously intends to present this not as a doctrine of his own, but as the current view of what takes place before our eyes. (In the same dialogue, he denies that earth is ever really transformed into the other three: 56d.5.) In the *Phaedo* also we find the change of one thing into another described as "going round as it were in a circle" (72b.1). This image, too, was already used by Empedocles, who claims, however, that such transformation constitutes only one aspect of the truth:

[1] *Μέλεα* Emped. B 27a, B 30.1, B 35.11; γυῖα B 31 (cf. B 27, B 29). This usage can be traced back to the poem of Parmenides if κρᾶσις μελέων πολυπλάγκτων in Parm. B 16 refers to the blending of world-members or elements, as several authors have suggested (see Jean Bollack, "Sur deux fragments de Parménide," *Revue des études grecques*, LXX [1957], 67). The corresponding expression in early technical prose is μοῖραι, portions or "shares" of the world. See Hp. *De Hebd.* 1–2; *De Carn.* 2.

[2] Emped. B 38, translated below, p. 125.

They rule in turn as the wheel revolves, and wane into one another and wax as their turn comes round . . . in so far thus as they are wont to grow into one from many, or, as the One grows apart, they become many once more, so far they are generated and possess no lasting lifetime; but in so far as these things never cease their perpetual change, so far they are for ever, unmoved throughout the circle.[1]

Against a different philosophic background, the cycle of elemental change appears to Aristotle also as an approximation to immortality. Not only does the eternal revolution of the heavenly sphere serve for him as motive cause of sublunary change, but it offers at the same time a goal of complete corporeal actuality, towards which all bodies strive:

Therefore all other things which change into one another according to their properties and powers, as do, for instance, the simple bodies—all these imitate the circular motion. For when air is produced out of water and fire out of air, and when water arises again from fire, we say that generation has gone round in a circle, since it turns back to where it began. Thus even linear motion is continuous by imitating motion in a circle. (*Gen. Corr.* 337ᵃ1–7)

This continuous transformation of one element into another is treated as an established fact of observation even by those thinkers for whom the four elements as such are of no fundamental importance. Thus Melissus argues that the apparent plurality of the natural world cannot be real, for if "earth and water and air and fire . . . and the rest" were true realities, they would never change; but it appears to us "that all these things are in process of change (ἑτεροιοῦσθαι) . . . and that earth and stone are produced out of water" (B 8). From a different but comparable point of view, Diogenes of Apollonia reasons that all these changing forms must be derivative and temporary modifications of one everlasting reality:

For if the things now existing in this world, earth and water and air and fire and all other things which are observed to exist in this world, if any one of these were different from another—really different in its own nature, and not the same real thing which changes and is altered in many ways—then they would be unable to mingle with one another at all, or to be any help or harm to another; neither would any plant grow from the earth nor any animal or any other thing be born, if they were not so constituted as to be really the same thing. But all these things arise by alteration (ἑτεροιούμενα) out of the same thing, become different at different times, and return back to the same thing. (B 2)

We shall have occasion later to return to these statements of Diogenes

---

[1] B 26. I read a comma after αἰὲν ἔασιν (v. 12) to give the Homeric expression of immortality its full weight (cf. θεοὶ αἰὲν ἐόντες; so ἔμπεδος αἰών here in v. 10).

and Melissus. Here it may be remarked that the two men proceed to draw diametrically opposed conclusions from a common observed fact. Melissus argues that if the multiple things were real they could not change; Diogenes' point is that if these things were *really different* from one another, they could not change or combine to produce anything else. But the minor premise is identical for each: the change of natural things into one another is a direct datum of experience. In both cases this process of change is expressed by the same word (ἐτεροιοῦσθαι), and the four elements are named each time as one example (among others) of things undergoing mutual transformation.

It would be possible to argue that Diogenes has been influenced here by Melissus. But such an hypothesis is superfluous, since the view which the two men share is truly universal in Greek thought. Besides the passages of Aristotle and Plato just cited we may recall the words of the *Theaetetus*, which inform us that "Protagoras and Heraclitus and Empedocles and all the wise men except Parmenides" believe that the world is in a state of motion and flux (152e). And the flux of nature is above all an incessant course of the elements into one another.

In this connection the four elements appear less as the *maxima membra mundi* than as the principal phases or forms of natural change. And this view of them is perhaps even more widely held than the other. For although earth, water, air, and fire are named in canonical order by both Melissus and Diogenes, neither treats these four terms as an exhaustive table of contents for the visible world.

ELEMENTS IN GENERAL. So far, we have been dealing with "what are called the elements" without in fact regarding them as such. In the full sense of the word, an element is more than a member of the world or a factor in natural change. Στοιχεῖον, says Aristotle, is "that out of which a thing is composed, which is contained in it as primary constituent, and which cannot be resolved further into something different in kind."[1] This definition is systematic rather than historical. It is, in fact, so rigorous that the four primary bodies are not true elements for Aristotle, who, as we have seen, normally refers to them as the "so-called elements."

But Aristotle's definition suggests something which is also essential for Empedocles. The latter's "four roots of all things" (B 6) are not identical with the great cosmic masses. In the first place, they are more general: the element of fire appears in the domestic hearth, the smithy's

---

[1] *Met.* Δ 3; cf. *De Caelo* 302ᵃ15.

forge, and the altar flame, as well as in the lightning flash or the sun, just as elemental water is found in wells and mountain springs no less than in the sea. Furthermore, they are more primary and fundamental than the bodies in nature; hence their description as the "roots" from which all things are sprung.

In this sense, the elements are clearly distinguished by Empedocles from the cosmic masses which represent them. The text of fragment 38 is partially corrupt, but the general sense is not in doubt:

Come then, I shall tell you what things are first and of one age from the beginning, out of which lo! is arisen all that we see now before us: Earth and the many-wavèd Sea and moist Air and the Titan Sky binding the whole circle fast about.[1]

The visible *membra mundi* are here set over against their source, the primeval elements, of which they constitute the most divine manifestation in this mortal world where the deathless gods put on perishable forms (B 35.14).

This priority of the true elements is evident above all in the role they play in combination. Μίξις τε διάλλαξίς τε μιγέντων, "mingling and the separation of things mixed"—such is for Empedocles the theme of elemental change.[2] The existence of compound things is implied by the very notion of an element: that out of which such things are composed. "For out of these [arises] all that is and was and will be" (B 21.9). So Empedocles compares the endless variety of physical combination to the manifold forms brought forth by the painter, all of which issue from a small number of colors (B 23). The human body and its parts are formed from the same source as the massive world (B 20, B 96–98). As has been seen, the atomists replace Empedocles' illustration from painting with one from writing: opposite things can arise from a slight rearrangement of particles, just as "tragedy and comedy are formed out of the same letters" (*Gen. Corr.* 315^{b}14). And such a comparison gives the "elements" their name.

If this doctrine of mixture and separation is an essential feature in the Empedoclean concept of the elements, it appears at the same time independently of his view. The concepts of μίξις and διάκρισις are no less essential for Anaxagoras and the atomists, in whose doctrines the four elements as such are of no primary significance. On the other hand, the

---

[1] B 38. Developing the suggestion of Diels, the first verse may be restored approximately as follows: Εἰ δ' ἄγε τοι λέξω τά τε πρῶτα καὶ ἥλικα ἀρχήν. In the second verse I follow P. Friedländer in keeping the MS. reading, ἐξ ὧν δὴ ἐγένοντο. [2] B 8. The correct sense for διάλλαξις ("separation") is given by LSJ, against Diels and Burnet ("interchange").

Empedoclean tetrad may also appear in a context from which any notion of elemental combination is excluded. Thus the Hippocratic treatise *De Natura Hominis* opens with an unexpected denial: "I do not say that man is altogether air nor fire nor water nor earth"; and the author goes on to pour out his contempt upon those theorists, "one of whom says that the One and the whole universe is Air, another says Fire, another Water, another Earth . . ." (ch. 1). We see that this writer of the late fifth century (who was identified by Aristotle and by his disciple Meno as Polybus, son-in-law of Hippocrates[1]) mentions the canonical four not in reference to the Empedoclean theory at all, but in describing monistic doctrines of the type proposed by Diogenes of Apollonia. In such a case, the four appear as "elements" only in the sense that one or the other of them serves to represent a reality more fundamental than the visible multiplicity of things. Here again we see that the doctrine of Empedocles gives a special interpretation to ideas which were widely current in other forms.

THE OPPOSITES. In so far as a theory of the elements seeks to give not only a description but a causal explanation of natural change, it is incomplete without an account of the opposites (τὰ ἐναντία). For it is they which represent the powers (δυνάμεις) by which one element acts upon another. The importance of this conception in Greek thought has often been recognized but rarely discussed.[2] It must therefore be treated here at some length.

If we disregard the curious table of ten pairs ascribed by Aristotle to certain Pythagoreans (*Met. A* 5), the opposites cannot in general be limited to any fixed number. Nevertheless, a unique importance attaches to the two couples of Hot-Cold and Dry-Wet. It is in terms of these four primary opposites that Aristotle defines the elemental bodies. It is in fact these two pairs of principles which for him most truly deserve the name of "elements."[3] Their derivatives, the simple bodies, are formed by the linking together of one member from each pair: fire is constituted by the hot and the dry; air by the hot and the wet; water, the cold and the wet; earth, the cold and the dry (*Gen. Corr.* II.3).

---

[1] Arist. *Hist. An.* 512[b]12; *Anonymus Londinensis* XIX.2, edited by W. H. S. Jones as *The Medical Writings of Anonymus Londinensis* (Cambridge, 1947), p. 74. (The apparent ascription of the same work to Hippocrates at *Anon. Lond.* VII.15, p. 40, Jones, represents not the view of Meno but an uncritical addition of the excerptor.) The Aristotelian attribution to Polybus was rejected by C. Fredrich, *Hippokratische Untersuchungen* (Berlin, 1899), pp. 50 ff.; successfully defended by K. Deichgräber, "Die Epidemien und das Corpus Hippocraticum," *Abhandlungen der preussischen Akademie der Wissenschaften*, 1933, pp. 105 ff.

[2] For the notion of natural powers, see J. Souilhé, *Étude sur le terme δύναμις* (Paris, 1919), especially the Hippocratic texts cited pp. 32–56.

[3] *Gen. Corr.* 330[a]30, 33: cf. 329[a]29–35.

Thus each simple body has one decisive quality in common with, one opposed to, its neighbor on either side. The two extreme bodies (fire and earth) also have a common feature, while there are two pairs which are formed only by opposing qualities: fire (hot and dry) and water (cold and wet); earth (cold and dry) and air (hot and wet).

The system of Empedocles does not seem to have been so neat. It is at any rate only imperfectly known to us from the fragments. But one of these makes clear that his elemental bodies were also characterized by qualitative opposites, including the two primary pairs:

First the Sun, bright to behold and hot in every way; then the Deathless Ones drenched in warmth and in the brilliant beam; and Rain, darkish and chill in all things; while from the Earth stream forth things rooted and solid (B 21.3–6).

If we may judge from these lines, water ("Rain") and fire (the "Sun") are defined by opposite qualities as for Aristotle. These qualities include hot and cold in both cases, but for Empedocles the second pair is bright-dark instead of dry-wet. The air, or rather its particles, bathed in the heat and light of celestial fire, are strangely referred to as ἄμβροτα, "deathless ones."[1] The earth, as source of solidity and of the roots of growing things (including animals, whose origin was from earth, B 62), seems to stand apart from the other three, just as it does in the *Timaeus*.

If the complete poem of Empedocles had survived, we might see that his theory was as fully articulated as that of Aristotle. It would in any case be more complex. Other fragments permit us to catch a glimpse of the causal role ascribed to the hot and cold, the dense and rare, and to the qualities of taste—bitter, sweet, and others.[2] The Aristotelian doctrine of the primary opposites probably took shape as an intentional simplification of this Empedoclean scheme. But, if so, it was certainly not the first adaptation of this kind. The Hippocratic treatise *De Carnibus*, for example, identifies celestial fire (called αἰθήρ) as chief concentration of the hot, earth as cold and dry, air as hot and wet, while water (which is not expressly named in the extant text) is described as "what is dampest and thickest."[3] A still simpler view is assigned to

---

[1] This expression seems to imply that the air is the seat of life for Empedocles, and presumably the source of the life-spirit or ψυχή (see above, p. 114). In a sense, all living things can be called deathless by one who holds the doctrine of transmigration.

[2] See Emped. B 65, B 67, B 75, B 90, B 104, etc.

[3] *De Carn.* 2 (Littré, VIII, 584). Probably no

one would any longer defend Zeller's view (II.ii², 441, n. 2) that this doctrine of the elements is borrowed from Aristotle. The latest editor of the *De Carnibus* places it at the end of the fifth century; see K. Deichgräber, *Hippokrates über Entstehung und Aufbau des menschlichen Körpers* (Leipzig, 1935), p. 27, with n. 4.

Philistion by the *Anonymus Londinensis*: fire is hot, air cold, water moist, and earth dry.[1]

The use of the opposites, and above all of the primary pairs, is much more widespread than any particular theory of the elements. The author of *De Victu* wishes to explain all biological processes in terms of fire and water alone, but he too defines the former as hot and dry, the latter as cold and wet.[2] The doctors who are mentioned in *De Natura Hominis* as ascribing man's nature to a single constituent part believe that this "changes its form and power under the necessity of the hot and the cold, and becomes sweet and bitter, bright and dark, and of every sort" (ch. 2; Jones IV, 6). The writer himself (Polybus) declares that "there are many things present in the body which produce diseases when they are heated by one another contrary to nature, or cooled or dried or moistened" (*ibid.*). He is referring not to the cosmic elements, but to the four fluids or "humors" of classical medicine, of which phlegm is the coldest, blood is moist and warm. According to Polybus, each of these four humors varies with the heat and moisture of the different seasons (ch. 7; Jones, IV, 18 ff.).

The opposites in some form are invoked by every writer in the Hippocratic Corpus who attempts a causal explanation. Their use may be seen, for instance, in the account of epileptic seizure given by the author of *The Sacred Disease*:

[The symptoms occur] when cold phlegm streams into the blood, which is warm; for it chills the blood and stops its flow. And if the stream is great and thick, death takes place immediately; for it overpowers the blood by its coldness and solidifies it. But if the stream of phlegm is less considerable, it overpowers the blood temporarily and cuts off respiration; then as it is gradually dispersed into the veins and mingled with a great deal of warm blood, if it is itself overpowered in this way, the veins receive air and consciousness is restored. (ch. 10; Jones, II, 160–62)

The morbid effects are ascribed to the paralyzing coldness of the

---

[1] *Anon. Lond.* xx.25, Jones, *Medical Writings*, p. 80. (It may, I think, be doubted whether Philistion's view can have been quite so crude. How, for example, could steam be explained if the air were *only* cold?) Ἀήρ was conceived as primarily cold in opposition to αἰθήρ. Its coldness reappears in the Pythagorean doctrine at D.L. viii.27 (= *Vors.* 58 B 1a): καλοῦσι δὲ τὸν μὲν ἀέρα ψυχρὸν αἰθέρα, τὴν δὲ θάλασσαν καὶ τὸ ὑγρὸν παχὺν αἰθέρα. (The last point recalls *De Carn.* 2, where we have ὑγρότατόν τε καὶ παχύτατον for the watery element.) Philistion's doctrine of the elements seems to have

been the one taken over by the Stoics, judging from D.L. vii.137. But for the additional qualities of air in the Stoic scheme, see the other texts cited by Zeller, iii.1³, 183, n. 2.

[2] *De Victu* 4, Jones, IV, 232. Compare the role of hot and cold, accompanied by dry and wet, for Petron of Aegina (*Anon. Lond.* xx.2, Jones, *Medical Writings*, p. 78); the hot and cold for Menecrates Zeus (*ibid.* xix.24, p. 76); the hot alone for Philolaus (*ibid.* xviii.10, p. 72); the moist and dry for Hippon (*ibid.* xi.23, p. 52), etc.

phlegm. They may be counteracted by the vital heat of the blood. Even an author like that of *Ancient Medicine*, who rejects all doctrinaire usage of the hot, cold, wet, and dry (chs. 1 and 15), and who claims paradoxically that "hot and cold have the least dominion of all powers in the body" (ch. 16; Jones, I, 42)—even he must attribute disease not only to diverse bodily structures, but also to "the powers of the humors"; that is, to an excess of the sweet, bitter, salty, sharp, or other qualities, which change into one another (chs. 22 and 24). For him, the hot and cold do not exist apart but only combined with these other "powers standing in opposition to one another" (δυνάμιας ἑωυτῇσιν ὑπεναντίας, ch. 15; Jones, I, 40).

It is in this general way that Plato can speak of the material causes used by most thinkers (which are for him only subsidiary causes, συναίτια) as "that which cools and heats and solidifies and dissolves, and other things producing results of this kind."[1] The cold is universally conceived as the power leading to contraction and solidification; the hot produces dissolution, motion, and expansion.[2] Therefore in Aristotle's scheme the hot and cold are active forces, while the wet and dry are acted upon by them (*Meteor.* IV.1). In this central role which he ascribes to the primary opposites, Aristotle is following and systemizing the purest tradition of Ionian natural philosophy. His doctrine of the elements in general is more true to the spirit of early Greek thought than is usually realized. It is only Democritus and Plato who (in principle, at least) reject the qualitative explanation of Nature and insist that, since this aspect of things is relative to human sensation, the rational knowledge of the world must go deeper: to atoms and the void for Democritus (B 9, B 125), to the geometrical structure of the elements for Plato in the *Timaeus*. In this respect Democritus and Plato anticipate the modern point of view, while Aristotle is a true "ancient." This revolutionary character of the atomic theory was well appreciated by Theophrastus, who stated that "Democritus had recourse to the atoms on the grounds that those who explain causation according to the hot, the cold, and other things of this sort give an unscientific account."[3] This attitude of Democritus was not only a novelty, but also a rarity in

---

[1] *Tim.* 46d.2. The primary opposites also represent the forces of physical necessity (ἀνάγκη) at *Laws* 889b.5 ff.

[2] See, e.g., Archelaus B 1a: ἡ ψυχρότης δεσμός ἐστιν (cf. A 4.2); *De Carn.* 3 (Littré, VIII, 588): τὸ μὲν ψυχρὸν πήγνυσιν· τὸ δὲ θερμὸν διαχέει; also Arist. *Gen. Corr.* 336ª3, etc.

[3] *Phys. Opin.* fr. 13 (*Dox.* 491): Δημόκριτος δέ, ὡς Θεόφραστος ἐν τοῖς Φυσικοῖς ἱστορεῖ, ὡς ἰδιωτικῶς ἀποδιδόντων τῶν κατὰ τὸ θερμὸν καὶ τὸ ψυχρὸν καὶ τὰ τοιαῦτα αἰτιολογούντων ἐπὶ τὰς ἀτόμους ἀνέβη. For the sense of ἰδιωτικῶς, "like a layman," cf. *Gen. Corr.* 315ᵇ1: οὐδεὶς οὐδὲν διώρισεν ... ὅ τι μὴ κἂν ὁ τυχὼν εἴπειεν.

ancient times. Even an atomist like Lucretius shows, in the whole fabric of his poem, that the imaginative basis of the old qualitative view of Nature had not been undermined by such an abstract denial.

In the theory of Aristotle the four elements are characterized by opposition to one another (*Gen. Corr.* 331ᵃ15). The transformation of one body into another takes place when one of the two essential qualities gives way to its opposite. Air becomes fire when its moisture is dried, as earth becomes fire when its coldness is heated. Now the metaphor which gave rise to the name τὰ ἐναντία is that of hostile warriors facing each other in battle: οἱ δ' ἐλελίχθησαν καὶ ἐναντίοι ἔσταν Ἀχαιῶν "The Trojans whirled about, and stood to face the Achaeans" (*E* 497). From such uses as this, οἱ ἐναντίοι comes to mean "the opponents," "the enemy." General expressions such as τἀναντία εἰπεῖν, ποιεῖν are current from the time of Aeschylus for doing or saying what is hostile, i.e., contrary, to something else done or intended.[1] But if the opposites are really "opponents," their confrontation is a battle. Even in the scholarly language of the Lyceum this imagery persists. If, says Aristotle, fire becomes air and air becomes water, it is because the dry has been "overpowered" (κρατηθέν) by the damp, the hot by the cold (*Gen. Corr.* 331ᵃ28–35, and *passim*).

Such a reference to the prevailing (κρατεῖν) of one opposite over another implies the old conception of them as δυνάμεις or active powers. It is a similar metaphor which appears when the suppression of any quality is called its "ruin" or "destruction," φθορά. This idea too has, of course, left its trace in Aristotle's technical treatises, where φθαρῆναι is the reciprocal of κρατεῖν (*Gen. Corr.* 331ᵇ1, 8, 9, 12, etc.). The metaphor is naturally much more conspicuous in the style of Plato:

And again, when a small amount of fire is surrounded by a great deal of air or waters or some form of earth, and is carried among them in their own motion, when it is thus embattled and defeated, it is shattered to pieces, and two bodies of fire combine to form one of air. And as air is mastered and dashed to bits, from two-and-a-half pieces of air one of water will be composed. . . . As long as an element comes into contact with another, and being weaker yields to the stronger in battle, it is unceasingly dissolved. (*Timaeus* 56e ff.)

In the conflict of opposites—and of the elements which they characterize—the weaker power will require succor or support (βοήθεια) if it is not to meet destruction at the hands of the stronger. The author of

---

[1] τἀναντί' εἰπεῖν, Aesch. *Ag.* 1373. Cf. *Sacred Disease* 4 (Jones, II, 148): τἀναντία τούτων ποιεῖν; Democr. B 234 τἀναντία πρήσσοντες.

Ancient Medicine reports that those innovators who believe that it is hot or cold or dry or wet which harms a man's body infer that the proper function of the physician is "to come to the aid of the hot against the cold, the cold against the hot," and so forth (ch. 13; Jones, I, 34). The writer insists that this aid is produced spontaneously within the body, and that there is therefore no need of help from the doctor (ch. 16). It must be in the same sense that Diogenes speaks of the elemental bodies receiving "benefit" or "harm" from one another (B 2).

The doctrine attacked by the author of *Ancient Medicine* is defended in many other Hippocratic treatises, which insist that "opposites are cures for opposites" (*De Flat.* 1; Jones, II, 228). The task of the physician is in this case to stand up to the morbid power as to an enemy (ἐναντίον ἵστασθαι), and to treat it by opposite influences (*Nat. Hom.* 9; Jones, IV, 24). As the writer on epilepsy says, "One must, in this disease as in all others, not augment the morbid element but waste it away by applying what is most hostile to each disease, and not what is its associate. For by association it flourishes and is increased, but what is hostile causes it to wither away and become faint" (*The Sacred Disease*, ch. 21; Jones, II, 182). It is this philosophical view of medicine which is played upon in the *Symposium*, where Eryximachus defines the doctor's art as a capacity "to make friends of things inimical in the body and to oblige them to fall in love with one another. Now the things most inimical are those which are most opposite: cold to hot, bitter to sweet, dry to wet, all things of this kind" (186d.5).

The physical role of Eros in the *Symposium* reminds us that Φιλότης also stands beside Νεῖκος in the scheme of Empedocles, the force of elemental attraction balancing the principle of conflict and strife. The most vivid sense of μίξις is that of union in the bonds of love; it is in this way that one elemental deity mingles with another (κατὰ μεῖζον ἐμίσγετο δαίμονι δαίμων, B 59.1). The author of *De Natura Hominis* has the same idea in mind when he asserts that no single principle can explain natural change: "It is necessary that generation take place not from one thing alone. For how could one single thing produce offspring if it were not coupled (μιχθείη) with another?" (ch. 3; Jones, IV, 8). Once more the traditional imagery is most elaborately developed in a Platonic text:

It seems to me that each one of these thinkers tells us a tale as if we were children, one saying that there are three real things of which some occasionally war against one another, and again become friends and offer marriages and offspring and nourishment for their children; but another tells us that there are two things, Wet and Dry or Hot and Cold; and they join these together and marry them off. (*Sophist* 242c–d)

The generation and nourishment which the opposing elements offer to one another or to their children compensates, as it were, for their mutual destruction. In its most banal and widespread form this principle applies to the nourishment of fire or the hot by its opposite, the moist.[1] But the author of *The Sacred Disease* says in general, "One thing is food for another" (ἕτερον γὰρ ἑτέρῳ τροφή ἐστι, ch. 21; Jones, II, 182); and again (under the influence of the south wind), "dull things arise from bright ones, hot things from cold, damp from dry" (ch. 16; Jones, II, 172). So in the *Phaedo*: "In the case of all animals and plants and in general for all things that take part in generation, we see that all come to be in this way: opposites out of opposites and from no other source" (70d–e). For this reason, says Aristotle, "the destruction of one thing is the generation of another."[2]

There are other facets to this many-colored view of natural forces acting together in hostility or collaboration. Friendship, for instance, may bring together not only opponents but also those of one mind, and hence we have the great principle, of universal application: "Like to like."[3] For Empedocles, Love combines unlike things precisely by making them similar to one another (B 22.5). A smooth blending is thus produced in which potentially hostile forces are reconciled like the high and low notes in a musical ἁρμονία. On the basis of this musical analogy, "Harmony" can serve as well as "Aphrodite" to designate the principle of creative unison by which bones, blood, flesh, and living things in general are compounded (Emped. B 20, B 96, B 98, etc.). The ψυχή or life-principle might itself be explained as such a "mixture and harmony" of the primary opposites (*Phaedo* 86b). The theory of health utilized by nearly every Hippocratic writer is of the same form: a normal functioning of the body depends upon the moderate blending and balance of contradictory forces; disease arises when one element oversteps the measure in an aggressive way.[4] Nor is this relationship

---

[1] *De Victu* 3 (Jones, IV, 232) and *passim*; cf. *De Flat.* 3 (Jones, II, 230), where πνεῦμα is the food of fire. See also Thales A 12–13. It is obvious that fire must be fed by something.

[2] τὴν τοῦδε φθορὰν ἄλλου εἶναι γένεσιν, *Gen. Corr.* 318ᵃ23. For the generation of opposites from opposites, see *ibid.* 331ᵃ14, and the parallels cited Bonitz, *Index*, 148ᵃ5 ff.

[3] For the attraction of like to like (and the corresponding repulsion of unlikes) see Emped. B 62.6, B 90, B 110.9; Anaxag. B 15; Democr. B 164; Plato *Tim.* 53a.4–6; *De Victu* 6 (Jones, IV, 238–40).

[4] For the doctrine of health as an equilibrium, see, e.g., *Nat. Hom.* 4 (Jones, IV, 10 f.): *Anc. Med.* 16 (Jones, I, 42); Plato, *Tim.* 82a; it can be

restricted to the human body. The condition of living things depends upon the influence of the cosmic forces, which vary according to the year, the season, and the local climate.[1] In the healthiest climate (such as that of Ionia) no single force is dominant, but there prevails an equal distribution (ἰσομοιρίη) of hot, cold, and the rest.[2]

There is practically no limit to the number of texts which could be cited in illustration of this view of nature as a dynamic interplay between conflicting powers. Nothing could be more misleading than to treat it as an external embellishment, the dramatic embroidery set by Empedocles and Plato upon an essentially prosaic view of mechanical causation. The most abundant texts are precisely those in which the spirit of fifth-century naturalism expresses itself most fully and most simply: the medical writings of the Hippocratic Corpus. As Diels pointed out, the Greek theory of the elements is founded upon the notion of opposites, from the earliest extant fragments until late antiquity.[3] But the opposites themselves imply a world full of conflict and full of life.

The Origins

Turning now to the sources of this theory, we are obliged to begin with the beginning, that is to say, with Homer and Hesiod. An omission of this pre-philosophic background could only result in a double distortion of the historic picture. In the first place, we know as a general principle in the history of ideas that the appearance of complete novelty *ex nihilo* is a thing to be looked upon with great suspicion. The idea of Greek rationalism suddenly bursting forth from sixth-century Ionia, like Athena from the brain of Zeus, is one of those historical naïvetés which are no longer very much in fashion. This birth no doubt followed in the normal way, upon conception; the maternal soil of Hellas was fertilized by Mesopotamian seed. On the other hand, the hereditary features of Ionian thought were not obliterated in any lifetime or even in any century. The originality which any one man can

traced back as far as Alcmaeon B 4. A full discussion is offered by A. Keus, *Ueber philosophische Begriffe und Theorien in den hippokratischen Schriften* (Bonn dissertation, 1914), pp. 58–66; see also G. Vlastos, *CP*, XLII (1947), 156 ff.

[1] *De Aëribus* 1 (Jones, I, 70); *Epid.* iii.16 (Jones, I, 256); *Nat. Hom.* 7 (Jones, IV, 18 ff.); *De Victu* 2 (Jones, IV, 228); etc.

[2] *De Aëribus* 12 (Jones, I, 106); Hdt. 1.142; cf. Plato, *Tim.* 24c.6.

[3] "Beachtenswert ist, daß Heraklit die Gegensatzpaare Kalt-Warm, Naß-Trocken bereits typisch zusammengestellt hat (fr. 126). Das ist die reale Grundlage der Elementarphysik im ganzen Altertum geblieben." (Diels, *Elementum*, p. 15, n. 3.)

show is astonishingly small, when measured against the enormous mass of ideas for which he is dependent on the past. And the past upon which the Milesians drew was still very largely the world of Homer and of Hesiod.

It is not only the historical plausibility of the picture that would suffer from a treatment that begins with Thales. The very possibility of understanding sixth-century ideas, where the documentation is so sadly lacking, depends upon our fuller knowledge of the older poetic outlook. It is only by placing the Milesians in between the two regions of light provided by archaic poetry on one hand and classical philosophy on the other—by thus illuminating them, as it were, from above as well as from below—that we may have any hope of seeing a bit deeper into this dark period of transition and creation.

The discussion then must lead back to the epic. But there can be no question here of analyzing all the cosmological ideas of the old poets. An exhaustive analysis is in any case probably impossible, for the essence of a poetic view is its extreme suppleness and adaptability to the mood and intention of the poet. In a sense, there are as many views of the universe in Homer and Hesiod as there are passages where the poets touch upon such matters. All we can do here is to consider a few texts of special interest for the later conception of the elements, and to determine the original sense of certain key words. We may best deal in turn with the three aspects of the classic theory which have already been distinguished, and attempt to retrace the stages by which each one of these notions reached its mature form.

THE FOUR ELEMENTS (ORIGINS). The conception of the natural world as composed essentially of earth, water, air, and fire is not of immemorial antiquity. The only obvious and universal division of the world is into Heaven and Earth. The parallel between these two is, of course, familiar to mythic thought in many lands, which loves to depict them as a divine couple whose fruitful union leads to the birth of the other gods and of everything that exists. The polar contrast between the two realms was emphasized in Indo-European tongues by a name for the gods derived from the root "heaven," and by one for men from that of "earth."[1] In recognition of this fact, Hesiod speaks of οὐρανός as "a seat for the blessed gods set firm for ever" (*Theog.* 128), just as γαῖα is

[1] See the discussion of Meillet, *Introduction à l'étude comparative des langues indo-européennes*[8] (Paris, 1949), pp. 399 f.; also *Linguistique historique et linguistique générale* (Paris, 1921), pp. 274 ff., 326 ff. The idea remains alive in Greek, despite the weak etymological link; e.g., *Theog.* 272; Hom. ζ 153, θ 222, λ 461.

"a seat for all set firm forever" (*Theog.* 117). When represented concretely, heaven serves as a kind of earth for the gods, who are οὐρανίωνες, "dwellers in heaven," while mortals are characteristically ἐπιχθόνιοι, "those who tread upon the earth" (cf. *Theog.* 372 f.).

These two great "seats" are obviously separated by a zone or region less easy to define, which is designated in the Rigveda by the happy expression *antárikṣa*, "the dwelling-place in between." In this ancient Indian view we can recognize a neat classification of the world into ascending regions or strata. "The triple division is the favorite one in the Rigveda, which loves triads, and, when it is accepted, the solar phenomena are assigned to the heaven, and those of lightning, rain, and wind to the atmosphere, while in the simpler twofold division all are ascribed to the sky."[1] Similar notions occur in ancient Egypt and Mesopotamia, where a divinity of the storm or wind stands between the gods of heaven and earth.[2]

Such a scheme can acquire little importance in the face of the extreme anthropomorphism which characterizes the epic view of the gods. Zeus is, of course, supposed to be a cloud-gatherer whose delight is in the thunderbolt, but the poets rarely depict him in such activities, unless the interests of his particular friends or enemies are at stake. The Homeric gods, even those whose cosmic responsibilities are most obvious, are generally loath to take part in the ordinary operation of the universe. As far as the natural world is concerned, they are well on their way to becoming the *dei otiosi* of the Epicureans. The winds, in the *Odyssey*, are kept by Aeolus—that is, by a mortal rather than a god.[3] Furthermore, when heaven and earth are increased to a triad, it is not the atmosphere but the sea which supplies the third member for the Greeks. Thus Hephaestus figures γαῖα, οὐρανός, and θάλασσα on the Shield of Achilles (Σ 483). The sea is a factor which cannot be neglected in a land where almost every city is a port whose horizon is shared between the mountains and the vast expanse of Aegean blue.

A somewhat more speculative, or at any rate more mythical, view of the world appears in the much discussed mention of the δασμός, the great division of the spoil among the three sons of Cronus. Poseidon protests that Zeus has no right to interfere with his actions on earth:

---

[1] A. B. Keith, *The Religion and Philosophy of the Veda and Upanishads* (Cambridge, Mass., 1925), p. 77.
[2] Cf. the role of Shu in Egypt and that of Enlil in Mesopotamia: John A. Wilson and Thorkild

Jacobsen, in *The Intellectual Adventure of Ancient Man* (Chicago, 1946), pp. 46, 137, 140 ff.
[3] κ 2, Αἴολος Ἱπποτάδης, φίλος ἀθανάτοισι θεοῖσι.

τρεῖς γάρ τ' ἐκ Κρόνου εἰμὲν ἀδελφεοί, οὓς τέκετο 'Ρέα,
Ζεὺς καὶ ἐγώ, τρίτατος δ' Ἀΐδης, ἐνέροισιν ἀνάσσων.
τριχθὰ δὲ πάντα δέδασται, ἕκαστος δ' ἔμμορε τιμῆς·
ἤτοι ἐγὼν ἔλαχον πολιὴν ἅλα ναιέμεν αἰεὶ
παλλομένων, Ἀΐδης δ' ἔλαχε ζόφον ἠερόεντα,
Ζεὺς δ' ἔλαχ' οὐρανὸν εὐρὺν ἐν αἰθέρι καὶ νεφέλῃσι·
γαῖα δ' ἔτι ξυνὴ πάντων καὶ μακρὸς Ὄλυμπος. (O 187 ff.)

Therefore, says Poseidon, let Zeus stay in his place.

It must at once be remarked that the three parts into which all things were divided do not constitute a stratified scheme for the visible world. The essential reference point, the earth, is entirely excluded from the δασμός as such. In here recalling or inventing such a division of the spoil, the poet's intention is not speculative but dramatic. He is less concerned to organize the world than to explain why Poseidon should have a free hand to do as he pleases on the earth. A system of strata or regions is suggested only imperfectly, if at all. Hades' realm of darkness and death, for example, seems to lie in the west, as well as beneath the earth.[1]

Nevertheless, if we neglect the ambiguous conception of Olympus (wavering between the Thessalian mountain and an invisible peak in heaven), we see that the poet vaguely presupposes a division of the world into Earth, Sea, Underworld, and Heaven. The same foursome recurs in Hesiod's introduction to the *Theogony*, this time not as passive "lots," but as the primeval powers from which the gods are sprung:

οἳ Γῆς ἐξεγένοντο καὶ Οὐρανοῦ ἀστερόεντος,
Νυκτός τε δνοφερῆς, οὓς θ' ἁλμυρὸς ἔτρεφε Πόντος. (106 f.)

The dismal powers of the dark are in this case represented by Night, the mother of Death and his associates (211 ff.). As in the δασμός episode, the damp element is not water in general but the concrete body of Pontos, the salt sea. Only the Earth possesses here the same name as the later element. A similar fourfold scheme plays a prominent part in several other passages of the *Theogony*, where, because of the context, it is Tartarus who is chosen to represent the dark underworld.[2]

The precedent of this poetic tetrad, familiar to every Greek schoolboy

---

[1] Thus Odysseus can reach the land of the dead by sailing across Ocean, λ 13 ff. The Elysian plain is in the west (δ 563 ff.), and ζόφος ἠερόεις is an expression for the west (M 240), as well as for the share of Hades in the δασμός. The extreme west, beyond the setting of the sun, was—for the Greeks as for other peoples—a mysterious region resembling the equally dark and unknown spaces beneath the earth. (See the similar view of the west at *Theog.* 274 f., 294, 746 ff.)

[2] *Theog.* 678–82, 736 f., 807 f., 839 ff.

from the recitations of Homer and Hesiod, must help to explain how the later doctrine of the four elements as *maxima membra mundi* could meet with such rapid and widespread approval. It is even likely that this traditional notion was instrumental in bringing Empedocles himself to fix upon the number four.[1] But we must not underestimate the deep gulf which separates the old poetic scheme from the classic theory. If the continuous importance of the earth is self-evident, and if the replacement of Sea by "water" scarcely calls for comment, the conception of the other two elements is another thing again. There is as yet scarcely a trace of fire in the Homeric οὐρανός; and it is a long road from ζόφος ἠερόεις to the ἀήρ of fifth-century natural philosophy.

In attempting to follow along this road, we may begin with a consideration of the Homeric οὐρανός, an essential term in every description of the universe. The word has no convincing etymology, and its full meaning can only be gathered from the various contexts in which it is used. The most frequent epithets for the heaven are "broad" (εὐρύς) and "starry" (ἀστερόεις).[2] It is said to be wreathed or garlanded with the stars (Σ 485), or these simply stand "in heaven" (X 318). Not only do the stars appear in heaven, but the moon as well (Θ 555 f.); and the Sun also reaches the middle of οὐρανός in his course (Θ 68; cf. Π 777). So as a signal of disaster the sun is seen to disappear suddenly "out of heaven," either in eclipse or shrouded by dark clouds (υ 356 f.).

No boundary is drawn between celestial and meteorological events. On the contrary, the portion assigned to Zeus in the δασμός is specified as "the broad heaven in αἰθήρ and in the clouds." The activity of Zeus was, of course, always seen in cloud-gathering, in the thunder and lightning of a rainstorm, and indeed in any atmospheric event such as the appearance of a rainbow (Λ 27 f.). The wide extension of the term οὐρανός frequently permits it to be used by the poet with some exaggeration. Thus not only high cliffs but also dust, smoke, and the scent (κνίση) of sacrifice are spoken of as "reaching to heaven."[3] It may be said that the οὐρανός designates in general everything that is above men's heads. In particular it indicates the zenith, the region above par excellence, as when Nestor and Agamemnon utter prayers to Zeus with their hands and eyes directed upwards "towards heaven" (O 371; T 254).

---

[1] The importance of the Homeric δασμός for the history of Greek philosophy was emphasized (and exaggerated) by F. M. Cornford, *From Religion to Philosophy* (London, 1912), pp. 15 ff., 21 ff., and *passim*.

[2] For the "starry heavens," see Δ 44, E 769

(= Θ 46), O 371. In each case the phrase is a conventional verse ending, without any particular reference to the night sky.

[3] μ 73, E 504, A 317, Θ 549; cf. B 457, P 425, etc.

A clear sky by day or, above all, by night seems to us to resemble a great vaulted dome, and it is often said that the Homeric οὐρανός too was conceived as a kind of hemisphere. There is, however, very little support for this view in the text of the epic.[1] On the contrary, to the poet's eye the visible sky presents no closed space, but fades imperceptibly into that distant region whose form can be discerned by the inspired imagination, and by it alone. When a Greek sought to picture this heaven of the gods, the image of a vaulted roof or dome would not occur to him as readily as to us. Homer has no word for such a vault. A Greek roof is normally flat or pitched.[2] In so far as heaven was visualized as a roof for the world, it would naturally be conceived as a plane rather than as a curved surface. This is confirmed, for instance, by Hesiod's reference to οὐρανός as "a seat for the gods set firm forever." The gods would be safer on a flat roof than on a dome.

As we have mentioned, οὐρανός seems at times to float before the poet's mind like an invisible counterpart to the floor of the earth. The land of the gods, culminating in the mountain Olympus, resembles the land of men reproduced on an upper storey.[3] And this idea fits the

---

[1] The view of οὐρανός as a dome or vault is given, for instance, by E. Buchholz, *Homerische Realien* (Leipzig, 1871), I, 3, referring to J. H. Voss, *Mythologische Briefe* (Königsberg, 1794), p. 170, who in turn takes for granted "das öde Gewölbe des ehernen Himmels"; similarly Heath, *Aristarchus*, p. 7. The various references to the sun's rising and setting do not tell us anything about the shape of the οὐρανός. When Helios leaves Ocean, he simply climbs "up into heaven" (οὐρανὸν εἰσανιών, H 423) or "towards heaven" (στείχῃσι πρὸς οὐρανὸν ἀστερόεντα, λ 17, with parallels quoted by Merry and Riddell, *Homer's Odyssey* [2d ed.; Oxford, 1886], p. 444). After having reached the middle of his course at noon (μέσον οὐρανὸν ἀμφιβεβήκει, Θ 68, Π 777, δ 400), he turns back downwards from heaven to earth (ἂψ ἐπὶ γαῖαν ἀπ' οὐρανόθεν προτράπηται, λ 18). In each case οὐρανός is simply "the region above the earth." (So also *Theog.* 761.) The conception is slightly more concrete in the Homeric Hymn to Helios (xxxi.15 f.), where the Sun rests his chariot "at the summit of heaven" (ἄκρου ἐπ' οὐρανοῦ), then drives "through heaven to the Ocean" (δι' οὐρανοῦ). It is not clear just what image the poet has in mind who speaks of the converging "sources and limits" of earth, Tartarus, sea, and οὐρανός, at *Theog.* 736 ff. (= 807 ff.). The most vivid description is to be found at *Theog.* 126 f., where Gaia engenders starry Ouranos "equal to herself, so that he might cover her all about" (ἶσον ἑωυτῇ ... ἵνα μιν περὶ πάντα καλύπτῃ). Since the surface of

the earth is circular (limited by Ocean), the shape of its heavenly cover must of course correspond; but nothing is said of a dome or a vault.

[2] καμάρα, "arch, vault" is not Homeric; neither is ἁψίς in this sense. Plato, of course, is familiar with "the celestial vault" (ὑπουράνιος ἁψίς, *Phaedrus* 247b.1), but his cosmology is not that of Homer. Herodotus may have a hemisphere in mind when he speaks of τὸν κύκλον πάντα τοῦ οὐρανοῦ (1.131), but he too stands in the shadow of the Ionian natural philosophers.

For the Homeric roof, see H. L. Lorimer, *Homer and the Monuments* (London, 1950), pp. 418 f. The roof of a princely dwelling seems normally to have been flat, like those of the Cretan palaces, the house of Circe (κ 558, with Merry's note), and the roof on which the watchman is posted at the opening of the *Agamemnon*. The great Mycenean tombs are of course vaulted, but anyone who has been inside the so-called "Treasury of Atreus" will think rather of the House of Hades than of the starry heavens. Nor is the θόλος at χ 442, which was probably a granary with a peaked roof (Lorimer, *op. cit.*, p. 431), of any significance for the Homeric view of the heavens.

[3] This is the natural interpretation of expressions such as "Tartarus . . . as far below Hades as heaven is from earth" (Θ 16); divine horses, which "fly readily in between earth and starry heaven" (Θ 45, E 768); Eris, the sister of Ares, "who first stands short, but then plants her head

conception of οὐρανός as a kind of roof. Some structure of this sort is clearly implied by the pillars of Atlas, which "support heaven and earth on either side" as a colonnade supports a temple:

$$\text{ἔχει δέ τε κίονας αὐτὸς}$$
$$\text{μακράς, αἳ γαῖάν τε καὶ οὐρανὸν ἀμφὶς ἔχουσι.}^{1}$$

Whatever role the poet intends to assign to Atlas himself, the words make clear that he has in mind columns standing on at least two sides (ἀμφίς) of the earth. They may very well have been set all round the earth, or at least in each corner, like the four great posts which prop up a flat heaven in the ancient Egyptian scheme:

The simplest mechanism [of support] was four posts set on earth to carry the weight of heaven. These were at the outer limits of the earth, as is indicated by such texts as: "I have set ... the terror of thee as far as the four pillars of heaven," and the number four suggests that they were placed at the four points of the compass. Fortunately, this arrangement appealed to the Egyptian as being both strong and permanent: "(As firm) as heaven resting upon its four posts" is a simile used more than once.[2]

The Greeks seem to have received from Egypt their old celestial architecture, as well as that of their temples. It is only when conceived in this way, as a roof, that the οὐρανός can be described as "brazen" or (in the *Odyssey*) as made of iron.[3] The reference is no doubt to the great solidity of the edifice. Hesiod has much the same thing in mind when he calls it "a seat set firm."

It is clear, then, that the Homeric οὐρανός may designate either the entire celestial region (including that of the clouds), or the upper roof which serves as boundary to this vast space. The same ambiguity attaches to οὐρανός in the classic usage, where the word denotes both the outer periphery of the universe and also the whole cosmic body contained within this limit (*De Caelo* 278b11 ff.). But by then the ill-defined

---

in heaven and walks upon the earth" (Δ 440 ff.). In each case οὐρανός is best conceived as a plane parallel to the surface of the earth. So it is a roof which is implied in Zeus' boast that not all the gods could drag him down from heaven to the earth's floor, "if they hung a golden rope from heaven" (Θ 19 ff.).

[1] α 53 f. It is probable that ἔχει here means not that Atlas directly supports the columns, but that he "has them in charge," as the Horae "keep the gates of heaven" (Θ 393). In that case αὐτός is emphatic: "he, and no one else," as when Zeus

is said "to hold himself" the thunder and lightning (αὐτὸς ἔχων, *Theog.* 72). Hesiod on the other hand gives the classic picture of Atlas bearing the heaven on his head and shoulders (*Theog.* 516 ff. 746 f.). The pillars are now superfluous. Aeschylus follows Hesiod (*P.V.* 430), but also mentions *one* pillar (*P.V.* 348 ff.), apparently in an attempt to combine two incompatible views.

[2] John A. Wilson in *The Intellectual Adventure of Ancient Man*, p. 46.

[3] Brazen heaven: Ε 504, Π 425, γ 2. Iron heaven: ο 329, ρ 565.

outlines of a mysterious structure have given way before the clear spherical architecture of Anaximander.

It is within this new system of spheres and circles that the later elements of fire and air have their place. Their antecedents are to be found less in the notion of οὐρανός as such than in the subordinate ideas linked with it in the epic.

When οὐρανός appears in Homer as the roof of the world, the position below it is occupied by αἰθήρ, which we are accustomed to translate ambiguously as "the sky." Thus Athena springs down to the earth "from heaven, through the αἰθήρ" (Τ 351). The same journey is effected in the opposite direction by the far-flashing gleam of a fully armed host, which "reaches through αἰθήρ to heaven" (B 458). But if αἰθήρ is the normal representative for what lies below the firmament, there is one passage in which it seems to share the field with ἀήρ. In describing the highest fir tree growing on the slopes of Mount Ida, the poet says that "it reaches through ἀήρ to the αἰθήρ."

$$\mu\alpha\kappa\rho\sigma\tau\acute{\alpha}\tau\eta \ \pi\epsilon\phi\upsilon\upsilon\hat{\iota}\alpha \ \delta\iota' \ \mathring{\eta}\acute{\epsilon}\rho\sigma\varsigma \ \alpha\mathring{\iota}\theta\acute{\epsilon}\rho' \ \mathring{\iota}\kappa\alpha\nu\epsilon\nu. \ (\Xi \ 288)$$

The scholiast on Ξ 288 declares:

According to Homer, the place from earth to the clouds is "air"; the place above the clouds is "sky," and it is also called by the same name as the firmament, "heaven." Therefore he speaks of the clouds as "the gates of heaven."[1]

We see that this verse proved to the satisfaction of the ancient commentators that Homer was already familiar with the classic distinction between the atmosphere and the upper celestial region and that he normally referred to the two as ἀήρ and αἰθήρ respectively, just as does, for instance, the author of De Carnibus (ch. 2), and after him the Stoics. In order to pass judgment on this Hellenistic interpretation, we must consider the use of the same two words in other epic passages, and, first of all, their etymology.

Αἰθήρ is clearly derived from the root of αἴθω, "to blaze," but its formation is irregular, and paralleled only by that of ἀήρ. Some etymological dictionaries still connect this second word with ἄημι, "to blow," but Meillet pointed out thirty years ago that such a derivation explains neither the form of the word nor the sense it bears in the oldest texts.[2]

---

[1] ὅτι καθ' Ὅμηρον ἀὴρ ὁ ἀπὸ γῆς μέχρι νεφῶν τόπος· ὁ δὲ ὑπὲρ τὰ νέφη τόπος αἰθήρ, καὶ ὁμωνύμως τῷ στερεμνίῳ οὐρανός. διὸ τὰ νέφη λέγει πύλας οὐρανοῦ; cited with parallels in K. Lehrs, De Aristarchi studiis Homericis, (3d ed.; Leipzig, 1882), p. 163. Not all ancient commentators were satis-

fied with this explanation (ibid., p. 168), but it was adopted without hesitation by O. Gilbert, as indicating the Homeric origin of the element theory. (See his Die meteorologischen Theorien des griechischen Altertums [Leipzig, 1907], p. 18.)

[2] "Remarques sur l'étymologie de quelques

Meillet himself interpreted ἀήρ as a root noun from ἀείρω (which could explain the pseudo-suffix -ηρ). Its original meaning would be "suspension; what is in suspension." Thus ἀήρ in Homer designates haze or mist. A secondary connection with αὔρα, ἄημι, and ἄνεμος would explain the later meaning of "atmosphere, the material constituting the atmosphere," which is common in fifth-century Ionic and Attic, passes into the κοινή, thence into Latin, and survives in modern words for the "air." Αἰθήρ, on the other hand, seems to be a purely literary creation, formed by analogy with ἀήρ and never firmly established in the spoken language. In the view of Meillet, the Indo-European word signifying "dark space" (*regʷes-, Vedic rájas) had become specialized in Greek ἔρεβος for the darkness of the underworld. The old contrast opposing the obscure regions of the earth to the sunlit sky, which the Vedic poets express by rájas and divó rocaná ("region of darkness" and "bright space of heaven"), was therefore conveyed in Greek by two new formations, ἀήρ and αἰθήρ.[1]

Although Meillet's account of the prehistory of the two words has not as yet been accepted by all linguists, it is at any rate in full accord with the Homeric texts. Thus for Homer αἰθήρ is certainly not a fixed region of elemental fire; the term signifies primarily the light which streams through a bright sky. The verbal forms of αἴθω refer in fact not only to the heat of fire but also to its blazing light.[2] It is this meaning of the root which comes out, for instance, in αἴθοψ, αἴθων, πάναιθος in the sense of "flashing, glittering," and also in αἴθρη, "fair weather." The latter term reminds us that αἰθήρ implies not only a sunlit but also a cloudless sky. Hence the Homeric αἰθήρ can refer to the sky's nocturnal brightness (just as the later form αἰθρία often means a "clear night"):

ὡς δ' ὅτ' ἐν οὐρανῷ ἄστρα φαεινὴν ἀμφὶ σελήνην
φαίνετ' ἀριπρεπέα, ὅτε τ' ἔπλετο νήνεμος αἰθήρ·
[ἔκ τ' ἔφανεν πᾶσαι σκοπιαὶ καὶ πρώονες ἄκροι
καὶ νάπαι· οὐρανόθεν δ' ἄρ' ὑπερράγη ἄσπετος αἰθήρ,]
πάντα δὲ εἴδεται ἄστρα, γέγηθε δέ τε φρένα ποιμήν. (Θ 555 ff.)

mots grecs," *Bulletin de la Société de Linguistique*, XXVI (1925), 7 ff., followed by P. Chantraine, *Formation des noms en grec ancien* (Paris, 1933), p. 219. In the new *Griechisches etymologisches Wörterbuch* of H. Frisk (Heidelberg, 1954-), *s.v.* ἀήρ, the old explanation from ἄημι has been dropped, but Meillet's alternative view is cited with reserve.

[1] In support of Meillet's view, it may be added that αἰθήρ must have been introduced as the normal word for the luminous sky by the same

poets for whom ζεύς, διός had become too vividly personified. The old sense of διός, "sky", still appears (next to αἰθήρ) at N 837; cf. also T 357.

[2] αἴθω γὰρ οὐ μόνον τὸ καίω ἀλλὰ καὶ τὸ λάμπω, Eustathius *ad. Il.* 249.23, cited in Ebeling, *Lexicon Homericum*, *s.v.* αἰθόμενος. Hence αἰθομένας δαΐδας, α 428, etc.; λαμπτῆρσι αἰθομένοισιν, σ 343. Pindar means, of course, that gold is a blazing (not a burning) flame: χρυσὸς αἰθόμενον πῦρ, O. 1.1.

Ignoring for a moment the athetized lines, we see that οὐρανός here is the place in which the stars are seen; αἰθήρ is not a region, as the scholiast claims, but the still clarity which has arisen (ἔπλετο) in heaven and which makes things visible. The word has exactly the same sense in another simile (whose last two lines are repeated by the manuscripts in the passage just cited):

ὡς δ' ὅτ' ἀφ' ὑψηλῆς κορυφῆς ὄρεος μεγάλοιο
κινήσῃ πυκινὴν νεφέλην στεροπηγερέτα Ζεύς,
ἔκ τ' ἔφανεν πᾶσαι σκοπιαὶ καὶ πρώονες ἄκροι
καὶ νάπαι, οὐρανόθεν δ' ἄρ' ὑπερράγη ἄσπετος αἰθήρ. (Π 297 ff.)

It is again obvious that αἰθήρ is not a place, but a certain condition of the sky, and, as it were, an active force,[1] which "breaks through" from the οὐρανός above and causes every crag and glen of the mountain to be seen.

The most precise sense of αἰθήρ is therefore not "sky" but "celestial light": that which is shut out when the sky is overcast. It is the active, causal nuance of αἰθήρ which seems to distinguish it from αἴθρη, the sky's clarity conceived as a more passive state or condition:

ποίησον δ' αἴθρην, δὸς δ' ὀφθαλμοῖσιν ἰδέσθαι. (P 646)

Of course, such a distinction between an active force and the state which it produces, or the space which it fills, is not always observed by the poet. But the original contrast between οὐρανός as a place and αἰθήρ as a particular condition appears again in another simile, where a sudden storm cloud is said "to invade heaven out of a bright αἰθήρ; that is to say, 'out of a clear sky'."[2] The etymological sense of "brightness" is still implied when a battle is said to take place "under the αἰθήρ," i.e., with full visibility, under a clear sky (P 371). On the other hand, the idea of clarity and light tends to fade away before the purely spatial

---

[1] So in describing the view of Anaxagoras, Aristotle refers to αἰθήρ as a "power" rather than a body or place: κἀκεῖνος τὴν ἐκεῖ (sc. ἄνω) δύναμιν αἰθέρα καλεῖν ἐνομίσεν, Meteor. 339ᵇ24.

In Π 300, ὑπερράγη is, of course, intransitive, not passive as one might infer from Leaf's rendering: "The aither is burst open" (The Iliad [2d ed.; London, 1900], I, 369). For the value of this aorist, see E. Schwyzer, Griechische Grammatik I (Munich, 1953), 757.

[2] ὡς δ' ὅτ' ἀπ' Οὐλύμπου νέφος ἔρχεται οὐρανὸν εἴσω
αἰθέρος ἐκ δίης, ὅτε τε Ζεὺς λαίλαπα τείνῃ.
(Π 364)

The obscurity which the commentators find here is largely due to their insistence on interpreting αἰθήρ as a place. Once this snare has been avoided, the meaning is plain: Olympus is the distant mountain around which Zeus gathers his clouds, and from which he sends one to produce a storm. All at once it appears within the visible heaven (ἔρχεται οὐρανὸν εἴσω), "out of a blue sky." The only ambiguity is in the conventional verse ending οὐρανὸν εἴσω, which normally describes movement upwards from the earth. (Cf. Hdt. 1. 87: ἐκ δὲ αἰθρίης τε καὶ νηνεμίης συνδραμεῖν ἐξαπίνης νέφεα καὶ χειμῶνά τε καὶ καταρραγῆναι . . . .)

conception of "sky," when the metallic noise of combat is said to pass "through αἰθήρ to brazen heaven."[1] The parallel thus established between αἰθήρ and οὐρανός becomes so complete that the former can simply be substituted for the latter: the rising smoke, the mighty battle cry, the distant gleam of armor, and the high-flying eagle, all are said to reach not heaven itself, but the bright sky.[2] In the same way, the action of Zeus proceeds "in the αἰθήρ" or "from the αἰθήρ." And even a wind may be said to rush "through the αἰθήρ" (o 293). But the sense of "brightness" is never quite lost. If the lot of Zeus is specified as "broad οὐρανός, in αἰθήρ and in the clouds" (O 192), the last two contrasting terms form as it were an exhaustive table of contents for the upper region: the luminous sky and the opaque clouds.

The history of ἀήρ is characterized by a similar extension of meaning which never quite loses sight of its starting point. This word also designated originally neither a place nor a specific substance, but a force or condition, to wit, one which makes things *invisible*. If it is light which permits us to see, it is mist or haze or some similar screen which prevents us from doing so. Hence ἀήρ is closely related in sense to "cloud" (νέφος, νεφέλη), as well as to darkness (ζόφος, νύξ)—this latter being conceived not as the privation of light, but as a positive reality.

The connection of ἀήρ with cloud and mist, as well as the corresponding contrast with αἰθήρ, is brought out very clearly in the battle scene around the body of Patroclus. In order to protect the corpse from the Trojans, Zeus "poured an abundant ἀήρ about the helmets" of the Achaean warriors standing around it (P 268 ff.). Their view was so obstructed in consequence that "one would say that neither sun nor moon was safe and sound; for they were oppressed by ἀήρ," while the other warriors continued to fight at ease "under a clear sky (ὑπ' αἰθέρι), where the piercing beam of the sun was spread abroad, and no cloud appeared on all the earth or even on the mountains" (P 366 ff.). Unable to see the field around him, Ajax calls upon father Zeus: "Deliver the sons of the Achaeans out from under the ἀήρ; make the sky bright (ποίησον δ' αἴθρην), and grant us to see with our eyes. Yea, destroy us in the light, if such is now thy pleasure" (P 645 ff.). Zeus had pity on his prayer and his tears, "and straightway scattered the ἀήρ and pushed

---

[1] P 425. Cf. B 458, T 351. In the first passage cited, the epithet ἀτρύγετος seems to assimilate the αἰθήρ to a sea, but the original meaning of the epithet is uncertain. Cf. ἄσπετος αἰθήρ, Π 300; νήνεμος αἰθήρ, Θ 556; αἰθέρα δῖαν, τ 540.

[2] The αἰθήρ is attained by smoke (Σ 207); by the glorious beam (σέλας) from the countenance of Achilles (Σ 214) or from his shield (T 379); by the shout of Ajax (O 686); and by an eagle (τ 540). Zeus dwells "in the αἰθήρ" (B 412, etc.) and acts "from the αἰθήρ" (O 610; cf. Λ 54).

away the mist; then the sun shone again, and the whole battle lay clear before them" (649 f.).

The ἀήρ which is thus dispelled by Zeus is plainly a kind of "suspension" like haze or fog. It is contrasted not only with the brightness of a clear sky (αἰθήρ, αἴθρη), but also with the light of the sun (vv. 372, 647, 650).

The link between ἀήρ and the clouds reappears in a curious simile in the fifth book of the *Iliad*, where the furious retreat of Ares (who has been wounded by Diomedes) is compared to a summer haze: "Like a dusky ἀήρ which appears from the clouds when the strong west wind blows after great heat, such did brazen Ares appear to Diomedes son of Tydeus as he went together with the clouds into the broad heaven" (*E* 864 ff.). The point of the simile is that both ἀήρ and the disappearing Ares are associated with the clouds, and that both are indistinctly seen. The epithet "dusky" (ἐρεβεννή) here applied to the ἀήρ seems to denote less its color than its impermeability to sight. The visual beam which leaves the eye and strikes its object plays a great part even in the later Greek theories of vision; it is clearly presupposed from the earliest times. Thus the Greek names for color do not indicate inert qualities, but certain ways of reacting to light or to the rays of sight. The etymological sense of λευκός is not simply "white" but "bright, translucent" (from the same root as Latin *lux*); and the corresponding sense of μέλας is "dark, opaque." In this way, the ἀήρ or haze which the gods regularly pour over persons or things to render them invisible is conceived as a shield which protects them from the gaze of men, or prevents their inner light from reaching human eyes.[1] For particular privacy, Zeus makes use of a golden cloud through which not even the sun's light can penetrate (*Ξ* 343). A more banal case is that of Diomedes, who cannot distinguish gods from mortal warriors until Athena removes the ἀχλύς or dark mist from before his eyes (*E* 127).

In such cases the ἀήρ (or its substitute) is certainly no metaphor. The haze in which Apollo hides Hector is described as "deep" or thick, and Achilles strikes it three times with his spear (*Υ* 446). In exactly the same way, the ἀήρ which Hera spreads out along the river Xanthus is thick enough to impede the Trojans in their flight (*Φ* 6 ff.). Such a haze is even conceived as capable of supporting objects belonging to the gods. Thus Ares, when he rests from battle, deposits his spear and chariot in an ἀήρ, just as mortals lay their arms upon the ground.[2] In such a case

---

[1] *Γ* 381, *E* 776, *I* 571, etc.   [2] *E* 356, where ἠέρι is locative, like χθονί in *K* 472.

the word still denotes an opaque "suspension," but the context is such that later Greeks may easily have understood a reference to the atmosphere.

The same is true of the verse with which we began, where a fir tree is said to reach "through the ἀήρ to the αἰθήρ" (Ξ 288). The ancient commentators were certainly mistaken in reading into this passage the classic doctrine of cosmic places. Here again ἀήρ is the opaque haze hovering in the vicinity of the earth or the clouds (like the ἀήρ in which Hera and Sleep have just been said to wrap themselves to escape notice, Ξ 282), whereas αἰθήρ is the bright, translucent sky overhead. Sleep has picked the tallest tree as his lookout post precisely because it is free of all impediments to the sight. For it is essential to the success of his scheme that his glance strike the eyes of Zeus before the latter sees him (Ξ 285). The primary contrast between ἀήρ and αἰθήρ is therefore still a question of visibility, not of relative location.[1]

It is true that ἀήρ as haze is necessarily to be found in the region of clouds and earth, while αἰθήρ as celestial brightness is at home in the upper sky. This was already evident from the verse cited earlier, where αἰθήρ is said to break through from heaven above (Π 300). So much and no more is implied by the fir tree which reaches "through ἀήρ to the αἰθήρ." It is because of its brightness that the αἰθήρ is above the clouds, just as the ἀήρ is below because it is like haze. Their spatial relationship is incidental, and the boundary line between them is altered by every change in the weather. Nor do these two items together occupy all the space between heaven and earth; the meaning of ἀήρ is still too specialized. The two may be distinguished as cosmic bodies, filling separate regions, only when the denotation of ἀήρ is extended to include the air we breathe and in which the birds fly, as well as the substance of the winds and of the clouds.

This extension of meaning has not yet taken place for Hesiod. In a vivid passage of the *Works and Days* the poet describes a fruitful mist (ἀήρ) which hangs upon the fields on winter mornings, drawing water from the rivers, rising above the earth with a gust of wind; and which then sometimes falls as rain at eventide or blows with the north wind,

---

[1] The original sense of ἀήρ is also clear from its adjectival derivatives, which mean "murky, gloomy, hazy": ἠερόεις is an epithet of Tartarus (Θ 13), of darkness (M 240, etc.), and of the paths of the sea (ν 64); ἠεροειδής also applies to the sea (Ψ 744), to a grotto (μ 80, etc.), and to the dimly visible form of Scylla (μ 233). In Ξ 770, ὅσσον δ' ἠεροειδές describes the vague line of the horizon as it appears to a lookout gazing off to sea.

descending in a dark cloud to drench the imprudent farmer who returns too late to his cottage.

> ψυχρὴ γάρ τ' ἠὼς πέλεται Βορέαο πεσόντος·
> ἠώιος δ' ἐπὶ γαῖαν ἀπ' οὐρανοῦ ἀστερόεντος
> ἀὴρ πυροφόρος τέταται μακάρων ἐπὶ ἔργοις,
> 550 ὅς τε ἀρυσσάμενος ποταμῶν ἀπὸ αἰεναόντων,
> ὑψοῦ ὑπὲρ γαίης ἀρθεὶς ἀνέμοιο θυέλλῃ,
> ἄλλοτε μέν θ' ὕει ποτὶ ἕσπερον, ἄλλοτ' ἄῃσι
> πυκνὰ Θρηικίου Βορέω νέφεα κλονέοντος.
> τὸν φθάμενος ἔργον τελέσας οἶκόνδε νέεσθαι,
> 555 μή ποτέ σ' οὐρανόθεν σκοτόεν νέφος ἀμφικαλύψῃ,
> χρῶτα δὲ μυδαλέον θήῃ κατά θ' εἵματα δεύσῃ.[1]

All the roots of the later theory of the atmosphere are apparent in this passage: the conception of ἀήρ as moisture derived from the water of the earth; the connection of it with wind and rain as well as with the clouds; and, above all, the transition from one of these forms to another in an alternate movement up and down between heaven and earth. Nevertheless, Hesiod is expressing no theory but a fact of everyday life in Boeotia. And ἀήρ for him means not "air," but "mist."

The earliest surviving text in which ἀήρ has its new and larger meaning seems to be a fragment of Xenophanes: "This upper limit of the earth is seen by our feet, striking against the ἀήρ; that below reaches to the boundless."[2]

The ἀήρ which is in contact with the surface of the earth is clearly "air," not "haze." This sense is frequent in fifth-century philosophical fragments, in the Hippocratic Corpus, and in Herodotus.[3] We have already encountered it in the Aristophanic Clouds. The new usage is somewhat slower to make its appearance in a completely poetic context. It is no doubt the concrete meaning of ἀήρ in the language of the epic which leads both Aeschylus and Euripides to prefer the vaguer expression αἰθήρ, even when they clearly mean "air." The same con-

---

[1] Op. 547 ff. Hesiod apparently associates ἀήρ both with ἀρθείς (v. 551) and with ἄῃσι (v. 552). It is not only dark (555), but also cold (547) and damp (550, 552, 556), exactly as is the later element (except in the theory of Aristotle, where ἀήρ is essentially hot).

[2] Xenoph. B 28, where ἠέρι is the convincing emendation of Diels for the MSS. καὶ ῥεῖ. The proposed alternative αἰθέρι is much less plausible. Could Xenophanes have said the earth touches the "sky" at our feet?

[3] The Herodotean use of ἀήρ is not noted in LSJ, but eight examples are given by J. E. Powell, A Lexicon to Herodotus (Cambridge, 1938), e.g., IV.7.3: πτερῶν γὰρ καὶ τὴν γῆν καὶ τὸν ἠέρα εἶναι πλέον; V.105: ὀϊστὸν . . . ἐς τὸν ἠέρα βάλλοντα.

siderations of style probably explain why Empedocles generally refers to the divine atmospheric element as αἰθήρ, although he sometimes uses ἀήρ in the normal way for "air," as does Sophocles.[1]

How did this new sense of ἀήρ develop from the idea of "mist"? There are at least two possibilities. In the first place, passages such as that cited above from Hesiod show how the old meaning of ἀήρ brought it into inevitable contact with the notions of cloud, wind, and atmospheric dampness. It is therefore conceivable that a gradual extension of meaning took place within the spoken language of Ionia and Athens.[2] In that case the philosophic concept of ἀήρ would be directly based upon a current usage of the word. But it may also have been the philosophers who first felt the need for a term to correspond to the new conception of the atmosphere, and they themselves may have taken the initiative in expanding the sense of the word. It is difficult to choose between these alternative explanations, for every author who makes use of ἀήρ in the larger sense has also been influenced by the Ionian philosophy of nature.

But if the purely linguistic career of the word must remain in doubt, there can be no question as to its early use by the philosophers. We know that Anaximenes, in the sixth century, conceived of ἀήρ as a universal force or principle from which all natural phenomena could be derived. Furthermore, if it is only with Anaximenes that "air" attains such predominance, the idea itself was equally familiar to Anaximander. We saw in the last chapter that his explanation of the

---

[1] Αἰθήρ is "air" in Aesch. P.V. 125, 280, 394; it stands vaguely between heaven and earth in the famous fragment (70 Nauck):

Ζεύς ἐστιν αἰθήρ, Ζεὺς δὲ γῆ, Ζεὺς δ' οὐρανός,
Ζεύς τοι τὰ πάντα χὦτι τῶνδ' ὑπέρτερον.

In Euripides, fr. 941, the reference is clearly to the atmosphere:

ὁρᾶς τὸν ὑψοῦ τόνδ' ἄπειρον αἰθέρα
καὶ γῆν πέριξ ἔχονθ' ὑγραῖς ἐν ἀγκάλαις;
τοῦτον νόμιζε Ζῆνα, τόνδ' ἡγοῦ θεόν.

This must be the passage Aristophanes has in mind when he invokes ἀμέτρητ' Ἀήρ (not Αἰθήρ) at Nubes 264. Aristophanes faithfully mocks the tragic preference for αἰθήρ when he presents Euripides in propria persona: ὄμνυμι τοίνυν αἰθέρ' οἴκησιν Διός, Thesm. 272. Cf. Ranae 892, and the Euripidean parallels cited by Van Leeuwen on Nubes 264.

Ἀήρ appears as an elemental power in Sophocles El. 86: ὦ φάος ἁγνὸν | καὶ γῆς ἰσόμοιρ' ἀήρ. The various terms for "air" relay one another in Emped. B 100 (where there is no reason to change

the MS. reading ἀέρος in v. 13; cf. πνεύματος v. 15). We have also κατ' ἠέρα B 77.2; and ἀήρ at B 38.3. Either ἠέρος or αἰθέρος is possible at B 17.18.

[2] Meillet judged differently: "Il n'a pu y avoir un passage du sens attesté par la langue épique à celui d' 'atmosphère, matière constituant l'atmosphère' qui se trouve en ionien et en attique, sens auquel la philosophie ionienne a donné du reste une précision nouvelle et qui a évolué par là-même. Le sens du mot ionien et attique se rattacherait directement au sens de 'suspension' et non au sens particulier observé dans la langue homérique" (Bulletin de la Société de Linguistique, XXVI, 8). In fact the transition is not as abrupt as Meillet suggests. Both senses may be used by the same writer, even in the same sentence. (See the passage from De Aëribus, n. 3, pp. 161–62.) Plato still associates ἀήρ with mist, darkness, and water (Phaedo 190b.6–7; cf. Tim. 58d.1–3), while Aristotle says expressly that it is "like vapor" (οἷον ἀτμὶς ὁ ἀήρ, Gen. Corr. 330b4).

heavenly bodies, as well as of thunder, lightning, and the rest, pre-supposes a view of the ἀήρ which begins with terrestrial vapors, but extends outwards to the circles of the sun and stars. Just as it is Anaxi-mander who replaces once and for all the old view of οὐρανός as a towering, vaguely roof-like edifice by a spherical structure of geometric form, so it is he who (as far as we know) first explained all events between this outer limit and the central earth by an interaction of fire, air, and terrestrial water. In order to make any sense at all of his cosmology and meteorology, one must credit Anaximander with the Ionian notion of the earth's environment as a vast expanse of atmospheric air, stretching outwards to the limit of the world, issuing in wind, rain, cloud, or fire according to the circumstances.[1]

Once this new conception of ἀήρ had been introduced, the decisive bridge was crossed which separated the old ideas from the classic view of earth, water, air, and fire as the great "members" of the world. For the obvious link between αἰθήρ and αἴθω made it an easy matter to reinterpret the epic "sky" as a region of pure fire. This new philosophic significance of the αἰθήρ is well attested for Anaxagoras.[2] It is likewise implied by the "aetherial fire of flame" in the cosmogony of Parmenides (φλογὸς αἰθέριον πῦρ, B 8.56), which is also designated as "light" (B 9) and as "unmixed fire" (B 11), and is represented in the visible world by the αἰθήρ, that is, by the upper sky in which the stars are situated (B 10.1, B 11.2). It is clear that both Parmenides and Anax-agoras have made a conscious effort to reconcile the new philosophic conceptions with the Homeric terminology. Such an endeavor remains characteristic of Ionian naturalism, and in all likelihood it continues the original point of view of the Milesians.[3] The rationalizing interpre-

---

[1] See above, pp. 93, 100–9.

[2] Anaxagoras' interpretation of the αἰθήρ as celestial fire is mentioned by Arist. De Caelo 270ᵇ24; Meteor. 339ᵇ23 (cf. Anaxag. B 1–2, B 15, etc.). It is echoed by the author of De Carnibus (ch. 2, Littré, VIII, 584): δοκέει δέ μοι ὁ καλέομεν θερμὸν, ἀθάνατόν τε εἶναι καὶ νοέειν πάντα καὶ ὁρῆν καὶ ἀκούειν καὶ εἰδέναι πάντα ἐόντα τε καὶ ἐσόμενα . . . καὶ ὀνομῆναί μοι αὐτὸ δοκέουσιν οἱ παλαιοὶ αἰθέρα (where the "ancients" are the poets, not the philosophers).

[3] See, for example, the allegorical interpreta-tion of Zeus as the ἀήρ in Democr. B 30: τῶν λογίων ἀνθρώπων ὀλίγοι ἀνατείναντες τὰς χεῖρας ἐνταῦθα, ὃν νῦν ἠέρα καλέομεν οἱ Ἕλληνες, πάντα Δία μυθέονται, καὶ πάνθ᾽ οὗτος οἶδε καὶ διδοῖ καὶ ἀφαιρέεται καὶ βασιλεὺς οὗτος τῶν πάντων. (For μυθεῖσθαι, μυθέεται in the MSS., I read the Ionic

third person plural in the historical present: "They declare as a myth that all the air is Zeus" [compare the sense of μυθοπλαστέοντες in Democr. B 297]; whereby the conjectures φασίν and εἶπαν may be avoided.) Compare the similar doctrine and phrasing of Diog. B 5: καί μοι δοκεῖ τὸ τὴν νόησιν ἔχον εἶναι ὁ ἀὴρ καλούμενος ὑπὸ τῶν ἀνθρώπων . . . αὐτὸ γάρ μοι τοῦτο θεὸς δοκεῖ εἶναι; and the parallel use of καλέομεν in De Carn. 2 (see the previous note). The formula can be traced back to the sixth century (i.e., presumably to Anaximenes) if, as seems likely, the lines of Ennius cited by Diels, Vors. 23 B 53, are really imitated from Epicharmus: istic est is Iupiter quem dico, quem Graeci vocant aërem. (On the connections between Epicharmus and the Milesians, see also the following note.) A comparable interpretation of Zeus, this time as celestial fire, is hinted at by

tation of the epic is at least as old as Hecataeus, who was probably
following here, as elsewhere, the path traced out by his predecessors and
compatriots, the natural philosophers.

Whatever terminology may have been used by the sixth-century
Milesians, it is certain that their conception of the natural world contained, in potential form, a view of earth, water, air, and fire as "members" or "portions" of the cosmos. However, it does not follow that they
formulated this view in the way which is later customary. The characteristic feature of the Empedoclean doctrine is its emphasis on the *four*
roots of all things (B 6), and the sufficiency of these four alone (B 17.30,
B 21.9, B 23.9 f., B 71). So for Plato, Aristotle, and later thinkers, the
same four elements exhaust the contents of the cosmos or (in the case of
Aristotle) those of the sublunary sphere. In all likelihood, this exclusive
role was assigned to earth, water, air, and fire by Empedocles for the
first time. What little we know of the element theory of the Milesians
suggests a different and less systematic view. Thus Theophrastus (in the
excerpt of Hippolytus) gives the following account of the theory of
Anaximenes.

He said that the ἀρχή was boundless ἀήρ; out of which arise what is becoming,
what has become, and what is to be, and gods, and things divine; the rest arise
from the progeny of the ἀήρ. Its form is as follows: when it is most uniform, it is
not apparent to the sight, but it is made distinct by the cold and the hot and the
moist and by what is in motion. It moves incessantly; for it would not change
as much as it does, if it were not in motion. For when condensed or rarefied, it
appears as different; thus when it is dissolved into rarer form, it becomes fire;
and the winds are ἀήρ condensed again; from ἀήρ cloud is produced by compression; water by still more compression; when further condensed it becomes earth
and, in its most condensed form, stones. Thus the most decisive causes of generation are opposites: hot and cold. (Anaximenes A 7)

It is no doubt Theophrastus himself who draws attention to the
primary opposites in his concluding remark. On the other hand, in the
preceding sentences we seem to have a very close paraphrase of what
Anaximenes actually said. The accuracy of this report may be seen
precisely in the fact that Theophrastus has *not* imposed upon it the later
doctrine of the elements. Fire, air, water, and earth are all mentioned
of course; after Anaximander how could they be ignored? But they are

---

Heracl. B 32. Zeus is probably the sky in Pherecydes B 1; and cf. Ζεύς ἐστιν αἰθήρ in Aesch. fr.
70 (n. 1, p. 147). This new philosophic view of
Zeus is, as it were, a return to the pre-Homeric,

Indo-European conception of *dyeus* as the "sky";
cf. Hdt. 1.131.2: the Persians "call the whole circle
of the heavens Zeus."

integrated here into a fuller series, in which ἀήρ is represented both by winds and by cloud, while earth is followed by the independent form "stones." The last four members of the series—from clouds to stones—reappear in exactly the same context in fragment B 16 of Anaxagoras:

As these things [probably "the thick and damp and cold and dark" of B 15] are separated off, earth is formed out of them by condensation. For water is separated off out of the clouds, and earth out of water; while stones are formed out of earth by condensation under the action of the cold; the latter depart further than water [from their original source?].

The coincidence between this view and that of Anaximenes is complete. Both texts make clear that, for the Milesians and their earliest disciples, the four classic elements had not yet assumed a unique position. They figure side by side with stones, clouds, and wind among the basic constituents of the universe.

If we look back now on the fragments of Melissus and Diogenes which were cited earlier (p. 123), we see that even in the second half of the fifth century there are unmistakable signs of this old Ionian view. When Melissus, for example, mentions "earth and water and air and fire," these terms do not compose his entire list. On the contrary, he goes on without a break: "and iron and gold [i.e., the "stones" of the older series] and what is alive as well as what is dead, and dark and bright, and all other things which men say are true" (B 8). Our experience with the senses, says Melissus, leads us to believe not only that "hot becomes cold and cold hot," and that all things change into their opposites, but also that "iron and gold and stone and everything strong is rubbed away by contact, while earth and stone arise out of water" (ibid.). Here too the four "elements" have their place within a larger inventory of natural forms, whose final members are the same as those in the lists of Anaximenes and Anaxagoras.

The case of Diogenes is similar. He does not cite the four alone, but "earth and water and air and fire and all other things which appear as real in this κόσμος" (B 2). One may perhaps recognize some influence of Empedocles here in the fact that Diogenes does not feel called upon to specify just what are the "other things" which compose the world. In this respect the decisive role of Empedocles was to crystallize attention on the four primary forms, and thus to replace a fuller Milesian series by the canonical tetrad.[1]

---

[1] The original Milesian view shows through in the imitation of Ennius cited as Epicharmus B 53, where the forms given for aër are: ventus, nubes, imber, frigus, then back to wind and air. (The winds appear in a similar context in Epicharmus B 8.) The absence of the tetrad in De Hebd. 1–2

With Melissus and Diogenes, as we have remarked, the elements do not appear as fixed portions of the universe but as phases in a continual process of transformation. This idea too is Milesian. It is precisely the theme of the series established by Anaximenes: fire, cloud, water, and the rest are for him not independent realities, but mere stages along the road in which ἀήρ passes unremittingly "up and down."

The origins of this view are in part very simple and very ancient. We may compare, for example, the "transformations" of Proteus: when grasped by Menelaus, he becomes "all things which creep upon the earth, and water, and wondrous-burning fire" (δ 417 f.). Such a magical series shows that there was no need of natural philosophy in order to recognize fire and water among the elemental appearances. (And one may compare the later use of earth and water as emblems of submission.) But it is the element unknown to Homer—the atmospheric ἀήρ— which is the real key to the classic view, just as it is above all this feature which distinguishes the Greek theory from its Indian parallel.[1] Now the interdependence of wind, cloud, water, rain, and ἀήρ was, as we have seen, already described by Hesiod in the *Works and Days*. It is just such seasonal phenomena of evaporation and precipitation which the Milesian theory took as its point of departure, when it set out to explain the whole world of nature according to a few simple principles. Thus winds and clouds arise by evaporation from the primeval moisture, while the dry earth is a by-product of the same process. Celestial fire grows out of the lower ἀήρ "like bark around a tree," and must apparently be nourished from the same source, that is to say, from evaporated moisture. Atmospheric fire, as it appears in the lightning bolt, is itself formed from wind—in other words, from a particularly dry, fine product of evaporation. Here we have the "way up" from terrestrial moisture to fire. That fire is quenched, wind compressed, cloud condensed, and moisture solidified to earth and stones is the central doctrine of Anaximenes; and this reciprocal "way down" must have been largely envisaged by Anaximander himself. The atmospheric river mentioned by Aristotle,[2] which flows in a yearly circle up and

---

may be a sign of relatively early date, although the need to find seven of everything could also be responsible here. The four μοῖραι of *De Carn.* 2, on the other hand, definitely suggest the influence of Empedocles.

[1] In the Indian theory, the corresponding element is *vāyu* or *vāta*, that is to say, the "wind": the active power, not the material substance, of the atmosphere. This essential difference shows that the Greek doctrine of the elements is not derived from India, nor the Indian from Greece. That earth, water, and fire should be recognized in both views is not very surprising. For the origins of the Indian theory, see H. Oldenberg, *Die Weltanschauung der Brahmana-Texte* (Göttingen, 1919), pp. 58 ff.

[2] Above, p. 106. For the Milesian meteorology, see above, pp. 100-4.

down, corresponds to the Milesian explanation of how the world took shape. The oldest theories of cosmogony and meteorology are indeed one and the same. The year imitates the life history of the universe, and both form a cycle of transformations revolving about the central concept of the ἀήρ.

It would be idle to speculate upon the relative extent of imitation and originality in the descriptions of the cycle of natural change which we have cited from Empedocles, Plato, and Aristotle. Since the sixth-century documents are almost entirely lost, we can do no more than recognize the essential line of continuity which leads from Anaximander to Aristotle and beyond. It is no doubt this Milesian view which is repeated and elaborated by Xenophanes, Heraclitus, Anaxagoras, Melissus, Diogenes, and the rest.[1]

Restricting ourselves for the present to the idea of the elements as members or sections of the world, and at the same time as the principal phases in its cycle of transformation, we may summarize the early history of the theory as follows.

The oldest Greek literary texts recognize a simple division of the world into four parts or portions: earth, sea, heaven (οὐρανός), and the nether darkness occupied by Hades and Night. This fourfold scheme can be assimilated to the classic doctrine of the elements, if οὐρανός is replaced by αἰθήρ, and darkness by ἀήρ. The first two terms already tend to become interchangeable in certain epic formulas, while the second substitution is prepared by the regular Homeric description of darkness as "aery" or "murky" (ζόφος ἠερόεις). This assimilation probably explains why the four elements are later called "portions" (μοῖραι), like the shares in the Homeric δασμός (O 195). It may also explain the introduction of the fourfold scheme by Empedocles, and its rapid success throughout the Greek world.

Nevertheless, a careful consideration of the sense of the epic terms shows that the classic theory could not possibly have developed directly out of these poetic ideas. For Homer's αἰθήρ is not composed of fire, and his ἀήρ is not "atmosphere" but "mist." As we shall see in a moment,

---

[1] Xenoph. B 30; Anaxag. B 15; Melissus B 8; Diog. B 2; Heracl. B 31, B 36, B 60, B 67; etc. In view of what has been said above about ἀήρ, I can see no reason to suspect the authenticity of Heracl. B 76 (in its most accurate version, of course, that of Plutarch). The ἀήρ is not Stoic, but Milesian, and the word is used in the regular sense by Xenophanes, Anaxagoras, and Empedocles.

The πρηστήρ of Heracl. B 31 refers precisely to an ignition of atmospheric substance, conceived either as cloud (Heracl. A 14) or as πνεῦμα (Arist. Meteor. 371ᵃ15). In either case it is ἀήρ, not water, which turns to fire. In general, the "exhalations" of Heraclitus are unintelligible except in the context of the Milesian theory of atmospheric transformation.

the archaic contrast of celestial brightness and terrestrial gloom continues to play a certain part in early Greek natural philosophy. But the direct accommodation of epic passages to the later scheme is a blatant anachronism. The Hellenistic interpretation of αἰθήρ and ἀήρ, reported by the scholiast, continues an old and honorable tradition which probably goes back to the earliest natural philosophers. Like his younger namesake, the first Anaximander of Miletus may also have been fond of discovering "hints" (ὑπόνοιαι) of the latest philosophical doctrines beneath the surface of the Homeric text.[1] The method remains in vogue throughout antiquity and passes directly into St. Augustine's exegesis of the Old Testament. From the historical point of view, however, it is neither more nor less legitimate to read the classic theory of the atmosphere into Homer than to find Neoplatonic metaphysics expounded in the Book of Genesis.

In fact, the conception of ἀήρ as the element of meteorological process is derived not from Homer, but from the observed facts of evaporation. These had already been remarked by Hesiod—and no doubt by many peasants and sailors before him—without giving rise to any particular philosophical scheme. The Milesian theory of the atmosphere was formulated by men who had pondered upon these facts, fused them into a single doctrine, and expanded this doctrine to include all natural phenomena whatsoever. The circular chain of transformation which leads from fire to water, earth, and stones—passing through wind, cloud, thunderstorm, and precipitation—may, in its fully articulated form, be the work of Anaximenes. All the individual links, at any rate, had been forged by his predecessor. Apart from Anaximander, each of the early theorists tends to emphasize a different member of the chain: Thales, we are told, preferred water; Anaximenes singled out air; Xenophanes, earth and water; Heraclitus, fire. The system which recognizes these four, and these four alone, is the innovation of Empedocles.[2]

[1] For the Homeric allegories of the younger Anaximander, see Xenophon, *Symp.* III. 6. (The identification with the second Anaximander of Miletus was established by E. Schwartz, in *RE*, I, 2086.14, followed by Jacoby, *F.Gr.Hist.* 9.T.3, with commentary.) Much the same rationalization of the epic was pursued by Democritus in his Homeric studies. His explanation of ἀμβροσία accommodates it to the Ionian cosmology (B 25), just as Pherecydes seems to have done before him (B 13a). The Democritean etymologies (see B 2 and B 142) must have been Plato's principal inspiration in the *Cratylus*. Such rediscovery of the lost wisdom of the past by an analysis of words is taken seriously by Aristotle, who cites it as proof of his cyclical view of the history of philosophy (*De Caelo* 270ᵇ16–25, *Meteor.* 339ᵇ21–30; cf. *Cratylus* 401b.6).

[2] Pherecydes A 8–9 seems to represent an old element theory, with Zeus interpreted as the upper heavens; the exact details cannot be reconstructed. Philolaus B 12, on the other hand, probably shows the influence of Empedocles, since the classical tetrad here exhaust the contents

Thus, both as components of the world and as phases in the cycle of change, the elements are of Milesian date. But they were not *four* until the time of Empedocles.

ELEMENTS IN GENERAL (ORIGINS). It is more difficult to trace the origin of the idea of an element as such. This very concept is to some extent defined anew by every systematic thinker, and its evolution can therefore scarcely be treated except in a general history of Greek philosophy. The true "elements" of Democritus, for instance, are the atoms, while even those philosophers who make use of the canonical four (as do Plato, Aristotle, and the Stoics) interpret them in quite different ways.

The four elements of Empedocles, for example, are defined by two primary characteristics: (1) they are ungenerated and imperishable, and (2) all natural change results from their mixture and separation (B 8–12, B 17.30–35, etc.). In neither respect does Empedocles open up a new path. These two doctrines (which really form one) had already been taught by Anaxagoras.[1] Both men are, of course, dependent here on Parmenides, whose polemic against γένεσις and ὄλεθρος constitutes the very heart of his doctrine (B 8.13 ff.). The theory of elemental mixture as a substitute for generation and corruption had also been worked out by him in the second part of his poem, to an extent which we can only guess from the miserable fragments that survive. It is clear, however, that not only the heavens, but also the human body, and even thought itself, were explained by him in terms of the blending of two elemental forms.[2] Anaxagoras found this pair of elements too few, and (like the atomists after him) extended the doctrine of Parmenides to an infinite number of diverse "things" or types of things. Here again, the originality of Empedocles lay in his insistence on four forms, and four alone.

The Parmenidean attack on generation and corruption dominates the entire development of natural philosophy in the fifth century. At the same time, it signifies a radical break with the older point of view. Aristotle sometimes speaks as if γένεσις and φθορά had never been taken seriously by the early philosophers,[3] but in that case the impassioned refutation of Parmenides would have no point. That "coming-to-be"

---

of the sphere. (The fact that the word στοιχεῖα is *not* used suggests a genuine, pre-Platonic origin for the fragment.)

[1] Anaxag. B 17, echoed by Emped. B 8–9. For the priority of Anaxagoras, see the Supplementary Note, p. 163.

[2] Parm. B 8.53 ff., B 9, B 12, B 16, B 18. The historical importance of Parmenides for the theories of mixture was rightly emphasized by Reinhardt, *Parmenides*, p. 75.

[3] *Met.* 984ª31 ff.

and "perishing" played an essential role in all previous doctrines is the natural conclusion to be drawn from a reading of his poem; and this view is fully confirmed by the fragments of Xenophanes and Heraclitus. In contrast to the denial of Parmenides, Anaxagoras, and Empedocles these earlier men speak unhesitatingly of "generation," "growth," and "death."[1] The fundamental difference between the sixth and the fifth centuries lies not in the abandonment of monism for plurality, but in the passage from a world of birth and death to one of mixture and separation.

We must not, therefore, confuse the imperishable elements of Empedocles with the generated and corruptible world bodies of sixth-century thought. On the other hand, the fifth-century denial of γένεσις and φθορά ceases once more to be essential for thinkers later than the atomists. For Plato, for Aristotle, and for the Stoics, the change of one element into another is not merely apparent. The cycle of generation and corruption is regarded as an irreducible fact of nature. In this respect the attitude of later times represents a return to the sixth-century view (which is, after all, the natural one), that birth and death are real.

Nevertheless, if the element concept of Empedocles and his contemporaries is something entirely new, in a larger sense the idea of elemental components is as old as human speculation. Hesiod, for instance, tells how Hephaestus fashioned the first woman by "kneading earth with water" (*Op.* 61 ff.; cf. *Theog.* 571), and the myth belongs to the oldest stratum of Mediterranean wisdom. Not only does the Book of Genesis know that Adam is formed "of the dust of the ground," but in Egypt too a god shapes mankind like a piece of pottery.[2] This primordial role of earth and water is never lost sight of in Greece, as we can see from the verses of Xenophanes, as well as from those of Semonides of Amorgus.[3] In this context earth and water are true elements, according

---

[1] Xenoph. B 27 (τελευτᾷ), B 29 (γίνονται ἠδὲ φύονται), B 30 (γενέτωρ); B 33. Heracl. B 31 (γενέσθαι γῆ), B 36, B 62, B 76, B 77, etc.

[2] "A ram-god, Khnum, is referred to as forming mankind on his potter's wheel," Wilson, in *The Intellectual Adventure of Ancient Man*, p. 54.

[3] Xenoph. B 29, B 33; Semonides of Amorgus fr. 7.21–42, Diehl, who has adapted it from Hesiod. It is not necessary to see any new speculative system here, as H. Fränkel suggests in his *Wege und Formen frühgriechischen Denkens* (Munich, 1955), pp. 276 f. There is nothing in Semonides which goes beyond the Pandora story. The idea of men

as formed of earth and water is also presupposed by the curse of Menelaus (*H* 99), which is a euphemistic reference to death: when the vital breath or ψυχή leaves men, they become mere earth and water again. (So Hector's corpse is described as "dumb earth," Ω 54.)

Fire also is recognized as an elemental power in the theft of Prometheus (*Theog.* 563; *Op.* 50). The myth rests, of course, upon the same facts which later serve as basis for the doctrine of natural places: fire's home is in heaven, where it appears as the dread bolt of Zeus; it is but a stranger and a sojourner upon the earth.

to the definition of Aristotle, that is to say, true "primary component parts" (*Met. Δ.* 3).

Although such ideas must have had some influence upon the speculation of sixth-century Miletus, it is above all the larger framework of the *Theogony* which serves as literary precedent for the new doctrines. We have already found the classical tetrad foreshadowed in the great primeval powers from whom, in successive generations, all the gods are born (*Theog.* 105 ff.). The enormous stress laid upon primogeniture in an archaic society leads Hesiod to treat with particular care the question, which god was born *first*, which afterwards (*Theog.* 44 ff., 108 ff.): it was Chaos who arose first of all, next Gaia, and so on through the Ouranides to Zeus, the younger gods, and, finally, the race of demi-gods and mortals (940 ff.).

Now the early cosmologists present a theory which they consider to be much more satisfactory, but which is still of the same outward form: cosmogony is the heir of theogony. Very little, unfortunately, is known of the initial phases in the cosmogony of Anaximander. We have nothing beyond the intriguing statement, that "something capable of generating hot and cold was separated off from the eternal [Boundless]" (**13.P**). It is perhaps no accident, however, that the word for "separating-off," ἀποκρίνεσθαι, is the normal term for the secretion or ejection of seed.[1] The first products of the Boundless must be its "children." At all events, the stylistic echoes of Hesiodic theogony are even more unmistakable in the case of Anaximenes. What is generated from his boundless Air is not only "all that is becoming, has become, and is to be" (cf. *Theog.* 32 and 38), but also "gods and things divine" (θεοὺς καὶ θεῖα). It must be these same divine beings which are referred to as the "offspring" (ἀπόγονοι) of the Air; it is from them in turn that all other things are born. (A 7.1). The context makes clear that these first divine children are above all fire, wind, cloud, water, earth, and stones.[2] What will later become the elements appear here as deities, the first-born of Air, who is himself no doubt the greatest god,[3] the invisible

---

[1] For the physiological sense of ἀποκρίνεσθαι, see Arist. *Gen. An.* 726ᵃ33: οὐδὲν σπέρμα ἀπο-κρίνεται ἀπὸ τοῦ θήλεος; Bonitz, *Index*, 82ᵃ9–41. The usage is frequent in Hippocratic discussions of conception and embryology; see, e.g., *De Victu* chs. 28–29 (Jones, IV, 266 ff.); *De Genit.* 1 (Littré, VII, 470) and *passim*.

[2] The reference of τὰ δὲ λοιπὰ ἐκ τῶν τούτου ἀπογόνων is vague in the text of Hippolytus (Anaximenes A 7.1), but specified by the parallel

in Simplicius (A 5): fire, wind, cloud, water, earth, stones, τὰ δὲ ἄλλα ἐκ τούτων. So also in Cicero (A 9): *gigni autem terram, aquam, ignem, tum ex iis omnia.*

[3] Cf. Xenoph. B 23: εἷς θεός, ἔν τε θεοῖσι καὶ ἀνθρώποισι μέγιστος. In all probability the plural "gods" of Xenophanes are the elements and the sun, moon, and stars; the greatest deity is the world itself, or its everlasting source. I cannot follow the modern interpretations of Xenophanes'

parent and father of all things. All beings compounded from the elements must represent his grandchildren or posterity. Much the same scheme was utilized by another sixth-century author, Pherecydes of Syros, whose theogony begins with "Zas and Time (Chronos) and Earth (Chthoniē)." These three are not born but "were forever" (B 1). Chronos then forms fire, πνεῦμα, and water from his seed (γόνος). The other gods arise out of these first two generations (A 8). It is probably just such a genealogy which Parmenides means to deny, by insisting that his ungenerated Reality is μουνογενές: "alone in the family; unique of its kind."[1]

We have here the sixth-century conception of the elements, in so far as it is known to us. The major components of the visible world are treated as elder children of the parental source, the first progeny in the life cycle which constitutes the natural world. It is from them that all else is sprung. Empedocles is no doubt carrying on with this archaic view when he speaks of the elemental powers as "equals in birth and of one age" (B 17.27), and as the "gods" (δαίμονες) from whom other things are born (B 59). The "gods" or "immortals" of Heraclitus who exchange life and death with mortals must also be the natural elements, water, earth, and the rest, from which living things arise and into which they are dissolved.[2] If the gods are identified with the powers of nature, it is obvious that, as Thales said, "all things are full of gods."[3]

---

deity which ignore its historical position between the cosmic θεῖον of Anaximander (8.Arist.1), on the one hand, and the divine Sphere of Empedocles (B 27-31; cf. B 134), on the other. These are better clues to the philosophic religion of an archaic Greek than all modern concepts of theism, pantheism, and the like. The cosmic deity of Heraclitus must be located within the same circle of ideas. His god takes many forms and is known by many names (B 67; cf. B 32 where "the wise alone" is said to be willing and unwilling to be called by the name of Zeus), but is above all the father and king of the universe (B 53), who guides it with his thought (B 41) and law (B 114), as does the deity of Xenophanes with his mind (B 25). Similarly in the view of Empedocles, φρὴν ἱερή (B 134) and πάντων νόμιμον (B 135) seem to be parallel expressions for the one divine principle which penetrates and governs the entire universe.

[1] For οὖλον μουνογενές in Parm. B 8.4 Kranz now prints ἐστι γὰρ οὐλομελές, although this reading is inferior in every respect. Clearly, the pointless repetition of ἐστι from the end of the previous line is not the work of Parmenides, but of a copyist.

The corrupt οὐλομελές can easily have arisen from οὖλον μουνογενές, but not vice versa; while the γάρ is meaningless here. A supposed contradiction with the preceding ἀγένητον is only apparent: μουνογενής does not mean "only-begotten" but "alone of its kind," "sui generis"; it is formed from the neuter substantive γένος, "race, kind," not directly from the verbal root *γεν- "to be born." (See Chantraine, Formation des noms, p. 424.)

[2] See Heracl. B 62 and B 77. I think the parallel of B 36 makes clear that these θεοί and ἀθάνατοι, whose life is our death, are in fact the elements: "It is death for ψυχαί to become water . . . but from water ψυχή is born." Since all nature is animate, its major elements and powers are the everliving "gods." According to Epicharmus too these were the true divinities (B 8 = Menander, fr. 537 Kock):

ὁ μὲν Ἐπίχαρμος τοὺς θεοὺς εἶναι λέγει
ἀνέμους, ὕδωρ, γῆν, ἥλιον, πῦρ, ἀστέρας.

[3] Thales A 22. The same conception of divinity is implied by the author of The Sacred Disease, who says: "This disease arises from the same

Thus from the Milesians to Empedocles there is a common theological scheme answering to what will later be called "the elements". This scheme takes the form of a reinterpretation of the mythic cosmogony, in which the fundamental cosmic principle is father and ruler of the gods, the elemental powers his divine offspring and parents, in their turn, of mortal things. It is precisely this scheme which Plato develops in the *Timaeus*. The old mythic formula reappears in his description of the ideal model and material receptacle of creation as the father and mother of the cosmic child (*Tim.* 50d.3). The physical world is itself a god, while Earth, in reminiscence of the Hesiodic account, is styled "first and eldest of the gods born within the heavens" (40c.3). It is from these secondary gods of nature, and not from the supreme Demiurge, that human beings and mortal creatures are formed, and to these they return at death (41d.1–3).

Because of the almost complete disappearance of the sixth-century texts, it is impossible for us to say just where genuine myth comes to an end and where allegory begins. In regard to the Milesians, it would certainly be a mistake to overestimate the "primitive" aspect of such formulas; the fragments of Pherecydes are there to show us just how literary the whole procedure may be. On the other hand, the serious use of similar expressions by Empedocles and Plato warns us against dismissing this mythic fabric as a mere trick of style. Behind the constant Greek tendency to dress the newest speculative ideas in the hoariest garments of antiquity lies a deep sense of continuity with the past. Since the early philosophers clearly regarded the world as alive, its emergence was a genuine *birth* in their eyes. The two senses of γίγνεσθαι were still one and the same. Furthermore, by describing the universe and its parts in the solemn language of traditional religion, these men invoked the ancestral pomp and ceremony—and the accompanying sentiment of awe before what is greater than mankind—in honor of their new conception of reality. The divinity whom Xenophanes proposes to celebrate at a feast of wise men (B 1) is certainly not Zeus son of Cronus, but the ungenerated god of the natural philosophers. And when Xenophanes thus seeks to replace the crude old stories by a truer account of what is most grand and fundamental in the world of Nature, we have every reason to recognize here, in the person of one of their earliest

---

causes as the others: from what comes in contact with the body and what leaves it, from cold and sun and the continually changing winds. But all these things are divine." Hence, he concludes, one disease is no more divine than another (ch. 21; Jones, II, 182).

disciples,[1] a typical example of the Milesians' attitude in the presence of their new gods.

THE OPPOSITES (ORIGINS). Thus far we have been concerned to show that the ideas of Empedocles are in essential continuity with those of the first Greek natural philosophers. Only in his dependence on Parmenides (and, hence, in the substitution of mixture for generation) does a fundamental difference appear between his presuppositions and those of the sixth century. His personal contribution lies above all in the classic simplicity of the fourfold scheme, and this he probably adopted in direct reaction against the infinite forms of Anaxagoras.[2] It is perhaps unfair to describe the resulting system as "an interesting eclecticism."[3] The view of Empedocles has after all a unity and a driving passion which are his own. But, in order to understand the earlier doctrines, we must not overestimate the originality of such fifth-century theories.

In regard to the causal role of the opposites, it scarcely needs to be argued that Empedocles and Aristotle are dependent on older ideas, for we have the words of Heraclitus, reflecting the importance of the primary opposites in his time: τὰ ψυχρὰ θέρεται, θερμὸν ψύχεται, ὑγρὸν αὐαίνεται, καρφαλέον νοτίζεται. "Cold things grow warm, hot cools, moist is parched, dry dampens" (B 126). Heraclitus' designation of War as king and father of all (B 53) is meaningful only in terms of the doctrine of elemental strife.[4] Also at the end of the sixth century comes the theory of Alcmaeon, defining health as an "equal distribution" (ἰσονομία) or proportionate blend (κρᾶσις σύμμετρος) of opposite powers, whose excess or "monarchy" is cause of disease (B 4). From Alcmaeon descends the standard causal doctrine of the Hippocratic authors, which we have considered. So the two basic forms of Parmenides are "set opposite to one another" (B 8.55), and have each one its several powers (δυνάμεις, B 9.2): their μίξις is symbolized by the male's pursuit of the

---

[1] Phys. Opin. fr. 6a (Vors. 28 A 1.21): τοῦτον (sc. Xenophanes) Θεόφραστος ἐν τῇ Ἐπιτομῇ Ἀναξιμάνδρου φησὶν ἀκοῦσαι.

For the religious color of certain phrases in the early fragments, see K. Deichgräber, "Hymnische Elemente in der philosophischen Prosa der Vorsokratiker," Philologus, LXXXVIII (1933), 347 ff.

[2] Arist. Phys. 189ᵃ16: "He thinks to account for all things [with a limited number of principles] that Anaxagoras explains from an infinite number." The rebuttal is provided by the atomists, who insist upon the need for an unlimited number of elements to explain the endless variety of appearances (Democr. A 38).

[3] Diels, "Gorgias und Empedocles," Sitzungsberichte der Preussischen Akademie, Berlin, 1884, p. 343. H. Fränkel says more justly of this period that "jeder neue Umbau des Weltbildes zugleich als konservierender, fast pietätvoller Ausbau, und als trotzige, selbstsichere Zerstörung und Neubau erscheint" (Frühgriechisches Denken, p. 187).

[4] Cf. Kirk, Heraclitus, pp. 241 ff., 401. Kirk takes a narrower view of B 53, but admits (p. 249) that there must be some connection with the cosmic strife of B 80.

female, and the "opposite" (that is, answering) reaction of the other sex (B 12). For Parmenides, too, the healthy formation of the body depends upon the proper blending of opposites (B 18.3: *temperies*, i.e., κρᾶσις).

The ancient roots of this view are easy to recognize. A cosmic Eros was familiar to Hesiod, even if he does not make much of him in the *Theogony* (120 ff.). The interdependence of opposing powers is anticipated in mythic terms by the birth of Day and Αἰθήρ out of Night (*Theog.* 124). Strife too is a great power in the early poetry (Hes. *Op.* 11 ff.). Nor did it require a natural philosopher to discover the enmity between fire and water, proverbial in the days of Theognis and Aeschylus.[1] A designation of water as "the wet" appears in the stylized Homeric mention of the magic sandals of the gods, which bear them "as well over dampness (ἐφ᾽ ὑγρήν) as over the boundless earth" (Ω 341, α 97, etc.). And the attraction of like to like is a familiar theme from the *Odyssey* (ρ 218).

Nevertheless, the use of the opposites in causal explanation, as known to Heraclitus, Alcmaeon, and Parmenides, derives less from these old ideas than from the new application which they receive in Milesian cosmology. The primary role of Hot and Cold in the formation of Anaximander's heaven is, as we saw, echoed by the action of these and of other opposing principles in the detailed account of meteorological events.[2] Indeed the very concept of "separating-out" (ἀπόκρισις) implies the emergence of unlike, contrasting forms.[3]

Which opposite powers played the greatest role in Milesian thought? The account of Theophrastus emphasizes above all the hot and the cold (**13.P.**), and Anaximenes seems in fact to have made use of these two in their classic function, as powers of rarefaction and condensation (B 1, A 7.3). But, of course, the wet and the dry were also required in any scheme where the processes of evaporation loomed so large.[4] It is, as we have seen, precisely these two couples which are singled out by Heraclitus in fragment B 126. The Parmenidean emphasis on male and female may imply another echo of Milesian ideas, reflecting the concrete sense of cosmogony as the fruit of sexual union. The contrast of

---

[1] Theognis 1245 f.; Aesch. *Ag.* 650.

[2] See above, pp. 101, 109.

[3] For ἀποκρίνεσθαι in the sense of a qualitative separation of unlike things from one another, see Hdt. 1.60; Thuc. 1.3.3; Democr. B 11. The root idea of *krei-* implies qualitative "discernment"; see Ernout-Meillet, *Dictionnaire étymologique de la*

langue latine, s.v. *cerno*; and in Greek, the sense of κριτός, "select." It is precisely the opposites which are "separated-out" from one another in the fragments of Anaxagoras (p. 161, n. 2).

[4] One may compare the role of moisture and desiccation in the Milesian theory of earthquakes (20a; above, p. 104).

bright and dark must also have been more prominent in early times than in the scheme of Aristotle. The importance of this couple may be seen, for instance, in Anaximander's account of the lightning flash (**19**), as well as in Anaximenes' explanation of the rainbow:

A rainbow arises from the radiation of the sun in contact with a cloud which is dense, thick, and dark, since the beams become entangled with the cloud and are not able to break through. . . . The first part [of the ἀήρ or cloud]¹ appears as brilliant red (φοινικοῦν), burnt through by the sun's rays, the rest as dark (μέλαν), overpowered by moisture. And he says that a rainbow arises at night from the moon, but not often because . . . its light is weaker than the sun's. (A 18)

There is a clear struggle of opposing forces here, where only the strong light of the sun is capable of victory over the resistant power of moisture. Furthermore, we see that solar heat is essentially bright for Anaximenes, while the moist condition of the ἀήρ is intrinsically dark. It is impossible not to think in this connection of the ἠέλιος λευκός and ὄμβρος δνοφόεις of Empedocles B 21 (above, p. 127), where again luminosity and darkness are parallel to heat and cold.

This gives us three opposing couples as certainly Milesian: hot-cold, dry-wet, bright-dark, and perhaps a fourth, male-female. This last pair reappears in the Pythagorean table, together with darkness and light (*Vors.* 58 B 5). It is, however, dropped by Anaxagoras, whose more severely scientific scheme is based upon the three inanimate couples just named, together with a fourth, rare-dense (ἀραιόν, πυκνόν).² These terms were also listed by Parmenides among the primary "signs" (σήματα) of his two fundamental forms (B 8.57–59). Has Anaxagoras borrowed his scheme directly from Parmenides, or do both men draw upon the Milesian tradition? There is little ground for hesitation here. The multiformity of ἀήρ for Anaximenes would be inexplicable without this notion of condensation and rarefaction, expressly attributed to him by Theophrastus (A 5) as well as by Plutarch (B 1). Indeed, the "thickness" of the cloud and the "fineness" of the wind are also essential in the meteorology of Anaximander (**17–19**). And this couple regularly reappears with the other three in fifth-century accounts of evaporation.³

---

¹ *Vors.* 13 A 18: ὅθεν τὸ μὲν πρότερον αὐτοῦ [τοῦ ἡλίου] φοινικοῦν φαίνεται, διακαιόμενον ὑπὸ τῶν ἀκτίνων, τὸ δὲ μέλαν, κατακρατούμενον ὑπὸ τῆς ὑγρότητος. I bracket the words τοῦ ἡλίου as a misplaced gloss on τῶν ἀκτίνων; cf. αἱ τοῦ ἡλίου αὐγαί in the preceding sentence. The reference of αὐτοῦ is to the ἀήρ, which has just been mentioned, for it is obviously not the sun which is

"burnt through by the rays." For the doctrine, cf. Xenoph. B 32; Anaxag. B 19, A 86; Arist. *Meteor.* 374ᵃ1 ff.
² Anaxag. B 4 (moist-dry, hot-cold, bright-dark); B 8 (hot-cold); B 12 (rare-dense, hot-cold, bright-dark, wet-dry); B 15 (dense, damp, cold, dark, opposed to rare, hot, dry).
³ See, e.g., *De Aëribus* 8 (Jones, I, 90–92):

Thus, behind the fourfold scheme of Empedocles we catch sight of an older, less elaborate pattern of elemental dualism. This tendency towards polar opposition is most fully documented in the fragments of Parmenides and Anaxagoras, but is also familiar to Heraclitus and Alcmaeon. It is regularly ascribed to the Milesians in the doxographical tradition. In virtue of this convergent testimony from different sources, we may reconstruct the Milesian view of elemental opposites approximately as follows: on the one hand stand hot, dry, bright, and rare; on the other, cold, damp, dark, and dense. The first series is naturally connected with the sun, and with the upper heavens in general; the second with terrestrial moisture and its solidified residue, the earth. The fundamental phenomenon of natural change is thus an ἀπόκρισις or separating-out of one opposite form from the other, typified in the acts of evaporation and combustion. But this process is, of course, reversible, and the nether powers take their revenge in the σύγκρισις (contraction or compression) of hot to cold, dry to damp: thus the brightness of the sun's ray may be overpowered by the thick moisture of a cloud, and the cloud itself condenses into rain.

These two opposing principles—the powers of heaven and of earth—are symbolized for Parmenides by Fire or Light on the one hand, Night on the other. In the fragments of Anaxagoras, the same position is occupied by the αἰθήρ and the ἀήρ.[1] The Milesians no doubt also regarded celestial fire as an elemental power or portion of the world, concentrated principally in the sun. The thick and opaque lower forces may very well have been identified by Anaximander with the ἀήρ, for here the link with the Homeric sense of the word is perfectly clear. The absence of direct documents makes it, of course, very difficult to visualize the exact Milesian terminology. But in regard to the opposites, at least, we have every right to look upon the cosmology of Anaxagoras as but a slightly modernized version of the sixth-century scheme. The fundamental dualism which Anaxagoras shares with Parmenides may be due in part to the systematic genius of the latter; the roots at any rate go back to Miletus.

ἐπειδὰν ἁρπασθῇ καὶ μετεωρισθῇ (sc. τὸ ὄμβριον ὕδωρ) περιφερόμενον καὶ καταμεμιγμένον ἐς τὸν ἠέρα, τὸ μὲν θολερὸν αὐτοῦ καὶ νυκτοειδὲς ἐκκρίνεται καὶ ἐξίσταται καὶ γίνεται ἠὴρ καὶ ὀμίχλη, τὸ δὲ λαμπρότατον καὶ κουφότατον αὐτοῦ λείπεται καὶ γλυκαίνεται ὑπὸ τοῦ ἡλίου καιόμενόν τε καὶ ἑψόμενον. In the first instance, τὸν ἠέρα means, of course, "the air," but the second ἠήρ is "mist."

[1] To the ἀπόκρισις of the opposites from one another (Anaxag. B 12, B 4: πρὶν ἀποκριθῆναι...; cf. B 8) corresponds the separating-out of αἰθήρ and ἀήρ (B 2, B 12). The actual process is described in B 15. The four opposing couples clearly define the ἀήρ and the αἰθήρ for Anaxagoras, just as the two "forms" of Parmenides (B 8.53) are distinguished by their respective δυνάμεις (B 9).

Returning now to our point of departure, we see what historical reality must lie behind the statements of Simplicius and Aristotle that Anaximander "observed the change of the four elements into one another," and so "did not think fit to make any one of these the material substratum," but chose instead "an infinite body . . . beside the elements," out of which he could "generate the latter."[1] In such a report the *four* elements are an anachronism, just as it is unhistorical to project the Aristotelian ὑποκείμενον back into the sixth century. The point of view described may nevertheless be recognized as that of a Milesian. The cyclical interchange of elemental forms was familiar to Anaximander and Anaximenes, and naturally led them to seek a more permanent source of cosmic evolution. Like the ἄπειρον itself, the boundless ἀήρ of Anaximenes is also really "different from the elements," since it is defined as imperceptible in its own form, distinguishable as wind or cloud only under the action of the hot, cold, or other active powers. Aristotle's statement that the elements were "generated out of the ἄπειρον" corresponds to their designation as "offspring of the Air" in the case of Anaximenes. What little we know of Anaximander's cosmogony suggests that Hot and Cold, the basic constituents of the heavens, appeared as the eldest progeny of the Boundless.

We cannot pretend to say just how many primary powers or portions were generated by Anaximander out of the ἄπειρον. Not only hot and cold, but the other major pairs of opposites must also have figured among them, incorporated in (or acting upon) the visible bodies of the natural world. Here, in addition to the sun, moon, and stars, Anaximander probably recognized the αἰθήρ as well as the ἀήρ and the six forms mentioned by Anaximenes: fire, wind, cloud, water, earth, and stones.

Supplementary Note: On the Chronological Relationship Between Anaxagoras and Empedocles

The priority of Anaxagoras is asserted by Aristotle, *Met.* 984[a]11: Ἐμπεδοκλῆς δὲ τὰ τέτταρα (sc. ἀρχὰς τίθησι) . . . Ἀναξαγόρας δὲ ὁ Κλαζομένιος τῇ μὲν ἡλικίᾳ πρότερος ὢν τούτου τοῖς δ' ἔργοις ὕστερος ἀπείρους εἶναί φησι τὰς ἀρχάς. The statement concerning their relative age is confirmed by Theophrastus, who, with his usual precision, adds that Empedocles was "born not much later than Anaxagoras" (*Phys. Opin.* fr. 3; *Dox.* 477.17). According to the Hellenistic chronology,

_____
[1] See the passages cited at the beginning of this chapter, p. 119.

Anaxagoras was the senior by about seventeen years: his birth was placed in 500/499 B.C., that of Empedocles in 483/2 (see "Fasti Apollodorei," in F. Jacoby, *Apollodors Chronik* [Berlin, 1902], p. 407). Of course, such dates must be taken with a grain of salt. But it would be futile to pretend to any greater accuracy by arbitrarily raising or lowering one of the figures, and a difference of seventeen years is compatible with the οὐ πολὺ κατόπιν γεγονώς of Theophrastus—Empedocles was younger by less than a generation.

In view of all this, it seems somewhat perverse of Zeller (I⁵, 1024–26) to argue that the points of contact between the two philosophers must be due to the influence of the younger man. One would naturally suppose the contrary to be true. We need not, like Alcidamas, make Empedocles a "hearer" of Anaxagoras (D.L. VIII.56), but we may reasonably assume that he had read the latter's book.

On the other hand, Ross (probably with Zeller's view in mind) renders as follows the text of the *Metaphysics* quoted above: "Anaxagoras of Clazomenae, who, though older than Empedocles, was later in his philosophical activity." Zeller's theory has thus succeeded in implanting itself in our sources. But in fact this cannot be what Aristotle means by τοῖς δ' ἔργοις ὕστερος, for in the same chapter he clearly assumes that not only the birth but also the doctrine of Anaxagoras was prior in time. The motive cause made its first real appearance with Anaxagoras' concept of Nous (984ᵇ15–22), while Empedocles was the first to conceive this cause as double, in Love and Strife (985ᵃ2–10, 29–31; similarly 985ᵃ18–23: Ἀναξαγόρας τε γὰρ μηχανῇ χρῆται τῷ νῷ . . . καὶ Ἐμπεδοκλῆς ἐπὶ πλέον μὲν τούτου χρῆται τοῖς αἰτίοις, οὐ μὴν οὔθ' ἱκανῶς). The same order is presupposed by Theophrastus: Ἀναξαγόρας . . . πρῶτος μετέστησε τὰς περὶ τῶν ἀρχῶν δόξας καὶ τὴν ἐλλείπουσαν αἰτίαν ἀνεπλήρωσε (fr. 4; *Dox.* 478.18).

The temporal priority of Empedocles' doctrine is therefore excluded. What then can Aristotle mean by saying that Anaxagoras is τοῖς δ' ἔργοις ὕστερος? The obvious answer is given by Alexander (*in Met.* 28.1–10): ὕστερος here means "inferior, second-rate." Aristotle often expresses his preference for the few principles of Empedocles over the infinite number introduced by Anaxagoras (*Phys.* 188ᵃ17, 189ᵃ15). As Alexander remarks, just such a contrast between the number of principles is suggested here by the context.

The meaning of the phrase in question is thus simply: "Anaxagoras comes before Empedocles in time, but after him in his philosophical achievements." The remark is offered as a kind of apology for having mentioned Empedocles before Anaxagoras. Such a stylistic contrast or parallel between priority in time and superiority in rank or quality is a standard device in Greek, answering to the double sense of πρῶτος: "first" and "best." Compare D.L. III.48: [who first wrote dialogues is a matter for dispute] δοκεῖ δέ μοι Πλάτων ἀκριβώσας τὸ εἶδος καὶ τὰ πρωτεῖα δικαίως ἂν ὥσπερ τοῦ κάλλους οὕτω καὶ τῆς εὑρέσεως ἀποφέρεσθαι. And Theophrastus probably had our passage from the *Metaphysics* in mind when he contrasted Plato with the earlier philosophers: τούτοις ἐπιγενόμενος Πλάτων τῇ μὲν δόξῃ καὶ τῇ δυνάμει πρότερος τοῖς δὲ χρόνοις ὕστερος (fr. 9; *Dox.* 484.19).

III

ANAXIMANDER'S FRAGMENT: THE UNIVERSE GOVERNED BY LAW

HAVING done what we can to reconstruct the historical context of Milesian thought, we must see what sense can be made of the only original document surviving from this period. It will be well to recall once more the doxographical framework within which Anaximander's fragment has been preserved.

Ἀναξίμανδρος . . . ἀρχήν τε καὶ στοιχεῖον εἴρηκε τῶν ὄντων τὸ ἄπειρον, πρῶτος τοῦτο τοὔνομα κομίσας τῆς ἀρχῆς· λέγει δ' αὐτὴν μήτε ὕδωρ μήτε ἄλλο τι τῶν καλουμένων εἶναι στοιχείων, ἀλλ' ἑτέραν τινὰ φύσιν ἄπειρον, ἐξ ἧς ἅπαντας γίνεσθαι τοὺς οὐρανοὺς καὶ τοὺς ἐν αὐτοῖς κόσμους· ἐξ ὧν δὲ ἡ γένεσίς ἐστι τοῖς οὖσι, καὶ τὴν φθορὰν εἰς ταῦτα γίνεσθαι κατὰ τὸ χρεών, διδόναι γὰρ αὐτὰ δίκην καὶ τίσιν ἀλλήλοις τῆς ἀδικίας κατὰ τὴν τοῦ χρόνου τάξιν, ποιητικωτέροις οὕτως ὀνόμασιν αὐτὰ λέγων. δῆλον δὲ ὅτι τὴν εἰς ἄλληλα μεταβολὴν τῶν τεττάρων στοιχείων οὗτος θεασάμενος οὐκ ἠξίωσεν ἕν τι τούτων ὑποκείμενον ποιῆσαι, ἀλλά τι ἄλλο παρὰ ταῦτα.

Anaximander . . . declared the Boundless to be principle and element of existing things, having been the first to introduce this very term of "principle"; he says that it is neither water nor any other of the so-called elements, but some different, boundless nature, from which all the heavens arise and the κόσμοι within them; out of those things whence is the generation for existing things, into these again does their destruction take place, according to what must needs be; for they make amends and give reparation to one another for their offense, according to the ordinance of time, speaking of them thus in rather poetical terms. It is clear that, having observed the change of the four elements into one another, he did not think fit to make any one of these the material substratum, but something else besides these. (*Phys. Opin.* fr. 2, *Dox.* 476, cited above, **1-6. S**)

It is the mention of Anaximander's use of poetical terms which proves that we have here, at least in part, a verbatim citation. From the grammatical point of view, the more obviously "poetic" expressions cannot be isolated from the long sentence in indirect discourse, which is introduced by the word λέγει and concluded by its repetition λέγων. The continuity of the thought as well as of the form is underlined for us by the following remark: it is precisely because the elements change into one another, that the ἀρχή was not identified with any one of them. These words direct us back to the very beginning of the indirect citation (μήτε ὕδωρ μήτε ἄλλο τι . . .).

For Simplicius, then, the fragment illustrates one idea and one alone: why the source from which "all the heavens" arise cannot be one of the so-called elements. That the "poetical terms," in particular, are taken to refer directly to the elements, is evident from the phrase ποιητικω-τέροις οὕτως ὀνόμασιν αὐτὰ λέγων. The neuter plural pronoun can only refer back to the στοιχεῖα, which are immediately mentioned again in the next sentence. This phrase tells us that Simplicius understood the preceding αὐτά (subject of the poetic διδόναι δίκην ἀλλήλοις) in the same way. For him, it is the *elements* which are picturesquely described as "making reparation to one another for their offense." But this first use of the pronoun, in the phrase διδόναι γὰρ αὐτὰ δίκην, implies that they have been mentioned in what immediately precedes. Did Simplicius intend the antecedent of αὐτά to be τοῖς οὖσι or the neuter pronouns ἐξ ὧν and εἰς ταῦτα? The second alternative seems the more likely when we recall the Aristotelian definition of an element as "that out of which a thing is composed and into which it can be resolved" (cf. οἷον φωνῆς στοιχεῖα ἐξ ὧν σύγκειται ἡ φωνὴ καὶ εἰς ἃ διαιρεῖται ἔσχατα, *Met.* 1014ᵃ27). A close reading of the passage shows that Simplicius' whole attention is focused on the notion of elements, and that the poetic phrase which he quotes from Anaximander explains the generation of τὰ ὄντα out of, and their dissolution into, the elements as a reparation which the latter make to one another for their offense.

There is, I submit, no other interpretation of this passage which is suggested by the immediate context, and therefore no reason to suppose that either Simplicius or Theophrastus (who are in this instance indistinguishable from one another) understood the words of Anaximander in any other way. The whole meaning of the passage—and, in particular, the identity of τὰ ὄντα—is still by no means clear. What does seem evident is that there is no place, either in the wording of the fragment or in the immediate context, for any penalty or wrongdoing which could involve the Boundless. The "poetic expressions" clearly point to a relationship of the elements among themselves (ἀλλήλοις). Merely on grammatical grounds, there is no term in the fragment which could refer to the ἄπειρον.[1]

---

[1] The inaccurate translation of ἐξ ὧν . . . εἰς ταῦτα . . . by "into that from which things arise . . ." (as if we had ἐξ οὗ . . . εἰς τοῦτο . . .) was universally prevalent until twenty years ago, when

Such a view should occur to anyone who examines the text of Simplicius without knowing in advance what it is supposed to say. If a very different interpretation has been adopted by most commentators, including Nietzsche and Diels, it is perhaps because they were so fascinated by the concept of *das Unendliche* as the source of all that exists that they never seriously considered the possibility that τὸ ἄπειρον might not even be mentioned in the only sentence surviving from Anaximander's book. Furthermore, they probably had in mind the parallel version of Aëtius: φησὶ τῶν ὄντων ἀρχὴν εἶναι τὸ ἄπειρον· ἐκ γὰρ τούτου πάντα γίγνεσθαι καὶ εἰς τοῦτο πάντα φθείρεσθαι. But this formula represents nothing more than a banal and inaccurate rendering of the same text which is much more faithfully preserved by Simplicius.[1] Once this fact is recognized, no motive remains for finding any reference to the Boundless in Anaximander's words.[2]

Before pressing any further into the problems of an *explication de texte*, we must first see just how much of a text we have. Where does the literal quotation begin and where does it end? The only methodical approach to this question is necessarily a long one. It leads us to a minute analysis of certain points of style.

The Language of the Fragment

The language in which Anaximander wrote was not the artificially archaic dialect of the epic tradition, but the spoken tongue of sixth-century Ionia. This inference may be drawn directly from his use of prose, but it is confirmed for us by the very expressions which the

---

H. Cherniss drew attention to the plural forms in *Aristotle's Criticism of Presocratic Philosophy* (Baltimore, 1935), p. 377. The error is now being corrected, but slowly. The latest editions of Diels–Kranz still translate "Woraus aber . . . in das hinein . . . ."

At the same time, Cherniss understood the plurals as referring to the ἄπειρον, and thus maintained the interpretation which stood behind the faulty translations in the first place. On this point he has been followed by G. Vlastos, *CP*, XLII, 170 ff., and by H. Fränkel, *Dichtung und Philosophie des frühen Griechentums* (New York, 1951), p. 347, n. 19. But any explanation of a plural form—even a neuter plural—as if it were a singular must inevitably arouse some misgiving, and such devices become unnecessary if, as I suggest, the plurals offer a natural and satisfactory sense.

[1] See the commentary on 4.A.

[2] A brief review of the older interpretations of the fragment, and of my reasons for rejecting

them, will be found in the Supplementary Note on p. 193.

The phrase which immediately precedes the fragment (ἐξ ἧς ἅπαντας γίνεσθαι τοὺς οὐρανοὺς καὶ τοὺς ἐν αὐτοῖς κόσμους) refers indeed to generation out of the Boundless. There is furthermore a certain resemblance between the two formulas: ἐξ ἧς γίνεσθαι, and ἐξ ὧν δὲ ἡ γένεσίς ἐστι. These facts may serve to explain—but not to justify—the insistence on understanding ἐξ ὧν . . . εἰς ταῦτα in the same way. But the relative clause ἐξ ἧς ἅπαντας γίνεσθαι τοὺς οὐρανούς is a parenthetical expression, specifying the role of the φύσις ἄπειρος, while the particle in ἐξ ὧν δὲ ἡ γένεσίς ἐστι τοῖς οὖσι introduces a new development, continued by γάρ in the following clause. That Simplicius here turns his attention back to τὰ καλούμενα στοιχεῖα is proved by αὐτὰ λέγων at the end of the sentence. It is to these again that he refers with δῆλον δέ in the next sentence.

doxographer describes as "poetic." This remark must apply above all to the phrase διδόναι δίκην καὶ τίσιν ἀλλήλοις τῆς ἀδικίας. Now the words δίκη and τίσις are both known to the old epic language, but neither appears there with the verb διδόναι in the sense required here. When, for example, Hesiod says δίκας διδοῦσιν, he means, not "they pay the penalty," but "they render judgments" (Op. 225). His expression for "making amends" is δίκην παρασχεῖν.[1] On the other hand, this construction of δίκην (or τίσιν) διδόναι, with the genitive of the offense committed and the dative of the person to whom retribution is due, is a regular feature of Attic and Ionic poetry and prose in the fifth century:

$$τοιᾶσδέ τοι$$
$$ἁμαρτίας σφε δεῖ θεοῖς δοῦναι δίκην. (Aesch. P.V. 8)$$

$$οὐδὲ ἐκεῖνοι \text{'}Ιοῦς τῆς Ἀργείης ἔδοσάν σφι δίκας τῆς ἁρπαγῆς· οὐδὲ$$
$$ὧν αὐτοὶ δώσειν ἐκείνοισι. (Hdt. 1.2.3)$$

$$ἵνα \ldots ἀπολαμφθέντες ἐν τῇ Σαλαμῖνι δοῖεν τίσιν (sc. τοῖσι Πέρσῃσι)$$
$$τῶν ἐπ᾽ Ἀρτεμισίῳ ἀγωνισμάτων. (Hdt. VIII.76.2)$$

Thus the fragment of Anaximander represents the earliest example of what must have been a very common phrase in the law courts.

The case of ἀδικία is similar. This word is frequent in early Attic and Ionic for the "wrongdoing" or "offense" of one who inflicts harm upon another (ἀδικεῖν τινα), and in particular for an offense which lies within the scope of legal action and compensation (δίκη). Later, of course, it comes to mean injustice or unrighteousness in general, the contrary of δικαιοσύνη. But it is unattested in any sense before the time of Anaximander.[2]

In its most unmistakably genuine portions, the fragment is thus the oldest known specimen of the classical tongue of Athens and Ionia, apart from the inscriptions. It has a much more direct kinship with the dialect of Herodotus and of the Hippocratic Corpus than with the old poetry based stylistically upon the epic. If we could read the treatises of sixth-century Miletus, the syntax would no doubt strike us as archaic (as does that of most Ionic compositions); the vocabulary, however, would be largely that of the fifth century.

This relatively modern linguistic character of the fragment appears

---

[1] Op. 712. Homer's phrase is πάντ᾽ ἀποδοῦναι (Σ 499; cf. β 78), πάντ᾽ ἀπέτισε (α 43), or simply τίσις ἔσσεται (α 40, β 76). At hymn. ad Merc. 312, δὸς δὲ δίκην καὶ δέξο is addressed to the plaintiff, not to the defendant, and means "submit the case to judgment."

[2] See LSJ s.v. ἀδικία.

in another expression which can hardly be due to the pen of a doxographer: κατὰ τὸ χρεών. The form χρεών is used impersonally by Solon (23.18, Diehl) and by Theognis (564), but the phrase with the article is not attested before Anaximander.[1] (We are not surprised to find the article employed by an author who spoke of τὸ ἄπειρον, and probably also of τὸ θερμόν, τὸ ὑγρόν, and the rest.) This construction is of course current in the fifth century:

κάνες τὸν οὐ χρῆν, καὶ τὸ μὴ χρεὼν πάθε. (Aesch. *Cho.* 930)

οὐ γὰρ ποιῆσαί μιν τὸ χρεὸν ἦν ποιέειν. (Hdt. 11.133.3)

οὔτε . . . καταπροΐξεαι ἀποτρέπων τὸ χρεὸν γενέσθαι.

(Hdt. vii.17.2)

Thus far, the literal citation from Anaximander is beyond dispute. The authenticity of the concluding phrase, κατὰ τὴν τοῦ χρόνου τάξιν, should be equally clear. The word τάξις is not attested before Anaximander, but fifth-century examples of the legal or military usage of the term are too numerous and too well known to require citation.[2] The full sense of the word is "an arrangement prescribed with authority; an order which is morally binding"; hence λιπεῖν τάξιν is an act of shame. In the present case such authority is exercised by Time.[3] The judicial color of διδόναι δίκην is maintained in the "ordinance" or "ordainment" by which the penalty is fixed, and Time appears as the magistrate who determines what the retribution shall be.

Now the personification of Chronos as a mighty power in human and cosmic affairs is a constant theme of archaic and early classical literature. Time is already a judge in one of Solon's poems, and he is regularly personified by the Attic tragedians as well as by Pindar.[4] His

---

[1] χρεών is a (late) variant for χρεώ at α 225 and ο 201. See the discussion of G. Redard, *Recherches sur χρή, χρῆσθαι* (Paris, 1953), pp. 70 ff. It is only the infinitival construction of χρεών (like χρή) which occurs in Aristotelian prose, as was pointed out by G. S. Kirk, *CQ*, XLIX, 33; see Bonitz, *Index*, 853ᵇ35.

[2] It may be recalled that τάξις designates the ordering of the seven cosmic regions in *De Hebd.* 1–2; and compare *De Victu* 8 (Jones, IV, 242): χρόνον δὲ τοσοῦτον ἕκαστον τὴν αὐτὴν τάξιν ἔχει, ἄχρι μηκέτι δέχηται ἡ χώρη μηδὲ τροφὴν ἱκανὴν ἔχῃ ἐς τὸ μήκιστον τῶν δυνατῶν (according to the text of Diels, *Vors.* 22 c 1).

[3] The genitive of κατὰ τὴν τοῦ χρόνου τάξιν is obviously "subjective": that is, it does not represent the accusative which receives the action

of the verb (as if we had κατὰ τὸν χρόνον τὸν τεταγμένον), but the nominative which exerts this action: κατὰ τὴν τάξιν ἦν ὁ χρόνος τάττει. Kirk compares κατὰ τὴν Ἀριστεί[δου τάξιν], "the assessment of Aristides" (Meritt, Wade-Gery, and McGregor, *The Athenian Tribute Lists*, II [Princeton, 1949], p. 61, no. D 13). Jaeger had already cited Plato, *Politicus* 305c.1 : παρὰ τὴν τοῦ νομοθέτου τάξιν.

[4] Solon 24.3 (Diehl): ἐν δίκῃ χρόνου compared by Jaeger, *Theology*, p. 207, n. 60, with references back to his earlier discussions. Cf. Aesch. *P.V.* 981: ἀλλ᾽ ἐκδιδάσκει πάνθ᾽ ὁ γηράσκων χρόνος; Soph. *O.T.* 614, *Ajax* 645; Eur. fr. 303, etc. One of the most striking Pindaric examples is fr. 14 (Bowra): ἄνακτα τὸν πάντων ὑπερβάλλοντα Χρόνον μακάρων.

importance as a primary figure in cosmogony is echoed with emphasis by Anaximander's younger contemporary, Pherecydes, whose philosophical fable begins with these words: Ζὰς μὲν καὶ Χρόνος ἦσαν ἀεὶ καὶ Χθονίη.[1]

It is therefore surprising that the phrase in question has recently been ascribed not to Anaximander but to his excerptor.[2] Τάξις, some critics argue, is a term frequently employed by Aristotle in reference to a temporal sequence. We have, for example:

πάντων γάρ ἐστι τάξις καὶ πᾶς χρόνος καὶ βίος μετρεῖται περιόδῳ.

(Gen. Corr. 336^{b}12)

κατὰ μέντοι τινὰ τάξιν νομίζειν χρὴ ταῦτα γίγνεσθαι καὶ περίοδον.

(Meteor. 351^{a}25)

ἄρχειν . . . ἢ κατ᾽ ἐνιαυτὸν ἢ κατά τινα ἄλλην τάξιν ἢ χρόνον.

(Pol. 1261^{a}34)

Indeed, the thought of the fragment is rendered by Simplicius elsewhere in nearly the same words:

ἡ γένεσις διὰ τὸν χρόνον ἐν τάξει διακέκριται. (in Cat. 356.26)

When, therefore, we find a similar phrase in the doxography for Heraclitus, it is reasonable to suppose that we are dealing not with the original words of the philosopher, but with a Peripatetic paraphrase:

ποιεῖ δὲ καὶ τάξιν τινὰ καὶ χρόνον ὡρισμένον τῆς τοῦ κόσμου μεταβολῆς κατά τινα εἱμαρμένην ἀνάγκην.

(Heracl. A 5 = Phys. Opin. fr. 1)

The final phrase of Anaximander's fragment, κατὰ τὴν τοῦ χρόνου τάξιν, must (it is argued) be a similar paraphrase, of which the original has been lost.

---

[1] Pherecydes B 1. In his discussion of "Die Zeitauffassung in der frühgriechischen Literatur" (Frühgriechisches Denken, p. 19), H. Fränkel suggested that the reading Χρόνος in D.L. does not represent the text of Pherecydes, but a later interpretation of the original Κρόνος such as is given in the summary of Hermias (Vors. 7 A 9): Κρόνον δὲ τὸν χρόνον. Pherecydes himself may of course have written both forms, just as he sets Χθονίη next to Γῆ. But, in such matters, D.L. is after all a better source than Hermias. Even if Pherecydes had written Κρόνος, he obviously meant it to be understood allegorically by "those who know." What else could be the sense of Father Cronus next to the ungenerated Ζάς?

This enigmatic use of Cronus for Time is (as Cornford pointed out) also familiar to Pindar; cf. O. 11: Χρόνος ὁ πάντων πατήρ (v. 17), παρὰ Κρόνου τύρσιν (v. 70), πόσις ὁ πάντων 'Ρέας (v. 77).

[2] F. Dirlmeier, "Der Satz des Anaximandros von Milet," RM, LXXXVII (1938), 376, and the same author in Hermes, LXXV (1940), 329; followed by O. Gigon, Der Ursprung der griechischen Philosophie (Basel, 1945), p. 81, n. 16; and also by Martin Heidegger in Holzwege (Frankfurt, 1950), pp. 296 ff. Dirlmeier's conclusions were rejected by K. Deichgräber in "Anaximander von Milet," Hermes, LXXV, (1940), 10, and recently by Kirk, CQ, XLIX, 35.

Despite its apparent rigor, this argument is rather like a will-o'-the-wisp which vanishes when one comes up for a closer look. In the first place, can such a striking parallel between the statement of Anaximander and the doctrine of Heraclitus be explained merely by the fact that in both cases Theophrastus is our source? Surely the possibility exists that Heraclitus was influenced by the thought of his predecessor and fellow Ionian.

In regard to style, on the other hand, the parallels cited prove the exact opposite of what they are intended to show. In the texts of Aristotle and Simplicius, as in the doxography for Heraclitus, τάξις and χρόνος are pale abstractions, set on an equal footing side by side, in order to designate a fixed temporal sequence. Here indeed we have the colorless prose of the schools.[1] The concrete sense of τάξις in the fragment, like the personification of χρόνος, only emerges more vividly from such a comparison.

We may therefore regard the following words with confidence, as Anaximander's minimum text: κατὰ τὸ χρεών, διδόναι γὰρ αὐτὰ δίκην καὶ τίσιν ἀλλήλοις τῆς ἀδικίας κατὰ τὴν τοῦ χρόνου τάξιν. But the text so established is clearly incomplete. The phrase κατὰ τὸ χρεών and the conjunctive γάρ are both meaningless without what precedes. From the point of view of grammar as well as logic, we require the first clause: ἐξ ὧν δὲ ἡ γένεσίς ἐστι τοῖς οὖσι, καὶ τὴν φθορὰν εἰς ταῦτα γίνεσθαι.

At this point the question of authenticity becomes very delicate. There is nothing sufficiently unusual in the words under consideration to guarantee their complete stylistic faithfulness. And we must bear in mind that the difference between free paraphrase and indirect quotation is only a matter of degree. The instinct of every epitomist is not only to abbreviate, but occasionally to vary his original, if only as a means of relieving the boredom of copying what someone else has written. Hence, until that unlikely day when the text of Anaximander is rediscovered, no method exists for determining with certainty which words did or did not stand in the original text.

Once this has been said, we must also point out how inconclusive are most of the objections which have been raised against the clause ἐξ ὧν ... εἰς ταῦτα. ...[2] Although γένεσις, φθορά, and τὰ ὄντα are frequently

---

[1] Compare the paraphrase of the fragment given by Hippolytus: λέγει δὲ χρόνον ὡς ὡρισμένης τῆς γενέσεως καὶ τῆς οὐσίας καὶ τῆς φθορᾶς (5.H.). Some of Anaximander's thought has been preserved, none of his style.

[2] Burnet (p. 52, n. 6), for instance, refers to "the Greek practice of blending quotations with the text," and adds: "It is safer not to ascribe the terms γένεσις and φθορά in their technical Platonic sense to Anaximander; and it is not likely that Anaximander said anything about τὰ ὄντα."

used by Plato and by later authors, these terms were not invented in the fourth century. It is one thing to admit that Theophrastus *might* have supplied them himself, and something else again to insist that he *did*. When the balance is struck here between paraphrase and faithful citation, the scales seem to me to dip on the side of fidelity.

The evidence for this view consists essentially in three points: 1) the accuracy with which the *preceding* words have been paraphrased, 2) the direct link to what follows (underlined by γάρ), and 3) the rhythmic balance of the clause, implying its organic unity with the second member of the fragment. Before enlarging upon these points, we must first demonstrate that Anaximander might in fact have made use of such expressions as γένεσις, φθορά, and τὰ ὄντα.

Γένεσις appears in Homer:

Ὠκεανοῦ ὅς περ γένεσις πάντεσσι τέτυκται. (Ξ 246; cf. 201)

It is noteworthy that the word is here associated with the dative, as in the fragment, whereas the genitive is more normal in Aristotle and later writers. (Alone, this would of course prove nothing. Together with other considerations, it weights the scales for authenticity.) Furthermore, in this epic passage γένεσις means not merely "birth," but "causal origin," the creative source of coming-to-be.

It is this same active sense which is implied by the refutation of Parmenides:

τὼς γένεσις μὲν ἀπέσβεσται καὶ ἄπυστος ὄλεθρος. (B 8.21)

The generation of things is a raging fire, which has been put out. An equally general reference to the coming-to-be of all things occurs in the poem of Empedocles:

δοιὴ δὲ θνητῶν γένεσις, δοιὴ δ᾽ ἀπόλειψις. (B 17.3)

The list could be lengthened, in particular from the Hippocratic Corpus. But these examples should suffice to show that the philosophic use of the word did not originate with Plato.

Φθορά is not attested before Aeschylus and Herodotus. (This is no argument against its possible use by Anaximander; the case is the same for ἀδικία, τὸ χρεών, and τάξις, as has been seen.) The verb φθείρω "to ruin, destroy, waste away," is, of course, current from the oldest period.

The first known uses of φθορά are for civil and military calamities (Hdt. II.161.4; VII.18.3; Democr. B 249; cf. Aesch. *Ag.* 814, where the text is doubtful). When did the word become current in the general sense of physical "wasting"? We do not know. The author of the *De Victu* (*c.* 400 B.C.?) opposes this concept to that of "growth, waxing" (αὐξάνεται or αὔξη):

φθορὴ δὲ πᾶσιν ἀπ' ἀλλήλων, τῷ μέζονι ἀπὸ τοῦ μείονος καὶ τῷ μείονι ἀπὸ τοῦ μέζονος. (ch. 5, Jones, IV, 238)

When Plato speaks of "undertaking a causal study of γένεσις καὶ φθορά," he refers immediately to "this wisdom which, as you know, they call περὶ φύσεως ἱστορία" (*Phaedo* 95e–96a). He seems to be making an intentional use of expressions already familiar in Ionian natural science. A similar phrase occurs again in the *Laws*, when the doctrines of the physicists are quoted for refutation: ὃ πρῶτον γενέσεως καὶ φθορᾶς αἴτιον ἁπάντων . . . (891e.5; cf. 894b.11).

It is then conceivable that φθορά was also used by Anaximander in the work which brought Ionian prose into being. The same idea, at any rate, is expressed by ὄλεθρος in the verse just quoted from Parmenides, and by ἀπόλειψις in that of Empedocles, while for Heraclitus the pendant to γένεσις is θάνατος (B 36, B 76). Anaximander may have used any one of these words, or another: τελευτή, for example, or one of its verbal forms. (We find τελευτᾶν in Xenoph. B 27 and Parm. B 19; θανάτοιο τελευτή in Emped. B 8; τελευτᾶν and τελευτή in Melissus B 2; τελευτᾶν in *Nat. Hom.* 3, Jones, IV, 10; etc.) Anaximander's original word has perhaps been replaced here by the canonical φθορά; but the idea has scarcely been distorted.

The use of τὰ ὄντα for "the things that are" is again of Homeric antiquity:

ὃς ᾔδη τά τ' ἐόντα τά τ' ἐσσόμενα πρό τ' ἐόντα. (Α 70)

In the epic this expression refers to all events known to an inspired seer, who, like Isaiah, can declare "former things that are come to pass, and new things before they spring forth." The old phrase is applied by Hesiod to the contents of the *Theogony* (32; cf. 38), and, as we have seen, it was apparently echoed by Anaximenes in describing the cosmogonical procession out of the Air: ἐξ οὗ τὰ γινόμενα καὶ τὰ γεγονότα καὶ τὰ ἐσόμενα . . . (Α 7.1). This solemn formula for past, present, and future is employed again by Anaxagoras for the totality of things set in order by Nous (B 12).[1] The neuter plural participle is found not only among the Eleatics[2] but also in Empedocles:

ῥεῖ' ὅ γε τῶν ὄντων πάντων λεύσσεσκεν ἕκαστον. (B 129.5)

in Protagoras:

πάντων χρημάτων μέτρον ἐστὶν ἄνθρωπος, τῶν μὲν ὄντων ὡς ἔστιν, τῶν δὲ οὐκ ὄντων ὡς οὐκ ἔστιν. (B 1)

in Diogenes:

πάντα τὰ ὄντα ἀπὸ τοῦ αὐτοῦ ἑτεροιοῦσθαι καὶ τὸ αὐτὸ εἶναι. . . . εἰ γὰρ τὰ ἐν τῷδε τῷ κόσμῳ ἐόντα νῦν, γῆ καὶ ὕδωρ καὶ ἀὴρ καὶ πῦρ καὶ τὰ ἄλλα ὅσα φαίνεται ἐν τῷδε τῷ κόσμῳ ἐόντα . . . . (B 2)

and in the Hippocratic treatises:

εἰ δέ ποτε κρατηθείη καὶ ὁκότερον [πρότερον], οὐδὲν ἂν εἴη τῶν νῦν ἐόντων ὥσπερ ἔχει νῦν. (De Victu 3; Jones, IV, 232)

The ἐόν of Parmenides is itself no technical expression, but means "what is in fact the case, what is real and true," just as in Herodotus: τὰς δίκας ἀποβαίνειν κατὰ τὸ ἐόν (1.97.1). Parmenides' attack on the plural ὄντα of the Ionians gains in sharpness, if we suppose such expressions to have been used by them in the sixth century.[3]

It is not only the individual terms of Anaximander's proposition which are familiar to early Greek thought. The rhetorical balance of generation and corruption is itself an ancient theme of poetry, as well as of religion. The idea finds its natural symbol in the yearly cycle of vegetation:

οἵη περ φύλλων γενεή, τοίη δὲ καὶ ἀνδρῶν.
φύλλα τὰ μέν τ' ἄνεμος χαμάδις χέει, ἄλλα δέ θ' ὕλη
τηλεθόωσα φύει, ἔαρος δ' ἐπιγίγνεται ὥρη·
ὡς ἀνδρῶν γενεὴ ἡ μὲν φύει ἡ δ' ἀπολήγει. (Z 146 ff.)

---

[1] Anaxag. B 12: πάντα ἔγνω νοῦς. καὶ ὁποῖα ἔμελλεν ἔσεσθαι καὶ ὁποῖα ἦν, ἄσσα νῦν μὴ ἔστι, καὶ ὅσα νῦν ἐστι καὶ ὁποῖα ἔσται, πάντα διεκόσμησε νοῦς. Compare the parallel in De Carn. 2: ὃ καλέομεν θερμόν . . . εἰδέναι πάντα ἐόντα τε καὶ ἐσόμενα, where the reading πάντα καὶ τὰ ἐόντα καὶ τὰ μέλλοντα ἔσεσθαι is preferred by K. Deichgräber, Hippokrates über Enstehung und Aufbau des menschlichen Körpers (Leipzig, 1935).

[2] Zeno B 3; Melissus B 8.3. Even here the sense is not "technical." Cf. φοβούμενος δὲ μὴ οἱ πεμπόμενοι . . . οὐ τὰ ὄντα ἀπαγγέλλωσιν, used as equivalent to ἡ ἀλήθεια, Thuc. VII.8.2.

[3] See ἀπεόντα, παρεόντα in Parm. B 4.1; μὴ ἐόντα in B 7.1. Both passages are polemical.

It is just such seasonal change from which exemption is granted by the magical air of Phaeacia:

τάων οὔ ποτε καρπὸς ἀπόλλυται οὐδ' ἀπολείπει
χείματος οὐδὲ θέρευς, ἐπετήσιος· ἀλλὰ μάλ' αἰεί
Ζεφυρίη πνείουσα τὰ μὲν φύει, ἄλλα δὲ πέσσει. (η 117 ff.)

The idea of alternate growth and waning is applied by the philosophers not only to human life, but to all natural processes:

ὕδατι δὲ θάνατος γῆν γενέσθαι, ἐκ γῆς δὲ ὕδωρ γίνεται
(Heracl. B 36)

καὶ τὸς ἀνθρώπως· ὁ μὲν γὰρ αὔξεθ', ὁ δέ γα μὰν φθίνει
(Epicharmus B 2.7)

οὕτω τοι κατὰ δόξαν ἔφυ τάδε καί νυν ἔασι
καὶ μετέπειτ' ἀπὸ τοῦδε τελευτήσουσι τραφέντα (Parm. B 19)

τῇ μὲν γίγνονταί τε καὶ οὔ σφισιν ἔμπεδος αἰών (Emped. B 17.11)

τῶν δὲ τὰ μὲν γίνεται, τὰ δὲ ἀπολείπει (Diog. B 7)

In all these passages there is an implicit or express contrast with the imperishable life of divine beings.[1] At the same time, the natural philosophers are concerned not merely to emphasize the passing-away of mortal things, but also to define the process in terms of its source and its destination:

ἐκ γαίης γὰρ πάντα καὶ εἰς γῆν πάντα τελευτᾷ. (Xenoph. B 27)

συνεκρίθη καὶ διεκρίθη κἀπῆλθεν ὅθεν ἦλθεν πάλιν
γᾶ μὲν εἰς γᾶν, πνεῦμα δ' ἄνω. (Epicharmus B 9)

πάντα ταῦτα ἐκ τοῦ αὐτοῦ ἑτεροιούμενα ἄλλοτε ἀλλοῖα γίνεται καὶ εἰς
τὸ αὐτὸ ἀναχωρεῖ. (Diog. B 2)

The statement of Anaximander, which describes the necessary dissolution of all generated things back into their source of birth, forms a natural link between such expressions and the Homeric antecedents quoted above.

There is therefore no cogent objection, either linguistic or historical, to the authenticity of the first portion of the fragment. And these

---

[1] Although the echo of Plato has a distinctly Parmenidean ring, we see that the tradition is both older and wider: τι καλὸν . . . ἀεὶ ὂν καὶ οὔτε γιγνόμενον οὔτε ἀπολλύμενον, οὔτε αὐξανόμενον οὔτε φθίνον (Symp. 211a.1).

general considerations are reinforced by certain positive features of the text, which we have mentioned:

1. The unusual phrase which immediately precedes the fragment, ἅπαντας τοὺς οὐρανοὺς καὶ τοὺς ἐν αὐτοῖς κόσμους, also suggests a very faithful rendering of Anaximander's original.[1]

2. After this Anaximandrian phrase, Theophrastus passes directly to ἐξ ὧν δὲ ... εἰς ταῦτα ..., ending his clause with the poetic κατὰ τὸ χρεών, and recalling the link with a γάρ in the next (and clearly genuine) part of the citation. The likelihood of any important reformulation of what lies in between seems therefore slight.

3. The first clause of the fragment forms a symmetrical balance to what follows: κατὰ τὸ χρεών is clearly answered by κατὰ τὴν τοῦ χρόνου τάξιν; and, to all appearances, the γένεσις and φθορά of the first member must somehow correspond to the δίκη and ἀδικία of the second. This careful period does not suggest the work of an excerptor.

On the contrary, we know how a student of Aristotle would have formulated the same idea:

ἐξ οὗ γὰρ ἔστιν ἅπαντα τὰ ὄντα καὶ ἐξ οὗ γίνεται πρώτου καὶ εἰς ὃ φθείρεται τελευταῖον. (Met. 983ᵇ8)

πάντα γὰρ φθείρεται εἰς ταῦτ᾽ ἐξ ὧν ἔστιν. (Met. 1000ᵇ25)

So Simplicius, following Theophrastus:

καὶ ἐκ πυρὸς ποιοῦσι τὰ ὄντα πυκνώσει καὶ μανώσει καὶ διαλύουσι πάλιν εἰς πῦρ. (Phys. Opin. fr. 1; Vors. 22 A 5)

As we have seen, the fragment itself has been recast by Aëtius in the same mold:

ἐκ γὰρ τούτου πάντα γίγνεσθαι καὶ εἰς τοῦτο πάντα φθείρεσθαι. (4.A.)

Set against such a drab background, the style of Anaximander can speak for itself.[2]

ἐξ ὧν δὲ ἡ γένεσίς ἐστι τοῖς οὖσι, καὶ τὴν φθορὰν εἰς ταῦτα γίνεσθαι κατὰ τὸ χρεών . . . .

We have not proved that the fragment of Anaximander is a verbatim citation from his book. It is in fact difficult to believe that Theophrastus

---

[1] See above, pp. 49 f.

[2] This stylistic contrast was rightly characterized by Cornford: "Theophrastus, a very terse and economical writer, would not write ἡ γένεσίς ἐστι τοῖς οὖσι for γίνεται τὰ ὄντα or τὴν φθορὰν γίγνεσθαι for φθείρεσθαι" (CQ, XXVIII, 11, n. 2).

can have cast these sentences into indirect discourse without altering a jot or tittle of the text. We have seen that the habitual φθορά might easily have taken the place of an older term, such as τελευτή. But it is at most a word that has been changed, not an idea. We have the fragment of Anaximander in a form at least as faithful as that of the longer excerpts from the *Timaeus*, which Theophrastus has reproduced for us almost word for word in the *De Sensibus*.[1]

A Literal Interpretation

According to Simplicius, the entities which make reparation to one another for their wrongdoing are the elements. Is there any good reason to reject this view?

We have seen in the previous chapter how the "elements" must be understood for Anaximander: they are the opposite powers of cold and heat, moisture and dryness, darkness and light, and also the main portions of the visible world, regarded as embodiments of these universal factors. Now it was long ago pointed out that only such opposing forces could reasonably be said to inflict damage on one another, and to make recompense "according to the ordinance of Time."[2] The opposites indeed are inevitably and continually at war with one another, and the advantage of one is the disaster (φθορά) of its rival.[3] Nothing can be more in harmony with this vivid picture of cosmic strife than to speak of the vanquished party as "offended," and of his periodic triumph as "revenge" or "compensation."

Since the old cosmological texts are lost, it is above all from the medical literature that we can illustrate such expressions. The doctors regularly refer in this way to the internal struggle of forces in the body, as well as to the action of external factors upon the microcosm. Thus the verb ἀδικεῖν describes the effect of a morbid agent: "One should continue to make use of the same modes of regimen, when they clearly do no harm (οὐδὲν ἀδικέοντα) to the man's body" (*Nat. Hom.* 9; Jones, IV, 28). The excessive strength of any power is considered a wrong (ἁμάρτημα) for which punishment is due;[4] hence one factor is said to

---

[1] See, e.g., the epitome of *Tim.* 67b.2 ff. in *De Sensibus* 6 (*Dox.* 500.14 ff.): φωνὴν γὰρ εἶναι πληγὴν ὑπ' ἀέρος ἐγκεφάλου καὶ αἵματος δι' ὤτων μέχρι ψυχῆς, τὴν δ' ἀπὸ ταύτης κίνησιν ἀπὸ κεφαλῆς μέχρι ἥπατος ἀκοήν, where the spaced words are identical with Plato's own text (although their order has been slightly simplified). On this literal accuracy in Theophrastus' excerpts,

see above, pp. 17–24.

[2] Burnet, pp. 53 f.; W. A. Heidel, "On Anaximander," *CP*, VII (1912), 233 ff. Similarly Cornford, *Principium Sapientiae*, p. 168; Kirk, *CQ*, XLIX, 33 ff.

[3] See above, p. 130.

[4] For the ἁμάρτημα inflicted by hostile forces on the body, see *De Hebd.* ch. 19.31.

chastise another (κολάζειν), or to avenge its intemperance (τιμωρεῖν).[1] The wronged party is in this case not so much the weaker element, as the healthy state of the whole body. The aggressor may be conceived either as the hot or moist within the body, or as its cosmic "ally."[2] Hence it is the spring which kills men in an epidemic, and the summer which "benefits" them.[3] Plato's doctor in the *Symposium* is speaking the language of the medical textbooks when he refers to "the hot and cold, and dry and wet," which, when blended and harmonized with one another, bring a season of health and prosperity to men, animals, and plants, "and cause no offense" (οὐδὲν ἠδίκησεν). But when ὕβρις reigns among the seasons of the year, these same powers

destroy many things and are cause of harm (διέφθειρέν τε πολλὰ καὶ ἠδίκησεν). For plagues generally arise from such circumstances, and many other irregular diseases for beasts and for plants as well. And indeed frosts and hailstorms and plant blights come from the excessive and unruly lust of such things for one another. (*Symp.* 188a–b)

The doctors are, of course, concerned with the damage inflicted by these powers upon the human body. The fragment of Anaximander speaks instead of the wrong (ἀδικία) perpetrated by the cosmic powers upon one another. His words suggest an exchange of crimes like that which Herodotus presents as the antecedent for the Persian War, in which Greeks and Orientals are alternative offenders against one another: τῶν ἀδικημάτων πρῶτον τοῦτο ἄρξαι . . . μετὰ δὲ ταῦτα Ἕλληνας αἰτίους τῆς δευτέρης ἀδικίης γενέσθαι (Hdt. 1.2.1). In such a context, the balance is restored when the wronged party retaliates in full (ταῦτα μὲν δὴ ἴσα πρὸς ἴσα σφι γενέσθαι). The crime establishes a debt, which the guilty party must "pay"; hence the phrase for rendering compensation: διδόναι δίκην καὶ τίσιν.[4] In the fragment, the conditions of payment are fixed by the arbiter Time, and his law is a periodic pendulum of give and take.

[1] Wind and water inhaled in breathing cool the body, and thus serve as retaliation (τιμωρίη) against congenital heat (*De Cord.* 3, Littré, IX, 82). Since the lung is cold by nature, and further cooled by respiration, its presence around the heart κολάζει τὴν ἀκρασίαν τοῦ θερμοῦ (ch. 5). The thickness of the heart's wall serves as protection (φυλακή) against the strength of this heat (ch. 6, Littré, IX, 84). The same kind of compensatory action (τιμωρέων) is provided by the brain against moisture (*De Gland.* 10, Littré, VIII, 564). The comparison between these passages and Anaxi-

mander's doctrine was first drawn by Heidel, "Hippocratea, I," in *Harv. Stud.* XXV (1914), 188 f.

[2] *De Hebd.* 19.21: τὸ γὰρ τῆς τοῦ ἀνθρώπου φύσιος θερμὸν ξύμμαχον ἑωυτῷ ἔλαβεν τὸ παρὰ τοῦ ἡλίου θερμόν.

[3] *Epid.* III.15, Jones, I, 254: χαλεπώτατον μὲν τὸ ἔαρ καὶ πλείστους ἀπέκτεινε. . . . δοκεῖ δέ μοι προσωφελῆσαι κατὰ λόγον τὸ γενόμενον θέρος.

[4] For δίκη as a debt due, cf. Aesch. *Ag.* 534: ὀφλὼν γὰρ ἁρπαγῆς τε καὶ κλοπῆς δίκην.

In this second, unmistakably authentic portion of our text, there is no real ambiguity. In a general way the relevance of the first part also seems clear: it is in the alternate generation and corruption of things that both wrong and retaliation must be found. The phrase κατὰ τὸ χρεών may contain a secondary allusion to the idea of retribution as a debt, since χρέος, χρέως, "debt" is of course from the same root. But the primary force of χρεών combines the ideas of right and of necessity: death succeeds to birth in the course of time, *because it must*. In Anaximander's phrase κατὰ τὸ χρεών we have the most impersonal Greek formula for Fate.

But what are the ὄντα whose generation and destruction represent such a relentless treadmill of offense and compensation? It is here that the problems of a literal interpretation become acute. Most modern commentators assume that τὰ ὄντα must be the individual things of the visible world: the men, animals, and plants whose waning occurs after a fixed period of growth, and whose death balances their birth. These may, of course, be said to return back "into those things from which they came to be," and the expression is classic in Greece from an early period. Xenophanes, as we have seen, insists that all things arise from earth and all return there in the end (B 27); he is probably thinking of the fate of mankind. That is certainly the case for Epicharmus, in the verse which has already been cited: "Earth to earth, πνεῦμα aloft" (B 9)—a thought that finds many echoes in the fifth century.[1] The author of *De Natura Hominis* formulates the doctrine in general terms. The genesis of things, he says, can take place only from an equitable blending of elemental opposites:

And it is necessary that they return each to its own nature when the man's body comes to an end: wet to wet, dry to dry, hot to hot, and cold to cold. Such is the nature of animals and of all other things; all come to be in the same way and end in the same way. For their nature is composed out of all the aforesaid things and ends, as was said, in the same thing whence each was composed (τελευτᾷ . . . ἐς τὸ αὐτὸ ὅθεν περ συνέστη ἕκαστον). (ch. 3; Jones, IV, 10)

Clearly this gives us a possible sense for the ἐξ ὧν . . . εἰς ταῦτα of the fragment. But such an interpretation of τὰ ὄντα, as individual beings

---

[1] See Eur. fr. 839, vv. 8–11, cited *Vors.* 59 A 112; paralleled by *Suppl.* 532–34 and by the famous inscription for those who fell at Potidaea: αἰθὴρ μὲμ φσυχὰς ὑπεδέχσατο, σώμ[ατα δὲ χθών] (M. N. Tod, *A Selection of Greek Historical Inscriptions* [2d ed.; Oxford, 1946], No. 59 = *I.G.* I². 945). It is because of this return of like to like that, according to the "Orphic" gold plates, the dead arriving in Hades must say "I am child of Earth and of starry Heaven, but my race (γένος) is heavenly" (*Vors.* 1 B 17.6).

such as men and animals, encounters a serious obstacle in the γάρ
which follows. For the explanatory statement introduced by this word
says nothing of particular, compound things, but refers instead to a
reciprocal action of the elemental powers upon one another (ἀλλήλοις).
How can an exchange of offense and penalty between the elements
explain why compound things are dissolved back into the materials
of which they were composed? In this view, the apparent parallelism
of the two clauses loses its *raison d'être*, as does the binding γάρ. We
would have two independent propositions, and no visible link between
them.[1]

One may, of course, imagine various devices for bridging the gap
which this view opens up. We might assume, for example, that the
excerpt of Theophrastus has suppressed one or more steps of the original
reasoning which is represented in our text by the γάρ: Anaximander
may have argued that the formation of individual things involves the
temporary supremacy of one power over another, perhaps in the form
of a debt to be paid back when the compound is resolved into its
elements.[2] Yet even with a great deal of ingenuity, we will hardly
succeed in explaining why the payment is then made, not by compound things back to their elements, but by the latter "to one another."
Furthermore, the use of a pronoun such as αὐτά (in the phrase διδόναι
γὰρ αὐτὰ δίκην καὶ τίσιν ἀλλήλοις) naturally leads us to suppose that the
things which exchange wrong and reparation are the same as those
whose generation and destruction has just been mentioned. Can this
have been the original thought of Anaximander, distorted by the
doxographical citation?[3]

Now there is another interpretation of the words τὰ ὄντα which
would permit us to understand the text in just this way, without any
additional conjectures and without supposing the sense to have been
altered by Simplicius or Theophrastus. Simplicius, we remember, thinks
that the fragment refers to the transformation of elements into one

---

[1] This apparent irrelevance of the two clauses
to one another is emphasized by J. B. McDiarmid,
"Theophrastus on the Presocratic Causes," *Harv.
Stud.*, LXI, 97.
[2] The loan of elements in the formation of the
human body is alluded to by Plato *Tim.* 42e.9:
ἀπὸ τοῦ κόσμου δανειζόμενοι μόρια ὡς ἀποδο-
θησόμενα (cf. φθίνοντα πάλιν δέχεσθε, 41d.3). The
same metaphor seems to have been applied by
Philolaus to the intake of air in breathing: πάλιν
καθαπερεὶ χρέος ἐκπέμπει αὐτό (sc. τὸ ἐκτὸς
πνεῦμα), *Anon. Lond.* XVIII.23; Jones, *Medical*

Writings, p. 72.
[3] Thus Kirk suggests that the original assertion
paraphrased by Theophrastus "might have been
to the effect that each opposite changes into its
own opposite and into no other, for example the
hot is replaced by the cold and not by the wet
or the soft" (*CQ*, XLIX, 35). I largely agree
with Kirk as to what Anaximander said, but see
no reason to believe that either Theophrastus or
Simplicius interpreted his words in a different
way.

another, and it has been seen that the idea of a seasonal (as well as of a cosmogonic) cycle of elemental change was familiar to the Milesians. It would be natural for them to speak of the formation of moisture in the rainy season as a birth of the wet out of the dry, just as the fiery element of summer is born and nourished from the moist.[1] May not these very principles be the ὄντα which, in the process of elemental change, perish again into the things from which they have arisen?

The expression τὰ ὄντα is so general that it may just as well apply to natural compounds as to the elements of which they are formed. Strictly speaking, the text of the fragment is compatible with either view. On the other hand, a glance at the oldest recorded usage of the term in philosophical contexts will suggest that it refers to elemental powers rather than to unique, individual bodies. In the fragment of Diogenes, for example, τὰ ἐν τῷδε τῷ κόσμῳ ἐόντα νῦν are specified as "earth and water and air and fire and the other things which are observed to exist in this κόσμος" (B 2). In the De Natura Hominis, the parallel phrase πάντων τῶν ἐνεόντων ἐν τῷδε τῷ κόσμῳ follows directly upon a mention of τῶν θερμῶν καὶ τῶν ψυχρῶν καὶ τῶν ξηρῶν καὶ τῶν ὑγρῶν (ch. 7; Jones, IV, 22). The πάντων (sc. χρημάτων) ὁμοῦ ἐόντων of Anaxagoras B 1 are of course not the individual bodies of men and animals, but ἀήρ, αἰθήρ, and the various powers and materials of things yet to be produced. For him also τὰ ἐν τῷ ἑνὶ κόσμῳ are exemplified by the hot and the cold (B 8). Anaxagoras is the philosopher whom we would expect Protagoras to attack, and it is probably in terms of such physical elements that we must understand the latter's opening reference to πάντα χρήματα, τὰ μὲν ὄντα, τὰ δὲ οὐκ ὄντα (B 1). When Plato propounds the Protagorean thesis in the Theaetetus, his first example is precisely the difference between a hot and a cold wind. So the pretended ὄντα which Melissus is concerned to refute, and "which men say to be true," are not individual things but "earth, water, air, fire, iron, gold, the living and the dead, dark, bright, and the rest," including hot and cold, hard and soft (B 8).

It is therefore most probable that the expression τὰ ὄντα in the fragment also refers to such elemental powers. It is they who are one another's source of generation, just as they are the mutual cause of death. On the grammatical level, it is these opposing principles, and these alone, which are implied by the neuter plural pronouns: ἐξ ὧν, εἰς ταῦτα, αὐτά, ἀλλήλοις. The wet is generated from the dry, the light

---

[1] See above, p. 132.

from the darkness. But the birth of such a thing involves the death of its reciprocal, and this loss must eventually be repaired by a backward swing of the pendulum. Thus it is that "from a single necessity all things are composed and nourished by one another."[1]

This compensation of death for birth is absolutely necessary; it takes place κατὰ τὸ χρεών. The following γάρ shows that this very inevitability is expressed again in the idea of διδόναι δίκην. The archaic view of ἀδικία is just this, that one who is guilty will always pay the penalty. It is probably misleading to lay too much stress on the moral or eschatological aspect of "cosmic injustice" for Anaximander. If the dominion (κρατεῖν) of one party over another is described as a wrong, this need not imply a different, pre-mundane or post-mundane state of harmony such as is dreamt of by Empedocles. The victory of one element over another is ἀδικία because the weaker party suffers, and because of the disastrous consequences which must ensue for the offender. The words and imagery of the fragment indicate above all that the exchange of birth and death is sure, remorseless, inescapable, like the justice which the gods send upon guilty men. It will come at last, when its hour is full. For Necessity enforces the ordinance which Time lays down.

The Philosophic Sense of the Fragment

According to the interpretation here proposed, the meaning of the two portions of the fragment is one and the same. The first member states the necessary return of mortal elements back into the opposite powers from which they are generated; the second clause explains this necessity as a just compensation for the damage done at birth. The elements feed one another by their own destruction, since what is life to one is death for its reciprocal. The first law of nature is a *lex talionis*: life for life.

Thus the fragment does not announce a last end of things, when the elemental powers will return into the Boundless from which they have arisen (despite the number of modern interpretations which presuppose this view). Neither does it contain a particular reference to the dissolution of men and animals back into the materials of which they are composed, although such an idea was frequently expressed by other

---

[1] ἀπὸ γὰρ τῆς αὐτῆς ἀνάγκης πάντα συνέστηκέ τε καὶ τρέφεται ὑπ' ἀλλήλων, *Nat. Hom.* 7; Jones, IV, 22. For the full context, see below, p. 189.

Greek thinkers. This brief text of Anaximander most naturally refers simply to that continuous change of opposing forms or powers into one another which is the common theme of Heraclitus (B 126, B 88, etc.), Epicharmus (B 2), Melissus (B 8), and Plato (*Phaedo* 70d–72). The most significant case for a Milesian cosmologist was no doubt the interchange of the major elements. "It is death for water to become earth," says Heraclitus, "but out of earth water arises" (B 36); the death of fire is birth for air, and the death of air is birth for water (B 76). "These live the death of those, and die their life" (B 62, B 77).

Anaximander must have seen this exchange transacted daily, in the alternation of light and darkness, of the fresh morning dew and the parched heat of noon. He must have recognized essentially the same process at work in the production of the fiery thunderbolt out of wind and cloud, themselves in turn produced from evaporating moisture. The downward return of quenched fire and condensing rain cloud will counteract the upward surge of dryness and heat, and thus preserve the balance of the whole. The waxing and waning of the moon's light fulfills in turn the lawful interchange of generation and corruption. If the celestial equilibrium was conceived by Anaximander as a stable sphere, it is the turning circle which best symbolizes this rhythm of elemental change. The image is preserved in our own terminology, which is in this respect still that of early Greece: "cycle" from κύκλος (originally "wheel"), "period" from περίοδος ("revolution"). In the Ionian view, the predominant cycle is that of the sun, since it is in step with this yearly movement that the seasons of heat and coolness, drought and rainfall succeed one another, while the dominion of daylight gives way before the long winter nights.[1] In Greece, even the winds are generally "opposite according to the opposite seasons" (Arist. *Meteor.* 364ᵃ34). And the mortal seasons of youth and age, growth and decay, exemplify the same periodic law.[2]

It is possible that Anaximander projected this pattern upon a still

---

[1] In *De Victu* 5, the θεία ἀνάγκη according to which all things come to pass is just such a rhythmic oscillation between maximum and minimum, illustrated by the periods of day and night, of the moon, and of the annual solar motion. And see above, pp. 104–6.

[2] "Old age arises from the loss of heat" (Parm. A 46a); "a man is hottest on the first of his days, coldest on the last" (*Nat. Hom.* 12; Jones, IV, 36). This idea, according to which man's life is a reduced model of the cosmic year (ending at the winter solstice), is developed at length by the author of *De Victu* (ch. 33; Jones, IV, 278), who adds the sequence wet, dry, and then wet again in increasing age (corresponding to the rains of both spring and fall).

In stating the general law of alternation between opposites, it is the seasonal changes which Plato mentions first: καὶ τῷ ὄντι τὸ ἄγαν τι ποιεῖν μεγάλην φιλεῖ εἰς τοὐναντίον μεταβολὴν ἀνταποδιδόναι, ἐν ὥραις τε καὶ ἐν φυτοῖς καὶ ἐν σώμασιν, καὶ δὴ καὶ ἐν πολιτείαις οὐχ ἥκιστα (*Rep.* 563e.9).

more majestic screen, and spoke (like Plato and his followers) of a Magnus Annus, in which the great astronomical cycles are to be accompanied by catastrophic transformations on the earth. Like Xenophanes, Anaximander may have taught that the progressive drying-up of the sea would eventually be reversed, so that the earth will sink back into the element from which it has arisen.[1] This would constitute the necessary "reparation" required by the fragment for any type of excess. The periodic destruction of mankind by fire and flood, to which Plato more than once alludes, seems to form part of the symmetrical pattern of this sixth-century world view.[2]

Did Anaximander envisage an even greater cycle, in which the appearance of this differentiated universe out of the Boundless would itself be periodically balanced by the return of all things, including the elements, back into their original source? This doctrine is ascribed to Anaximander by some doxographers, but there is no definite statement to this effect in our most reliable sources.[3] On the other hand, it seems difficult to deny such a view to the Milesians, if their belief in an "eternal motion" is to be taken seriously.[4] A periodic destruction of the world order might well follow from Anaximander's conception of symmetrical action and counter-action, continuing unhampered throughout endless time. But there is no place for this doctrine in the text of Anaximander's fragment, which does not mention the generation of things out of the ἄπειρον. There is therefore no reason whatsoever to

---

[1] Xenoph. A 33.5-6 (Hippolytus): "A mixture of earth with sea is taking place, and it will at length be dissolved by the moist . . . all men will be destroyed, when the earth collapses into the sea and becomes mud; then there will be a new beginning of generation; and this transformation occurs in all the κόσμοι." For the meaning of the last phrase see above, pp. 51 ff.

[2] The alternate destructions of human societies by fire and water are mentioned by Plato at *Tim.* 22c; frequent destructions in the past, particularly by floods, at *Laws* 677a; similar cycles of human and cosmic transformations at *Politicus* 269a.

Democritus was author of a work entitled Μέγας ἐνιαυτὸς ἢ Ἀστρονομίη; very little is known of its contents. For the astronomical meaning of the τέλεος ἐνιαυτός, see *Tim.* 39d.4, and Arist. fr. 25, where the version of Censorinus 18 adds: *cuius anni hiemps summa est cataclysmus, quam nostri diluvionem vocant, aestas autem ecpyrosis, quod est mundi incendium.* The concept of the *ecpyrosis* may have received a new interpretation from the Stoics, but the cosmic summer and winter are

obviously part of the original Great Year (cf. χειμών and καῦμα at *Tim.* 22e.6). They represent the alternate victory of Hot and Cold, in the most monumental of all struggles regulated by "the ordinance of Time." For a recent discussion, see B. L. van der Waerden, "Das Grosse Jahr und die ewige Wiederkehr," *Hermes*, LXXX (1952), 129.

[3] The destruction of the world (or worlds) appears in 2.P., 4.A., 7.P., 9.S.1, 9.A.4, 9.C., and 9.Augustine; no mention of it occurs in Hippolytus or in the primary excerpt of Simplicius (*in Phys.* p. 24 = *Phys. Opin.* fr. 2).

[4] An ἀίδιος κίνησις should imply that some change took place before the present world order began to arise, and that something else will follow its destruction (if any). The expression would not have been used if Anaximander, like Anaxagoras, had avoided any reference to events before the commencement of our cosmic order, or implied that no changes took place during this time; cf. Arist. *Phys.* 250ᵇ24, where the view of Anaxagoras is cited as an example of μὴ ἀεὶ εἶναι κίνησιν.

suppose that the destruction of the world is an "atonement" to be made for some kind of wrongdoing.

On the other hand, if a cycle of world formation and dissolution is not implied by this brief text, everything else we know about Anaximander's cosmology has its place here: astronomical cycles, the succession of the seasons, the phenomena of the atmosphere, the origin of dry land and living things, all converge in the element doctrine of the fragment. There is another idea which we may expect to find here, in view of our earlier discussion of Anaximander's theories, and that is the principle of geometric proportion. In order to see how Anaximander's mathematical conceptions are related to his statement in the fragment, we must consider some Aristotelian passages in which a similar view is described. We have already recognized the Milesian doctrine in Aristotle's reference to those who declare that there is "an infinite body, one and simple . . . besides the elements, out of which they generate the latter."

For there are some who make the ἄπειρον not air or water, but a thing of this sort, so that the other elements should not be destroyed by the one of them that is infinite. For they are characterized by opposition to one another; air, for instance, is cold, water is wet, fire is hot; if one of these were infinite, the others would now have perished. Hence, they say, the ἄπειρον is something else, from which these things arise. (*Phys.* 204ᵇ22; cited here as **6.Arist.3**)

There is no reason to doubt the substantial accuracy here of Aristotle's report.[1] This argument against the infinity of any single element corresponds exactly to the view expressed by the fragment: if there were no limits assigned to the supremacy of one of the participants in cosmic strife, its victory would never be compensated by the statutory

[1] See Simpl. *in Phys.* 479.32 ff., where the argument is expressly assigned to Anaximander. The doubts expressed in general terms by Zeller (I⁵ 215) and developed in detail by Cherniss (*Aristotle's Criticism of Presocratic Philosophy*, pp. 27 f., 367) do not seem cogent. As Vlastos has pointed out (*CP*, XLII, 168, n. 121), the balance between the elemental powers is not a new idea with Aristotle, but everywhere presupposed in the early medical literature (see above, p. 132, n. 4). Furthermore, a clear indication that the reasoning given here is not an invention of Aristotle may be seen in his reference to air as cold. This anomaly with regard to Aristotle's own theory—according to which air is defined as hot-moist (*Gen. Corr.* 330ᵇ4)—has often perplexed the commentators, both ancient and modern. The riddle disappears

if we remember that the ἀήρ was originally defined by his predecessors as cold in opposition to the fiery αἰθήρ. (In the scheme of Anaxagoras, for example, the ἀήρ is cold, damp, dense, and dark.) Aristotle seems to have borrowed these examples together with their argument.

Hence it is peculiarly appropriate that Aristotle should refute Anaximander's thesis by an adaptation of his own principle: "There is no such sensible body besides the so-called elements. *For all things are dissolved back into that out of which they are composed*; so that this body would then appear in addition to air and fire and earth and water; but nothing of the sort is to be seen" (*Phys.* 204ᵇ32, where the plural ἐξ ὧν of Anaximander has, of course, been replaced by the singular ἐξ οὗ).

defeat. It is this same idea which Aristotle has just adapted in his own proof that no element can be infinite: "The opposites must always be in a relationship of equality" (ἰσάζειν ἀεὶ τἀναντία); for an infinite elemental body will always exceed and destroy (ὑπερβαλεῖ καὶ φθερεῖ) one that is finite (*Phys.* 204ᵇ13–19). Much the same principle is invoked by him in the *Meteorologica* against those who believe that the entire celestial region is filled with fire and air (340ᵃ1 ff.). That cannot be, says Aristotle, for, in view of the relatively small dimensions of the earth in comparison with the whole heavens, fire and air "would then exceed by far the equality of a common proportion with regard to their fellow elements."[1] Aristotle is prepared to admit that there is more air than water in the universe, for he knows that water expands when evaporated. What he requires is therefore not a simple arithmetic correspondence, but an "equality of power" (ἰσότης τῆς δυνάμεως)—a geometric relationship which joins different quantities in a single proportion (κοινὴ ἀναλογία), just as a fixed amount of water produces a corresponding amount of steam (340ᵃ16).

Aristotle feels himself entirely justified in using this principle against his predecessors, for he is conscious of having taken it from them. He discusses elsewhere (*Gen. Corr.* 333ᵃ18 ff.) the statement of Empedocles that the elements are "equal in every way": Love is "equal in length and breadth" to the others, just as Strife is their "equipoise at every point" (Emped. B 17.19–27). For Empedocles as for Aristotle, this geometric equality between the elements is an expression of their equal power.[2] Such an equilibrium between opposing principles is no less important in the view of Anaxagoras, for whom "all things are always equal" (B 5; cf. B 3). To preserve this necessary balance, his ἀήρ and αἰθήρ must each be infinite, for they are the two greatest things in bulk (B 1). The same is true of the two symmetrical forms which together fill the cosmic sphere of Parmenides. They too are opposite to one another, and "both equal" (B 9.4). Although the form which this idea assumes for Anaxagoras and Empedocles may be due to the direct influence of Parmenides, the general principle is not new with him. For we also find it in the "measures" which regulate elemental transformation according to Heraclitus: when Fire in the turnings of its

---

[1] πολὺ γὰρ ἂν ὑπερβάλλοι τὴν ἰσότητα τῆς κοινῆς ἀναλογίας πρὸς τὰ σύστοιχα σώματα, *Meteor.* 340ᵃ4. According to the pseudo-Aristotelian *De Mundo*, the universe is preserved by such an agreement and balance of opposing forces: αἰτία δὲ ταύτης μὲν (sc. τῷ παντὶ σωτηρίας) ἡ τῶν στοιχείων ὁμολογία, τῆς δὲ ὁμολογίας ἡ ἰσομοιρία καὶ τὸ μηδὲν αὐτῶν πλέον ἕτερον ἑτέρου δύνασθαι (396ᵇ34).

[2] See the distribution of τίμη and κρατεῖν between the elements in Emped. B 17.28 f., correctly interpreted by Vlastos (*CP*, XLII, 159) as a dynamic equilibrium.

cycle (τροπαί) has become sea and then earth, once more "sea is poured out, and measured back into the same λόγος as before it became earth" (B 31).[1] This λόγος of elemental exchange is precisely a geometric "equality of common proportion" such as that which Aristotle postulates in the *Meteorologica*. It guarantees that the fundamental order of the universe will persist unchanged, despite its periodic transformations. From the modern point of view, it represents the earliest formula for the conservation of both energy and matter, since at this period bulk (μέγεθος) and power (δύναμις) are conceived as the two faces of a single coin.

The old Ionic theory of the elements is thus characterized by the same geometric symmetry which prevails in Anaximander's celestial scheme. The equilibrium of the earth at the center of a spherical world is reflected in the mathematical proportion by which the elements are bound to one another. These parts belong together in a unified whole, a community whose balance of power is maintained by periodic readjustments, in accordance with that general law of astronomical cycles which Anaximander conceived as an immutable τάξις of Time.

This is, I suggest, the conception which lies at the root of the Greek view of the natural world as a κόσμος, an admirably organized whole. The term κόσμος is interpreted by Plato as implying "geometric equality,"[2] and the word is bright with the combined radiance of the moral and aesthetic ideals of early Greece. No ancient author, it is true, tells us that Anaximander spoke of the world as a κόσμος. But the new philosophic sense of this term is as familiar to Heraclitus and Parmenides as it is to Anaxagoras, Empedocles, and Diogenes.[3] It is difficult to see where such a widespread notion could have arisen, if not in sixth-century Miletus—the mother city from which, like so many colonies, all the philosophic schools of early Greece are sprung.

Precisely considered, the κόσμος is a concrete arrangement of all things, defined not only by a spatial disposition of parts, but also by the temporal τάξις within which opposing powers have their turn in office. It is the spatial aspect (in which the κόσμος, identified with the οὐρανός,

---

[1] It is because of these equal measures, by which Fire is exchanged for all things and all for Fire (Heracl. B 90) that "the starting-point and the limit of the circle [of elemental transformations] are one and the same" (B 103).

[2] "The wise, Callicles, say that both heaven and earth and gods and men are held together by community and friendship, by orderliness (κοσμιότης) and temperance and justice (δικαιότης),

and for this reason they call this whole universe an Order (κόσμος), my friend, not disorder (ἀκοσμία) nor license. . . . But you have not noticed that geometric equality has great power both among men and among gods; and you think one should practice excessive greed (πλεονεξία), for you neglect geometry" (*Gorg.* 508a).

[3] See Appendix I, p. 219.

appears as a body whose limbs are the elements) which tends more and more to obscure the temporal order that prevailed in the earlier conception. Both ideas, however, are inextricably linked from the beginning to the end of Greek philosophy. The cosmos has not only an extended body, but also a lifetime (αἰών), whose phases are celestial cycles.[1]

Two Hippocratic texts may serve to illustrate this conception in the minds of men penetrated by Ionian science. The authors of the *De Natura Hominis* and the *De Victu* both employ the word κόσμος for the universal order, and apply this notion in detail to the structure and function of men's bodies. It was no doubt towards the end of the fifth century that Polybus, the son-in-law of Hippocrates, wrote as follows.

The body of man always possesses all of these [the four humors, characterized by the four primary opposites], but through the revolving seasons they become now greater than themselves, now lesser in turn, according to nature. For, just as every year has a share in all, in hot things as well as cold, in dry things as well as wet (for no one of these could endure for any length of time without all of the things present in this κόσμος; but if any one of these were to cease, all would disappear; for from a single necessity all are composed and nourished by one another); just so, if any one of these components should cease in a man, the man would not be able to live. (*Nat. Hom.* 7, Jones, IV, 20–22)

The year and the κόσμος each constitute an organized body, from which no vital member may be removed without catastrophe. Writing perhaps a few years later,[2] the author of the *De Victu* holds a similar

[1] This sense of αἰών, the world's lifetime, occurs in Arist. *De Caelo* 279ᵃ22–30 and 283ᵇ28 (for the idea, cf. 285ᵃ29, 286ᵃ9; similar uses of αἰών in Bonitz, *Index*, 23ᵇ19, 21). The meaning is probably the same in Emped. B 16. For reasons of his own, Plato has re-defined αἰών as the timeless eternity of the Forms, while χρόνος is its moving image in the heavens (*Tim.* 37d); Aristotle's use of the word is closer to the original meaning. The etymological sense of αἰών was "vitality, vital force" (see E. Benveniste, "Expression indo-européenne de l'éternité," *Bulletin de la Société de Linguistique*, XXXVIII [1937], 103). Hence it came to mean "duration of life, lifetime." The later sense of "eternity" is due to a philosophic reinterpretation of αἰών as equivalent to ἀεὶ ὤν. For the transitional use of the term for the everlasting life of the universe or cosmic god, see A.-J. Festugière, "Le sens philosophique du mot αἰών," *La Parola del Passato*, IV [1949], 172).

It is because Time (χρόνος), as the sequence of astronomical cycles, was also conceived as the vital motion of the universe that it could be "inhaled" from outside like a breath-soul (in the

Pythagorean view, *Vors.* 58 B 30), and be identified by some with the heavenly sphere itself, as well as with its motion (*Phys.* 218ᵇ1). Compare *Tim.* 38e.4, where the stars "produce Time," and 41e.5, where they are "instruments of Time."

[2] The date of the *De Victu* has been much disputed. Most authors assign it to the end of the fifth century, but Jaeger has put it in the middle of the fourth (*Paideia*, III, 33 ff., with notes), and Kirk even sees Peripatetic influence here (*Heraclitus*, pp. 27 ff.). Their arguments are, however, scarcely decisive. In regard to questions of cosmology, there is no trace of any influence later than Empedocles and Archelaus. The author cannot have read the *Timaeus*, or even the *Phaedo*. In view of his otherwise receptive attitude to the ideas of his predecessors, this makes it difficult to believe that he is younger than Plato. Anyone who compares *De Victu* 69 with the description of Herodicus of Selymbria at *Republic* 406a–b and *Anon. Lond.* IX.20 ff. (Jones, *Medical Writings*, p. 48) will wonder whether there can have been two doctors of the same period with such a similar εὕρημα. It will hardly do to claim the author of the

view of the interdependence of natural factors. A good doctor, he claims, "must be familiar with the risings and settings of the stars, that he may be competent to guard against the changes and excesses of food and drink, of winds, and of the κόσμος as a whole, since it is from these [changes and excesses] that diseases arise among men" (ch. 2; Jones, IV, 228). Such vicissitudes of nature, he says, are due to the alternate dominion not of four principles, but of two alone: fire and water.

Each one rules and is ruled in turn, to the maximum and minimum of what is possible. For neither one is able to rule altogether. . . . If either were ever dominated, none of the things which now exist would be as it is now. But as things are, these [fire and water] will be the same forever, and will never cease either separately or together (ch. 3, Jones, IV, 232).

For this author too the κόσμος takes the form of a rhythmically repeated cycle, executed by a system in dynamic equilibrium.

Perhaps the most striking expression of this old view of cosmic order is to be found in a relatively late text. Diogenes Laertius quotes from Alexander Polyhistor a cosmology which the latter is said to have found in certain "Pythagorean notebooks" (ὑπομνήματα). We do not know who these Pythagoreans were, or when they lived.[1] But the doctrine that follows clearly reflects the same conceptions that prevail in the Hippocratic Corpus:

Light and darkness, hot and cold, dry and wet obtain equal portions in the κόσμος; it is from their dominance that arises summer, from that of the hot, and winter, from that of the cold.[2] But when their portions are equalized, the year is at its finest; its flourishing season, spring, is healthy, but its waning season, autumn, productive of disease. Indeed, the day itself has a flourishing period at dawn, but wanes at evening, which is therefore the most unhealthy hour. (D.L. VIII.26 = Vors. 58 B 1a)

The medical theory of these three texts is, as far as we know, the creation of Alcmaeon and of the founders of the Hippocratic method.

De Victu as a "pupil" of Herodicus (as does Jones, Medical Writings, p. 48), since this is precisely the point where the writer insists upon his originality (ch. 69; cf. ch. 2). The argument of J. Jütner (Philostratos [Leipzig, 1909], pp. 15 ff.), that the "biting scorn" for gymnastics in De Victu 24 could not come from a former trainer, is one which cuts both ways.

[1] Diels followed M. Wellman, Hermes, LIV (1919), 225, in assigning the doctrine to a con-

temporary of Plato; Festugière has argued for a late fourth-century date in Revue des Études Grecques, LVIII (1945), 1.

[2] The "emendation" of Cobet ⟨ξηροῦ δ' ἔαρ καὶ ὑγροῦ φθινόπωρον⟩ (which is printed by Hicks in the Loeb Diogenes as part of the text) stands in flat contradiction to the following words: spring and fall are not subject to the domination of any power, but represent the "finest" time of the year because of their balance.

But the cosmology on which it is based—and of which it is a faithful reflection—is the common heritage of all Greek philosophers after the sixth century. Its earliest expression is to be found in the fragment of Anaximander.

There are other traces of this view in the extant philosophical fragments. Anaxagoras, for example, declares that Nous "has set all things in good order" (πάντα διεκόσμησε, B 12). It is clear from the context that the chief instrument of this order is the cosmic revolution (περιχώρησις) performed by the heavenly bodies, the source of a differentiated universe. Further details concerning the "order" brought about by Nous have been lost, but may to some extent be supplied from the doctrine of Diogenes. Like Anaxagoras, he too praises the intelligence (νόησις) of his cosmic principle, which "arranges all things" (B 5), and in his case, we have a text that states the concrete evidence of this ordering:

For it were not possible for all things to be so distributed (δεδάσθαι) without intelligence, that there should be measures of all things, of winter and summer, of night and day, of rainfall and winds and clear weather. And if one is willing to reflect on other things, he will find them also so disposed as to be the best possible. (B 3)

For this fifth-century Ionian, as for the Milesians before him, it is the seasonal regularity of celestial and meteorological processes which best exhibits the organic structure of the universe.

Here, at the starting-point of Western science and philosophy, we find the Order of Nature clearly conceived as an "ordinance of Time." This oldest formula of natural law thus emphasizes that same notion of periodicity which, in a much more elaborate form, plays such an important role in modern physical thought.[1] The early appearance of this idea is no cause for surprise; indeed the great periodic occurrences have never passed unnoticed. The cycle of the stars and seasons is the fundamental fact in any agricultural society, which must strive to establish some harmony between the works of man and the motions of the heavenly bodies. Such is the theme not only of Hesiod's poem, but of all ancient religions.

What is new in Anaximander's doctrine is neither the concern for

[1] "The birth of modern physics depended upon the application of the abstract idea of periodicity to a variety of concrete instances" (A. N. Whitehead, Science and the Modern World, ch. 2). The achievement of the Greeks was, of course, just the reverse: to pass from the experience of concrete periods to the idea of one principle governing all transformations whatsoever.

seasonal repetition, nor the application of moral and legal concepts to
the natural world. The idea that "man lived in a charmed circle of
social law and custom, but the world around him at first seemed law-
less,"[1] is based upon a total misconception. The earliest civilizations
had no notion of the distinction between Nature and Society which has
become habitual to us. In Homer, for example, no boundary is recognized between human usage and the order of the universe. In front of
man stands not Nature, but the power of the gods, and they intervene
as easily in the natural world as in the life of men. Poseidon is lord of the
sea, shaker of the earth, but he stands in battle next to the Greeks before
Troy. Zeus is god of the storm, and was once the personified power of
the sky itself, but when he casts his thunderbolt, it is to exact punishment from perjurers.[2] The Horae, who are the Seasons, and will become
the astronomical Hours, have for sisters the Moirae, the "fated portions" of mankind. Their common mother is Themis ("lawful establishment"), and their names are Justice, Peace, and Good Distribution
($εὐνομίη$) (Hes. *Theog.* 901).

These ideas are from the beginning so intimately linked that, in
lands where mythic speculation is highly developed, a single term for
"law" normally applies to ritual, to morality, and to the natural order.
Such, for instance, is the case for the Vedic concept of *ṛtá*, literally,
"what is adjusted, fitted together" (from the root **ar-* in $ἀραρίσκω$,
$ἁρμός$, $ἁρμονία$). The word designates not only ritual correctness—like
Latin *ritus*, from the same root—but moral order, and the regular
arrangement by which the gods produce the dawn, the movement of
the sun, and the yearly sequence of the seasons. The annual cycle itself
is pictured as "a twelve-spoked wheel of *ṛtá* which turns unaging round
the heaven."[3]

Such ancient conceptions show that it is not the assimilation of
Nature and Society which philosophy was called upon to establish, but
rather their separation from one another. These two ideas were first

---

[1] Burnet, p. 9. Similarly R. Hirzel, *Themis,
Dike und Verwandtes* (Leipzig, 1907), pp. 386 f.

[2] See, e.g., Aristophanes *Nubes* 397: τοῦτον γὰρ
(sc. τὸν κεραυνόν) φανερῶς ὁ Ζεὺς ἵησ' ἐπὶ τοὺς
ἐπιόρκους.

[3] Rigveda 1.164.11. On the conception of *ṛtá*,
see A. Bergaigne, *Religion védique*, III, 210 ff.; H.
Oldenberg, *Religion des Vedas*, pp. 195 ff. Compare
the Egyptian and Babylonian points of view
described in *The Intellectual Adventure of Ancient
Man* (Chicago, 1946), and the conclusion of the

Frankforts, p. 26: "The life of man and the
function of the state are for mythopoeic thought
imbedded in nature, and the natural processes are
affected by the acts of man no less than man's
life depends on his harmonious integration with
nature. The experiencing of this unity with the
utmost intensity was the greatest good ancient
oriental religion could bestow. To conceive this
integration in the form of intuitive imagery was
the aim of the speculative thought of the ancient
Near East."

defined, by mutual contrast, as a result of the fifth-century controversies regarding φύσις and νόμος.[1] But the concept of the world as a κόσμος or well-ordered constitution of things dates from the earlier period, when the two realms were still counted as one. It was then easy and natural for Anaximander to transfer terms like δίκη, τίσις, and τάξις from their social usage to a description of that larger community which includes not only man and living things on earth, but the heavenly bodies and the elemental powers as well. All philosophic terms have necessarily begun in this way, from a simpler, concrete usage with a human reference point. For example, the concept of a "cause," αἴτιον, is clearly a development from the idea of the "guilty one, he who is to blame," αἴτιος. Language is older than science; and the new wine must be served in whatever bottles are on hand.

The importance of the imagery of cosmic strife in early Greek thought should make clear that the rational outlook on the world did not arise by mere negation, by the stripping away of some primitive veil of pictures in order to lay bare *the facts*. In the historical experience of Greece, Nature became permeable to the human intelligence only when the inscrutable personalities of mythic religion were replaced by well-defined and regular powers. The linguistic stamp of the new mentality is a preference for neuter forms, in place of the "animate" masculines and feminines which are the stuff of myth. The Olympians have given way before τὸ ἄπειρον, τὸ χρεών, τὸ περιέχον, τὸ θερμόν, τὰ ἐναντία. The strife of elemental forces is henceforth no unpredictable quarrel between capricious agents, but an orderly scheme in which defeat must follow aggression as inevitably as the night the day.

The philosophic achievement of Ionia was no doubt made possible by the astral and mathematical science accumulated in the age-old Mesopotamian tradition. It is indeed the principles of geometry and astronomy which define the new world view. But the unity and the rational clarity of this conception are as completely Greek as is the term "cosmos" by which it continues to be known.

Supplementary Note: The Earlier Interpretations of the Fragment

As the oldest document in the history of Western philosophy, the brief fragment of Anaximander has been the object of endless discussion. Most of the interpretations proposed may be grouped under two categories.

---

[1] See the study of this antithesis by F. Heinimann, *Nomos und Physis* (Basel, 1945).

The first and, until recently, the most widely accepted view of the fragment is what can be described as a neo-Orphic interpretation: the ἀδικία for which penance is imposed consists in a kind of "falling-off" from the higher reality of the ἄπειρον into the imperfect, unjustified existence of individual things. Something of this sort was proposed by H. Ritter, in what seems to have been the first detailed exegesis of the fragment.[1] The most celebrated version of this view is that of Nietzsche,[2] but it has been presented in many forms, by many authors. Its essential features are still to be seen in the posthumous interpretation of Diels, where the analogy to the Orphic doctrine of the soul is explicitly maintained ("Anaximandros von Milet," *Neue Jahrbücher für das klassische Altertum*, LI [1923], 69).

Although this reading of Anaximander's "poetical words" may still find defenders, it is clearly wrong. In the first place (as Jaeger has already pointed out), the doctrine of Empedocles and of the Orphics mentioned by Plato and Aristotle is that we undergo this life as a punishment for some previous crime, while the "Orphic" interpretation of the fragment would imply that generation is the crime itself, to be punished by death. Furthermore this view cannot explain why compensation is paid by things *to one another* (ἀλλήλοις).

The word ἀλλήλοις was missing from the older printed texts of Simplicius, and was still omitted when Ritter offered his first interpretation. It was supplied from the MSS. of Simplicius a few years later by C. A. Brandis (*Handbuch der Geschichte der griechisch-römischen philosophie* [Berlin, 1835], I, 129, n. F). The correct text was therefore printed in the first edition of Ritter–Preller, *Historia philosophiae graeco-romanae* (Hamburg, 1838), p. 30. Yet, strangely enough, the incomplete version was still cited throughout the nineteenth century (e.g., by Nietzsche). This word ἀλλήλοις, and the plurals ἐξ ὧν . . . εἰς ταῦτα, led Ritter–Preller to offer a new interpretation of the fragment: "Poenas sibi invicem reddunt, quia caelum et mundus, *calor et frigus invicem velut conterunt quippe contraria,* eoque ut omnia in infinitam illam mixtionem absumantur efficitur" (italics added). The essential role of the opposites is recognized here, but was forgotten again until its rediscovery by Burnet and Heidel.[3] At the same time, the reference to the Boundless as a mixture

---

[1] *Geschichte der ionischen Philosophie* (Berlin, 1821), p. 188. The existence of the fragment had been remarked earlier by Schleiermacher, in "Ueber Anaximandros," *Königliche Akademie Berlin*, 1811, reprinted in *Sämmtliche Werke* (Berlin,

1838), 3. Abt., 2. Bd., pp. 171 ff.
[2] See *Philosophie im tragischen Zeitalter der Griechen*, in *Werke* (Leipzig, 1896), X, 22.
[3] See above, p. 78, n. 2.

anticipates the view defended by Cherniss a century later.[1] The plurals
ἐξ ὧν . . . εἰς ταῦτα are here explained by conceiving the ἄπειρον as a
plurality.

Unlike the neo-Orphic view (in which the Boundless must represent
a state of complete harmony and *unity*), this second theory can fit the
text of the fragment. It does not, I suggest, emerge from this text in a
natural way, but has the look of being imposed upon it from without.
Furthermore, the idea that things make amends to one another for
their mutual wrongs *by both parties ceasing to exist at the same time*, is a
strange one; and I think it would be hard to find a comparable
application of διδόναι δίκην (or τίσιν). We should expect the injured
party or his kinsmen to survive, in order to receive some benefit from
their compensation.

The decisive documentary fact—whose full importance has perhaps
not been generally recognized—is the absolute superiority here of
Simplicius' excerpt over that of the other doxographers. Diels' proof
that Aëtius is no independent source, but only a poorer extract from
Theophrastus, has left no justification for using **4.A.** as a basis for
interpreting the more accurate quotation of the fragment in **4.S.** (as
was consciously done by Ritter, unconsciously by many scholars since).
There is no external evidence that can decide the sense of Anaximander's words. The text of Simplicius is our one and only source.

Now most commentators, from Aëtius to Diels, have assumed that
the fragment must describe the generation of things out of the ἄπειρον.
But Simplicius, the only author who quotes the original words, tells
us that Anaximander had in mind "the change of the four elements
into one another."

I suggest that, once the slight anachronism of the *four* elements is
rectified (above, p. 163), the judgment of Simplicius must be accepted.
Whether he speaks here on his own initiative or on that of Theophrastus, he is better placed than we are to know the original context of the
words he cites. We would be justified in rejecting his testimony only
if it were refuted by the text itself. But this is not the case. On the contrary, the explanation of Simplicius permits us to avoid the grammatical
tour de force of explaining the plurals ἐξ ὧν and εἰς ταῦτα as if they referred
to a singular antecedent, τὸ ἄπειρον. And it tightens the logical knot
(γάρ) between the two clauses of the fragment: the mutual exchange of
wrong and reparation between the opposites corresponds exactly to their

---

[1] Above, p. 168n., where the parallel interpretations of Vlastos and Fränkel are also cited.

interchange in birth and death. Hot arises out of cold, dry out of damp, and each must perish into its source "according to necessity"; for they pay the penalty (of death) to one another for their transgression (at birth) "according to the ordinance of time," that is, according to the everlasting cycle which includes not only the seasons but all other rhythmic patterns of growth and diminution.

Substantially the same interpretation of the fragment has recently been proposed by W. Bröcker in his note "Heraklit zitiert Anaximander," *Hermes*, LXXXIV (1956), 382–84. Bröcker points out that Heraclitus B 126 ("Cold things grow warm, warm cools, moist is parched, dry dampens") corresponds exactly to the thought expressed by ἐξ ὧν δὲ ἡ γένεσίς ἐστι τοῖς οὖσι, καὶ τὴν φθορὰν εἰς ταῦτα γίνεσθαι in Anaximander's fragment: both texts refer to the necessary transformation of opposite things into one another. On this central point of interpretation we are in full agreement. On the other hand, I cannot follow Bröcker when he concludes that the fragment of Heraclitus does not really belong to Heraclitus at all, but constitutes a verbatim quotation from Anaximander—a quotation in fact of that very sentence for which ἐξ ὧν ... εἰς ταῦτα is merely "ein Referat in peripatetischer Sprache." Anaximander's doctrine of the interchange of opposites soon became a commonplace, and there is no reason why Heraclitus should not have reformulated it in his own words.

CONCLUSION

MILESIAN SPECULATION AND THE GREEK PHILOSOPHY OF NATURE

ANAXIMANDER's conception of the world is, we have seen, the prototype of the Greek view of nature as a cosmos, a harmonious realm within which the waxing and waning of the elemental powers march in step with the astronomical cycles. It is just such a rhythmic "order of time" which finds expression in his fragment. All later Greek formulas for the cosmos must accordingly be understood as developments or modifications of this Milesian view, and in so far as our own conception of the laws of nature is derived from that of Greece, its origins can be traced back to Anaximander. Indeed, the legal metaphor is explicit in his words.

However, the Milesian contribution to Greek thought is by no means limited to the idea of cosmic order or natural law, important as this may be. What Anaximander and his fellows brought into being is nothing less than the science and the natural philosophy of antiquity. The written work of Anaximander, represented for us by his fragment, constituted the earliest known Greek treatise "on the nature of things." A consideration here of the form of this new literary genre may help to suggest some of the wider implications of the Milesian view for the Greek study of nature in general.

If we may judge from the report of Theophrastus, and from the surviving portions of similar works by Parmenides and Anaxagoras, the arrangement of Anaximander's treatise followed an order which was essentially chronological. The life history of the world was described as a process of gradual evolution and differentiation out of the primordial ἄπειρον. First the fundamental forces of heat and cold are distinguished; then, through their interaction, the earth and heavens take shape. Living things arise in the sea, and later, as the dry earth emerges, adapt themselves to life on land. The appearance of man brings the development to its completion; but the sea is continuing to evaporate, will eventually be dry, and there is some hint of a retrograde process in which (as Xenophanes taught) the earth will subside into the sea, and life on land be extinguished once more.

This presentation of natural science as a kind of epic poem, with beginning, middle, and end, is characteristic of early Greek thought.

The book of Parmenides, for example, concludes with the statement:
"Thus, according to the views of men, have these things [of the natural
world] arisen and [thus] do they exist at present; and from this point
will they be nourished further and afterwards come to an end" (B 19).
For Empedocles the cycle is the same, but repeated indefinitely: "A
twofold tale will I declare: for now does one thing grow to be alone
out of many, now again do many draw their growth from one; there is
a double generation of mortal things, a double cessation" (B 17.1–6).
The atomists teach that "just as there are generations of the world, so
are there also waxings and wanings and destructions" (Leucippus A
1.33). And the exposition of Anaxagoras also begins from the beginning,
"when all things were together" (B 1).

There does not seem to have been the same unanimity in regard to
the ultimate destruction of things. Anaxagoras, for example, either
denied the doctrine, or left his opinion on the matter unclear.[1] But an
interest in the way things first arose is universal in this period, and its
importance is easily understood. The precedent for all Greek speculation is of course the *Theogony* of Hesiod, whose burning question is
"What gods were born in the beginning? Who first of all, who next?"
The eldest origin of things is indeed a primary subject for speculation
in all ancient societies. Just as the Old Testament opens with a creation
story, so in India the beginnings of philosophical discussion center
around the problem of cosmogony.[2] Greek philosophy is no exception
to the rule, and we may recall here the intimate link between Thales'
view that "all things come from water" and the similar starting point
for the great creation myths of the ancient Near East. If Anaximander's
solution to the problem is more complex, his interest in the ἀρχή of
things is no less conspicuous.

The extent to which the viewpoint of cosmogony dominated early
Greek natural thought is most clearly revealed in the attitude of
Parmenides. For him the physical origin of things is after all a problem
which makes no sense. The natural world arises because "mortals have
made up their minds to name two forms" of opposing powers, instead
of recognizing the one true Reality (B 8.53 ff.). The first section of his
poem is devoted precisely to the demonstration that any science based

---

[1] In *Vors.* 59 A 64, Simplicius supports the first
alternative, in 59 A 59, the second. In either case
Aëtius' listing of Anaxagoras among those who
hold "that the world is perishable" is altogether
misleading (59 A 65).

The question whether Heraclitus B 30 ex-

cludes the generation and alteration of the present world order will be discussed in Appendix I
(below, p. 225).

[2] See in particular the famous hymn Rigveda
x.129, and the discussion of K. F. Geldner, *Zur
Kosmogonie des Rigveda* (Marburg, 1908).

on the concept of generation (γένεσις) must be contradictory and falla-cious. Nevertheless, either because no better procedure occurs to him or because the rules of the genre are already fixed, he too announces his physical theory in the form of a regular development from the beginning:

You will know the φύσις of the Sky, and all the Signs within it, and the burning deeds of the pure lamp of the brilliant Sun, and *whence they came to be,* and you will learn of the wandering deeds of the cyclops Moon, and its φύσις, and you will know of the Heaven which holds them round about, *whence it arose* and how Necessity led and bound it to hold the limits of the stars. (B 10)

The other fragments of Parmenides (B 11–19) show that this promise was fulfilled, and that the φύσις of all things was explained by an account of how they arose from a combination of the two primary forms, Fire and Darkness. The term φύσις itself is set parallel to ἔφυ and ἐξεγένοντο in the fragment just cited, so that Parmenides makes clear that the word is to be taken in its strict sense, as an action noun from φύομαι.[1] What we translate by "nature" is here properly *the process of natural development*, or *growth*.

Φύσις is, of course, the catchword for the new philosophy. Heraclitus too begins his work by a promise that in his discussion he will "dis-tinguish each thing according to its φύσις and tell what is its [true] condition" (κατὰ φύσιν διαιρέων ἕκαστον καὶ φράζων ὅκως ἔχει, B 1). This expression of Heraclitus suggests that, in contemporary prose, the term φύσις had become specialized to indicate the *essential character* of a thing as well as the process by which it arose, and it is, of course, this derivative sense which dominates in the later history of the word.[2]

---

[1] The true verbal force of φύσις in this fragment of Parmenides has recently been emphasized by F. Heinimann, *Nomos und Physis* (Basel, 1945), pp. 90 f. But it would be misleading to draw any absolute distinction between this strict sense of "origin, development," and the more common one of "true character, nature." It is precisely the true nature of things which Parmenides will re-veal by telling how they have been formed: the composition from Fire and Darkness is their φύσις in both senses. The same convergence of the two meanings of φύσις is evident in the passage from the *De Victu*, cited on the next page.

[2] Even in the one Homeric use of the word there is no explicit reference to a process of growth; the φύσις of the moly plant is simply its bodily form at maturity (see above, p. 4, n. 1). That the usual sense of φύσις in Greek literature is not "growth," but "form, character, nature (of a given thing)" is abundantly illustrated in the recent study of D. Holwerda, *Commentatio de vocis quae est φύσις vi atque usu* (Groningen, 1955). But it is not true to add (as Holwerda and others have done, after Burnet) that the original sense of the root φυ- (Indo-European *bhu-*) was also "exist-ence, being" rather than "growth, biological development." This view is based upon the mean-ings which the root acquires in languages other than Greek. But from the standpoint of compara-tive linguistics, there can be no doubt that the concrete sense of "growth" is older and more fundamental than the use of the same root for "coming-to-be" or for "existence" in general. See, e.g., Meillet in *Dictionnaire étymologique de la*

But the choice of just this term to designate the true nature of a thing (in preference to such conceivable alternatives as εἶδος or μορφή) clearly reflects the importance attached to the process of development. The early philosophers sought to understand the "nature" of a thing by discovering *from what source* and *in what way* it has come to be what it is.[1] This was as true for the detailed study of man and of living things, as for the general theory of the world as a whole. A passionate interest in embryology in the one case matches the concern for cosmogony in the other.[2] The doctors, for example, seek to discover the decisive factors in the normal functioning of the body by observing which powers predominate in its original formation. A writer on regimen must

know and distinguish the φύσις of the whole man: know from what things it has been composed in the beginning (ἀπὸ τίνων συνέστηκεν ἐξ ἀρχῆς), distinguish by what parts it is dominated. For if he does not know the original composition, he will be incapable of recognizing their results (τὰ ὑπ' ἐκείνων γινόμενα); and if he does not know what is dominant in the body, he will not be able to apply the proper remedies.[3]

It is this interest in the origin of all things—of the world, of living beings, of man, and of his social institutions—which characterizes the scientific thought of early Greece. This attitude implicitly affirms the conviction on which the creation myths are based: that by discovering the original state of affairs one may penetrate to the secret core of things. Hence it is that φύσις can denote the true nature of a thing, while maintaining its etymological sense of "the primary source or process" from which the thing has come to be.[4] "Nature" and "origin" are combined in one and the same idea. This ancient principle is still respected by Plato in his use of the creation motif in the *Timaeus*. With Aristotle, however, such an approach to natural philosophy is

---

langue latine, s.vv. fuam, fui; the proof for the Greek forms is given by A. Burger, *Les mots de la famille de φύω en grec ancien*, Fascicule no. 246 de la Bibliothèque de l'École des Hautes Études (Paris, 1925), especially pp. 1–4. As an action noun in -σις, φύσις means properly "l'accomplissement (effectué) d'un devenir": E. Benveniste, *Noms d'agent et noms d'action en indo-européen* (Paris, 1948), p. 78. In the classic usage of the word as "form, true character," this etymological value had become largely obscured, but certainly not forgotten.

[1] Thus in fr. 910 (= *Vors.* 59 A 30) Euripides speaks of the philosopher who studies "the ageless κόσμος of undying φύσις, whence it was

composed and in what way": ἀθανάτου καθορῶν φύσεως κόσμον ἀγήρων, †πῇ τε συνέστη καὶ ὅπῃ καὶ ὅπως; despite the corrupt πῇ τε, there is no doubt as to the sense.

[2] See, e.g., Alcmaeon A 13–17; Parm. B 17–18; Anaxag. A 107–11; Emped. A 81–84.

[3] *De Victu* 2, Jones, IV, 226. This method is criticized in *Anc. Med.* 20 (Jones, I, 52) as that of Empedocles and others οἳ περὶ φύσιος γεγράφασιν ἐξ ἀρχῆς ὅ τί ἐστιν ἄνθρωπος, καὶ ὅπως ἐγένετο πρῶτον καὶ ὁπόθεν συνεπάγη.

[4] Plato *Laws* 892c.2 (speaking of the natural philosophers): φύσιν βούλονται λέγειν γένεσιν τὴν περὶ τὰ πρῶτα.

entirely abandoned. The order of the universe is declared to be eternal and ungenerated, and the traditional attempt to construct it from a hypothetical starting point (ἀρχή) is systematically rejected in favour of a new kind of ἀρχαί, the "fundamental principles" into which cosmic movement and change are to be resolved. The prevalence in Aristotle's works of this new meaning for the old term ἀρχή indicates a basic shift in his scientific outlook.[1]

In biology, the revolution of ideas is of the same kind. Whereas his predecessors investigated "the way each thing naturally comes to be rather than the way it is" (πῶς ἕκαστον γίνεσθαι πέφυκε μᾶλλον ἢ πῶς ἔστιν), Aristotle insists that it is not the unformed embryo but the full structure of the mature individual which calls for primary attention, "for the process of generation exists for the sake of the complete being (οὐσία), not the being for the sake of generation."[2] Aristotle himself links the biological method of his predecessors to their interest in cosmogony:

The ancients who first philosophized concerning nature investigated the material starting point (ἡ ὑλικὴ ἀρχή) and causation of the same type: what the starting point is, what are its properties, and how the universe arises from it, under the action of what motive force. . . . And in this way they generate the κόσμος.[3]

Aristotle's reaction against this basic tendency of early Greek thought was only partially successful. Neither of the two major Hellenistic schools accepted his proofs of the eternity of the world. Stoics as well as Epicureans continue "to generate the cosmos," and both schools teach its eventual destruction. To this extent, the Hellenistic cosmologies follow the Ionians rather than Aristotle.

But if the dogma of cosmogony persisted, the interest in the matter did not. It is revealing in this respect to compare the poem of Lucretius with that of Parmenides. The earlier work invites us to learn "how Earth and Sun and Moon and the common Sky, the Milky Way, outer Olympus, and the hot force of the Stars eagerly began to come into existence" (Parm. B 11). The origin of the universe is here the center of attention; the generation of living things and of the soul of

---

[1] This new usage of ἀρχή is directly paralleled by the more static sense of φύσις for Aristotle, which accounts for his misunderstanding of φύσις = γένεσις in the poem of Empedocles (see above, pp. 23 and 75).

[2] Part. An. 640ᵃ11–19.

[3] Ibid. 640ᵇ5–12. Of course, there are many traces of the older method in Aristotle, for instance, in his analytic-genetic study of the origins of a political community: εἰ δή τις ἐξ ἀρχῆς τὰ πράγματα φυόμενα βλέψειεν, ὥσπερ ἐν τοῖς ἄλλοις, καὶ ἐν τούτοις κάλλιστ' ἂν οὕτω θεωρήσειεν (Pol. 1252ᵃ25).

man appear in their proper chronological place, towards the end.[1] Lucretius still claims to discourse in general περὶ φύσεως (*de rerum natura*),[2] but his account of the Epicurean cosmogony is in fact delayed until Book v. After an exposition of the "principles" (Books i–ii) he passes directly to human psychology (Books iii–iv). The same lack of interest is revealed in Epicurus' own discussion of cosmological problems; all that matters for him is that one should not fear the thunder and lightning of Zeus.[3] In the changed intellectual conditions of the Hellenistic age, a theoretic interest in the natural phenomena for their own sake faded before the concern for a philosophy of man. It was only the latter that could replace the disintegrating religious order of the old city-state by a new way of life offering spiritual salvation.[4]

In one sense, therefore, the tradition initiated by the Milesians came to an end in the fourth century B.C. Plato, in the *Timaeus*, is one of its last conscious imitators. The thesis of Aristotle's *De Caelo* is an attack on the central doctrine of the old school, while the interest of the Hellenistic philosophers lies elsewhere.

Thus delimited, the Ionian investigation of nature can be described as the school of Anaximander. Anaximenes, Xenophanes, and Heraclitus are his disciples in a true sense; their conception of the physical universe differs from his only in detail. Too little remains of the physical writings of Xenophanes for us to judge the extent of his activity in this field. The more numerous fragments of Heraclitus suggest that he has largely taken for granted the cosmology of Anaximander (or at least the Milesian doctrine of regular elemental conflict and interchange), and that he is above all concerned to define the place allotted to man within this ordered universe. The ancient critic who said that the work of Heraclitus was not primarily about the physical world (περὶ φύσεως), but about man's life in society (περὶ πολιτείας), may not have been altogether mistaken.[5]

A much more creative figure in natural science was Anaximander's younger fellow countryman, Anaximenes. It is difficult to estimate the

---

[1] The order of exposition is indicated by Simplicius (under Parm. B 11) : καὶ τῶν γινομένων καὶ φθειρομένων μέχρι τῶν μορίων τῶν ζῴων τὴν γένεσιν παραδίδωσι. Plutarch (on Parm. B 10) also names the γένεσις ἀνθρώπων after the formation of earth, heaven, sun, and moon.

[2] 1.25: (*versus*) *quos ego de rerum natura pangere conor.*

[3] See, e.g., D.L. x.85–87.

[4] See Zeller III. 1³, 11–20 and the recent comments of A.-J. Festugière, "Le fait religieux à l'époque hellénistique," in *Épicure et ses dieux* (Paris, 1946), pp. 12–24.

[5] τῶν δὲ γραμματικῶν Διόδοτος [sc. μέμνηται Ἡρακλείτου], ὃς οὔ φησι περὶ φύσεως εἶναι τὸ σύγγραμμα, ἀλλὰ περὶ πολιτείας, τὰ δὲ περὶ φύσεως ἐν παραδείγματος εἴδει κεῖσθαι (D.L. ix. 15 = *Vors.* 22 A 1).

The childish innovations of Xenophanes and Heraclitus in astronomical matters have been noticed above, p. 92.

significance of his most famous innovation, the substitution of ἄπειρος ἀήρ for the simple ἄπειρον as source of the world process. Presumably this specification was designed to emphasize the vital role of his principle, as the inexhaustible "breath of life" for the universe. In any case, his derivation of all things from this source by the operation of heat (as the force of loosening and expansion) and of cold (as that of hardening and contraction) is in basic agreement with the physics of Anaximander. More radical are the innovations of Anaximenes with regard to the shape and order of the celestial bodies: the stars, not the sun, are farthest from the earth;[1] sun and moon are not "rings" but flat objects which float in the air, just as the earth itself is borne up by air (A 7.4, A 20). And it is in this form that the Milesian cosmology is transmitted to the Ionians of the fifth century.

The most conservative spokesman for the later Ionian school is of course Diogenes of Apollonia. He continues the general doctrine of Anaximenes, although the details of his cosmology are adapted from Anaxagoras and Leucippus.[2] Anaxagoras himself stands close to the viewpoint of the Milesians. His conception of the original state of things has been modified by the criticism of Parmenides, but what he says of the consecutive stages of cosmogony and of the ἀποκρίνεσθαι of elemental forces is scarcely new.[3] Furthermore, for the order of the heavenly bodies, for the reason why the stars give no heat, and for the explanation of the earth's position at the center, he follows Anaximenes. His doctrine of wind, thunder, lightning, and earthquake, as well as his view that living things first arose in moisture, are all clearly dependent upon the Milesians.

Somewhat apart from the Ionians stand the western philosophers: Parmenides, Empedocles, and the Pythagoreans. Empedocles is perhaps most clearly linked to the Ionian school. He, like Anaxagoras, seeks to lay a foundation for the traditional science which will be capable of withstanding Eleatic criticism. The originality of Parmenides' own view can scarcely be overestimated. Its influence on the development of Greek thought may perhaps be compared to that of Kant's *Critique* in modern philosophy. Nevertheless, we have seen that in the exposition of his physical theory Parmenides follows the familiar outline of Milesian cosmology. Even for the metaphysical section of his poem, it seems

---

[1] This follows from the statement that "they give no heat because of the magnitude of their distance" (Anaximenes A 7.8), and is implied by the description of them as "set in the crystalline [sphere]" (A 14).   [2] Diog. A 5 = *Phys. Opin.* fr. 2.   [3] See above, pp. 150, 161 f.

more illuminating to locate the polemical standpoint of Parmenides within the framework of Ionian theories of the type discussed above, than to represent him as launching a direct attack upon those contemporary Pythagorean teachings of which we know so little.

Pythagoras himself was of course an Ionian, and certain features of the Pythagorean cosmology, such as the idea of the heaven inhaling Breath from the surrounding Boundless (*Vors.* 58 B 30), show the unmistakable influence of Miletus. It is probable that western Greeks like Parmenides and Empedocles came into contact with Ionian science less by way of written works (such as those of Anaximander and Anaximenes) than by personal contact with the tradition as it was preserved in the Pythagorean brotherhood. In fact, the Hellenistic biographers assign Pythagorean teachers to both Parmenides and Empedocles. The originality of the school of Pythagoras lay above all in mathematics and in mathematical astronomy; yet its basic conception of the universe, as pervaded by a geometrical principle of harmony and equilibrium, is taken over from the Ionian scheme.[1]

The final and most durable achievement of the Ionian study of nature was the atomist system of Leucippus and Democritus. Their characteristic doctrines are, of course, new, but many a detail of the scheme, such as the shape and position of the earth, or the explanation of thunder and lightning, bears witness to its Milesian ancestry. Hence it has been said of Leucippus that he was "as reactionary in his detailed cosmology as he was daring in his general physical theory."[2]

Finally, the physical speculation of Plato in the *Timaeus* appears as a great attempt to counteract the materialistic tendencies of Ionian science—as embodied above all in the atomic system—by resuming and reinterpreting the achievements of the entire tradition. Plato bases his physical doctrine on the principle that Reason (νοῦς) and Life (ψυχή) are prior in nature to Body (σῶμα) and to blind physical causation (ἀνάγκη). This thesis of Plato is both a conscious reformulation of the

---

[1] See above, pp. 77 ff., 186 ff. The earliest known application of the Milesian cosmology to medical theory is due to Alcmaeon of Croton, who dedicated his book to members of the Pythagorean society (B 1; for the names, see Burnet, p. 194, n. 1). Alcmaeon taught that the "equal distribution" (ἰσονομία) of opposing "powers" is a condition of health in the body, while the "monarchy" of any one power causes disease (B 4). The influence of this idea can be traced not only in the theories of the "Pythagorean notebooks" (cited above, p. 190), but in practically every treatise of the (Ionian) Hippocratic Corpus. The arbitrary nature of any systematic distinction between the Ionian and the Italian schools is here apparent.

[2] Burnet, p. 339. The link between the atomists and Anaximander is particularly striking if the doctrine of infinite worlds can be attributed to the latter. But for doubts on this point, see above, pp. 47 ff.

doctrine of Anaxagoras and a vindication, as it were, of one of the earliest conceptions of Greek philosophy, that the powers of nature are instinct with divine life. For Plato as for Thales, "all things are full of gods."[1]

From the sixth to the fourth century, therefore, the Greek study of nature is a close-knit unity, and the originality of the individual thinkers is intelligible only against the background of a continuous tradition, that is to say, of a common set of problems, principles, and solutions. Our only complete scientific texts from this period—the earlier medical treatises of the Hippocratic Corpus—provide clear evidence of the overwhelming influence of the Ionian tradition on almost every page. For example, the connections between the cosmological preface to the *De Hebdomadibus* and the doctrines of the Milesians have often been stressed.[2] Similarly, the opening chapters of the *De Victu* contain clear reminiscences of Heraclitus, Anaxagoras, Empedocles, and perhaps of others. Many such medical texts might be cited, but none is more revealing than the introduction to the *De Carnibus*. The author excuses himself for making use of the "commonly held views" (κοιναὶ γνῶμαι) of his predecessors, but insists upon the necessity of "laying a commonly accepted foundation as starting point for one's ideas" in order to compose a technical treatise on the medical art.[3] These "common views" are given in the familiar form of a world arrangement which emerges progressively from an original state of mixture and confusion (chs. 2–3). The immediate model is probably the scheme of Anaxagoras (or of his pupil Archelaus), but the principles involved are, as the author says, "common": they are shared by the entire Ionian school.

Because the existence of this common body of ideas has been too often neglected, much effort has been poured into the fruitless attempt to trace the influence of a particular philosopher on a given page of the Hippocratic Corpus. Our knowledge of sixth- and fifth-century theories is rarely complete enough for us to draw any precise line between what each one owes to the tradition on a specific point of detail, and what is his private contribution.

Indeed, it is an essential feature of the Greek philosophical tradition that the effort for originality is concentrated on the doctrine of first

---

[1] *Laws* 899b.9.

[2] The case was overstated by W. H. Roscher, who thought that the author of this fragmentary treatise must be a sixth-century Milesian; see the commentary to his edition of the *De Hebd.* (cited in the Bibliographical Note). A more sober review of the facts was given by Diels in *Deutsche Literaturzeitung*, XXXII (1911), cols. 1861–66.

[3] *De Carn.* 1, Littré, VIII, 584: ἀναγκαίως γὰρ ἔχει κοινὴν ἀρχὴν ὑποθέσθαι τῆσι γνώμῃσι βουλόμενον ξυνθεῖναι τὸν λόγον τόνδε περὶ τῆς τέχνης τῆς ἰητρικῆς.

principles, or restricted to relatively minor features of the whole scheme. The atoms and the void, the four "roots" of Empedocles, the Nous of Anaxagoras, and the two "forms" of Parmenides claim our attention as great personal achievements. But, in every case, the concrete description of the world is drawn up along more traditional lines. Varying the metaphor of the *De Carnibus*, we may say that each one of these philosophers lays a new foundation for what remains essentially the same edifice. Most of the stones for his building and many of the structural ideas are those which have already been employed by his predecessors.

The activity of an ancient natural philosopher may thus be compared, *mutatis mutandis*, to that of the author of a textbook in modern science, who seeks primarily to offer a fresh approach to a familiar subject. The Greek thinker (unless he is an Eleatic) does not propose that *everything* must be considered anew, as Descartes or Hume would have us do. Like the author of the *De Carnibus*, the Ionian σοφιστής or φυσικός acts as heir to a common tradition, which it is his responsibility to preserve as well as to correct. What has been too hastily described as "eclecticism" or "reaction" in early Greek thought may be more properly interpreted as the influence of this abiding tradition. The study of nature is carried on as a τέχνη or specialized discipline, and, like the poet or the sculptor, the author of a treatise "on the nature of things" can claim the attention of his audience only by a mastery of the traditional forms. It is therefore in the renovation rather than in the destruction of these forms that his original genius seeks to express itself.[1]

Two quotations from the creative period of Greek science may serve to illustrate this attitude.

The investigation of truth (says Aristotle) is in one sense difficult, in another easy. An indication of this is that while no one is able to attain it properly, neither do

---

[1] This point was made by Diels in his article "Ueber die ältesten Philosophenschulen der Griechen," in *Philosophische Aufsätze Eduard Zeller gewidmet* (Leipzig, 1887), especially pp. 243 ff.
  A striking example of the parallelism (and occasional coincidence) of the role played by tradition in poetry and in natural science is provided by the "signs" of weather which Vergil has borrowed from Aratus (cf. *Georgics* 1.356–460 with *Phaenomena* 733–1141). The poet has exactly the same right here as when he imitates Hesiod, Theocritus, or Homer, but the student of nature is doubly justified, for Aratus himself has taken

the signs from some earlier author (just as Vergil in turn will be quoted as an authority). The abnormal greediness of pigs, for example, is noted as a warning of bad weather by Aratus (1123), Vergil (1.399–400), and Pliny (*H.N.* xviii.364), as well as by the Greek treatise περὶ σημείων, attributed to Theophrastus. In this case we can apparently trace the observation back to Democritus, that is to say, to the last great representative of the Ionian school. (See Democr. B 147, and the remarks of P. Maas in his edition of Aratus [2d ed.; Berlin, 1955], p. xxvi.) The chain does not necessarily end here, for it seems that Democritus may have had in mind a phrase of Heraclitus (B 13).

they all miss the goal, but each one says something [positive] about the nature of things ($\pi\epsilon\rho\grave{\iota}$ $\tau\hat{\eta}s$ $\phi\acute{\upsilon}\sigma\epsilon\omega s$). Thus, although individually they make little or no contribution to the truth, the sum of all their efforts is a result of some magnitude.[1]

In this statement of principle (and in his practice in the *Meteorologica*, for instance, or in the biological works) Aristotle agrees with the medical author of the *De Victu*:

In so far as the facts have been correctly stated by my predecessors, it is not by treating of them in a different way that I should treat of them correctly. . . . Therefore I shall add my agreement to those things which have been properly explained; but in what has been incorrectly stated I shall make clear the true facts. And I shall also set forth the nature of those things which no one of my predecessors has even attempted to explain.[2]

Such science is not a personal creation but a group undertaking, and it must have been handed down in some regular manner, as were the other $\tau\acute{\epsilon}\chi\nu\alpha\iota$. Perhaps the accumulation and transmission of the knowledge of nature was, from the earliest times, the work of an organized association.[3] In this case the Pythagorean brotherhood and the Athenian schools would continue the example of Miletus. The group around Thales and Anaximander must at least have had the social coherence of the Socratic circle; while the maximum of formality is represented by the Hippocratic Oath, which binds the apprentice "to treat my teacher in this art as equal to my parents, and his offspring as equal to my brothers." Whatever the original mode of transmission may have been, it was certainly more exclusive than the professional popularizing of the later "sophists"—although these too drew their knowledge from the philosophical tradition: Gorgias was a pupil of Empedocles, and Protagoras came from the city of the atomists.

The tradition which we have sketched above is a recognizable historical unit from the time of Anaximander to that of Democritus and Plato. The constant goal of this common intellectual enterprise is to

---

[1] *Met.* 993ª30 (adapted from the Oxford translation of W. D. Ross).

[2] *De Victu* 1, Jones, IV, 224–26 (after the translation of Jones). The attitude of a Pythagorean mathematician is, of course, even more reverent towards the tradition. "Those who have concerned themselves with mathematics," says Archytas, "have discovered an excellent kind of knowledge, and it is no surprise that they have rightly under-

stood each thing as it [truly] is. . . . Indeed, they have handed down to us clear and distinct knowledge of the speed of the heavenly bodies, and of their risings and settings, as well as of geometry, numbers, the analysis of the sphere, and, not least, of musical theory" (B 1).

[3] As Diels suggested, in the article cited above, p. 208, n. 1.

explain how the world and all that it contains have reached their
present form. Hence the disintegration of the tradition in the second
half of the fourth century may be symbolized by Aristotle's rejection
of cosmogony as a valid principle of scientific explanation. In more
historical terms the unified τέχνη or science of nature (περὶ φύσεως
ἱστορία) gives way before the competitive activity of the various schools,
with their primary interest in moral questions and in the refutation of
their opponents.

In this as in other respects, Aristotle stands between two worlds. The
spirit of his work has more in common with that of his predecessors than
with the philosophy of the Hellenistic Age, and it is in fact in his school
—for a few generations, and in a more specialized way—that men like
Theophrastus and Strato will continue the study of nature in the
Ionian sense. But Aristotle himself is as yet no specialist, and, when he
surveys the field of natural philosophy, the entire περὶ φύσεως ἱστορία
presents itself to him as a single discipline. His study of plants and
animals is to crown an investigation of the whole of nature, beginning
from first principles and the abstract study of motion (*Physics*), passing
through the structure of the upper heavens (*De Caelo* I–II) and the
elements of sublunar change (*De Caelo* III–IV, *De Generatione et Corrup-
tione*), to the phenomena of the atmosphere and the earth (*Meteorologica*),
and, finally, to the principles of life itself (*De Anima*).[1] Both the scope
of this enterprise and the general order in which the subjects are treated
are entirely parallel to the old cosmogonical development which Plato
follows in the *Timaeus*.

The natural philosophy of the Hellenistic schools adds little that is
essentially new to the body of Greek ideas on the subject, although a
physical doctrine is still felt to be indispensable. The atomism of Epicurus is borrowed from Democritus with only minor adaptations, while
the Stoic cosmology is so intimately akin to that of Heraclitus (and
hence to that of the entire Ionian school) that it is often difficult to
disentangle one from the other. In general, the Stoics have altered the
Ionian scheme only by the infusion of Platonic and Aristotelian ideas.

Thus, if from one point of view the direct tradition of Milesian
inquiry into nature comes to an end with Democritus and the contemporaries of Plato, in a broader perspective the entire natural philosophy of antiquity appears as one continuous, developing tradition.

If we seek to define the inherent unity of this tradition, we can

---

[1] See *Meteor.* I.I for this outline of the physical treatises.

perhaps do so most adequately by invoking that concept of elemental balance and cosmic periodicity which the preceding chapters have described. In one sense, of course, the Greek conception of a rationally ordered universe is also that of modern science. But the characteristic features of the ancient view become clear precisely when we contrast it with the idea of Nature to which we have become accustomed.

In the physical scheme which has dominated modern thought since the days of Galileo and Descartes, the object of science is defined in strictly mathematical or quantitative terms. The picturesque, qualitative diversity of things which forms the texture of our daily experience is held to be "subjective" in origin, and of no significance for the scientific analysis of nature. The laws of the universe are mechanical or abstract in character, without any visible resemblance to the concrete pattern of our personal existence and our life in society. The ancient view, on the contrary, is centered on the realm of living beings, its κόσμος is composed of qualitative powers (such as *hot* and *cold*, *dry* and *wet*) that are thoroughly familiar to our everyday experience, and its unifying structure takes the form of a harmonious community of opponents dwelling together under law. The Greek view of the cosmos thus preserves that sense of the link between man, society, and nature which lies at the heart of the old myths.

Wherever we find a general similarity between the ancient and the modern view, a closer glance will assure us that the Greeks had in mind something quite different from our post-Cartesian scheme. The Pythagorean doctrine that "things imitate numbers," for example, presents a certain analogy to modern mathematical physics, but the ancient view certainly included "the shape-iness of shape, which is an impure mathematical entity."[1] Moreover, it is precisely because of this qualitative aspect of early Greek arithmetic and geometry that the Pythagorean correspondences are meaningful. The examples given by Aristotle for this doctrine include "justice," "soul," "reason," and "due measure" or "opportunity" (καιρός). Justice, for instance, is the number 4, the simplest product of equal numbers multiplied together.[2] What the Pythagoreans had in mind here is what we express by the word "foursquare," and the connections between mathematics, man, and society remain intact.

[1] A. N. Whitehead, *Science and the Modern World* (New York, 1948), p. 42.
[2] Arist. *Met.* 985ᵇ29–30 and fr. 203. For the good man as τετράγωνος, see Simonides fr. 5 Bergk (Plato, *Prot.* 339b).

There is, on the other hand, a direct historical link between ancient atomism and the modern view of nature as a mechanism. In fact the idea of a distinction between "subjective" and "objective" reality is borrowed from Democritus, who said: "By usage[1] there is sweet, by usage bitter, by usage hot, by usage cold, by usage color; but in truth there are atoms and the void" (B 9). Theoretically, then, the universe of the Greek atomists is as unlike our world of everyday experience as is the intricate geometry of modern atomic theory. In fact, however, the ancient atomists never achieved that rigorously quantitative conception of the world which modern physics takes for granted—and perhaps they could not do so with the still "qualitative" mathematics of fifth-century Greece. Thus the ancient atoms are characterized by "shape" or "form" (ῥυσμός, ἰδέα, σχῆμα) as well as by position and arrangement. In one of his rare fragments concerning the theory of nature, Democritus compares the flocking together of animals of like kind ("doves with doves, cranes with cranes") to the discrimination of different sorts of grain in winnowing and to the selective placing of round and oblong pebbles on the beach, "as if the similarity in things possessed some power tending to draw them together" (B 164). The attraction of like to like (which first appears in the *Odyssey* as drawing together like-minded *men*) is conceived by Democritus as applying in a parallel way to the behavior of living things and to mechanical motions. We are far from the Cartesian field of extended matter from which all signs of life have been banned.

Still more patent is the bond between man and nature in the only complete statement of the atomic doctrine which has come down to us. The poem of Lucretius is suffused throughout by the idea of nature as a realm of color, passion, and eagerness for life:

> omnibus incutiens blandum per pectora amorem
> efficis ut cupide generatim saecla propagent. (1.19–20)

It is not the conservation of inert matter or measurable energy which vindicates for Lucretius the orderly operation of natural law. For him, as for Anaximander, the *foedera naturai* constitute an organic "ordering of Time," exemplified in the regular reproduction and growth of living things and in their unfailing harmony with the cycle of seasonal change:

> praeterea cur vere rosam, frumenta calore,
> vitis autumno fundi suadente videmus,
> si non, certa suo quia tempore semina rerum

[1] Or "by convention," νόμῳ.

cum confluxerunt, patefit quodcumque creatur,
dum tempestates adsunt et vivida tellus
tuto res teneras effert in luminis oras? (1.174–79)

We may recall that, from Anaximander to Plato, the origin of the universe is compared to the formation and birth of a living being. This ancient pairing of cosmogony and embryology explains why the elemental bodies are referred to by Anaxagoras and Empedocles as the "seeds" or "roots" of all things.[1] So for Lucretius the atoms are not only *primordia rerum* or *corpora prima*, but also *genitalia corpora* and *semina rerum*,

> unde omnis natura creet res auctet alatque
> quove eadem rursum natura perempta resolvat. (1.56–57)

Although such a systematic analogy between the history of the physical world and the life cycle of plants and animals was not recognized by Aristotle, the world is no less a living thing in his eyes.[2] The most fundamental principle in Aristotle's philosophy of nature, the development from potentiality (δύναμις) to realization (ἐνέργεια), embodies the law by which a fruit tree blossoms from its seed, and a human embryo grows to maturity as a rational being.

Thus, at the heart of the ancient conception of φύσις, the etymological link with growth and vital development is preserved. There is no unbridgeable gulf between man and nature, and the larger order of the universe is one in which the "little cosmos" has its natural place. For the course of man's life keeps step with the seasons and with the ceaseless pacing of the stars, while the elemental forces dwell, as he does, within an ordered community that holds their antagonism in check.

We are so habituated to the lifeless mechanism of our physical science that we scarcely realize its relative novelty, nor the extent to which the ancient view was still current even in the age of Newton. For poetical reasons, Milton could ignore the new cosmology of his contemporaries and depict the Chaos prior to creation as

> The Womb of nature and perhaps her Grave,
> Of neither Sea, nor Shore, nor Air, nor Fire,
> But all these in thir pregnant causes mixt
> Confus'dly, and which thus must ever fight.[3]

---

[1] σπέρματα πάντων χρημάτων, Anaxag. B 4; πάντων ῥιζώματα, Emped. B 6; cf. the oath by Pythagoras, who revealed to us the τετρακτύν / παγὰν ἀενάου φύσεως ῥίζωμά τ' ἔχουσαν (Vors.

58 B 15).
[2] ὁ δ' οὐρανὸς ἔμψυχος, De Caelo 285ᵃ29.
[3] Paradise Lost 11.911–14.

Not only has Milton taken his doctrine from classical antiquity, but the true spirit of the ancient view still breathes through his description:

> For hot, cold, moist, and dry, four Champions fierce
> Strive here for Maistrie, and to Battel bring
> Thir embryon Atoms; they around the flag
> Of each his faction, in thir several Clanns,
> Light-arm'd or heavy, sharp, smooth, swift or slow,
> Swarm populous.[1]

Within the order of the created world, Adam and Eve invoke

> Aire, and ye Elements the eldest birth
> Of Natures Womb, that in quaternion run
> Perpetual Circle, multiform; and mix
> And nourish all things.[2]

The description of the act of creation itself follows of course the Hebrew account in Genesis, but the details are clearly Greek: the Spirit of God "his brooding wings outspred,"

> And vital vertue infus'd, and vital warmth
> Throughout the fluid Mass, but downward purg'd
> The black tartareous cold infernal dregs
> Adverse to life: then founded, then conglob'd
> Like things to like, the rest to several place
> Disparted, and between spun out the Air,
> And Earth self-ballanc't on her Center hung.[3]

If for the Spirit of God we were to read something like "the upward surge of fire in the universe," Milton's cosmogony would be largely identical with that of the ancient Ionians. Indeed, it is as if the ghosts of Anaximander and Pythagoras had been summoned through a space of twenty-two centuries to favor Milton with their inspiration, when he portrays the cosmic sphere as an emblem of complete symmetry and proportion.

> And in his hand
> He took the golden Compasses, prepar'd
> In Gods Eternal store, to circumscribe
> This Universe, and all created things:
> One foot he center'd, and the other turn'd
> Round through the vast profunditie obscure,

---

[1] *Paradise Lost* ii.898–903.
[2] *Ibid.* v.180–83.
[3] *Ibid.* vii.236–42.

And said, thus farr extend, thus farr thy bounds,
This be thy just Circumference, O World.[1]

Paradise Lost is evidence not only for the poetic excellence of the ancient cosmology, but also for the conservative character of the tradition. Whether Milton was inspired by Plato, Aristotle, Lucretius, or the Stoics—or by all of them and others as well—is of no consequence. The schools do not differ from one another on such questions as the cycle of elemental change, the balance of hostile opposites, the attraction of like for like, and the rhythmical adjustment of the universe in a structure of dynamic harmony and proportion.

[1] *Paradise Lost* VII.224–31. Milton must have seen an illuminated Bible of the type illustrated in Plate IIB. The motif of the compasses was frequently used in thirteenth-century manuscripts. It is generally traced back to Proverbs VIII.27 (Wisdom speaks): "When He prepared the heavens, I was there: when he set a compass upon the face of the depth." But neither in Milton nor in the Bible illustration are the compasses set on the face of the deep in order to trace the circle of land and sea (as in the Babylonian map, Plate I). What they do is to mark out the whole universe as a perfect sphere. The medieval clerks inherited this conception from Plato and Aristotle; it seems to be neither Babylonian nor Hebrew but purely Greek.

For Anaximander's use of the celestial sphere, see above pp. 77 ff.

APPENDICES

APPENDIX I

THE USAGE OF THE TERM ΚΟΣΜΟΣ IN EARLY GREEK PHILOSOPHY

IT is of some importance for the history of Greek cosmology to know just what meaning was attached to the word κόσμος by the first philosophers who employed it to designate "the world." Exactly when and how this usage of the term arose, we do not know. There is no direct proof that κόσμος in this sense formed part of the Milesian vocabulary (unless Anaximenes B 2 ὅλον τὸν κόσμον πνεῦμα καὶ ἀὴρ περιέχει represents a direct quotation, which is not likely). But there is good circumstantial evidence in favor of a Milesian origin. In the first place, κόσμος is the word invariably used by later authors to denote the organic view of the natural world which we have traced back to Miletus and to the fragment of Anaximander. In the second place, the philosophic sense of κόσμος is attested for almost every author who stands in the Milesian tradition. It is difficult to imagine that the Milesians developed the idea of the κόσμος without using this word, and that Heraclitus, Parmenides, Anaxagoras, Empedocles, and the rest have all received their terminology from another source. As Jaeger has put it, the philosophy of Anaximander represents "the discovery of the cosmos,"[1] and there is no good reason to suppose that this discovery was ever called by any other name.[2]

The early philosophic use of κόσμος has often been discussed.[3] For our purposes, however, a sufficiently clear distinction has not been drawn between 1) the ordinary meanings of κόσμος from Homer onwards, and 2) the special sense current among the philosophers.

The use of κόσμος for the universal order which "holds together heaven and earth, men and gods," is referred by Plato to "the wise," who have made a study of geometry (*Gorg.* 508a, cited above, p. 188,

---

[1] *Paideia*, I, 160.

[2] The statement of D.L. VIII.48, cited above, p. 115, that Pythagoras "was the first to name the heaven κόσμος," comes apparently from Favorinus, and has no historical value. But of course it is likely that Pythagoras and his associates, as heirs to the Milesians, would also have made use of the term. It appears with unusual frequency in the fragments attributed to Philolaus.

[3] See the literature cited by W. Kranz in his two articles "Kosmos als philosophischer Begriff frühgriechischer Zeit," *Philologus*, XCIII (1938), 430; and "Kosmos," *Archiv für Begriffsgeschichte*, II, 1 (Bonn, 1955). Also Kirk, *Heraclitus*, pp. 311–15.

n. 2). Xenophon treats the term in a similar way, when he insists that
"Socrates did not have the habit of discussing the nature of all things,
as do most of the others, inquiring into the circumstances of what the
experts call the κόσμος, and into the necessary causes why the different
phenomena of heaven take place as they do" (οὐδὲ γὰρ περὶ τῆς τῶν
πάντων φύσεως, ἧπερ τῶν ἄλλων οἱ πλεῖστοι, διελέγετο σκοπῶν ὅπως ὁ
καλούμενος ὑπὸ τῶν σοφιστῶν κόσμος ἔχει καὶ τίσιν ἀνάγκαις ἕκαστα
γίγνεται τῶν οὐρανίων. Mem. I.I.II).

These two texts make clear that, for an Athenian of the early fourth
century, κόσμος in the philosophic sense was not a normal part of the
spoken language, but a peculiar expression heard most often in lectures on natural philosophy. What seems to be the only instance of the
term in Attic literature of the previous century confirms this view, for
when Euripides speaks of "the unaging κόσμος of deathless φύσις," it is
precisely to characterize the object of Ionian science (fr. 910 = Vors.
59 A 30, probably with reference to Anaxagoras).

Κόσμος has no etymology worthy of the name, and the original
meaning of the word must be extracted from its use in the texts. (The
root *κεδ-, "to order," is a mere flight of fancy, and the alternatives
which have been offered are hardly better.) In Homer and in the other
early literature, κόσμος, κοσμέω, and their derivatives denote in general
any arrangement or disposition of parts which is appropriate, well-
disposed, and effective. The primary idea is of something physically
neat and trim rather than morally or socially "correct." For κοσμέω in
Homer may apply not only to the marshalling of the host (as in the
reference to the Atreidae as κοσμήτορε λαῶν), but also to the fitting of
an arrow to one's bow (αἶψα δ' ἐπὶ νευρῇ κατεκόσμει πικρὸν ὀϊστόν, Δ
118), to the preparation of a meal (ἥ οἱ πῦρ ἀνέκαιε καὶ εἴσω δόρπον
ἐκόσμει, η 13; cf. εὖ κατὰ κόσμον at Ω 622), and to the cleaning of a
house (πάντα δόμον κατακοσμήσησθε, χ 440, 457; ἀμφίπολοι δ' ἀπεκό-
σμεον ἔντεα δαιτός, η 232); so the "well-kept" vegetable beds of Alcinous
are κοσμηταὶ πρασιαί (η 127). This physical sense is also apparent in
the later usage, as when Herodotus employs the phrase κόσμῳ ἐπιτιθέναι
to describe the laying of the timbers and brushwood in place, in the
construction of the bridge over the Hellespont (VII. 36. 4–5).

From this meaning of "neat arrangement" the transfer is an easy one
to the wider decorative sense of κόσμος as "finery, rich adornment,"
which is so frequent in classic Greek. Examples in Homer are the

toilette of Hera (πάντα περὶ χροῒ θήκατο κόσμον, Ξ 187), and the description of a crimson-stained ivory bridle as "an ornament (κόσμος) to the horse and a glory to his driver" (Δ 145). Poetry too may be thought of as an elaborate work of "adornment," and later writers speak of song as a κόσμος ἐπέων (Solon 2.2; cf. κόσμος ἀοιδῆς from "Orpheus," *Vors.* 1 в 1). So Democritus says of Homer that he "framed a glorious structure of manifold verse" (ἐπέων κόσμον ἐτεκτήνατο παντοίων, в 21). It is probably such a work of cunning art that Homer has in mind when he describes the Trojan horse as ἵππου κόσμον . . . δουρατέου, τὸν Ἐπειὸς ἐποίησεν σὺν Ἀθήνῃ (θ 492 f.).

On the other hand, κόσμος, κοσμέω also refer, of course, to the good order of the assembled host, in which "the leaders marshal (διεκόσμεον) the men in this place and in that, as goatherds easily separate their flocks when they have mingled in pasture" (Β 474–76). Although the physical sense is still clear, the "arrangement" in question is of a larger social significance, as when Rhodes is said to be inhabited by men "arranged in three groups . . . dwelling apart by tribes" (Β 655: διὰ τρίχα κοσμηθέντες; cf. Β 668: τριχθὰ δὲ ᾤκηθεν καταφυλαδόν). In such a case we are not far from the general moral connotation of "good order." In Homer (and also in later Greek) this sense of κόσμος is represented above all by the adverbial constructions κόσμῳ or κατὰ κόσμον, for anything which is done properly, decorously, *comme il faut*. The same idea is expressed by the Attic adjective κόσμιος "well-behaved." So κόσμος may refer to the good order or discipline of an army: κόσμον καὶ φυλακὴν περὶ παντὸς ποιούμενοι καὶ τὰ παραγγελλόμενα ὀξέως δεχόμενοι (Thuc. II.11.9). In the myth of Protagoras, Zeus sends αἰδώς and δίκη to men "so that there may be orderly ways of life in cities (πόλεων κόσμοι) and bonds of friendship drawing men together" (Plato, *Prot.* 322c.3).[1]

At the same time, κόσμος in the social sphere may denote an arrangement of some particular kind, rather than good order in general. It is contrasted not merely with anarchy and disorder, but with a constitution in which things are disposed otherwise. Thus Herodotus says κόσμον τόνδε . . . καταστησάμενος in introducing his narrative of the establishment of Median court etiquette under Deioces (1.99.1), and Lycurgus is supposed to have learned from the Pythia τὸν νῦν κατεστεῶτα κόσμον Σπαρτιήτῃσι (1.65.4; the idea of εὐνομίη is here implied

---

[1] This political sense of κόσμος is reflected by the curious Cretan usage of the term for the magis-trate himself (references in LSJ, *s.v.* κόσμος III).

by the context). Thucydides describes a change in constitution as μεταστῆσαι τὸν κόσμον (IV.76.2; cf. ἐκ τοῦ παρόντος κόσμου μεταστῆσαι, VIII.48.4; μένειν ἐν τῷ ὀλιγαρχικῷ κόσμῳ, VIII.72.2).

Such is, in brief, the range of meanings for κόσμος outside of natural philosophy. The peculiar richness of the term lies in its capacity to denote a concrete arrangement of beauty or utility, as well as the more abstract idea of moral and social "order." We may suppose that it was, first of all, the physical sense of "arrangement, neat disposition" which led to the use of κόσμος to designate the natural order of the universe, but the "goodness" of the order was immediately implied. This double value of the term may be illustrated by the phrase which Herodotus gives as an etymology for θεοί: the gods were so named because "after disposing all things in order they also had possession of all the shares [into which things were distributed]": ὅτι κόσμῳ θέντες τὰ πάντα πρήγματα καὶ πάσας νομὰς εἶχον (II.52.1). The idea comes from Hesiod, who says of Zeus, "He properly disposed the portions for the immortals, and assigned them their privileges": εὖ δὲ ἕκαστα / ἀθανάτοις διέταξεν ὁμῶς καὶ ἐπέφραδε τιμάς (Theog. 73 f.; cf. 112: ὥς τ᾽ ἄφενος δάσσοντο καὶ ὡς τιμὰς διέλοντο). In Hesiod's phrase, the excellence of the order is explicit. And Herodotus' use of κόσμος is a simple equivalent for εὖ διατάσσειν. Neither here nor elsewhere does he employ the term in its fully philosophic sense.[1]

With the philosophers we find this ancient idea of the δασμός consciously reinterpreted to apply to the rational order of the heavens. When Anaxagoras says πάντα διεκόσμησε νοῦς, his primary example is the celestial rotation (B 12); and when Diogenes speaks of all things "being distributed (δεδάσθαι) so that there are measures of all things," he mentions "winter and summer, night and day, rainfall and winds and clear weather" (B 3; cf. πάντα διατιθέναι in B 5). It is this new notion of the δασμός, the division of shares among the gods now understood as natural powers, which Heraclitus has in mind when he insists that "the Sun will not overstep his measures" (B 94).

The κόσμος of the philosophers, then, is an "arrangement" of all things, in which every natural power has its function and its limits assigned. As in the case of any good arrangement, the term implies a systematic unity in which diverse elements are combined or "com-

---

[1] For the intimate connection between κόσμος and δασμός see Theognis 677 f.:

χρήματα δ᾽ ἁρπάζουσι βίῃ, κόσμος δ᾽ ἀπόλωλεν,
δασμὸς δ᾽ οὐκέτ᾽ ἴσος γίνεται ἐς τὸ μέσον.

posed." The verb with which κόσμος is most frequently associated is συνίστασθαι: τῶν πραγμάτων ἐξ ὧν συνέστα ὁ κόσμος, Philolaus B 6; κόσμον ἀγήρων, †πῇ τε συνέστη, Eurip. fr. 910; σύστασις καὶ κόσμος, *De. Hebd.* 1; ἡ τοῦ κόσμου σύστασις. . . . συνέστησεν αὐτὸν ὁ συνιστάς, Plato *Tim.* 32c.5–7; etc.

Of course the word preserves all its connotations from the older literary usage. The social overtones were particularly important, and it may be that, from the beginning, κόσμος was applied to the world of nature by conscious analogy with the good order of society. This connection of ideas is suggested by the regular use of moral and political terminology in early Greek philosophy (e.g., διδόναι δίκην and ἀδικία in Anaximander's fragment, νόμος in Heracl. B 114, ἰσονομία and μοναρχία in Alcmaeon B 4). And it is borne out by the way in which διακοσμεῖν and διατιθέναι are supplemented by such expressions as δεδάσθαι, κυβερνᾶν, and κρατεῖν (Anaxag. B 12; Diog. B 5; etc.). So when Plato introduces the philosophic term in the *Gorgias*, he explains it by reference to κοσμιότης καὶ σωφροσύνη καὶ δικαιότης.[1]

Later, it is true, the conception of the world as an object of beauty comes to the fore, so that the Romans translate κόσμος by *mundus*, "adornment." But there is little or no evidence of this aesthetic view in the older texts; and it can at first have played only a subordinate role. The Aeschylean invocation of Night as μεγάλων κόσμων κτέατειρα (*Agam.* 356) is sometimes cited as proof that the stars were considered the "ornaments" of the night sky (e.g., by LSJ *s.v.* κόσμος IV). Even if this were Aeschylus' meaning, it would by no means follow that κόσμος as used by the early philosophers implies an aesthetic conception of the universe. And in fact "the great κόσμοι acquired by favoring Night, who has spread her net upon the towers of Troy" must be simply the rich treasures captured in the sack of the city.[2]

In any case, it is certain that when Plato, Xenophon, and Aristotle speak of the heaven as a κόσμος they do not have in mind the immediate spectacle of the night sky, but an all-embracing order of things, of which the celestial motions offer only the most conspicuous and most

---

[1] The parallel between the world of nature (κόσμος) and the community of men (πόλις) was, of course, elaborately developed in Hellenistic times: on the one hand we have the concept of the κοσμοπολίτης; on the other, a description of the natural order in terms of the πολιτικὴ ὁμόνοια, as in [Arist.] *De Mundo* 5, 396ᵃ33 ff.

[2] "Κτέατειρα non *domina* est, sed quae paravit seu conciliavit μεγάλους κόσμους h.e. victoriae gloriam, praedae magnitudinem": Schütz on *Ag.* 356, cited with approval by E. Fraenkel, *Agamemnon* (Oxford, 1950), II, 189.

It should be noted that Aëtius II.13.15 (*Dox.* 343), which is sometimes quoted as a parallel to this verse, does not say that Heraclides and the Pythagoreans named the stars κόσμοι, but that they considered them to be world systems.

noble manifestation. It is therefore by a natural specialization of meaning that κόσμος can be used as a stylistic variant for οὐρανός (as in Isoc. 4.179: τῆς γῆς ἁπάσης τῆς ὑπὸ τῷ κόσμῳ κειμένης). On the other hand, it can also be used for a more restricted portion of the atmosphere or sky—in Aristotle's *Meteorologica*, for the sublunary world: ὁ περὶ τὴν γῆν ὅλος κόσμος, 339ᵃ19; τῷ περιέχοντι κόσμῳ τὴν γῆν, 339ᵇ4 (and the other passages cited by Bonitz, *Index*, 406ᵃ46–49). In the *De Hebdomadibus* (chs. 1–2) we have ὁ ἄκριτος κόσμος and ὁ ὀλύμπιος κόσμος for the outer celestial "order" or sphere, ἡ τοῦ ἠέρος σύστασις καὶ κόσμος for the region of air, οἱ ὑπὸ τῇ γῇ κόσμοι for the elemental portions or "arrangements" under the earth, and οἱ τῶν ξυμπάντων κόσμοι for the sum of all the portions. The Platonic *Epinomis* points out that the term κόσμος is particularly appropriate to the sphere of the fixed stars (987b.7); here the concrete sense of beauty coincides with an arrangement of mathematical perfection. The κόσμος is in fact normally defined by reference to the stellar sphere in astronomical works such as Euclid's *Phaenomena*.[1]

It is possible that these different uses of κόσμος for particular portions of the world are all to be derived from a basic sense of "world-ordering" or "universal arrangement," since this wider usage is best attested in the early fragments. On the other hand, the variety of meanings for κόσμος is so great at every period that the word may always have been used by the natural philosophers in a number of different ways, all based upon the physical notion of "arrangement." The Milesians, like the author of the *De Hebdomadibus*, may very well have spoken of πάντες οἱ κόσμοι for the world portions, as well as of ὅλος ὁ κόσμος or ὅδε ὁ κόσμος for the world order as a whole.[2] We have seen that certain items in the doxography for Anaximander, Xenophanes, and Anaxagoras are best explained as referring to κόσμοι in some more restricted sense, rather than to a plurality of worlds (above, pp. 47–53).

We may conclude with a list of the relevant examples of κόσμος in the early philosophic texts. The sense of "universal arrangement, universe" is attested from Heraclitus onwards.

1. Heraclitus B 30: "This κόσμος neither any one of gods nor of men

---

[1] Κόσμου περιστροφῆς χρόνος ἐστίν, ἐν ᾧ ἕκαστον τῶν ἀπλανῶν ἀστέρων ἀπ' ἀνατολῆς ἐπὶ τὴν ἐξῆς ἀνατολὴν παραγίνεται, *Phaenomena*, ed. Menge (Leipzig, 1916), p. 8.29. So Pliny speaks of the fixed stars as "fastened to the *mundus*" (*H.N.* 11.8.28: *sidera quae adfixa diximus mundo*).

[2] *De Hebd.* ch. 2.24: κατὰ μέσον δὲ τὸν κόσμον

ἡ γῆ κειμένη. Κόσμος in the larger sense is also implied by the Latin translation of the (lost) opening sentence: "*Mundi* forma sic omnis ornata est"; similarly in ch. 6, "inseparabilis soliditas quae mundum continet omnem" must represent ἄκριτος πάγος ὃς ὅλον τὸν κόσμον περιέχει.

has made, but it always was and is and will be, an ever-living fire, kindled by measures and by measures put out."[1] *Κόσμος* here must be the entire organized cycle of elementary and vital transformations, the world of nature taken in its widest sense. The point of Heraclitus' emphatic denial seems to be that, unlike most "arrangements," the *κόσμος* to which he refers (ὅδε) is not a product of art either human or divine. In this case there is no *κοσμήτωρ*, for the world order has its own unique, self-governing wisdom (ἒν τὸ σοφόν) which steers all things (B 41 ; so *πῦρ φρόνιμον* in B 64–66). The contrast intended is not between an eternal world and one created in time, but between a living, immortal being, and an inert object on which a plan might be imposed from without. A fire which regularly bursts into flame and dies out again is the natural symbol for a world order that alternates between extreme heat and extreme cold. The tradition which connects Heraclitus with the doctrine of a Magnus Annus (culminating in a Great Summer and a Great Winter) is therefore thoroughly credible. Only here *κόσμος* must be understood as referring to the entire sequence of world conditions, and not to any one.

This fragment has sometimes been interpreted as denying any origin or end of the *present* world order, and Heraclitus thus appears as anticipating the Aristotelian doctrine of the eternity of the world.[2] But that is hardly suggested by his image of a fire dying out, and there is definite external evidence against such a view. If Aristotle had understood Heraclitus to assert the eternity of the world in its present condition, he would certainly have mentioned this precedent for his own doctrine. What he says, however, is the reverse, namely, that Heraclitus, like Empedocles, held that "the condition of the *οὐρανός* alternates, so that it is now in one state, now in another, and this process of corruption

---

[1] *κόσμον τόνδε* [τὸν αὐτὸν ἁπάντων] οὔτε τις θεῶν οὔτε ἀνθρώπων ἐποίησεν, ἀλλ' ἦν ἀεὶ καὶ ἔστιν καὶ ἔσται πῦρ ἀείζωον, ἁπτόμενον μέτρα καὶ ἀποσβεννύμενον μέτρα. I follow Reinhardt and Kirk in treating the words *τὸν αὐτὸν ἁπάντων* as a later addition to the sentence of Heraclitus. Even so, they indirectly confirm the authenticity of εἰς καὶ κοινὸς κόσμος in B 89; see the next page.

[2] The various arguments pro and con are summarized by Kirk, *Heraclitus*, pp. 335–38. I do not mean to prejudge the question of whether the Stoic *ecpyrosis* is a mere repetition of the Ionian doctrine of world periods, or whether it is an essentially new variation on an old theme. In either case the historical link must have been real. I can see no reason to suppose that the Stoics based their cosmology upon an Aristotelian mis-

interpretation of Heraclitus which they found in Theophrastus, rather than upon their own study of Heraclitus and his fellow Ionians. Above all, I would insist that there is no good evidence that Heraclitus denied the most fundamental tenet in all early Greek thought: that the universe undergoes a process of generation and growth comparable to that of living things. The principle of cosmogony was rejected by no one before Aristotle, not even by Parmenides, and it has perhaps been rejected by no one since, except under Aristotelian influence. The scientists who write on "the birth of the solar system" are only giving us the latest version of the creation story.

(Compare now the article of R. Mondolfo, "Evidence of Plato and Aristotle Relating to the *Ekpyrosis* in Heraclitus," *Phronesis*, III [1958], 75.)

continues forever" (*De Caelo* 279^{b}14–16 = *Vors.* 22 A 10). And it is clear that Theophrastus, in his more detailed account of Heraclitus' teaching, concurred in Aristotle's view (*Vors.* 22 A 1.8; A 5).

There is a Platonic passage which distinguishes the doctrines of Heraclitus and Empedocles, and which, although it has no bearing on the eternity of the world, has been used to discredit the testimony of Aristotle and Theophrastus. The question discussed by Plato is: How many real things (ὄντα) are there, and of what sort?[1] Some say there are three real things, some two, the Eleatics only one.

> But some Ionian Muses [Heraclitus] and some later ones from Sicily [Empedocles] have understood that it is safer to combine both views, and to say that reality is both one and many, held together by love and [separated] by hostility. "In distinction it is always united" (διαφερόμενον ἀεὶ συμφέρεται), say the stricter Muses; but the milder ones have relaxed this condition of its being always so, and say that by turns the All is now one and loving under the influence of Aphrodite, and then again many and inimical to itself because of some sort of strife. (*Soph.* 242d–e)

Plato does not say, or even suggest, that Heraclitus thought the world always was and always will be in its present condition. He is discussing the ways in which Unity can be combined with Plurality. Empedocles' doctrine of alternating world states is introduced merely as a "mild" solution to this problem, which Heraclitus had treated in a more rigorous way. The point of the contrast is not that Heraclitus rejected the world periods of the Sicilian, but simply that he had no need to raise such a question in order to reconcile the opposites. In his view, the latter exercise their influence simultaneously and *continuously* (ἀεί). To read this as a denial of cosmogony and world periods for Heraclitus is to give Plato's words a meaning which they do not bear.

The word κόσμος also appears in three indirect citations from Heraclitus. In B 75 ("Heraclitus says that those asleep are workers and accomplices in what goes on in the κόσμος"), the term may have been supplied by our informant, Marcus Aurelius; in the other two cases it seems to have been used by Heraclitus himself. Its authenticity in B 89 ("Heraclitus says that the waking have one κόσμος in common, while the sleepers turn aside each to his own") is confirmed by the appearance of a similar phrase (κόσμος ὁ αὐτὸς ἁπάντων) in one version of B 30. And the play on the sense "ornament" in ὁ κάλλιστος κόσμος in B 124 must come from Heraclitus, not Theophrastus. These examples, and above

---

[1] *Soph.* 242c.5–6.

all B 89, suggest that Heraclitus was the first to give the new conception of "natural order" a direct meaning for man's own life and experience. (We may suppose that Pythagoras, in his semi-religious fraternity of scientists, might to some extent have anticipated Heraclitus in developing the moral and social implications of the new philosophy).

2. Parmenides describes his system of the natural world as a διάκοσμος: τόν σοι ἐγὼ διάκοσμον ἐοικότα πάντα φατίζω (B 8.60). The context shows that he means the "arrangement" or "disposition" of all things, according to the combination of the two primary forms, Fire and Night. Therefore, when he introduces his cosmology with the ambiguous phrase κόσμον ἐμῶν ἐπέων ἀπατηλόν (B 8.52), he certainly means not only "the treacherous tricking-out of my verses," but also "the deceitful world order" which they present. Precisely the same ὑπόνοια or "hint" is given by the Homeric clausula κατὰ κόσμον in B 4: οὔτε σκιδνάμενον πάντῃ πάντως κατὰ κόσμον / οὔτε συνιστάμενον—since the real does not divide from what is real, there can be no alternate process of separation and contraction "according to a cosmic order." The ambiguity of Parmenides' style is intentional. He writes like Pindar "for those who understand" (for the εἰδὼς φώς, B 1.3, not the βροτοὶ εἰδότες οὐδέν, B 6.4).

3. In Anaxagoras B 8 τὰ ἐν τῷ ἑνὶ κόσμῳ, which are "not separated from one another nor chopped apart with an axe," are exemplified by the hot and the cold. The κόσμος here is clearly the world arrangement of which the elemental powers are the constituent parts. It is probably called "the one κόσμος" because it is a unity whose parts are bound together (and, perhaps, to distinguish it from subordinate κόσμοι or "world portions," which Anaxagoras may also have mentioned—not, however, to distinguish it from other "worlds"). The word designates the result of Mind's activity: πάντα διεκόσμησε νοῦς, B 12.

(It is probably from Anaxagoras that Euripides has learned to speak of "the unaging κόσμος of deathless φύσις," fr. 910.)

4. In Empedocles B 134.5 the φρὴν ἱερή which is the highest form of divinity "flits with nimble thoughts through the whole κόσμος." Of all the early uses of the word, it is here that the original idea of "arrangement" is most completely neglected. This κόσμος seems to be simply "the world," or universal body extended in space (like κατὰ μέσον τὸν κόσμον for the earth's position in De Hebd. 2). We see that the standard philosophic usage of the term was well established by the middle of the fifth century.

It must therefore be the same orderly universe which Empedocles has in mind when he speaks of the elements coming together εἰς ἕνα κόσμον (B 26.5). Like Anaxagoras, Empedocles specifies the unity of this world order (εἷς κόσμος). Unlike Heraclitus, he seems to contrast the organized κόσμος of the elements with their polar conditions of complete separation and total fusion (whereas for Heraclitus κόσμος stands for the entire system of transformations).[1]

5. In Diogenes B 2 we have the classic conception of the κόσμος, as the organic whole of which the elements are the parts (cf. *Tim.* 32c.5; *De Caelo* 301ᵃ19; etc.). The repeated phrase τὰ ἐν τῷδε τῷ κόσμῳ ἐόντα νῦν designates "earth and water and air and fire and the rest" as concrete portions of the visible universe. The parallel to Anaxagoras B 8 is obvious, as well as to the Hippocratic uses cited in the text (above, p. 182).

The expression ὅδε ὁ κόσμος is the same as in Heraclitus B 31 and *De Natura Hominis* 7 (Jones, IV, 22). With Diogenes it might conceivably refer to "this world" as opposed to others, but that is not its most likely sense. The same phrase often appears in contexts where there can be no question of other worlds (see, e.g., Plato *Tim.* 29a.2). The demonstrative pronoun seems to indicate the world as a concrete presence, with a gesture of the hand as it were. So Plato paraphrases κόσμος by τὸ ὅλον τοῦτο.[2] The world is "the whole" or "the arrangement" par excellence.

6. The fragments of Philolaus, whose authenticity has been much disputed, contain repeated mention of a κόσμος within which all of nature is organized (B 1: ἁ φύσις δ᾽ ἐν τῷ κόσμῳ ἁρμόχθη, like φύσεως κόσμος of Eurip. fr. 910). This arrangement includes all things, and in particular all things "limitless and limiting" (ἄπειρα καὶ περαίνοντα), for these are the foundations or starting points (ἀρχαί) of the universe (B 2, B 6). The κόσμος is a "fitting-together" (ἁρμονία) in which the opposing principles are organized (κοσμηθῆναι), reconciled (ἁρμοχθῆναι), combined (συγκεκλεῖσθαι), and held in check (κατέχεσθαι). On the other hand, the concrete body of the world, of which the parts are elements, is referred to as ἁ σφαῖρα (B 12). In this respect, the terminology of these fragments seems at least as archaic as that of Empedocles and Diogenes, for here the original sense of κόσμος as "arrangement, organized whole" is even more vividly preserved. (For the mathematical

---

[1] Both uses of κόσμος are preserved by the Stoics, who apply the term to the ungenerated, immortal world-divinity, as well as to the perishable order of the heavens (D.L. vii. 137).

[2] *Gorg.* 508a.3. Precisely the same expression is used in early Sanskrit for "the universe": sárvam idám, "all this," Rigveda x.129.3.

connotations of κόσμος in Philolaus, compare Hp. *Prognosticon* 20, Jones, II, 42, where the periodic rise and fall of fevers according to fixed numerical intervals is referred to as οὗτος ὁ κόσμος.) In short, the language of these fragments seems to be that of the fifth century. A consciously archaic use of κόσμος—and a systematic avoidance of such fourth-century terms as στοιχεῖα—is difficult to imagine at a later date.

7. The cosmological writings of Leucippus and Democritus are cited respectively as Μέγας and Μικρὸς Διάκοσμος. The second title presupposes, of course, that the first was already known as "the διάκοσμος," just as Parmenides refers to his own cosmology by this name. Democritus' description of man as a μικρὸς κόσμος comes down to us only as a late and indirect citation (B 34), but the phrase in this sense is familiar to Aristotle (see *Phys.* 252ᵇ26, where there is, however, no clear reference to Democritus).[1]

8. The usage of Melissus (B 7) has been reserved for the last, since it is polemical in nature and must be defined by reference to the examples listed above. His aim is not to refute the "ordering" (διακοσμεῖσθαι) of the world, but its transformation (μετακοσμεῖσθαι) from one organized state (ὁ κόσμος ὁ πρόσθεν ἐών) to another (ὁ μὴ ἐών). This does not correspond exactly to any of the other early uses of the term κόσμος, and it is therefore misleading to interpret the Ionian concept from the point of view of its Eleatic critics, as Reinhardt wished to do (*Parmenides*, pp. 50, 174 ff.). If κόσμος has any positive sense for Melissus, it can only be the immutable structure of the one Being, eternally identical with itself.

Thus all extant examples of κόσμος and διάκοσμος in the early philosophical fragments illustrate the idea of an all-embracing "arrangement" or ordering of parts: the natural world is conceived of as a structured whole in which every component has its place. According to the context or the author's philosophic bent, the emphasis may fall upon the everlasting duration of this order despite radical change (Heraclitus B 30; cf. Euripides fr. 910), the universal scope of the world-order in which all things are bound together (Anaxagoras, Diogenes, Heraclitus B 89), the rational, harmonious structure of the arrangement (Philolaus), or the fact that it constitutes only one phase in a larger cycle (Empedocles

---

[1] In Democr. B 247 the whole κόσμος is said to be the country of a noble soul. It has been doubted whether this use of κόσμος for the "inhabited world" (which is otherwise not known before Hellenistic times) can represent an authentic quotation from Democritus.

B 26.5). The term may even refer to the world as a concrete whole, with no apparent emphasis on its ordering (Empedocles B 134), or to the structure of an immutable Reality which can scarcely be described as a world at all (Melissus B 7). But the common basis which clearly underlies all of these conceptions is the Milesian view of the natural world as an organized system, characterized by symmetry of parts, periodicity of events, and equilibrium between conflicting factors.

THE ΑΠΕΙΡΟΝ OF ANAXIMANDER

SINCE Aristotle's review of his predecessors in the first book of the *Metaphysics*, the study of early Greek philosophy has been focused upon the question, what each thinker had to say on the subject of ἀρχαί or "first principles." That topic has been largely neglected here. It invariably serves to oppose the philosophers to one another, whereas our concern has been to discover the common conceptions which bind them together. But Anaximander's "principle," the ἄπειρον, has after all its role to play in his cosmology, and that role must be briefly considered here.

Unfortunately, what Aristotle and Theophrastus tell us about Anaximander's ἄπειρον is so meager, and so dependent upon their own conceptual scheme, that a review of the evidence will raise more questions than it can resolve. There is, however, one good source of information outside of the doxographic tradition, and that is the meaning attached to the word ἄπειρος in early Greek literature.

Ἄπειρος (together with its Homeric equivalents ἀπείρων, ἀπείριτος, ἀπειρέσιος, ἀπερείσιος) is obviously a compound with a- privative, but the precise form of the simplex is not quite so clear. Is it correct to assume (with LSJ and others) that ἄπειρος is derived from the noun πεῖραρ, πέρας, "limit"? In that case the literal meaning of the adjective would be "devoid of limits, boundless." But although "boundless" is often a convenient translation for ἄπειρος, it does not really answer to the usage of the term. In the epic, ἀπείρων is the characteristic epithet of earth and sea, particularly the former.[1] Neither earth nor sea is devoid of limits, and in fact the poet speaks repeatedly of the πείρατα of both.[2] So Hesiod describes the place where the "sources and limits" (πηγαὶ καὶ πείρατα) of Earth, Tartarus, Sea, and Heaven converge (*Theog.* 736-38 = 807-9), although for him too both Earth and Sea are ἀπείριτος (*Theog.* 109, 878, etc.).

It may, of course, be argued that the old poets are not in love with

---

[1] The phrase ἐπ' ἀπείρονα γαῖαν often ends the verse, e.g., H 446, o 79; so A 350 ἐπ' ἀπείρονα πόντον.

[2] Πείρατα of earth: Ξ 200 = 301, δ 563, cf. ι 284; of earth and sea: Θ 478.

consistency, and could have referred to the earth as "limitless" without hesitating to mention its limits a few verses later. But there are other uses of the term which are difficult to explain by the derivation from πέρας. Not only are circles and rings described as ἄπειρος or ἀπείρων, but the word is also used of garments or nets "in which one is entangled past escape".[1]

This last sense suggests that it is not the noun πέρας which is negated by the α- privative, but the verbal root *per- represented in πείρω, περάω, and περαίνω, as well as in a number of Indo-European adverbs and prepositions, all referring in some way to the direction "forward, in front" (Greek πρό, Latin per, prae, etc.). The verbal forms indicate a movement in this direction, and the group of περάω, πέραν, περαίνω, πεῖραρ envisages the point at which the forward motion comes to an end. Thus περάω (like περαιόω) is regularly used of passing over a body of water to reach the other side; the adverb πέραν refers precisely to what lies "across," as the Echinades islands lie over the water from mainland Greece:

νήσων, αἳ ναίουσι πέρην ἁλὸς Ἤλιδος ἄντα. (B 626)

Πεῖραρ is the limit or goal of a given passage—the point at which the forward movement comes to an end. So the word regularly occurs in Homer together with a verb of motion.[2] (With the usual vowel gradation, the same root appears in the nouns πόρος, πορθμός designating either the motion as such, or the passage through which one moves.)

It is this basic verbal idea which is negatived in ἀπείρων, ἄπειρος, exactly as the synonymous ἀπέραντος is formed from the verbal stem of περαίνω (aorist ἐπέρανα). The true sense of ἄπειρος is therefore "what cannot be passed over or traversed from end to end." When earth and heaven are called ἀπείρων, there is no contradiction; both have πείρατα, but few mortals can travel like Hera "to the ends of the earth" (Ε 200). It is understandable that something circular "cannot be passed through to the end," for, as the geometers point out, a circle has beginning and end at every point (see Heracl. β 103). Above all, there is no doubt why a wrapping from which one cannot escape is called "impenetrable."[3] Any remaining doubts as to the true meaning of ἄπειρος may be dispelled by a glance at Aristotle's discussion of the term (Phys. 204ᵃ2–7),

---

[1] LSJ s.v. ἄπειρος (B) 2 and 3; s.v. ἀπείρων (B) 3.   ἤλθομεν, ψ 248–49; πέμψουσι, δ 563–64.
[2] Θ 478: εἴ κε τὰ νείατα πείραθ' ἵκηαι / γαίης καὶ   [3] Thus Aeschylus says ἄπειρον ἀμφίβληστρον πόντοιο; similarly with εἶμι, Ε 200; ἵκανε, λ 13;   at Ag. 1382, like ἀπέραντον δίκτυον at P.V. 1078.

where the idea is rendered by contrast to διελθεῖν, διιέναι, and διέξοδος; Aristotle's synonym is ἀδιεξίτητος (204ᵃ14). The point is no less obvious in the lengthy commentary of Simplicius (*in Phys.* 470–71), who opposes ἄπειρος to διεξοδευτός, διαπορευτός.

The literal sense of "what cannot be traversed to the end" easily passes into that of "immense, enormous." This transfer of meaning is complete in many Homeric passages, which speak of a "countless ransom" (ἀπερείσι' ἄποινα), of "innumerable goats" (ι 118: αἶγες ἀπειρέσιαι), of an "immense crowd" of mourners (Ω 776: δῆμος ἀπείρων), and even of the "endless sleep" of Odysseus, arriving exhausted on the coast of Phaeacia (η 286: ὕπνον ἀπείρονα). In all such exaggerations the idea of great length, mass, or quantity persists.

It is this spatial or quantitative sense which predominates in early Greek philosophy, as the fragments show: "The earth stretches away below ἐς ἄπειρον" (Xenoph. B 28); "Things must be on the one hand so small as to have no magnitude, on the other, so large as to be ἄπειρα" (Zeno B 1); "That which surrounds [the world] is ἄπειρον in amount" (Anaxag. B 2). As a result of the philosophic usage which begins with Anaximander, the term is systematically opposed to πέρας and πεπερασμένον in such a way that it accumulates the senses of "unlimited," "mathematically infinite," "qualitatively indeterminate," or "indefinite."[1] But before the philosophers set to work, ἄπειρος implied concrete bulk, magnitude, and extension.

The ἄπειρον of Anaximander is then primarily a huge, inexhaustible mass, stretching away endlessly in every direction. It has the epithet (and the majesty) which Earth and Sea possess for Homer. And we see at once why such a source is required for the sustenance of the world, "in order that the generation of things may not cease" (**6.A.** with **Arist.2**). Equally intelligible is Anaximander's view that the ἄπειρον clips the heavens in its vast embrace (περιέχειν πάντας τοὺς οὐρανούς, **8.Arist.4**; cf. **8.H.**). The Boundless is in fact what we call infinite space, the antecedent for the atomistic void as well as for the Receptacle or Nurse of generation in Plato's *Timaeus*. But this space is not as yet thought of in abstraction from the material which fills it. Place and body are here combined in a single idea.

---

[1] Anaximander probably defined τὸ ἄπειρον by opposition to πέρας; compare the arguments which Aristotle gives for his view at *Phys.* 203ᵇ7 (cited under 8). The same opposition played a considerable role in Pythagorean speculation, judging from its appearance at the head of their list of opposing principles (*Met.* 986ᵃ23) as well as from its importance in the fragments of Philolaus (B 1, B 2, etc.). This Pythagorean usage clearly implies a mathematical conception of "infinity" (as also in Zeno B 3 and Anaxag. B 1: καὶ γὰρ τὸ σμικρὸν ἄπειρον ἦν).

The conception of the ἄπειρον as a universal body or mass surrounding the world is a permanent feature of Ionian cosmology. We have quoted Xenophanes' description of the earth reaching out below ἐς ἄπειρον. Presumably he had the theory of Anaximander in mind, but exactly what he meant is as obscure to us as it was to Simplicius (Xenoph. A 47). The survival of Anaximander's conception is more obvious in the ἄπειρος ἀήρ of Anaximenes, which encompasses the whole world (B 2). This view differs from its predecessor only by an explicit assimilation of the extra-mundane mass to the atmospheric environment which encloses the earth. The Milesian περιέχον reappears in the system of Anaxagoras, who describes it (as we have seen) as "inexhaustible in amount" (ἄπειρόν ἐστι τὸ πλῆθος), and speaks of the ἀήρ and αἰθήρ of our world as separated off from this cosmic envelope (B 2). Anaxagoras gives as a complete enumeration of things: "the great περιέχον, the things which have been united with it, and those which have been separated off" (B 14). Like many other aspects of the Milesian cosmology, the boundless περιέχον is also preserved in the doctrine of the atomists. When a world is formed, it is from this unlimited mass of atoms in the void that a "shearing-off" (ἀποτομή) of certain minute bodies takes place, and it is from the same external regions that a sufficiently violent blow will one day arise to cause the destruction of the world.[1]

Thus, in the Ionian view of the universe which descends from Anaximander, the ἄπειρον is the great cosmic mass encircling the spherical body of our star-studded heaven,[2] and this conception is retained not only in the Epicurean cosmology, but likewise in that of the Stoics.[3] For Plato and Aristotle, on the other hand, there is neither matter nor "place" for anything outside of the spherical οὐρανός. This alternative conception of the physical universe as a finite sphere seems to have begun with Parmenides.[4] A similar view is held by Empedocles, who pointedly applies the Milesian epithet ἀπείρων to the "immense sphere" formed by the union of all things in the sway of Love (B 28).

[1] The world is formed by atoms separated off ἐκ τοῦ ἀπείρου (MSS. τῆς), Leucippus A 1.31; ἐκ τοῦ περιέχοντος, A 10; ἀπὸ τοῦ παντός, Democr. B 167. Its destruction is due to ἰσχυροτέρα τις ἐκ τοῦ περιέχοντος ἀνάγκη παραγενομένη, Democr. A 37.

[2] Of course, for Anaximander it is not the stars but the sun which is placed closest to the outer sphere of the οὐρανός or περιέχον. The classical view seems to have originated with Anaximenes.

[3] According to the Stoics, the extra-mundane region is a κενὸν ἄπειρον; see D.L. VII.140, Aëtius II.1.7 (Dox. 328).

[4] See Parm. B 8.42–49; so in B 10.5 there is no place for anything outside of the οὐρανός which holds the stars. This idea is not derived from the Pythagoreans (or at any rate not from those known to Aristotle), for their cosmology is of the Ionian type, with an ἄπειρον πνεῦμα outside the heavens (Vors. 58 A 30, with A 26 and A 28).

The fact that the term ἄπειρος may refer to something circular or spherical has led some scholars to suggest that Anaximander also thought of his "boundless" as a sphere, or at least as capable of rotary motion. The ἄπειρον would be what Pascal said all of nature was, "une sphère infinie dont le centre est partout, la circonférence nulle part." The ceaseless turning of this immense sphere upon itself would represent that "eternal motion" which, according to the doxographers, played a great role in the cosmology of both Anaximander and Anaximenes.[1] It might also be tempting to assimilate this motion to the universal rotation (περιχώρησις) which produces similar results in the cosmogony of Anaxagoras (B 9, B 12–13). But of course the rotation of Anaxagoras is not eternal, since it arose only when "Nous began to move things." Although circular motion is the only type which Aristotle would recognize as eternal, the phrase ἀΐδιος κίνησις means after all no more than ἀεὶ κινεῖσθαι, and does not in itself imply circular motion.[2] This expression of Theophrastus merely tells us that, for the Milesians as well as for the atomists, there never was (and never will be) a time when motion did not exist. This probably means that the formation of our heavens represents only one stage in a continuing cosmic cycle, and "eternity" here should be interpreted in connection with the Greek concept of Time as an endless series of astronomical recurrences.[3] But with regard to the shape and motion of the ἄπειρον itself, our information justifies no more than a verdict of *non liquet*.[4]

What we do know is that the ἄπειρον surrounds the world at present, and originally served as the ἀρχή or starting point in its formation. The primary connotations of this term ἀρχή are probably as much spatial as temporal. Just as the basic sense of the verb ἄρχω is "to lead [troops to

---

[1] 7; Anaximenes A 5, A 7.2. For the interpretation of the ἄπειρον as a sphere, see Cornford, *Principium Sapientiae* (Cambridge, 1952), pp. 176–78. The Milesian "eternal motion" was also understood as circular by W. A. Heidel, "The δίνη in Anaximenes and Anaximander," *CP*, I (1906), 279.

[2] Cornford (*op. cit.*, p. 181) claimed that ἀΐδιος κίνησις "had become practically a technical term for the revolution of a sphere in particular of the heavenly spheres." But in the doxography for Anaximenes ἀΐδιος κίνησις (A 5) alternates with κινεῖσθαι ἀεί (sc. τὸν ἀέρα; A 7.2); while the random movement of the atoms in all directions is also described as ἀεὶ κινούμενα (Leucippus A 8, A 10; cf. Arist. *Phys.* 250ᵇ20: ἀεὶ εἶναι κίνησιν; *De Caelo* 300ᵇ9: ἀεὶ κινεῖσθαι τὰ πρῶτα σώματα).

[3] See above, p. 189, n. 1. For some suggestions on astronomical time and eternity in early Greek thought, see my discussion of "Anaximander and the Arguments Concerning the ἄπειρον at Physics 203ᵇ4–15," in *Festschrift Ernst Kapp* (Hamburg, 1958), pp. 26–29.

[4] There is some indirect evidence that the ἄπειρον was *not* in motion. There is no indication in the fragments of Anaxagoras that his boundless περιέχον takes part in the cosmic rotation; while the outer, "unseparated" sphere of the *De Hebdomadibus* is expressly described as στάσιμος and ἀκίνητος (ch. 2.17 and 2.43); and the "greatest god" of Xenophanes is also immobile (B 26). Since all three of these ideas reflect, at least in part, the conception of Anaximander, they suggest that his surrounding Boundless was likewise stationary.

battle],"¹ whence it can mean "to rule" as well as "to go first, to begin" in any action, so the fundamental idea of ἀρχή is that of the first member in a chain of events,² whence it can also mean the foundation upon which all else rests.³ In Aristotle's discussion of the term, the first meaning given is a spatial one: the point from which a road or a line begins.⁴

In the context of a cosmogony, of course, this idea of "starting point, foundation" has also a direct temporal sense: the ἀρχή is the first and eldest of things, from which all others arise in the course of time. More exactly, for Anaximander the ἄπειρον "secretes" (ἀποκρίνεσθαι) the seed out of which emerge the opposing principles whose interaction constitutes the world. Many modern interpreters, following a remark of Aristotle, have supposed that these principles must themselves have been present in their source before generation, and that the ἄπειρον was therefore a kind of mixture, similar to the primeval mingling of things in the cosmogony of Anaxagoras.⁵ But such a view of Anaximander's Boundless is basically anachronistic, in that it presupposes the criticism of Parmenides. After him, the generation of something essentially new was considered an impossibility, but in the sixth century γένεσις was taken for granted as an obvious fact of nature. Furthermore, Theophrastus assures us that the ἄπειρον was no mixture, but "one φύσις" (*Phys. Opin.* fr. 4, cited under 7). From the Aristotelian viewpoint, the opposites were of course potentially present in their source. But for a Milesian they were no more pre-existent in the ἄπειρον than children pre-exist in the body of their parents before conception.

From our own point of view, the logical difficulties of such a doctrine are naturally very great. It may be that they are no greater than those of any other theory of the origin of the universe,⁶ but at any rate they

¹ E.g., *O* 306: Τρῶες δὲ προὔτυψαν ἀολλέες, ἦρχε δ' ἄρ' Ἕκτωρ / μακρὰ βιβάς. Similarly in the Catalogue, *B* 494, 512, etc.

² The crime of Paris is νείκεος ἀρχή (*X* 116; at *Γ* 100, simply ἀρχή), "origin of the quarrel"; the first moment in the series of events leading to Patroclus' death is κακοῦ ἀρχή (*Λ* 604); the contest of the bow is φόνου ἀρχή for the suitors of Penelope (φ 4 and ω 169).

³ This sense of ἀρχή is not recognized by LSJ, but see Plato *Laws* 803a.3: ναυπηγὸς τὴν τῆς ναυπηγίας ἀρχὴν καταβαλλόμενος τὰ τροπιδεῖα ὑπογράφεται τῶν πλοίων σχήματα; Hp. *De Carn.* 1 (Littré, VIII, 584): κοινὴν ἀρχὴν ὑποθέσθαι. Aristotle lists among the basic meanings of ἀρχή: οἷον ὡς πλοίου τρόπις καὶ οἰκίας θεμέλιος (*Met.* 1013ª4), while Demosthenes says that τῶν πράξεων τὰς

ἀρχὰς καὶ τὰς ὑποθέσεις must be right and true, comparing them to the foundations of a house and the keel of a ship (2.10).

⁴ *Met.* 1012ᵇ35. So in Hp. *Anc. Med.* 2 (Jones, I, 14): ἰητρικῇ δὲ πάλαι πάντα ὑπάρχει, καὶ ἀρχὴ καὶ ὁδὸς εὑρημένη.

⁵ This point has been discussed above, p. 41. The most prudent statement of the mixture theory is Cornford's: "We must imagine them [the opposites in the Unlimited stuff] as fused, like wine and water, which are different, but not separate as water and oil are when you try to mix them" (*Principium Sapientiae*, p. 178).

⁶ See Tannery's interesting comparison of Anaximander's view to modern theories of entropy and nebular evolution, *Science hellène*, pp. 104–18.

are more obvious to us. How do qualitative differences emerge from something which has no qualities? What is the mechanism behind the image of seed and secretion, or what exactly is meant by the ἀποκρίνε-σθαι of opposing natural principles? In short, what is the equivalent for Anaximander of the theory of Anaximenes, that Air by contraction and expansion can pass through diverse states?

In general, to pose such questions is to read the history of Greek philosophy backwards. Great as was the achievement of Anaximander, he could not foresee all of the problems that would arise as his successors continued along the road which he had traced. But he did see that the starting point was decisive in any explanation of the universe, and he chose an ἀρχή which, by its very nature, would be capable of generating the world. He accepted as an unquestioned fact that one thing could arise out of another, as day arises out of night and spring out of winter, and he expressed this fact in the most significant way he or any man of his time could imagine, by analogy with the generation of living things. He concluded that, since the constituent principles of the world as we know it are in a continuous and reciprocal process of transformation, they must themselves have arisen out of some more permanent source that is partially or wholly unknown to us, but which must be such as to offer an inexhaustible store of creative power and material. He called this unknown world source τὸ ἄπειρον, "that which is inexhaustible," and he identified it with the equally mysterious outlying body which holds the visible world in its embrace. The Boundless represents the unknown entity which encompasses the known world in time as well as in space. It is ἄπειρον and περιέχον in both respects, by contrast with the limited and perishable structure of the heavens.

A more detailed account of the ἄπειρον cannot be extracted from our sources. Nor is it at all obvious that Anaximander would have offered much more. In such ultimate questions the only cogent principle is that the cause must suffice for the effect: in this instance, that it must be adequate to generate the universe. In the nature of the case, any rational definition of the First Cause will be largely negative: we infer that it must lack those limitations by which lesser things are defined. It is for similar reasons that modern philosophers can speak of God as "the Infinite." Of course, Anaximander's conception of divinity is very different, and his mode of expression incomparably more concrete. The ἄπειρον is by definition "non-traversable" or "inexhaustible"; it is neither air nor water nor anything of the sort (3); unlike these

things, it does not change into something other than itself (**6.S.1**); its
motion or life-activity lasts forever (**7**); its existence is affected neither
by old age nor by death; it is in short immortal, uncorruptible, and
divine (**8**).

Clearly, the ἄπειρον of Anaximander cannot be reduced to material
or to quantitative terms. It is not only the matter but the motor of the
world, the living, divine force of natural change. In a passage where
Aristotle describes the Milesian doctrine at some length, he tells us that
this ἄπειρον, which has no limit and hence no origin (ἀρχή), is held to
be "ungenerated as well as imperishable."

It is believed to be the origin of other things, and to encompass all things
and guide them all (as those say who do not set up other causes besides the
Boundless, such as Mind or Love), and to be the divine; for it is immortal
and uncorruptible, as Anaximander says and most of the natural philosophers.
(**8.Arist.1.**)

It is probably Anaximander's view which Aristotle has in mind throughout this passage.[1] If so, Anaximander is responsible for the idea that the
divine principle must be not only imperishable but ungenerated, without any starting point or origin (ἀρχή) in the past. In contrast to the
ageless but generated gods of the epic, the philosophers of the late sixth
and early fifth centuries all proclaim a new conception of divinity,
which is free from birth as well as from death.[2] Aristotle's remarks here
permit us to infer that these philosophers were following in the wake of
Anaximander. Certainly no one but he could have said that the ἄπειρον
guides and governs all things (πάντα κυβερνᾶν).

Our discussion of Anaximander's fragment, and of the early conception of nature as a κόσμος, should have made clear what is implied
by such a universal government of things. We see that, in addition to
being the vital source out of which the substance of the world has come
and the outer limit which encloses and defines the body of the cosmos,
the ἄπειρον is also the everlasting, god-like power which governs the
rhythmic life cycle of this world. Thus it is not only the idea of the well-
regulated cosmos which Greece owes to Anaximander, but also that of
its regulator, the Cosmic God. And the two ideas belong together. For
the conception of the natural world as a unified whole, characterized

---

[1] I have stated in detail the case for ascribing
this whole chain of reasoning to Anaximander, in
the article cited above, p. 235, n. 3.

[2] See Pherecydes B 1; Xenoph. A 12, B 14;
Heracl. B 30 (ἦν ἀεί); Epicharmus B 1; Parm.
B 8.3 (ἀγένητον). Most of these passages were dis-
cussed and linked to Anaximander by Jaeger,
Theology, pp. 32, 67 f.

throughout by order and equilibrium, gave rise to the only form of monotheism known to classical antiquity. The god of the Greek philosophers is not identical with the world; but his Decalogue is the Law of Nature, and his revelation is to be read in the ever-turning cycles of the sun, the moon, the planets, and the stellar sphere.

NOTE: THE FIRST GREEK PROSE TREATISE

ON page 6 I take for granted that Anaximander was the first
Greek to write a prose treatise *On Nature*. However, my friend
William M. Calder III, who has been kind enough to read
the proofs, reminds me that Theopompus and most ancient authorities
held that Pherecydes of Syros was πρῶτον περὶ φύσεως καὶ θεῶν γράψαι.
(D.L. I. 116 = F Gr Hist 115 F 71; parallel statements are cited by
Jacoby, *Abhandlungen zur griechischen Geschichtschreibung* [Leiden, 1956],
p. 106, n. 22.)

Of course the dates of two lost works of the sixth century cannot be
fixed with any high degree of accuracy. We can be certain only that the
two authors were roughly contemporary. Nevertheless, there is good
reason to suppose that Theopompus (and the ancient sources who
follow him) may have been mistaken about the priority of Pherecydes.
Not too much stress can be laid upon the *floruit* dates assigned by
Hellenistic chronologists, but it is interesting to remark that that of
Anaximander (571/0) is nearly thirty years earlier than that of Pherecydes (544/1, according to Jacoby in the article cited). More signifi-
cantly, the intellectual position of Pherecydes seems to presuppose
Milesian speculation. Instead of relating the birth of the oldest gods as
Hesiod does, Pherecydes begins his fable with the assertion that "Zas,
Chronos, and Chthoniē have existed forever". Such an attitude implies
some knowledge of Anaximander's arguments for an eternal, un-
generated ἀρχή as the necessary starting-point for any cosmogony. See
Jaeger, *Theology*, pp. 67 f.; also *Festschrift Ernst Kapp*, p. 28.

Hence there is every reason to believe that Anaximander was the
author of the first Greek treatise in prose of which we have any knowledge.

INDEX OF SUBJECTS

INDEX OF GREEK TERMS